16,963

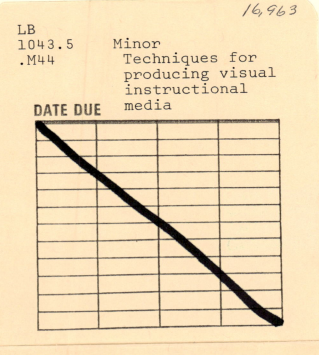

DATE DUE

Education
ms
is University
inois 62901

TECHNIQUES FOR PRODUCING VISUAL INSTRUCTIONAL MEDIA

TECHNIQUES FOR PRODUCING VISUAL INSTRUCTIONAL MEDIA

Ed Minor
Professor of Education and Director
Instructional Media Center
Florida A and M University

Harvey R. Frye
Associate Professor of Education and Supervisor of Graphic Arts
Audio Visual Center
Indiana University

McGraw-Hill Book Company
New York   St. Louis   San Francisco   Düsseldorf   London   Mexico   Panama   Sydney   Toronto

This book was set in News Gothic by Monotype Composition Company, Inc., printed on permanent paper by Halliday Lithograph Corporation, and bound by The Book Press, Inc. The designer was Richard Paul Kluga. The editors were Steve J. Melmeck and Molly Scully. Adam Jacobs supervised the production.

PREFACE

Never in the history of civilization have instructional media played such an important role in the communications processes as they do today. It was mainly upon this premise that this book was originally conceived, and it has been written to present, under one cover, techniques, methods, and processes for preparing modern visual instructional media.

This book is concerned in the main with simplified methods and it has been written both for the person without skills in art, graphic art, photography and for the professional seeking new approaches to production problems. The authors have intended the contents of this book to provide clear instructions and illustrations whereby the user might—with the aid of the most up-to-date equipment and materials available—create and produce modern instructional media. What has been written between these covers has been written with the belief that excellence need not be predicated upon complexity; therefore, complicated instructions and terminology often associated with many of the techniques, methods, and processes have been avoided.

If the reader is to make full use of this book, he must always keep in mind that the purpose of any worthwhile instructional material should be to communicate quickly, clearly, and memorably; thus, materials should be prepared and used only when they will do the job of communicating better and quicker than any other method of communication available.

To help solve problems of preparing instructional media, one needs a system or pattern to follow. This book documents the authors' pattern—a pattern which has been developed over a number of years of teaching and experimentation associated with techniques, methods, and processes required for creating and producing modern instructional media. Many of the techniques have been used for years to produce visual aids, and the authors have taken a number of these "old reliables" and presented them in a modern context and, even more important, related them to the preparation of modern instructional media.

The book is divided into six chapters. Chapter 1 deals with illustration as it applies to producing instructional media. Chapter 2 covers some of today's most modern and practical techniques for mounting and preserving materials. Chapter 3 presents the lettering and printing techniques which should be the answer to most lettering problems. Chapter 4 treats a number of unique coloring and shading techniques as they relate to opaque and transparent materials. Chapter 5 is a comprehensive treatment of techniques for producing projection and display transparencies. Also included in this section are suggestions for mounting, binding, and filing overhead projection transparencies and slides. Finally, Chapter 6 contains comprehensive references which include a glossary containing over five hundred terms related to the contents of the text; annotations of over two hundred publications related to the preparation of instructional media; annotations of over one hundred films, filmstrips, slides, and overhead transparencies; and an address directory of suppliers, manufacturers, and producers. A materials and equipment index appears in the back of the book.

All the techniques presented in this book have been used in one form or another to produce a major portion of the book's artwork. Thus, the authors have put into practice much of what they have been "preaching" over the years.

Actually, space forbids including all the techniques and processes now available for producing instructional media. However, what is presented here is a practical and tested approach to local production for the classroom teacher and producer of teaching aids. It is hoped that what the authors have shared with the readers will serve today and in the future as an inspiration and springboard for the creation and preparation of instructional media. The authors welcome comments and questions related to the contents of the book.

Obviously a book of this type could not have been written without assistance and moral support coming from several sources. Our many students from all over the world and staff associates over the years should receive a great deal of credit for motivating the two of us to put into print what we have been teaching for a number of years. We are most grateful to Dr. Richard B. Lewis for his advice, encouragement, and special concessions during the final stages of the book. Special thanks goes to Darryle Webb and Roger Glenn for their assistance with some of the artwork and suggestions for visualizing some of our concepts of local production. Appreciation is due to those companies who gave us permission to make use of photographs and technical information. Among the companies included are Artype, Inc.; Canon, USA, Inc.; Dymo Products Co.; Keuffel & Esser Co.; Polaroid Corp.; Reynolds Printasign Co.; Seal, Inc.; Scott Machine Devolopment Corp.; Varigraph, Inc.; and VariTyper Corp.

Finally, very special thanks to Bertha and Mary, two of the most understanding wives around. Their contributions exceeded those of the authors in so many ways.

Ed Minor
Harvey R. Frye

CONTENTS

HOW TO USE THIS BOOK

There are a number of different ways to use a book of this type. If it is used as a reference source, Chapter 6 would be the major focal point, since it is, in effect, a book within a book. Chapter 6 contains comprehensive references including a glossary; annotations of publications, films, filmstrips, slides, and overhead transparencies; sources of materials and equipment; and addresses of suppliers, manufacturers, and producers.

All the references in Chapter 6 relate to the preparation of instructional media. Should this book be used for self-instruction, as it is primarily intended, the suggested approach to its use follows. To simplify these suggestions, instructional media have been divided here into two categories: *opaque* (primarily nonprojected materials) and *transparent* (materials intended mainly for projection).

OPAQUE INSTRUCTIONAL MEDIA (*1*)

A large group of instructional media are classified under this heading. They include charts; graphs; diagrams; maps; posters; exhibits; displays; bulletin, magnetic, velcro, felt, and chalk boards; signs; logos; and duplication stencils. One or more of the techniques included in this book could be used to produce or modify any of these materials. First, determine which of the techniques will be required to produce a certain type of instructional aid, then refer to the chapter, page, or pages which illustrate and discuss the techniques designed or recommended for a particular phase of the production. For example, lettering is one of the techniques required for the poster or original illustrated, and lettering is covered in Chapter 3. If you turn to this chapter, you will find a chart which recommends the best lettering techniques for the preparation of a poster. Also included in this chapter are tips on spacing and letter design. Even more important is that in Chapter 3 a large number of lettering and printing techniques are fully illustrated and discussed. Each production requirement of each instructional material could be carried out in

this manner. Each of the chapters of the book has its own unique contribution to the total production of simple instructional media. Here are other suggestions for producing instructional media.

(1)

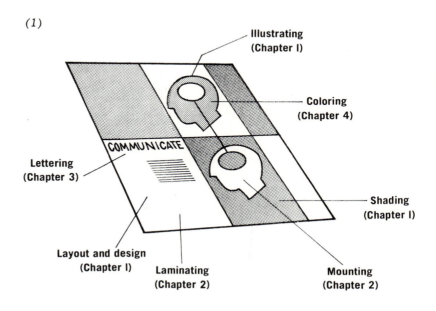

Illustrating (Chapter 1)

Coloring (Chapter 4)

Lettering (Chapter 3)

Shading (Chapter 1)

Layout and design (Chapter 1)

Laminating (Chapter 2)

Mounting (Chapter 2)

COMMUNICATE

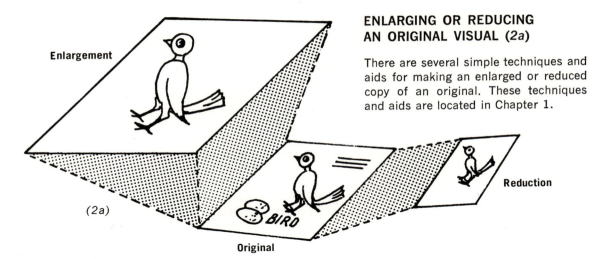

(2a)

ENLARGING OR REDUCING AN ORIGINAL VISUAL (2a)

There are several simple techniques and aids for making an enlarged or reduced copy of an original. These techniques and aids are located in Chapter 1.

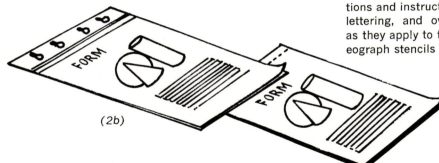

(2b)

STENCIL AND SPIRIT DUPLICATION (2b)

Chapters 1, 3, and 5 include illustrations and instructions related to artwork, lettering, and overhead transparencies as they apply to the preparation of mimeograph stencils and spirit masters.

TRANSPARENT INSTRUCTIONAL MEDIA (3)

These media include slides; overhead projection and display transparencies; motion picture, filmstrip, and slide titles (transparent); and transparent overlays of all types and sizes. One or more of the techniques included in this book could be used to produce any of the transparent media just listed. First, determine which of the techniques will be required to produce a transparent media, and then refer to the sections or pages indicated which illustrate and discuss the techniques which apply to a particular phase of the production. For ex-

ample, if drawing an image (visual) on prepared acetate is required or desired, refer to Chapter 5. Here you will find information on direct image on acetate transparency. The same approach should be used for all the techniques required to produce a certain type of visual aid.

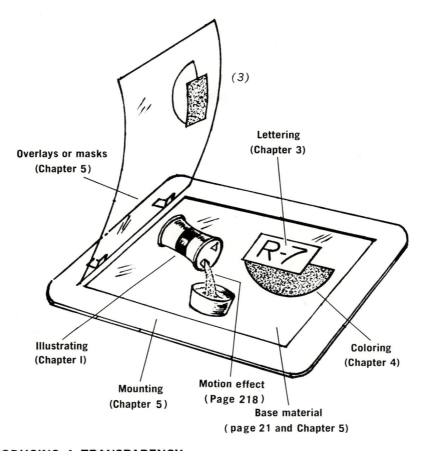

Overlays or masks
(Chapter 5)

Lettering
(Chapter 3)

(3)

Illustrating
(Chapter I)

Mounting
(Chapter 5)

Motion effect
(Page 218)

Coloring
(Chapter 4)

Base material
(page 21 and Chapter 5)

PRODUCING A TRANSPARENCY FROM AN ORIGINAL VISUAL (4)

Chapter 5 is made up of tested techniques and processes for producing many different types of transparencies from an original such as the one illustrated.

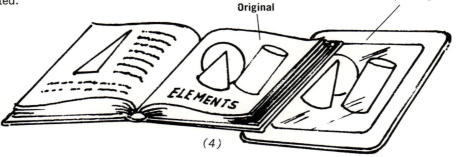

Original

Transparency

ELEMENTS

(4)

ILLUSTRATING TECHNIQUES

Pens and Markers

Drawing and Lettering Inks

Pencils and Crayons

Accessories and Devices for Illustrating

Basic Cutting Devices and Techniques
Special Cutting Devices
Basic Cutting Techniques
Other Cutting Devices

Drawing, Paste-up, and Lettering Surfaces

Preparation of Working Surface

Idea Sources for Visuals

Printed Art Aids
Charting (Drafting) Tapes
Shading (Texture) Sheets
Clip Art
ModulArt

Simplified Paste-up Techniques

Symbol Templates

Photosketching Techniques

Art Aids for Stencil and Spirit Duplication
Instructions for Drawing on Stencils
and Spirit Masters

Enlarging Visuals by Projection

Reducing Visuals by Reverse Projection

Enlarging and Reducing Visuals with a Pantograph

Enlarging Visuals with the Rubber Band Technique

Grid Drawing

Pounce Pattern for Image Transfer
Variations in Using
the Pounce Pattern

Visual Transfer Techniques

ILLUSTRATING TECHNIQUES

With an ever-increasing awareness of the many valuable visual materials now available in magazines, newspapers, and other printed sources, the creative individual using the visual approach to instruction will want to turn to the production of materials based on some of his own visual ideas. When the decision has been made to visualize an idea, and the purposes, content, and method of presentation have been decided upon, the problem of the basic illustration arises. The difficulty in physically forming the image on paper or acetate becomes so frustrating to some people that they give up the idea, and all the potentials of visual communication are lost. The inability to see form, the lack of knowledge of materials and equipment, a nervous hand, a dripping pen often force the individual into an avenue of escape. Except for the few who have the advantage of training in drawing, or have access to art services, creating the visual image will be one of the most serious problems in developing materials. In recent years great advancement has been made in developing equipment and materials to help those who are not adept at creating their own graphs, diagrams, maps, and illustrations. Not only do these new materials help the inexperienced person, but they also speed production for the professional artist.

A knowledge of some of the older techniques combined with a knowledge of the newly developed materials and equipment will expand tremendously the potential of the nonartist in developing visual imagery. It is, therefore, very important for the instructor to keep informed concerning the many production aids available for the process of visualization.

Hundreds of drawing templates are being produced to facilitate the drawing of symbols of various kinds. Drafting tapes in a wide variety of sizes and patterns help to simplify the visualizer's problems. A large assortment of shading sheets is available to shortcut the monotonous drawing of repetitive patterns and textures. Symbols of various objects printed on sheets enable the individual to obtain repetitive silhouette images for use on graphs and charts. Large assortments of prepared art to be used for paste-up are appearing in the form of sheets and booklets and may be subscribed to as one would a magazine to ensure a continuous, incoming flow of new and varied drawings and illustrations. It is the knowledge and use of these art aids that is vitally important to those interested in developing their own presentation materials. The greater the knowledge one has of these visual means of expression, the more flexibility one will have in expressing an idea.

Because of the variety of visual means of expression, size of the image becomes important. The size of image may vary from a large drawing on the blackboard to a small drawing on papers to be passed out. Methods of enlarging and reducing image size must be understood. Methods of transferring an image from one surface to another are important to know. As one's knowledge of these areas grows, the creation of meaningful visualizations becomes increasingly easy.

PENS AND MARKERS

There are various types of pens, each particularly suited to specific problems related to producing images on transparent and opaque surfaces. The pens and markers presented here should solve most problems where a line in black, white, or color is desired. Additional information on each of the pens can be obtained from sources listed in Chapter 6.

Speedball Lettering Pens (5)

Metal lettering and drawing pens that fit into a metal, plastic, or wood pen holder. Ideal for lettering in poster making, for example. Special pens are available for left-handed users. Four point styles available follow:

A. Designed to produce square poster-type letters with single stroke.
B. For single-stroke round Gothic letters. For drawing and sketching.
C. Will duplicate strokes of the flexible hand-cut reed pen. Used for Roman and italic alphabets with "thick" and "thin" elements.
D. With oval marking tip, used for bold poster Roman alphabet with "thick" and "thicker" elements.

Speedball Auto-feed Pen (6)

A fountain-type pen which feeds ink into regular Speedball lettering and drawing pens. Fill like a fountain pen and simply press the button on the side for more ink in the reservoir of the pen. Holder will accept all standard Speedball lettering and drawing pens.

Technical Fountain Pen (7)

A nonclogging fountain pen which uses india or regular drawing inks. Some

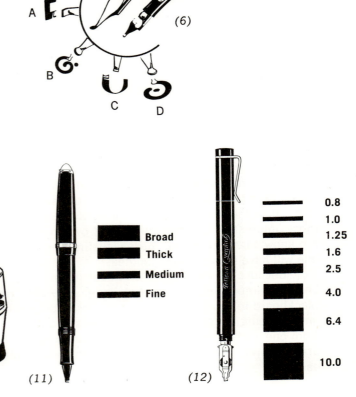

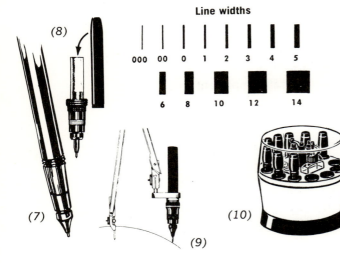

Line widths

000 00 0 1 2 3 4 5

6 8 10 12 14

Broad
Thick
Medium
Fine

0.8
1.0
1.25
1.6
2.5
4.0
6.4
10.0

(7) (8) (9) (10) (11) (12)

4

models will accept acetate inks. Pen line widths range from 00 to 5. This type of pen is ideal for drawing directly on clear or matte (frosted) acetate and for use with transparent irregular and ellipse guides.

Reservoir Pen (8)

A fountain-type pen designed for those doing a considerable amount of lettering or ink drawing. These pens have a translucent plastic reservoir that holds sufficient ink for many hours of lettering. Keuffel & Esser (LeRoy) and Letterguide pens will fit into mechanical lettering scribers also. Pen line widths range from 000 to 5. Keuffel & Esser pens are available in line widths 000 to 6 and 8, 10, 12, and 14.

Beam Compass Reservoir Pen Attachment (9)

Special attachment for a beam compass which permits the use of a reservoir pen.

Pen Humidifier (10)

Koh-I-Noor, Inc., manufactures a revolving humidified pen container for storing reservoir pens. The humidified interior of the container prevents ink points from drying out. The base section contains an integral sponge ring to maintain a humid interior atmosphere. Humectant (Koh-I-Noor product) is used to activate the sponge ring, or it can be moistened with water.

Brush-point Pen (11)

A nonclogging fountain pen that will accept drawing, writing, and acetate inks. The interchangeable points are made of nylon or flexible perlon fibers. Ideal for making wide lines and for filling in large areas and open letters.

Pelican Graphos Pens (12)

The Pelican (Pelikan) Graphos fountain-type pens, with their 60 interchangeable nibs (points), are suitable for technical drawing, freehand drawing, sketching, lettering, or ruling. The pen illustrated is the T ruling pen which is designed for broad lines and for poster work. The line widths for this pen are also illustrated.

Ruling Pen (13)

A drafting instrument designed for drawing precision ink lines on opaque and transparent surfaces. Ideal for drawing lines on prepared (special-surface) acetate. Drawing inks of various colors can be used in the pen.

Contour Ruling Pen (14)

A ruling pen for drawing curves; will follow irregular curves with ease. Can also be used as a pen for regular straight-line ruling.

Wricoprint Pen (15)

Special lettering pen designed for use with Wrico standard stencil lettering guides. Can be used as an india ink pen for ruling, irregular curves, symbol templates, etc. Line widths are illustrated.

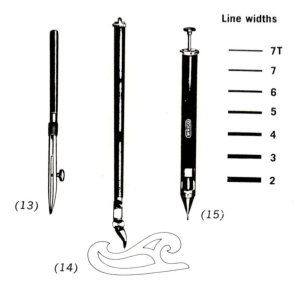

Line widths

7T
7
6
5
4
3
2

(13)

(14)

(15)

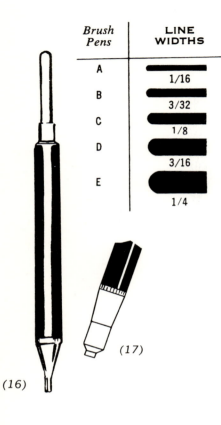

Brush Pens	LINE WIDTHS
A	1/16
B	3/32
C	1/8
D	3/16
E	1/4

(16)

(17)

Mechanical Scriber Lettering Pens (*18*)

India ink lettering pens designed for use in mechanical lettering scribers. Complete unit consists of a pen and cleaner pen. See chart for line widths. These pens can also be used in special holders for freehand lettering and drawing.

Mechanical Scriber Lettering Pen Holder (*19*)

Accepts standard mechanical scriber lettering pens. Designed so that when held comfortably in hand, the pen is perpendicular to the drawing or lettering surface. Ideal for freehand lettering, drawing, and ink line ruling. LeRoy (Keuffel & Esser) also manufactures a holder which will accept the larger pens (sizes 9 to 14).

Wrico Brush Pen (*16*)

A metal brush pen designed for use with Wrico Sign-Maker lettering guides. Ideal for producing ink lines from ⅟₁₆ to ¼ inch wide. Recommended for use with india ink only.

Wrico Adaptor Pen (*17*)

A special Wrico Brush pen used for obtaining different effects with the same Wrico Sign-Maker lettering guide. First letter of pen indicates width of line made by the pen; second letter indicates guide for which it is designed to be used. For example, pen No. AB makes an A-width line as shown in the chart with any lettering guide designed for Brush pen B.

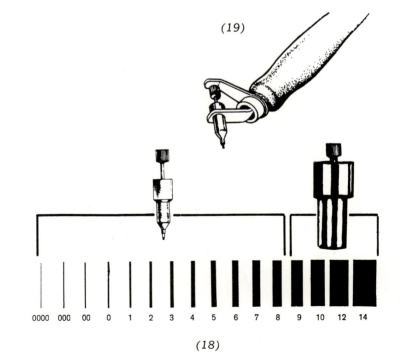

(19)

0000 000 00 0 1 2 3 4 5 6 7 8 9 10 12 14

(18)

Crow Quill Pen *(20)*

A very fine pen that has a flexible point with a tubular shaft that fits a special holder. Ideal for fine-line pen and ink drawing on opaque and transparent surfaces that will accept india-ink lines.

**Hunt Bowl Pointed Pen
Model 512** *(21)*

A bowl-pointed extra-fine pen recommended for lettering and drawing on prepared and matte (frosted) acetate.

Metal Brush Pens *(22)*

A unique concept in lettering pens. The pens are made of flexible layers of steel and produce lines with a single stroke from 1⁄16 to 1 inch wide. Pens are ideal for making large posters and signs. Speedball steel brushes (pens) are available in four sizes. Coit's pens are available in nine sizes.

**Mechanical Scriber
Ball-point Pen** *(23)*

A ball-point pen-stylus with black or red reproducing ink for offset (direct-image) masters, and blue ink for layout work. Also used as a stylus for direct lettering or drawing on duplicating stencils and masters.

Ball-point Pen *(24)*

Ink-controlled ball-point pen designed for smooth writing, drawing, and lettering. Ideal for use with cardboard and plastic stencil guides, die-cut letters, etc.

Nylon-point Pens *(25)*

Fountain-type pens with a specially tapered point made of nylon or fiber which produces a permanent ink line or a water-base ink line. Will write on most surfaces. Assorted colors available.

Felt-point Pens *(26)*

Plastic or metal fountain-type pens with a variety of point styles. Contain permanent or water-base inks in assorted colors.

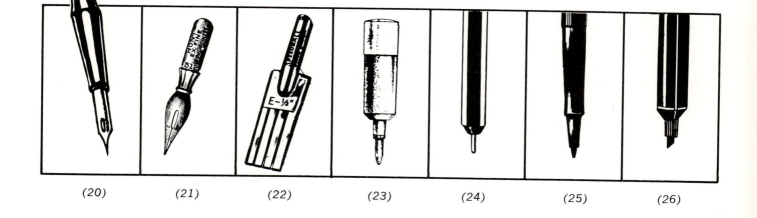

(20)　　(21)　　(22)　　(23)　　(24)　　(25)　　(26)

DRAWING AND LETTERING INKS

Many pages could be written just on the variety of inks available for drawing and lettering; inks for opaque surfaces such as paper, cardboard, chalkboards and inks for transparent surfaces such as clear or matte (frosted) acetate, glass. In selecting the best type of ink to use, one should take into consideration the type of surface on which inking is to be done, whether ink line is to be projected or not, permanent or water-base ink is desired, and so forth. The inks most widely used are briefly described here. Chapter 6 lists sources from which additional information can be obtained.

Acetate Inks

Opaque or transparent inks designed for use on acetate or plastic surfaces. Some inks are permanent; others are removable. Inks can be applied with brush, pen, or airbrush. Transparent inks project in brilliant color. Special fountain-type pens are available for use with acetate inks.

Chalkboard Ink

A white ink designed especially for the chalkboard. Will resist erasing or sponge washing with water. Color chalk marks are easily erased from ink lines. Ink is easily removed from chalkboard with a cloth dampened with solvent furnished with ink and pen set, or with most dry-cleaning solvents or cleaning powders.

Drawing Inks (Color)

Transparent, free-flowing color drawing inks. White is the only color that is not transparent. All colors are intermixable and work well in brushes, pens, and air-brushes.

Felt-point Pen Inks

Special inks for felt-point pens that can be refilled. Two types of inks are avail-

able: water-base, which can be removed with a damp cloth, and permanent-base. Assorted colors available.

Gold and Silver Inks

Ready-to-use gold or silver ink for use with pen or brush.

Hectograph (Gelatin) Ink

A specially formulated ink for use in the preparation of hectograph masters. Inked masters will produce up to sixty good copies. Available in assorted colors.

Lantern Slide Ink

A special transparent ink for use on etched lantern slide glass and matte (frosted) acetate. Assorted colors available.

Offset Master (Direct-image) Ink

A writing, drawing, and lettering ink for use on direct-image offset masters. Can be used in a ruling pen for precision lines. A knife blade or razor blade and special eraser are used to make corrections.

Stamp Pad Ink

Special ink for stamp pads. Assorted colors available. Sanford Ink Company manufactures a stamp pad ink in a roll-on bottle. Bottle inks often come with a handy brush cap applicator. Stamp pad ink for direct offset is also available.

Stencil Ink

Opaque ink in aerosol spray can or bottle for use with metal interlocking and oil-board stencil letters. A fast-drying, pigmented ink for all kinds of surfaces: wood, cardboard, and metal. Bottle inks can be applied with stencil brush or airbrush.

White Ink

For dense white mark on practically all surfaces. Will work on x-ray films, photographic negatives, plastics, leather, cellophane, glass, and wood. Can be thinned for use in lettering pens.

PENCILS AND CRAYONS

Pencils are not ordinarily thought of as a medium for finished artwork. However, they play a part in the preparation of a number of instructional media in one form or another. The pencils and crayons presented here relate in some degree to a number of techniques treated in this book. Additional information on pencils and crayons can be found in Chapter 6.

Thermocopy Reproducing Pencil (28)

Contains a special lead that can be reproduced in a thermocopy machine. Pencil lines give strong, clear copies. A soft lead pencil can also be used as a reproducing pencil.

Offset Master (Direct-image) Reproducing Pencil (29)

A high-quality medium lead pencil which produces a reproducing image on direct-image offset masters. Used for handwriting, ruling, drawing, or underscoring. Printed copy has the same pencil-like appearance as the original copy.

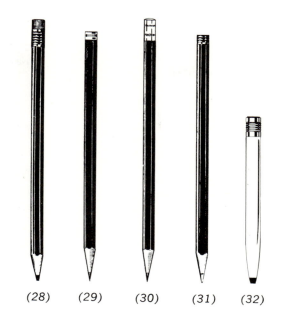

(28)   (29)   (30)   (31)   (32)

Spirit Duplicator Pencil (30)

An indelible copy pencil for use on spirit and hectographic duplicator masters. Writing, drawing, and lettering can be done directly on the master with this pencil.

Spirit Duplicator Correction Pencil (31)

A special pencil for making corrections on spirit and hectographic masters. Simply rub pencil over the error. Pencil contains a substance similar to the coating on the master. This substance combines with the carbon deposit on the master. For best results, remove raised carbon deposit with a razor blade.

Transparent Color Marking Pencil (32)

A pencil that has been especially created for use with overhead projection equipment. Leads are smooth and strong and appear in deep transparent color when projected. Markings can be removed with a damp cloth.

9

Opaque Color Marking Pencil (33)

Opaque color all-purpose marking pencil with a lead that writes in dense color on glass, plastic, acetate, cellophane, metal, etc. Marking pencils are also known as *grease* or *China* marking pencils. A damp cloth can be used to remove unwanted pencil marks from nonporous surfaces.

Color Drawing Pencil (34)

A water-soluble or special lead coloring pencil which permits writing, drawing, and coloring on matte (frosted) acetate. Clear plastic spray must be applied to the working surface to make the color transparent for projection. Excellent for making matte (frosted) acetate transparencies.

Nonreproducing Pencil (35)

Produces a light shade of blue which is nonreproducing in line work. This special color pencil is also used to block in and mark key lines on sketches and line mechanicals.

Lantern Slide Crayons (36)

Specially prepared crayons for applying transparent color to etched (matte or frosted) lantern slide glass and acetate. Crayons come in assorted colors.

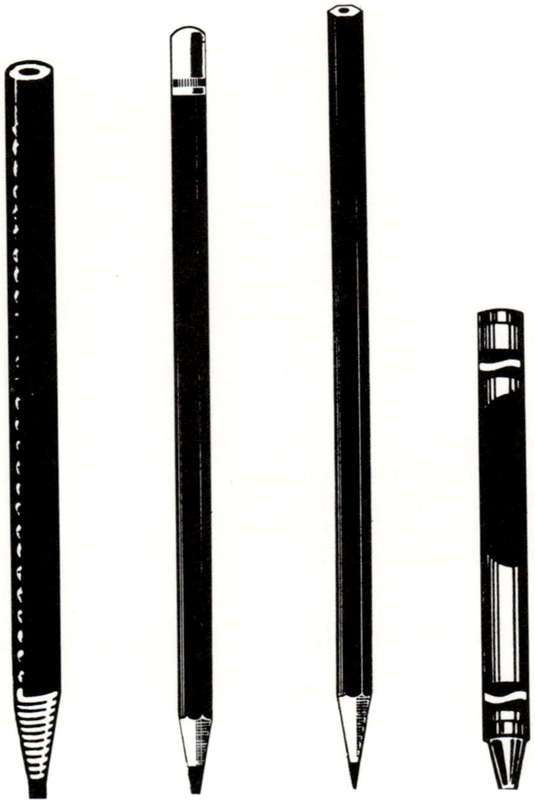

(33) (34) (35) (36)

Wax Crayons

Conventional wax marking (crayon) used for adding opaque color to such materials as paper and cardboard. See page 84 for application in the preparation of special effects in lamination.

ACCESSORIES AND DEVICES FOR ILLUSTRATING

Both the professional and nonprofessional artist and the producer of visual instructional media will find the accessories and devices illustrated and discussed here most helpful and time-saving.

Ellipse and Circle Templates (Guides) (37)

Transparent or translucent plastic templates for drawing perfect forms on paper, cardboard, acetate, duplication stencils, etc. When the drawing is to be in ink or color, pens such as ball-point, nylon-point, reservoir, technical fountain, and Wricoprint are recommended.

Adjustable (Flexible) Curve (38)

A plastic or metal device that easily can be bent into any desired curve or shape. Once bent, the curve holds its shape without being held. The smooth edge of the curve permits drawing with a pen or pencil. This device is also useful for the preparation of visual layouts.

Compasses (39)

Compasses are available for practically every illustrating requirement. (a) Chalk-board compass, made of wood or metal, which holds chalk, pencil, or crayon in an adjustable holder on one leg. Useful for making large circles on the chalk-board, on cardboard and wood; (b) ink compass designed for making circles in ink on paper, acetate, etc.; (c) pencil compass for making circles in pencil; (d) yardstick beam compass consists of two metal parts that fit a standard-size yardstick. Adjusts easily and makes accurate circles up to 66 inches in diameter.

Pantograph (40)

A precision-made drawing instrument consisting of a metal or wood frame with adjustable joints. Used to make enlargements or reductions of original art. Detailed instructions for the use of the pantograph can be found on page 44.

Circular Proportional Slide Rule (41)

A white plastic device for obtaining proportions on reducing or enlarging photographs, artwork. Gives number of times of reduction or enlargement of original size plus all possible new proportions.

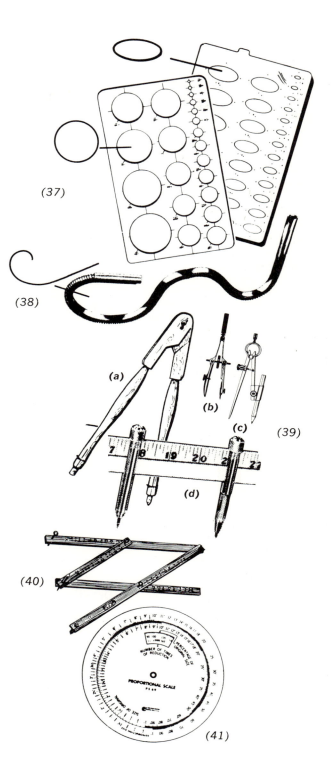

(37)

(38)

(a)

(b)

(c)

(39)

(d)

(40)

(41)

T square (42)

A T-shape metal, plastic, or wood ruler for drawing parallel lines. Also used as a support for lettering templates and devices. To use, hold the T-square head against the left side of the drawing board, for the top and bottom of the board may not be square. Line up drawing surface with top edge of blade. While holding T-square head firmly against the board, hold pen or pencil vertically and draw horizontal lines. Move T square downward for additional lines.

Plastic Triangle (43)

Transparent plastic triangular drafting device for drawing vertical and angle lines. To use, hold pen or pencil vertically and draw against the left edge as illustrated. Use the left hand to hold the triangle in place against the top edge of the T square. To raise the triangle off the working surface to prevent ink from smearing, tape small thin coins to the reverse side.

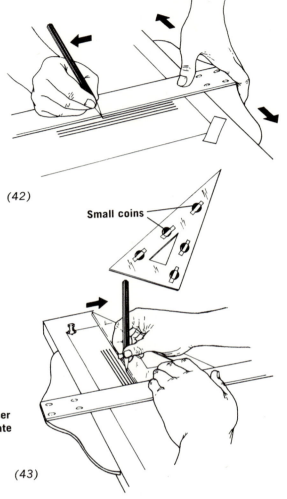

(42)

Small coins

Ink riser template

(43)

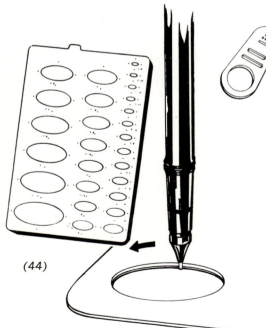

(44)

Drawing Ellipses (44)

Ball-point, nylon-point, reservoir, technical fountain, and Wricoprint pens can be used to trace ellipse and circle templates. Hold the pen in a vertical position and trace against the guide opening. To raise the template off the working surface while inking, use an ink riser template or tape small thin coins to the reverse side of the template.

Drawing Curves with Irregular Transparent (French) Curves (45)

Curves that cannot be made with a compass can be made with these drawing devices. First sketch the curve line in pencil, positioning the curve to get the desired line, then finish the line in a medium desired. Ball-point, contour, nylon-point, reservoir, technical fountain, and Wricoprint pens are recommended for use with irregular curves.

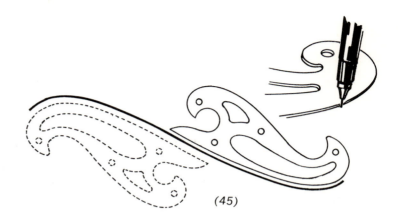

(45)

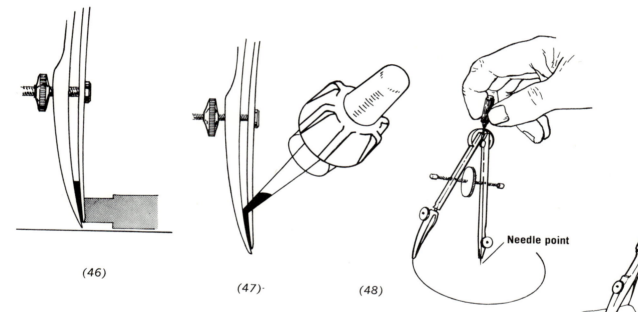

(46)

(47)

(48)

Needle point

(49)

Inking Instruments

The ruling pen is a drafting tool used for drawing accurately ruled lines on paper, cardboard, acetate. The adjustable screw can be set for different width lines. To use, hold pen in a vertical position against the drawing instrument (T square, triangle, etc.) as illustrated (46). The height of the ink supply should be about $\frac{3}{16}$ inch (47).

The ink compass is designed for making circles in ink. Ink filling should be the same as for a ruling pen. To use, set the needle point of the compass at center point of where circle is to be drawn, hold the pen vertical, and turn clockwise by twisting thumb and index finger as illustrated (48). To fill both the ruling pen and ink compass use a dropper-stopper or an eyedropper.

To clean pens, use a small piece of tissue, cloth, or chamois skin (49). If ink has dried, use a solution of household ammonia and water. Commercial pen cleaners are also available.

BASIC CUTTING DEVICES AND TECHNIQUES

SPECIAL CUTTING DEVICES

The common single-edge razor blade, because of its availability, is one of the most common cutting devices. Special inexpensive razor blades are available in quantity lots from art supply houses. The extensive use of the razor blade for scraping and cutting has led to the development of a great number of handles and holders to facilitate use.

Some holders have been developed for single-edge blades (50, 51), while others are to be used with double-edge blades (52). Although these holders are available, often the blade is used in its original form. When the single-edge blade is used without a holder, the index finger usually furnishes the necessary pressure for cutting. After a while, the pressure on the narrow top edge of the blade causes the finger to become quite sore. Several windings of drafting tape around the finger will help alleviate this irritation (53).

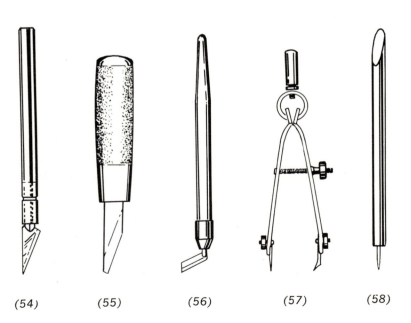

(50)   (51)   (52)   (53)

A great variety of special cutting knives is available from the stencil knife with a very delicately pointed blade (54) to the heavy-duty mat cutter (55). When it is necessary to a make a straight cut through heavy materials, the heavy-duty mat cutter works well. For greater maneuverability in cutting out delicate designs from lightweight paper, film, or tissue, a finely pointed knife is essential. Some specially designed cutting devices are available that satisfy the needs of specific cutting problems. The swivel knife is designed to cut lightweight materials (56). Because of the swivel head in the blade holder, it is possible to cut irregular curves with ease. A compass with attached cutting blade facilitates the cutting of circles of various sizes (57). When cutting odd shapes

(54)   (55)   (56)   (57)   (58)

from lightweight color or texture adhesive sheets, you will find that the cutting needle works well (58). A number of special cutting devices are designed to cut beveled edges (59). After the blade has been adjusted, they may also be used for scoring and straight cutting. No one cutting instrument will satisfy all needs.

No matter what type of cutting device is being used, it is essential to have the blades sharp at all times. The blades for some cutting knives are inexpensive and should be replaced as soon as they become dull. In other cases, the blade should be sharpened to keep it in good cutting condition at all times. A dull blade will tend to tear the paper. To protect the blade of the knife as well as ensure a clean, finished cut, one must always work on a smooth, firm surface that will not damage the blade as it passes through the material being cut. Scrap cardboard works well for this purpose.

BASIC CUTTING TECHNIQUES

When the cutting blade is properly used, the heavier cardboard materials can be cut with relative ease. Use a series of repeated cutting strokes and hold the blade at about a 30° angle for greatest efficiency (60). At this angle the blade tends to have a "sawing" effect and cuts

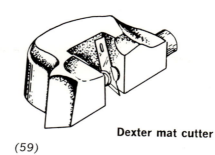

Dexter mat cutter

(59)

the more resistant paper fiber quite easily. Holding the blade in too vertical a position tends to cause a buildup of paper fibers in front of the cutting edge (61). The blade, instead of cutting the more resistant material, tears it, causing a roughly cut edge. This is especially true if the cutting edge of the blade is slightly dull. If the blade is held at a low angle, the cut will be quite satisfactory, but because of the extensive amount of cutting edge imbedded into the paper surface, maneuverability of the blade is impaired (62). Thus, it may be difficult to follow a prescribed line, especially if it is other than straight. Although the razor blade has been used to demonstrate these principles of cutting, they will apply to almost any single-edge cutting device.

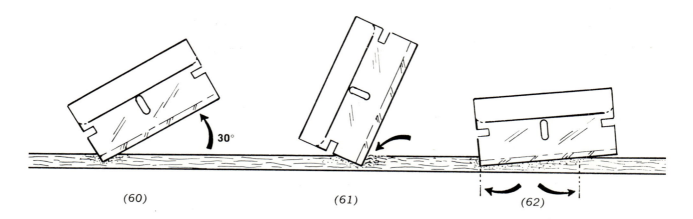

(60)   *(61)*   *(62)*

First stroke

(63)

After proper positioning of the blade, a second consideration is the application of even pressure on the blade as it is drawn along the paper or cardboard surface. With the heavier paper materials, the first cut should be made with a light, even pressure to create an accurate initial cut which will serve as a guide for repeated strokes of the blade in completing the cut. Each following draw of the blade should be made with a firm, even pressure so that each cut is of a uniform, even depth (63). The thickness of cardboard has been exaggerated in the diagram.

(64)

Often the applying of excessive pressure on the blade tends to lead to a variation in depth of cut. After repeated strokes of the cutting blade, the irregularities in cutting depth are amplified, causing irregular areas of paper fiber to accumulate (64). Then as the blade is forced through these heavy areas, tearing takes place; a roughly finished cut results. Where it is necessary to cut around extremely complicated forms, a sharply pointed blade, other than a razor blade, is recommended because of the greater maneuverability of a small blade in a depth of cardboard.

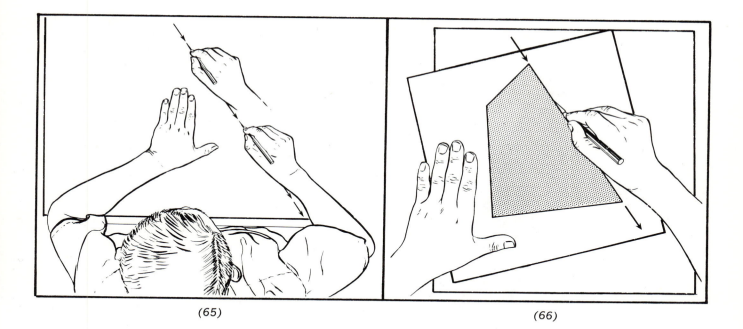

(65)

(66)

Obtaining a clean, flowing cut through cardboard or paper with a sharp blade is to a great extent dependent upon the position and movement of the arm in the cutting process. One of the most natural movements for the arm is moving in a straight diagonal line across the front of the body (65). Working with a cutting blade in this position helps ensure greater ease and accuracy in the cutting process (66). By rotating the artwork during the cutting process, it is possible to take advantage of this natural arm movement (67).

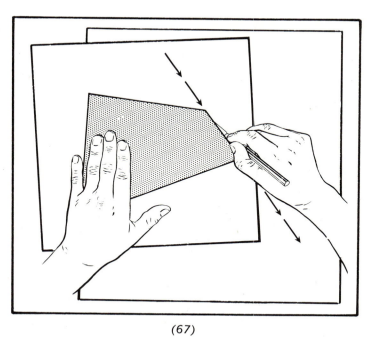

(67)

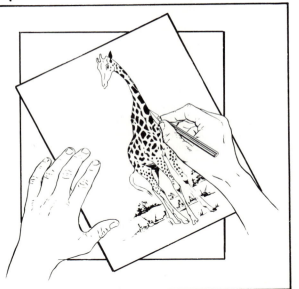

(68)

(70)

(69)

The process of cutting out irregularly shaped images will be greatly simplified if a few moments are taken to plan the cutting sequence. First, it is important to plan the direction of each cut. It is best when cutting irregular shapes to move the blade in an outward direction away from the center of the image. This will help prevent a possible slip of the cutting blade into the image area. The dotted lines on the diagram (68) suggest the direction of some of the basic cuts. Second, it is important to place the line to be cut in such a position that it approximates the natural movement of the cutting arm (69). This requires a new positioning of the image before each cut is made. In order to avoid rough or torn edges, it is important to use a sharp blade, especially when the image is printed on lightweight paper. If the cutout figure is to be mounted by the dry mounting process, the mounting tissue should be tacked to the back of the image before the cutting process is begun. In this way, the mounting tissue and the image will be cut simultaneously, guaranteeing perfect register of form (70).

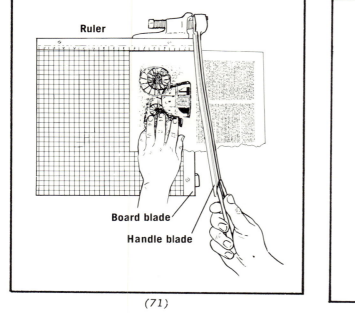

Ruler

Board blade

Handle blade

(71)

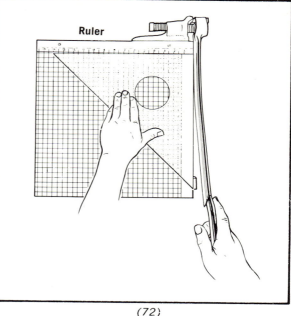

Ruler

(72)

OTHER CUTTING DEVICES

Paper Cutter

To most people the paper cutter is a simple cutting device, but it also is possibly the most misused and neglected. A carefully maintained cutter will ensure a clean, accurate cut through the weight and thickness of material for which it has been designed. Excessive thickness of paper or cardboard will tend to throw the cutting blade out of line. Cutting cheap cardboard and paper containing impurities should be avoided. Metal staples, often overlooked, can cause serious damage to a sharp blade. Excessive inward pressure on the blade handle will cause great wear on the board blade, gradually developing a slight curve in the blade; this makes cutting a straight edge almost impossible. When both the handle and board blades are sharp and in proper adjustment, the cut should be made with ease as the handle blade is lowered in a straight, downward movement. Spring adjustment in the handle should be carefully set to

avoid too strong an upward force. On large paper cutters excessive spring tension can cause the handle to spring back and cause injury to the operator. When cutting very lightweight tissue paper or similar material, it is often advantageous to place the material between two other lightweight sheets of scrap paper. This tends to avoid the tearing and shifting of the material being cut.

Generally, it is desirable to trim pictures, photographs, and magazine pages in a square or rectangular format. The paper cutter has been designed to do this with ease. When a known straight edge of the material being cut is placed against the ruler, the cutting blade should make a clean, right-angle cut (71). However, if you are working on an unfamiliar cutter, you cannot assume that the ruler is at a right angle to the cutting blade. A quick check can be made by placing a large triangle on the cutting board to determine if the ruler *is* at a right angle to the cutting edge (72). On most cutters the ruler can be

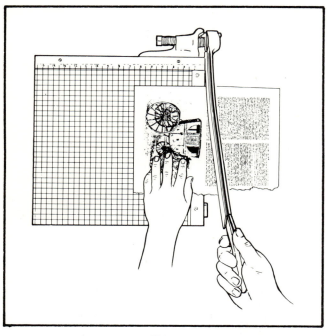

(73)

adjusted by loosening the screws which
hold it in place. Make the necessary adjustment and tighten the screws in
place. Where it is not feasible or possible to make adjustments on the ruler,
the grid lines on the surface of the
board will help in squaring the paper to
the cutting blade (73).

Make sure that a known straight
edge of the material being cut lines up
with the grid lines on the cutting board
for each cut. When the picture is rotated
each time a cut is made to make certain
the edge coincides with grid lines, a true
square or rectangular picture format results. (74).

When difficult paper or cardboard
is being cut or when the blade is dull,
there is a tendency for the material to
shift as the blade is lowered. This can be
prevented by pressing down firmly on a
strip of stiff cardboard or a straightedge
that has been placed over the material
close to the cutting edge.

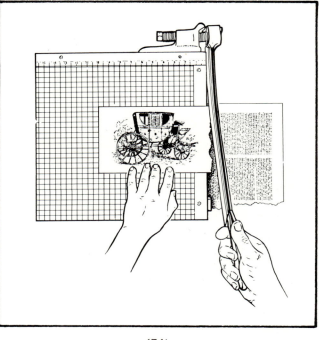

(74)

Circle Cutter (75)

A metal compass device for cutting perfect circles out of such materials as
paper, acetate, thin cardboard. It is used
much like a pencil or ink compass. The
cutting blade can be sharpened or replaced. The model illustrated can be ad-
justed to cut circles from $\frac{1}{16}$ to $3\frac{1}{4}$

inches in diameter with no overlap. Other models can cut circles up to 26½ inches in diameter.

Corner Rounder (76)

A metal cutting device for rounding corners of paper, cardboard, acetate, etc. Cutting blades are interchangeable. The model illustrated will accommodate 8½- by 11-inch stock conveniently.

Letterguide Scriber Cutting Knives

Swivel knife (77)

A special cutting knife for use in the Letterguide scriber and similar units. Designed to cut all types of silk-screen films, thin stencil paper and film, adhesive backed acetate, etc.

Silk-screen knife (78)

Designed mainly for use in the Letterguide scriber. A precision cutting device for cutting letters out of silk-screen film (open-letter templates must be used). Knife can be adjusted for desired cutting depth.

Electric Stylus (79)

A compact electrical device that writes like a pencil on acetate, plastic, glass, wood, duplication stencils. Engraves lines, letters, visuals.

DRAWING, PASTE-UP, AND LETTERING SURFACES

There are various types of surfaces on which one can draw, paste-up, and letter, each having characteristics suitable for a particular job. A few of the more commonly used materials will be described here and are included in this chapter because they relate directly or indirectly to many of the techniques discussed in this book. Sources for each of the materials described can be found in Chapter 6.

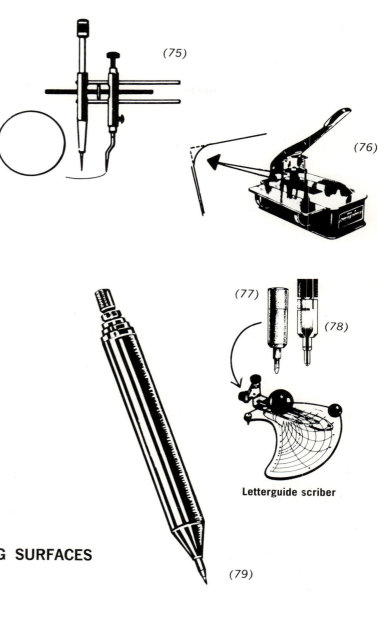

(75)

(76)

(77)

(78)

Letterguide scriber

(79)

Drawing Paper (80)

A high-quality paper for practically all drawing, paste-up, and lettering purposes. A variety of surfaces and weights is available. The use of drawing paper for paste-up art is recommended when the art is to be copied in thermocopy, diazo, or electronic stencil-cutting machines.

Illustration Board (81)

High-quality drawing paper mounted on cardboard backing. Generally recommended for finished artwork because it need not be mounted. Available in several weights and finishes.

Tracing Paper (82)

A high-quality translucent paper for all tracing purposes. Ideal for the preparation of diazo masters. Available in several weights, in rolls and sheets.

Matte (Frosted) Acetate (83)

A nonflammable cellulose acetate with a matte (frosted) surface on one side. Surface permits drawing, lettering, and coloring with pencil or pen. Projection slides and overhead transparencies can be made with matte acetate. Can also be used for the preparation of diazo masters. Available in pads, rolls, and sheets. See page 167 for instructions related to the use of matte acetate.

Carbon-coated Projection Acetate (Film) (84)

A lightweight acetate film coated with a black opaque carbon material. Lines scribed on the coated (dull) side with a pencil or other stylus-type instrument will show up as luminous white lines on a black background when used on the overhead projector. See pages 51 and 169 for instructions related to the use of this film.

Prepared (Specially Surfaced) Acetate (85)

A clear (transparent) acetate with a special coating on both sides that will accept poster paints, watercolors, inks, and dyes without crawling. Available in sheets and pads. Ideal for making handmade slides and overhead projection transparencies (see pages 166 to 168).

Clear Acetate Sheet or Roll (86)

An all-purpose transparent cellulose sheet or roll. Can be used much like an ordinary sheet of paper for drawing, writing, and so forth. Surface will accept a variety of drawing and marking devices. Also useful for making overlays for overhead transparencies. A clear acetate roll is available for use on the overhead projector, but it requires a special roll adapter.

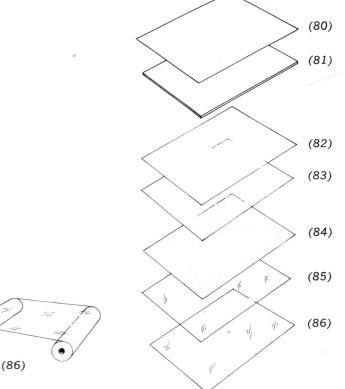

(80)
(81)
(82)
(83)
(84)
(85)
(86)

(86)

PREPARATION OF WORKING SURFACE

Whatever technique of lettering or illustrating is to be used, the preparation of the working surface is most important and should be given careful attention. Here are a few tips for preparing the working surface for use.

A good drawing board and T square are the basic tools required for preparing the working surface. A Cam-lock drawing board or a board to which a Cam-lock channel is attached and a Cam-lock T square are highly recommended in that the T square can be locked into working position.

Aligning and Securing the Working Surface (87)

1. Place the T-square head against the left side of the drawing board and move to position (A) as illustrated.
2. Line up the working surface (paper, cardboard, acetate, etc.) with the top edge of the T-square blade. Secure surface to board with plastic pressure-sensitive discs, double-coated adhesive tape, pressure-sensitive tape, or pushpins.
3. Move the T-square to working position (B). The desired instrument or device (such as a lettering guide or triangle) can be placed on the top edge of T-square blade.

Double-coated Adhesive Tape (88)

Attach strips or small pieces of this tape to the drawing-board surface at points where contact is desired. Peel off the protective paper; this will expose the other adhesive side. Attach the working surface to the board as instructed in steps 1, 2, and 3. If the working surface is paper or cardboard, spray where tape contact points are to be with clear plastic spray; this will prevent damage to the back of the working surface when it is removed from drawing board.

Pressure-sensitive Discs (89a)

Clear plastic, pressure-sensitive ⅝-inch diameter discs for holding drawing and drafting materials to drawing boards, tables, or other working surface. Simply insert a disc at corner contact points under the material to be attached to the drawing board.

Pressure-sensitive Tape (89b)

Any pressure-sensitive tape can be used to attach working surface to secure it to the drawing board. Roll 1-inch pieces of tape, "sticky" side out, the thickness of a small pencil and stick one to each corner contact point under the material.

Pushpins (90)

Metal or glass pushpins can be inserted at corner contact points of surface material.

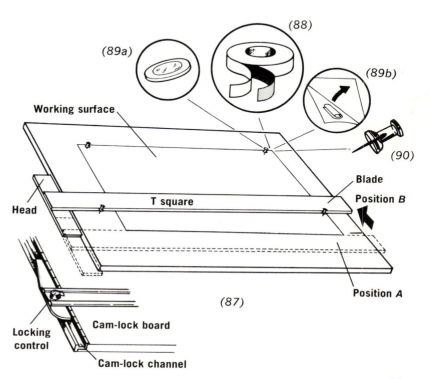

Magazine

(91)

GRAFIC SEX EXHIBITION JAN 2

Poster

NEWS

Newspaper

Brochure

Style

Rough sketch

Style
SHOW

Finished poster

IDEA SOURCES FOR VISUALS

Bear in mind that this book, directed primarily toward the nonprofessional artist and producer of visual instructional media, does not propose to teach the essentials of commercial art techniques. However, in Chapter 6 are a number of excellent publications that deal directly with commercial art and its many techniques. The major concern of this section is that of assisting the novice to find quick and easy solutions to planning and creating quality instructional media.

Once having decided what, in the way of content, is to be presented, the need for ideas related to layout, design, lettering, color, and so forth, is usually the first concern of the producer of instructional media. Here are suggested a few idea sources and their application to creating and preparing such materials as posters, charts, graphs, bulletin boards, displays, and transparencies.

Magazines, newspapers, picture brochures, travel posters, direct-mail pieces (91) are just a few of the many sources of excellent ideas that can be modified to create quality instructional media. Only one idea may come from a given source, such as an idea for the arrangement of lettering or pictures. A particular idea source may serve only to suggest possible color combinations, but this will be an important contribution to the finished product.

In many cases, however, one visual source, such as a picture brochure, may contain enough ideas to plan a poster. The first step, after consideration has been given to size, type of visuals, and lettering, is to make a rough sketch of the poster, using the brochure as guide. Modifications can be made to come up with the desired end product. Once the rough sketch has been finalized, the next step is that of actually producing the poster. A starting point might be to refer to page xi. Here you will find suggestions concerning how one might approach various problems of producing visual materials and references to certain sections of the book that illustrate and explain techniques designed to help solve a specific production problem. Another approach to producing the final product is to refer directly to the section of the book related to your specific production problem. For example, the lettering chart on page 100 suggests a number of techniques designed especially for poster making. All one needs to do is to follow the instructions and illustrations referred to in order to produce the lettering required.

Although this means of putting an idea to work may not seem "professional" in structure, it is a quick, easy way to produce a quality visual material.

Idea Source File (92)

To collect ideas related to layout, illustrations, color combinations, and lettering, start an idea file. It can include clips from magazines, newspapers, brochures, direct-mail advertisements, notices, announcements—literally any printed material.

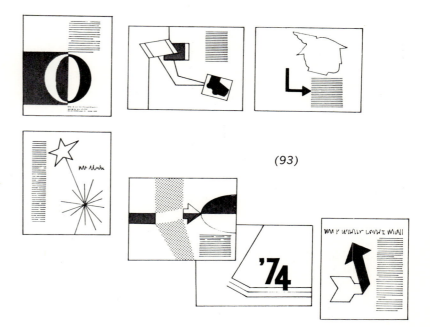

(93)

Example Layouts and Designs (93)

Here are a few example layouts and designs, all the results of ideas taken from the sources we have mentioned. Strict rules of layout have purposely been avoided so as not to confuse the beginning producer of visual media. The main concern in this case is to come up with a quick, attractive, and eye-catching visual.

(92)

PRINTED ART AIDS

CHARTING (DRAFTING) TAPES

Charting tapes include a wide variety of special tapes designed mainly for drafting and chart making. The use of these tapes has opened up a fresh new approach to a drafting task that in the past required many hours to perform. And the wide choice of tapes, many having different basic characteristics, enables one to produce visual materials of high quality without professional training. Charting tapes include color, shading, and symbol tapes in color and black and white. The printed surface of tapes is either transparent or opaque, either glossy or dull. The dull surface is preferred when the finished product is to be photographed. Tapes with a heat-resistant adhesive are designed for the preparation of art that is to be reproduced in a heat-type copying machine.

Charting tapes range in width from ¹⁄₆₄ inch to 2 inches. The wide-width tapes (94) are ideal for making bar graphs; the narrow-width tapes (95) are excellent for producing lines of various patterns.

Special tape dispensers are de-

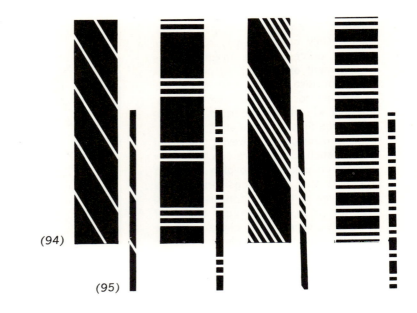

(94)

(95)

signed to produce tape lines with the aid of a straightedge (96). Flexible tapes in narrow widths can be used to make curved tape lines with the aid of an irregular (French) curve or an adjustable curve (97). When circles are to be "drawn," the flexible tapes can be attached to a special tape compass to produce tape circles of varied diameters.

Special tapes have been designed

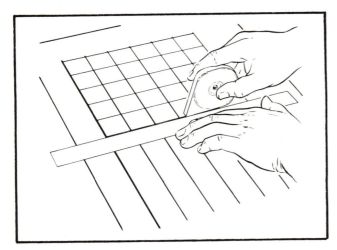

(96)

(97)

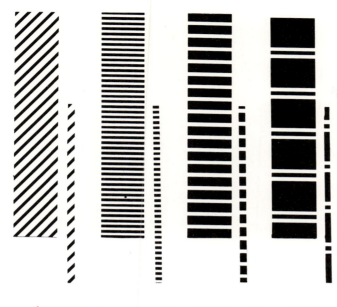

for use in the preparation of plant and office layouts, printed circuit designs, and many other special tasks. A wide variety of border-design tapes is available for artwork requiring professional-looking borders.

Symbol tapes, both adhesive-back and dry transfer, cover a variety of subject areas such as transportation, buildings, and human figures. Several manu-facturers offer custom-made symbol tapes as a special service.

Dry transfer symbol tapes are quite unique in that the symbols transfer from the tape to the drawing surface when a pencil or ball-point pen is rubbed over the symbol (98), and as the tape is lifted (99), the symbol remains on the drawing surface.

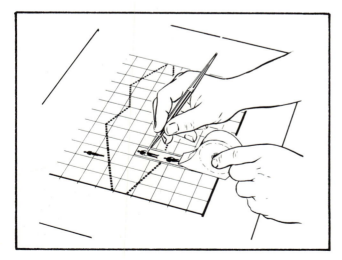

(98)

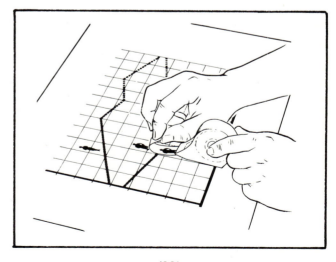

(99)

SHADING (TEXTURE) SHEETS

To help the user bypass extensive amounts of monotonous, repetitive drawing, adhesive-backed acetate sheets have been developed on which are printed repetitive opaque patterns (100). These sheets may be backed with a wax-type or pressure-sensitive, heat-resistant adhesive. Shading sheets used in heat copying machines must be of the heat-resistant variety. Shading sheets may be purchased with a glossy or matte finish. If the material is to be photographed, nonreflective matte finish is preferred. In some cases it is desirable to use these materials directly on transparencies. Should this be a requirement, the clear, transparent, heat-resistant material is recommended. It is important to place any unused material back on the support sheet for storage in a cool place.

The great variety of patterns (101) that can be obtained includes cross-hatch, stipple, diagonal lines, vertical lines, dot patterns, weaves, textures, and many others. Special patterns have been developed for draftsmen working in such areas as geography, geology, and architecture. Standard and graduate dot-screen patterns (102) may be obtained in a variety of line and density relationships. If shading sheets are to be used, it is very important to choose a pattern appropriate for the visual being constructed.

With the shading sheet still on its backing, lay it in position over the area of the illustration to be shaded and, being careful not to cut into the backing paper, cut an area of the shading material slightly larger than the area to be shaded (103). Peel the material from its backing. Place it over the drawing, lowering it onto the surface of the illustration (adhesive side down) so that air pockets and wrinkles do not form (104). Be sure to have a sharp cutting instrument. Carefully cut around the image and peel off the excess material (105). Press the shading material down for

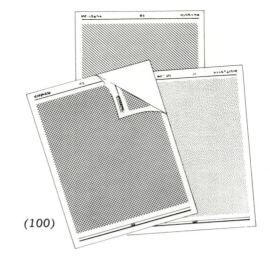

(100)

good adhesion. Other areas may be shaded in a similar manner.

Two variations should be mentioned. First, some shading materials are available which have the image printed on the top surface of the shading sheet. This permits the user to remove small areas of the pattern by etching off the surface with a sharp instrument. In this way, fine detail can be added that would be extremely difficult to add if the material had to be removed by cutting. The second variation involves

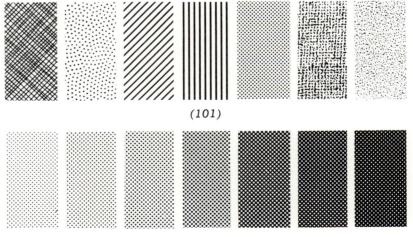

(101)

(102)

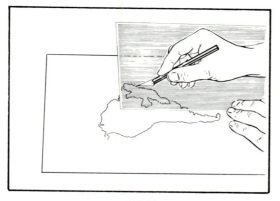

(103)

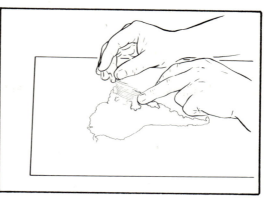

(104)

shading and texture sheet material of the dry transfer variety. When using this material, you must remove the printed sheet from its backing and place it over the area of the visual that is to be shaded. When the surface of the sheet is burnished, the printed pattern is transferred to the visual image (106). As the sheet is lifted from the visual, the printed pattern remains (107).

Wherever shading and texture patterns are needed, these adhesive-backed printed sheets can save time as well as furnish sharp, clean copy for a visual illustration.

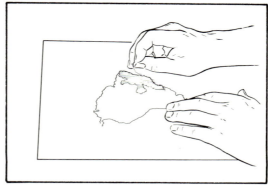

(105)

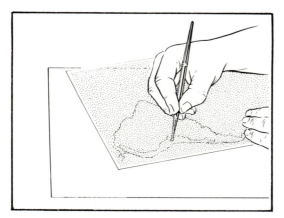

(106)

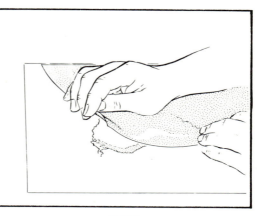

(107)

CLIP ART

When the person producing visual materials does not possess special drawing skill, or when time is a factor in the preparation of art, clip art may be the answer. Clip art is line and tone ready-to-use illustrations covering every practical subject classification from A to Z. Many clip art books (108) and sheets (109) contain symbols, decorative borders, and so forth. Several companies offer a subscription service through which subscribers receive updated and newly designed clip art periodically.

Some clip art is available in the form of sheets. These have a variety of drawings in various sizes and positions which can be manipulated with drawings or lettering from other sources to produce an original for electronic stencils, thermocopy, photographic, or other forms of reproduction. Old drawings, covering a wide range of subject matter, have been collected and reprinted in book form to serve as a source of ideas for the person having need for this type of art.

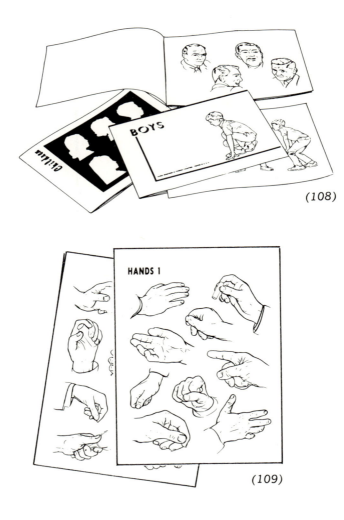

(108)

(109)

It is important to note that all the printed art aids, such as clip art, are closely related. Too often printed tapes, texture and shading sheets, and clip art are set off in separate, distinct categories, when actually they are very similar. First of all, these materials serve as some form of art aid in paste-up art. They may all be printed on transparent, translucent, or opaque base material. With some exceptions, most of these printed art aids adhere to a working surface (drawing paper, illustration board) with similar types of adhesives. Some of these art aids adhere by the dry transfer method: The art is printed on a translucent plastic carrier sheet and transfers to a working surface with the aid of a pencil, ball-point pen, or burnisher. Several companies offer a service for the printing of custom art in color or in black and white.

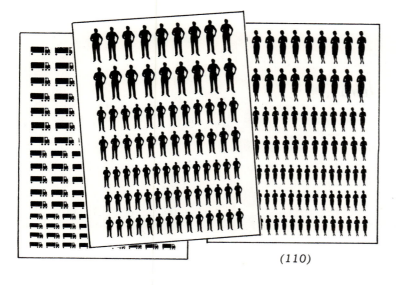

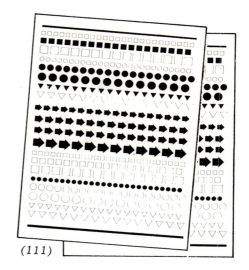

(110)

(111)

Printed sheets of repetitive sil-houette visuals (110) are available in a variety of subject areas. These sheets usually contain a choice of four or five sizes of visuals. They are ideal for use where repetitive symbols are required. Clip art also includes squares, circles, arrows, asterisks, stars, and so forth (111).

The paste-up of a simple poster might include a variety of art aids and techniques. In (112), the frame is printed tape, the map is hand-traced on lightweight paper, the shaded area is from a shading sheet, the zebra is clip art, and the spears of grass are hand-drawn. All these aids and techniques have been combined to create an original which can be reproduced by a variety of methods (113).

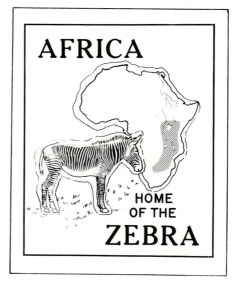

(112)

(113)

MODULART

A new and exciting art aid designed to give maximum flexibility to the designer and to furnish clean, crisp images for assembly is ModulArt. This technique consists of a variety of specially designed illustrative figures, costumes, animals, backgrounds, vehicles, and accessories—all in modular form (114). These modular images are printed on the underside of sheets of clear, matte-surfaced acetate in colors and in shades of gray. Each element is cut out separately and assembled on the drawing surface selected. Because of the transparent film base on which the images are printed, it is not necessary to cut the elements out exactly on the outline. The sheets are coated on the back with a transparent adhesive which, when lightly rubbed down, holds the image in place but also permits removal and new positioning if required. After final placement, the image is firmly burnished down on the surface. The burnishing process eliminates any sign of the cut edge of each element in the picture composition. ModulArt sheets are so designed that figures and backgrounds are interchangeable. The matte surface also permits the addition of detail to the picture composition with pen and ink or pencil. This allows unlimited freedom to create an endless variety of creative illustrations for all types of visual representation (115) (television, film, and slide titles; publication art).

(114)

(115)

SIMPLIFIED PASTE-UP TECHNIQUES

The term *paste-up* refers to art prepared in paste-up form specifically for any number of reproduction techniques (thermocopy, photocopy, electronic stencil copy, etc.). The true art of paste-up requires some professional know-how. However, an attempt has been made here to simplify the technique.

As a preliminary to the paste-up, it is a good idea to prepare a rough draft of what is intended to be the finished paste-up. This will help you visualize how the finished art will look and will serve as a guide in fitting all the art, lettering, shading, and so forth, together on the finished paste-up. The "rough" should be done on a sheet of paper the size of the finished art.

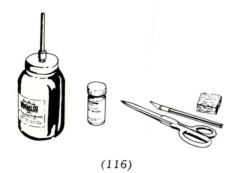

(116)

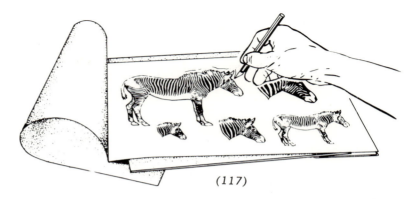

(117)

Basic Tools and Materials (116)

There are several basic tools and materials required for paste-up. They should include a drawing board, T square, triangle, cutting tools (such as scissors, razor blade, frisket knife), nonreproducing pencil, rubber cement, rubber cement eraser and correction material (liquid or paper). The nonreproducing pencil is for drawing any guidelines or marks on the finished artwork which will not be sensitive to most reproducing techniques or methods. A light-blue color pencil can also be used.

Instructions

1. Cut out the art (117) (clip art is illustrated here) with one of the cutting tools. Note that protective cardboard is being used to prevent cutting the next sheet in the clip art book.
2. Apply rubber cement to the reverse side of all paste-up art requiring adhesive (118). Next, apply cement to the areas on the working surface (paper, cardboard) where the art is to go (119). Allow both cemented surfaces to dry. The rubber cement should be thinned, 4 parts rubber cement to 1 part rubber cement thinner (solvent). This will allow the cement to flow freely from the brush.

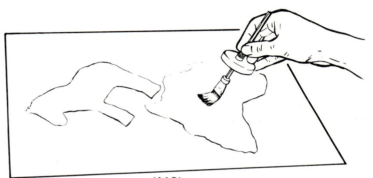

(118)

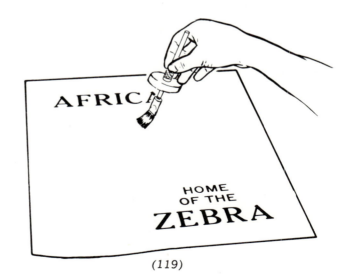

(119)

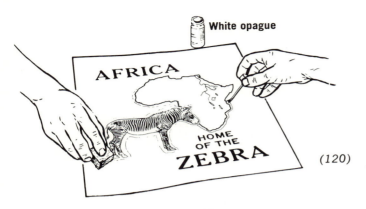

White opague

(120)

(121)

3. Attach the art to the working surface (*120*). Remove excessive cement from around the visual with a rubber cement eraser or rub off with a clean finger. Opaque out the cut line around the visual with white correction liquid. See pages 28-29 for instructions on adding shading.

4. Paste-up is ready for reproduction (*121*). Instructions for paste-up, related to a specific reproduction technique or method, should be followed very closely. What is presented here is only intended to be general instructions. Several good publications dealing with or containing information on paste-up technique are included in the Annotated Bibliography in Chapter 6.

SYMBOL TEMPLATES

Available on the market today are a variety of symbol templates (*122a*). These transparent plastic outline templates are made up of symbols that can be traced directly on a drawing surface with a variety of drawing instruments (*122b*). Templates covering almost every major subject area are available.

Drawing Symbols on Paper, Cardboard, Acetate

When drawing directly on paper, cardboard, and similar surfaces, pens such as ball-point, nylon-point, reservoir, technical fountain and Wricoprint are recommended, especially if a line in ink or color is desired. When drawing directly on prepared acetate, all the pens just mentioned, with the exception of the ball-point, can be used. The ink riser template is an ideal device for raising the symbol template far enough off the drawing surface to prevent ink from smearing while tracing the symbol.

Drawing on Stencils and Spirit Masters

Symbol templates are excellent drawing aids for stencils and spirit masters. A ball-point stylus or pen is recommended for tracing the desired symbol. Instructions for drawing on stencils can be found on page 40.

Mechanical Scriber Symbol Templates (*123*)

Special symbol templates designed for use with a mechanical lettering scriber equipped with a pen for ink line symbols, or with a special stylus for drawing symbols on stencils and spirit masters.

Ink riser template

Wricoprint pen

Ball-point pen

Technical fountain pen

(122a)

(122b)

(123)

PHOTOSKETCHING TECHNIQUES (124)

Often it is more desirable, or even necessary, to have a line or high-contrast drawing rather than an actual photograph for a visual presentation. This is often the case when developing masters or paste-up copy for various types of reproduction, such as used in the diazo, thermocopy, photographic silk screen, offset, letterpress, electronic stencil, spirit, and other duplicating processes used as printed or projected visuals. For the person with minimal art training who desires to make his own illustrations, the photosketching process may be a great aid. Even the professional artist may find this a way to expedite routine assignments or effect exact reproduction in size and detail.

By this method of drawing, the beginner can obtain very acceptable results. With some training and practice, he will find the drawing possibilities almost limitless, ranging from a simple outline drawing to one complete with shading. It is important to remember that with this method of illustration it is possible to omit or add detail; to clarify images that were indistinct or

(124)

too dark or light to be seen on the original photograph; to emphasize or de-emphasize parts of the imagery; to lose identity, as in the case of people appearing in the illustration; and to use an illustration which may in its original form not have been usable because of its poor photographic quality. By using

35

(125)

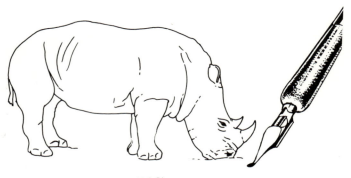

(126)

any of a wide range of pens and brushes, almost any effect in line drawing can be obtained from the simple line to stipple and crosshatched shading effects. This picture of the white rhinoceros (125) has been photosketched[(126) to (128)]using different drawing techniques with treatment ranging from a simple outline drawing to one complete in all detail.

The photosketches in (129) to (132) show a variety of subject matter treated in different ways. These illustrations were drawn by pen and brush or by a combination of both.

Instructions

1. Using waterproof india ink, sketch directly on the surface of the photograph. Although photographs with a glossy surface may be used, the ink will adhere better to one having a matte surface. If possible, it is recommended that a light photographic print be used. Detail in dark areas of a photograph will be easier to see if placed on a light box. Generally, the light passing through the back of the print will reveal detail hard to see by reflected light. If the glossy surface of the print tends to resist ink, or if it has oily fingerprints on its surface, rub the surface thoroughly with baking soda. If a mistake is made in the drawing, the ink may be removed immediately by wiping it off with damp cotton, or it may be allowed to dry and be painted out with white paint.

2. Allow the ink to dry thoroughly. This may require at least thirty

(129)

(130)

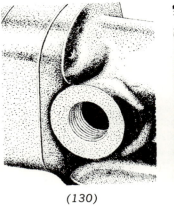

(131)

(132)

(127)　　　　　　　　　　　　　　　(128)

minutes. Often ink that appears to be dry may need more time. This is important since the image will be placed in liquid during the bleaching process (133).

3. Bleaching is the next step in the process. Regular iodine, procured from the local drugstore, may be used for the bleach solution. This iodine, as purchased, may be diluted with 2 to 3 parts of water. Place the photosketch into a pan of iodine solution (a) with the image side up. Avoid touching the ink image during the entire bleaching process. Be sure that the entire surface of the print is covered with iodine solution. Slight agitation helps speed up the process. The time the print remains in the bleach depends upon the characteristics of the photograph as well as the strength of the bleach solution.

4. When all traces of the dark photographic image have been replaced by one that is a dark brownish orange, remove the photosketch from the iodine solution and rinse the excess iodine off in cool water (b).

5. Place the print into a pan containing photographic fixing bath (hypo) (c). This chemical can be obtained at any photographic supply store. The solution will bleach out

the remaining iodine image, leaving a clean black-and-white drawing. Be sure that all traces of the yellow stain are removed before removing the print from the solution.

6. Place the photosketch in cool running water for about five minutes to remove the remaining chemicals (d).

7. Although this print can be dried on a regular photographic dryer, it may also be air-dried by simply laying it out on a clean piece of paper for a period of time (e). If care is taken, excess water may be blotted off the sketch by using newsprint or some other absorbent material. Some curling of the sketch during drying can be discouraged by placing a heavy porous cloth on top to straighten and hold it in a flat position.

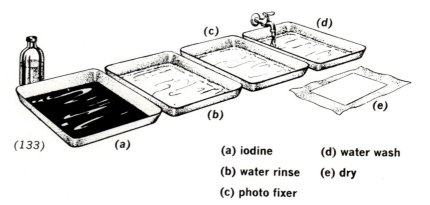

(133)

(a) iodine　　　　(d) water wash

(b) water rinse　　(e) dry

(c) photo fixer

37

(134)

The example in (134) shows a pencil drawing made from a continuous-tone photograph by the photosketching technique. It is possible to draw over a continuous-tone photograph with lead pencil and through the bleaching process convert the photograph to a pencil drawing. This may be necessary when changes or corrections are to be made on the original photograph but it is not desirable to convert the illustration to a line drawing. By using various grades of pencils, a good range of gray tones may be obtained giving all the characteristics of a continuous-tone picture. When using the pencil technique for photosketching, you will find it desirable to use a matte-surfaced photograph, because the rough surface will pick up the pencil carbon; it is almost impossible to draw on a glossy-surfaced photograph. The process of bleaching the photograph is the same when using pencil as it is when using ink.

There are times when it is desirable to photosketch only selected sections of a photograph to emphasize or clarify detail in a given area: because of poor lighting, distracting elements, or imperfections on the image being photographed, details may be difficult to see. Bleaching of these areas of the photograph is possible through the use of rubber cement, often used for mounting flat pictures. Any area of the photograph coated with this cement will not be affected by the bleaching solution. Thin the rubber cement so that it will flow freely from the brush. Good-quality cement will be made of genuine rubber and be very clear. This makes it rather difficult to see when it is being applied. To assure complete coverage of the area to be masked, a small amount of mimeograph ink or dark oil stain added to the rubber cement will make it easier to see. Apply two coats of rubber cement to assure complete coverage. In (135), (A) indicates the areas to be masked with rubber cement and (B), the area that will be photosketched. In (136) we see the final results after bleaching.

(135)

(136)

ART AIDS FOR STENCIL AND SPIRIT DUPLICATION

For the person lacking the necessary skills for producing art (visuals, symbols, etc.) for stencil or spirit duplication there exists a variety of art aids. The information that follows is intended to suggest aids and techniques that should make it easy for the nonprofessional artist to produce attractive and interesting art for duplication.

Stencil Duplicator Art (137)

Easy-to-use drawings created by professional artists for stencil and spirit duplication. Drawings are usually printed on one side of a white sheet that will permit enough light to pass through it for tracing on a viewing light box or a Mimeoscope. Stencil art books are also available for producing visuals. These books contain stencils of animals, space art, flowers, and numerous other objects.

Clip Art (138)

Clip art, in book or sheet form, can be traced for use on stencil and masters. Usually a tracing will have to be made on tracing paper first and then retraced on the stencil. In any event, clip art provides an excellent source of art and art ideas.

Symbol Templates (139)

Transparent plastic outline symbol templates (guides) for use on stencils and masters. The desired symbol can be traced with a drawing stylus or a ballpoint pen.

Plastic Shading Plates (140a)

When shading or texture is to be added to illustrations or lettering, plastic shading plates can be used. Stencil duplicator shading wheels can also be used to create the same effect on stencil and spirit masters. Plates and wheels are available in many attractive patterns. Shading plates require the use of a special burnisher (140b).

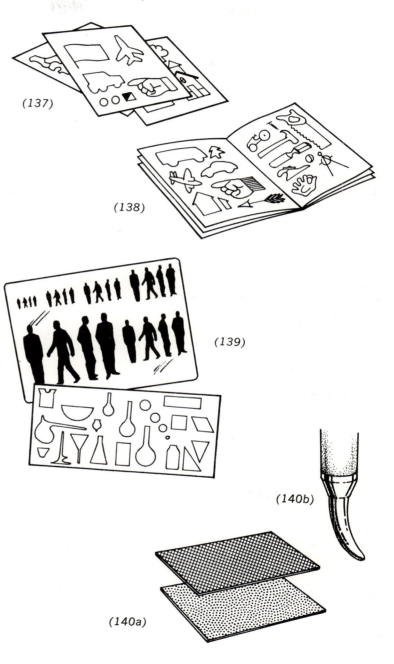

(137)

(138)

(139)

(140b)

(140a)

Wire-loop stylus

(141)

Writing plate

Backing sheet

Visual

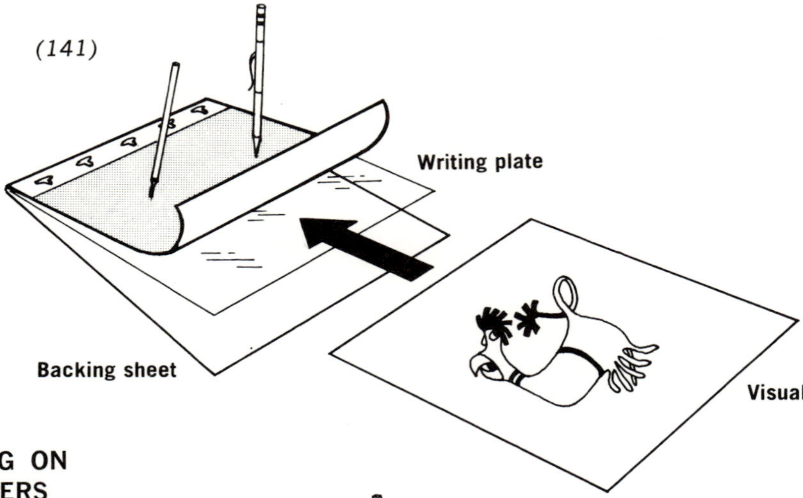

INSTRUCTIONS FOR DRAWING ON STENCILS AND SPIRIT MASTERS

To draw on a mimeograph stencil (141), first insert a plastic writing plate between the stencil and backing sheet, then draw, letter, or write directly on the stencil as recommended by the manufacturer. A wire-loop stylus is recommended for the tracing. If this type of stylus is used, hold it so that the thinnest part of the loop moves along the line being traced. Where possible, use a Mimeoscope as a working surface.

To draw on a spirit master (142), first insert a plastic writing plate under the carbon sheet, or place the master on a hard, smooth surface such as plate glass or linoleum; then draw, letter, or write directly on the master. Make certain the interleaf sheet of the master has been removed. *To add color*, simply remove the initial carbon sheet and replace it with the color carbon sheet desired (assorted colors available). The color carbon sheet must be the type designed for spirit duplication. The Mimeoscope (tracing scope) (143) is an illuminated drawing board. This device is used for illustrating, lettering, shading on stencils. It consists of a metal frame supporting a sheet of translucent glass. Usually an electric light is located under the glass surface.

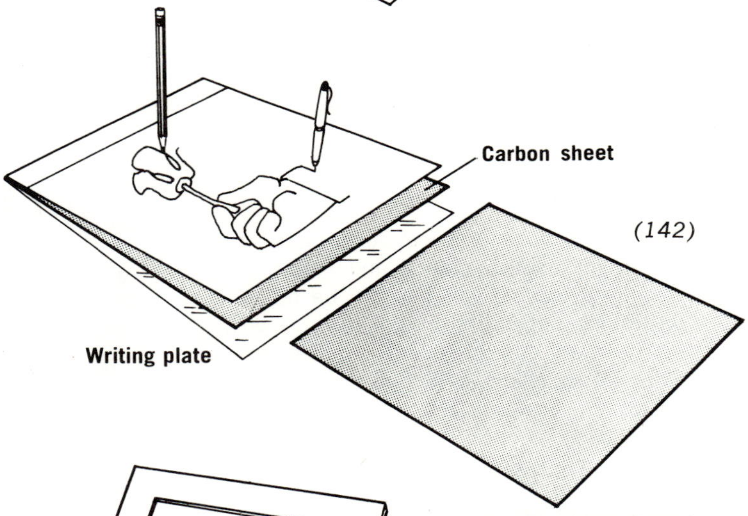

Carbon sheet

(142)

Writing plate

Second color carbon sheet

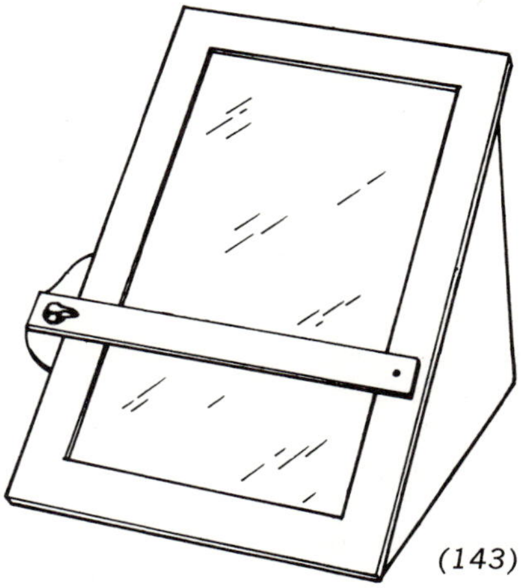

(143)

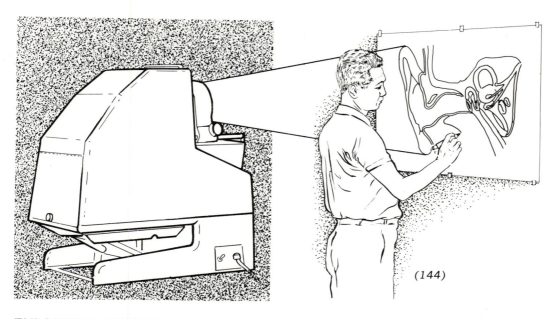

(144)

ENLARGING VISUALS BY PROJECTION (144)

The opaque projector is often used as a means of enlarging drawings. Not only can tear sheets and drawings be projected, but real objects having a certain limited third dimension can serve as subject matter for tracings. Interesting drawings for wall murals can be made by manipulating visual images taken from tear sheets, mounting them into a meaningful visual, and then enlarging the composite picture onto a large panel or chalkboard. Color may then be added by using chalk, crayon, watercolor, or any other medium desired. Special opaque projectors, simple in design, may be purchased specifically for use in making enlargements for signs and murals.

In situations where there is constant demand for the enlargement of opaque material, a simple opaque enlarger may be made (145). It is basically a box mounted to a wood track on the wall. Brackets clamped to the wood track support the main body of the projector. By loosening the bolts, the projector may be raised or lowered. The main box has

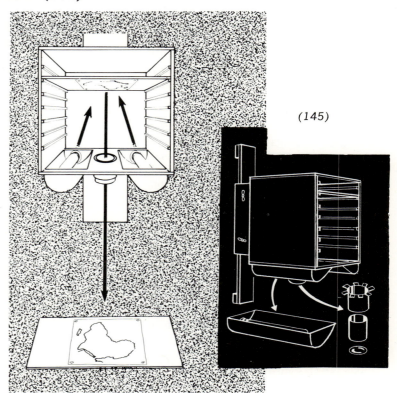

(145)

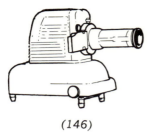

(146)

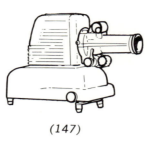

(147)

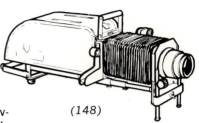

(148)

small strips fastened to two sides which permit the raising and lowering of the lightweight board, to the lower side of which the original drawing has been tacked. This helps in adjusting focus. To furnish the necessary illumination, two shiny tin reflectors containing lights are mounted in the bottom of the box on either side of the lens opening. The lens is a 2-inch magnifying glass mounted in a tin or aluminum sleeve which in turn is telescoped into a similar metal cylinder that has been fastened to the main body of the projector. By adjusting the lens, the drawing board, and the projector on its track, images of various sizes can be focused on the drawing board below. The tracing can then be made easily.

Almost any type of slide projector can be used as a device for producing enlarged drawings for such visuals as charts, posters, graphs, murals, chalkboard exhibits. Practically any subject matter in slide form can be projected on a desired surface and traced.

There are a limited number of slides or transparencies produced commercially for this technique of producing large visuals. However, it is relatively easy to copy drawings, photographs, etc., for the 2- by 2-inch slide projector (146) by using a 35mm still camera. In a like manner, special half-frame 35mm cameras can be used to produce filmstrips that can be used in a filmstrip projector to produce large illustrations (147). Standard 2- by 2-inch slides can be converted into filmstrips by a

number of companies offering this service. Slides for the 3¼- by 4-inch slide projector can be made photographically or by hand (see Chapter 5) (148).

The image area of the 10- by 10-inch overhead transparency is ideal for preparing hand-drawn materials to be enlarged with the overhead projector (149).

The photographic enlarger (150) can also be used as a projection device for preparing large visuals from a transparent or translucent original. The material to be enlarged is placed in the enlarger the way one inserts a regular photographic negative. Avoid leaving the lamp of the enlarger on for extended periods of time; this will cause extensive damage to the optical system of the enlarger. The enlarger can be adjusted to focus an image of the desired size down on the base of the enlarger.

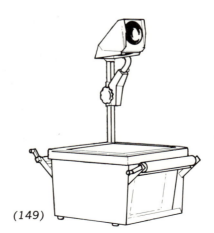

(149)

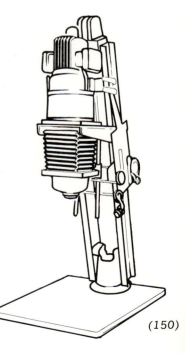

(150)

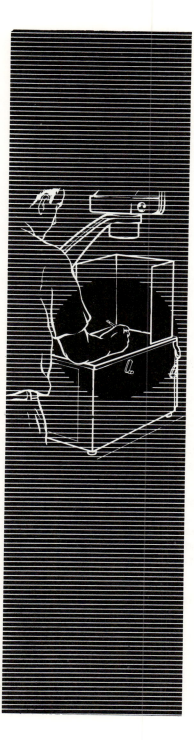

REDUCING VISUALS BY REVERSE PROJECTION

There are times when a large illustration, diagram, chart, or map might be more usable if it were reduced to the form of an opaque projection flat, a slide, or an overhead projection transparency. There are several ways this can be accomplished. However, if the image is such that it can be drawn readily, the reverse projection method may be the simplest approach.

In a slightly darkened room, place an overhead projector on a table or projection stand with the lens facing the visual to be reproduced. Illuminate the visual with a light source such as photofloods, lamps, reflector floods, or even floor lamps (151). Tape any opaque or translucent drawing material on the stage of the projector. The light reflection on the visual will reflect back through the projector's lens system onto the stage of the projector (152). Moving the projector away from the visual will reduce the size of the image on the projector stage; moving it closer will increase the size. The focusing device on the projector is used to sharpen the image as it is reflected onto the drawing surface. Extraneous room light may make it difficult to see the image on the stage of the projector. A simple light shield may be made out of cardboard, as illustrated (153). When everything is satisfactory, proceed by tracing along the lines of the reflected image (154). If it is desirable to draw on a transparent material, proceed as before, but place a piece of opaque white paper under the transparent surface on which the drawing is to be made.

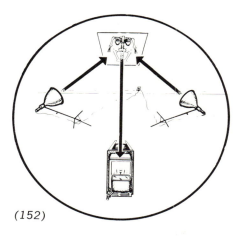

(151)

(152)

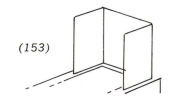

(153)

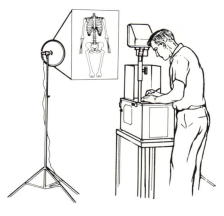

(154)

43

ENLARGING AND REDUCING VISUALS WITH A PANTOGRAPH

A pantograph is a simple drawing device used to make enlarged or reduced reproductions of drawings. It is made of four wood, metal, or plastic bars containing a series of holes so calibrated that by hinging these bars together at certain predetermined points, about twenty to forty different ratios in enlargement or reduction may be realized, depending on the particular model pantograph being used.

When working with the pantograph, a sufficiently large, smooth working surface is essential. If a drawing board is being used (155), the pivot point of the device (a) should be mounted firmly at the lower left-hand corner. Some pantographs have a simple clamping device which clamps to the edge of the board, and others are fastened by thumbtacks or more permanently mounted with nails.

To enlarge a drawing, the tracer point is attached at (b). At position (c) is located the pencil holder. How the device is operated depends upon the operator. Some people prefer to use the left hand to guide the tracing pin over the original drawing while the right hand guides the pencil. As illustrated, the tracing pin is guided by the right hand and the pencil is left free to make the enlarged drawing. In this case it is always wise to use a soft pencil lead to ensure a clean tracing. With some practice, a good reproduction can be made. It is important to guide the tracing pin smoothly to avoid exaggerated irregularities in the enlarged pencil drawing.

To reduce a drawing (156), the position of the pencil and the tracing pin are reversed. The pencil will be at (b) and the tracing pin will be at point (c). If an exact-size reproduction is desired, locate the pivot point at (b) and the

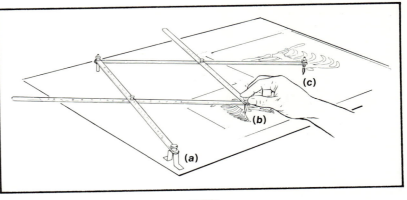

(155)

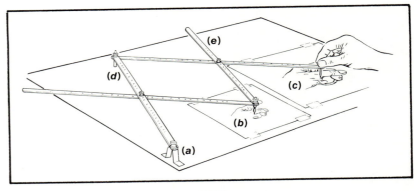

(156)

tracing pin at (a) with the pencil at position (c). When it is necessary to change the pantograph to different size ratios, the connecting points at (d) and (e) are moved to the desired ratio points.

ENLARGING VISUALS WITH THE RUBBER BAND TECHNIQUE

A simple and effective enlarging device can be made from [see (157)] a push-pin (a) or suction cup (b), a long piece of good-quality rubber band (c), a small wedge-shaped pointer (d), and a pencil (e) or ball-point pen. The rubber band should be of good quality and very elastic. The length of the band needed is dependent on its elasticity and the size of enlargements desired. On both ends of the rubber band form a small loop by folding the ends back and fastening them with narrow strips of tape or string. The loops should be small enough so they will fit tightly around the pencil and the pivot post, whether it be a suction cup or pushpin. Cut a small wedge-shaped pointer as shown in the illustration (f) from stiff paper or lightweight aluminum. A U-shaped cut in the upper portion will serve as a small clip to hold it onto the rubber band.

The sizes of enlargements can be figured quite accurately with this device (158). If the guide pointer (b) is placed midway between (a) and (c), the enlargement will be approximately two times. If the distance between (a) and (b) is one-fourth the distance between (a) and (c), the enlargement will be four times. Thus it is easy to set up a simple scale to help determine the setting for the guide pointer on the rubber band. Set up the original copy and the surface on which the enlargement is to be made, as shown in (159). The tip of the pointer should be just a little short of touching the paper surface when the pencil is in drawing position. Being sure that the pencil is absolutely vertical at all times, trace the original sketch with the pointer. Do not watch the drawing hand, but keep your eye on the pointer at all times. With a little practice, you will be able to execute excellent drawings by this method. After the drawing is completed and any small irregularities are corrected, the drawing is ready to use.

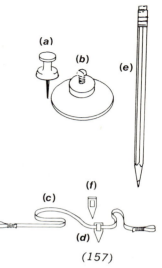

(157)

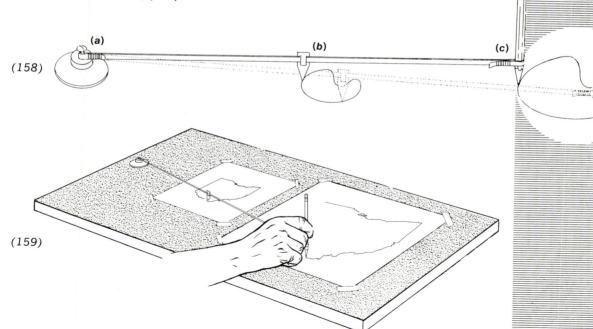

(158)

(159)

GRID DRAWING

An easy way to reduce and enlarge existing drawings, symbols, letters, and so forth, is by the squaring method. In effect, the original image is subdivided through a grid pattern into smaller, less complex areas. This enables a person with little or no drawing experience to reproduce the small squared sections of the drawing one at a time and, upon its completion, have effectively reproduced a rather complex image in any size desired from a direct reproduction to one either smaller or larger than the original.

The first step in the squaring process is to lay out a square grid pattern (160) over the image to be reproduced. The size of the squares will be determined by the complexity of the original, as well as the experience of the artist. Light pencil lines for the grid will make it easier to follow the lines of the image. A grid (161) of the desired proportion is next drawn on the surface on which the drawing is to be made. If the grid lines are erased after the drawing is completed, this may serve as the final product. However, if it is desirable to trace the finished drawing onto some other surface, tracing paper will serve as a good intermediate material upon which to place the drawing. If squared graph paper of the desired size can be obtained, the drawing of an original grid will be eliminated. After the grid is completed (162), transpose lines from the original drawing square by square. Lettering the border squares may help in maintaining the orientation. Trace the image (163) onto the desired surface. Clean up the basic lines of the drawing and render them in the desired medium, filling in shading and details as desired.

Often it is impossible or undesirable to draw the grid lines directly on the original. A simple time-saving aid can be made by scratching grid lines

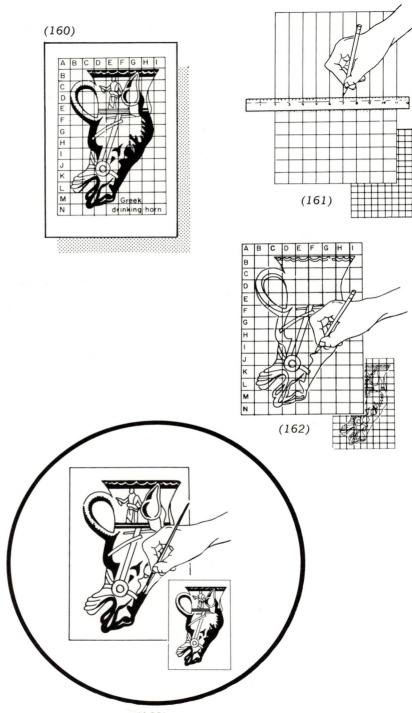

(160)

(161)

(162)

(163)

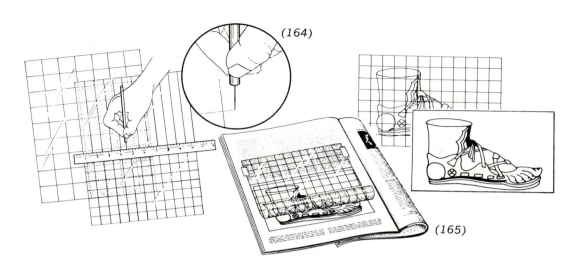

(164)

(165)

on a clear piece of acetate with a sharp stylus (164). It may be desirable to make several sheets having various-sized grids. By rubbing crayon or wax pencil into these etched lines, they become more visible. These acetate sheets may then serve as a grid over any printed visual without damaging the original material (165). At this point, proceed as before with the drawing process.

In order to make drawings from three-dimensional objects, a simple grid frame can be constructed. Small brads or tacks are inserted at a desired uni-form distance around the opening of a frame (166). The head of each brad is allowed to protrude at least ⅛ inch (167). Elastic string or rubber bands are stretched between protruding nail heads to form a square grid (168). It is often desirable to use smaller grids when working with complex subject matter. Therefore, when making the frame, make sure that the intervals between the nails are rather small to allow for stretching the string to form various-sized grids.

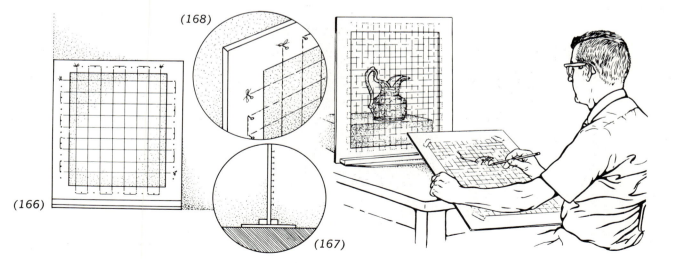

(168)

(166)

(167)

In the process of drawing from an original squared picture, it is important to analyze the basic form of the object and determine which lines will be of greatest value when reproducing this imagery. An actual photograph (169) has been used here to demonstrate how this problem might be approached. First, it is important to choose only those lines in the object that will give the most meaning. Often, the inexperienced person will attempt to reproduce the lines of an image without really understanding their function. One of the valuable by-products of drawing is the fact that, as the drawing is evolving, the artist must constantly analyze and understand the relative value of each line in contributing to the image formation. This is especially important when the final drawing is to be used for instructional purposes. The drawer must continually ask himself: Where does this line come from, where does it go, and what purpose does it serve? Even though the continuity of a line is obstructed by objects in the foreground, it is important to understand the continuity or flow of the line as it forms the image. An example of this is the line forming the folds of skin that pass behind the ear in the illustration. In reproducing the head of this rhinoceros, it is important to develop a feeling of solidity to the mas-

sive head. The ears must be cylindrical, with a cone-shaped opening. Lines showing the heavy folds of flesh are an important element in translating this photograph into a drawing. The thick folds of flesh around the nostril opening also add valuable information. In (170) black lines have been used to indicate some of the important lines in the photograph. Note in (171) how a few carefully chosen lines without shading give a feeling of the dimensionality of the ear. The grid (172) illustrates one method of locating the exact position of each line. As the arrows indicate, the draftsman first locates, by use of the grid, points of orientation. These usually fall on the grid lines. After this is accomplished, a smooth, flowing line is then used to connect the dots. After the drawing is inked in, the dots are erased. Note that even the invisible lines are drawn in (behind the ear) to help keep a smooth flow in the form being drawn. Of course, those which do not make a contribution to the final drawing are removed.

(171)

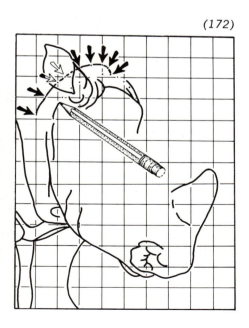

(172)

(169)

(170)

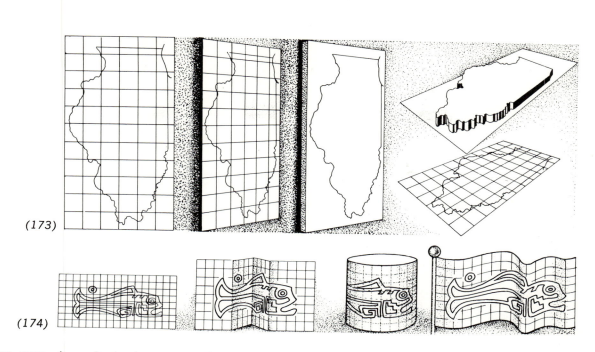

(173)

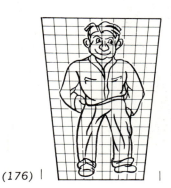

(174)

Other uses, beyond simple enlarging or reducing of a drawing, may be made of the squaring process. By using grids drawn in perspective, flat pictorial images may be drawn in perspective (173). Perspective grid paper may either be developed by the user or be purchased from drafting supply stores. Grids drawn on irregular surfaces may be a great help when attempting to draw images that must appear to lie on the irregular contour of the surface. The fish design is shown above on three different surfaces (174).

Distortion may be valuable in visualization. Several examples are shown. Horizontal grid distortion gives this cartoon character (175) a rugged, husky appearance by broadening the chest (176). The character takes on a thin, wiry appearance (177) when variations on the vertical grid are used. Note that the grids in areas A, B, C, D, and E all vary in size. Distortion, if carefully planned, can lead to very effective visualization.

(175)

(176)

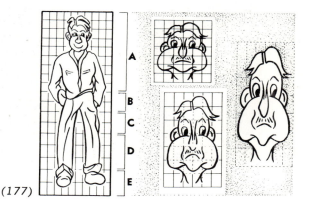

(177)

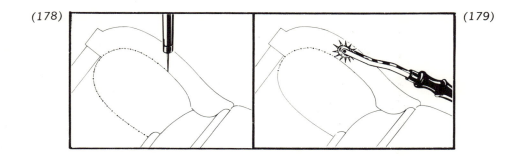

(178)   (179)

POUNCE PATTERN FOR IMAGE TRANSFER

An extremely old technique of transferring an image from one surface to another is through the use of a pounce pattern. This is especially effective when producing large images, such as for chalkboard drawings, signs, and murals.

Perforations are made along the lines of the original drawing using a sharp, pointed tool such as a cutting needle (178) or pounce wheel (179). A sewing machine from which the thread has been removed also serves well for this purpose. The finer the detail, the closer together the perforations are made. When all the lines on the original have been perforated, the pattern is ready for use. This perforated drawing may be transferred to any other surface by patting over the lines with powder or chalk dust. A powder puff or blackboard eraser works well for this process

(180). When transferring the image to a light surface, a dark-colored chalk dust must be used. After all lines have been carefully covered with dust, check to see that a complete dot pattern has been transferred (181). Then complete the visual image by drawing along the dotted lines (182). A pounce pattern made on good-quality heavyweight paper coated with shellac or plastic spray will give years of use.

VARIATIONS IN USING THE POUNCE PATTERN

An application of the pounce pattern can be made in the production of transparencies for the overhead projector. The use of this technique permits the instructor actively to develop a visual image as a lecture progresses. The orig-

(180)

(181)

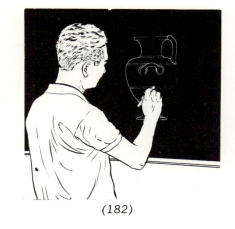

(182)

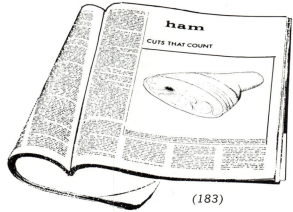

ham

CUTS THAT COUNT

(183)

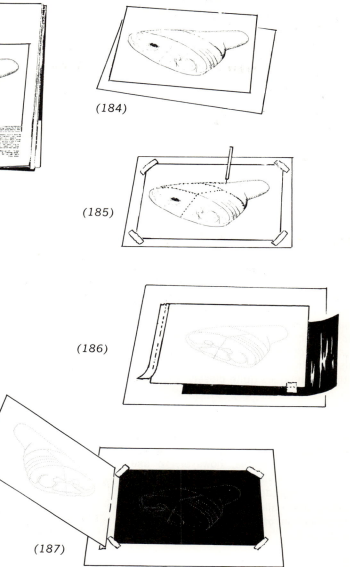

(184)

(185)

(186)

(187)

inal visual may be chosen from any source available, as long as it is of the appropriate size to fit on the stage of the overhead projector. For sake of explanation, assume that a tear sheet in a magazine (183) contains the visual that is desired. Remove the page from the magazine and trim the visual to the desired size. Place the visual on a piece of tagboard or similar strong, lightweight material (184) which has been cut to a dimension slightly larger than the projection area of the projector. This may be approximately 11 by 11 inches. Carefully center the visual on the tagboard (185) and tape it in place. With a sharp cutting needle perforate the lines of the drawing. Be sure to work on a soft surface that will not be damaged by the point of the needle. Scrap cardboard or sheet cork will work well for this purpose. When all lines are perforated, remove the original. Take the perforated tagboard and hinge it with tape to the overhead transparency mount (186). Now place a sheet of carbon-coated projection acetate under the perforated image with coated side up. This film is a lightweight acetate film coated with a black opaque carbon material. When it is used on the overhead projector and scribed on the coated side with a pencil (or other stylus-type instrument), a white luminous line will appear on a black background. For ease

of use, this film should be taped to the mount. With the perforated visual image over the carbon film, pat the image with a chalk eraser. The white chalk dust will record the perforated image on the black carbon film. Flip the original pounce pattern back out of the way (187). Now as the instructor lectures, he can draw along the white dotted lines. As his drawing instrument scrapes away the black carbon, an animated white line will appear on the projection screen. The perforated pattern may be used over innumerable times, but the carbon film must be changed each time this projected visual is used.

The pounce pattern technique can also be used to transfer drawings, diagrams, and so forth, onto duplicator masters and stencils, wood surfaces, and cloth (188).

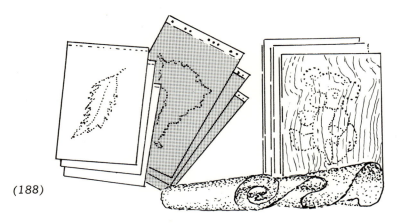

(188)

VISUAL TRANSFER TECHNIQUES

It is often necessary to trace a visual on tracing paper and transfer it to another surface. One technique for doing this is pounce pattern. However, this may not always be the most convenient or desirable way because of the lack of facilities or certain characteristics of the visual being transferred. There are three other techniques quite closely related to pounce pattern, any of which have certain advantages over it. With any of these techniques it is important to start with a carefully drawn original visual on lightweight drawing or tracing paper (189). It is possible, however, to use the original visual if damaging is not of serious consequence. Making an original tracing does allow for clarification and simplification of the image, which may be desired.

Pencil Carbon Technique

A common technique for making a visual transfer is the use of pencil carbon. With the visual's drawing face down on a clean, smooth working surface, apply a heavy layer of soft pencil lead to the image lines of the visual (190). Be sure all lines are completely covered with lead. Turn the visual over and tape to the surface on which the transfer is to be made (191). Using a stylus, pencil, or ball-point pen, carefully trace over the lines of the visual. Be careful not to use too much pressure, because this will leave an indentation on the transfer.

As the drawing instrument traces over the drawing, the pencil carbon on the back of the drawing will be transferred. When all lines have been traced, carefully lift one corner of the drawing to check the quality of the transfer

(189)

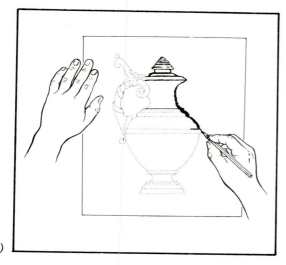

(190)

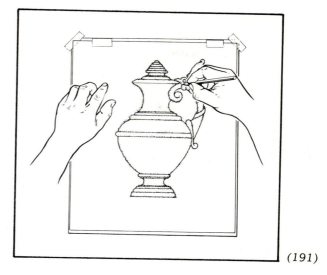

(191)

(192). To ensure reregistration, if required (repeating lines not transferred as desired), simply lower the drawing back down on the surface. If the transfer is satisfactory, remove the original and complete the transferred drawing in whatever medium desired. Although this technique works quite well, there is a tendency for extraneous carbon to rub off causing smudges on the final drawing.

Chalk Technique

Closely related to the pencil-carbon technique is one using pastel crayon or chalk. These materials adapt better to large materials and are somewhat cleaner when making the transfer. If light-color chalk is used, the transfer can be made on dark surfaces. Coat the reverse side of the image with a generous layer of chalk (193). After the

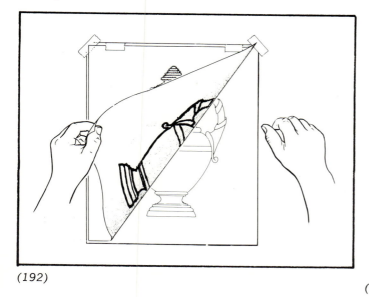

(192)

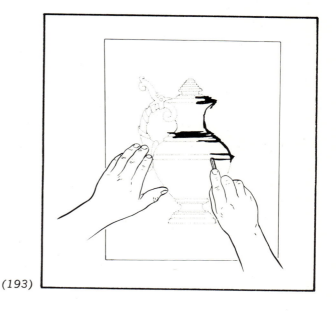

(193)

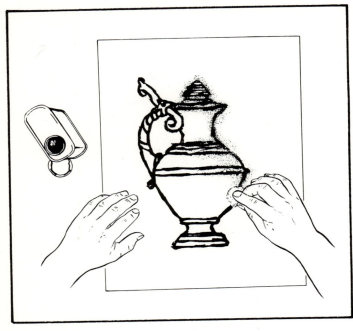

(194)

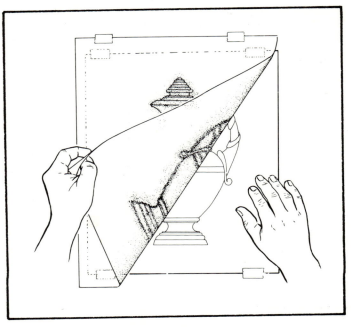

(195)

image is completely coated, take a ball of cotton moistened with rubber cement thinner and gently pat it over the chalk surface (194). This moistening sets the chalk so that smudges will not form on the surface on which the image is to be transferred.

Tape the original to the surface selected. Trace over the outline with a pencil, stylus, or ball-point pen (195). Check the quality of the transfer (196). If it is satisfactory, remove the original and complete the transfer as desired. Avoid using chalk with wax or oil content. Under some conditions oil and wax repel other forms of art media and cause difficulty when completing the final artwork.

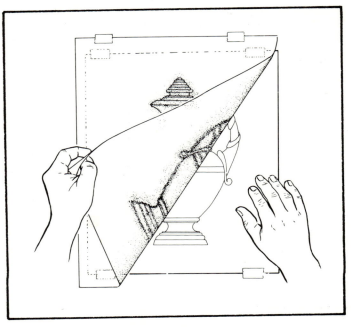

(196)

(197)

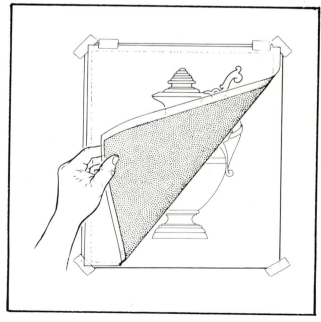

(198)

Transfer Carbon Sheets

Another technique for producing sharp, clear transfer visuals is the use of transfer carbon sheets. These sheets, coated with a special type of carbon, come in assorted colors. To use, insert a sheet of carbon (carbon side down) under the original and tape both sheets to the surface of material selected (197). Next, trace over the original with a pencil, stylus, or ball-point pen. Make certain no lines are missed (198). When the tracing is completed, check quality of transfer (199). If all detail is satisfactory, remove the carbon sheet and original, then complete the transferred visual as desired. It is important to draw carefully when making transfers; small inaccuracies multiply in each generation of the technique, so it is important to minimize defects in tracing.

(199)

MOUNTING AND LAMINATING TECHNIQUES

Cold Mounting
    Rubber Cement Mounting
    Wax Mounting
    Double-coated Adhesive Acetate
    Wet Mounting

Heat Mounting
    Dry Mounting Tissue
    Dry Mounting Cement
    Plastic Spray (Aerosol Can)
    Dry Backing Cloth

Laminating
    Cold Laminating Acetate
    Laminating Machine (Cold Process)
    Laminating Machine (Heat Process)
    Dry Mounting Press Laminating
    Thermocopy Machine Laminating

Passe-partout Mounting

Display Easels
    Attached Easel (Sample Wing)
    Attached Easel (Lock Wing)
    Folding Easel

Mounting Aids

MOUNTING AND LAMINATING TECHNIQUES

Attaching one surface or material to another surface or material such as mounting paper on paper, cardboard, cloth, or acetate; laminating acetate on paper or cardboard; mounting precut letters and other three-dimensional materials and objects on a variety of surfaces—these are just a few of the many situations in which a mounting or laminating technique or material of one type or another is required.

This chapter on mounting and laminating techniques is divided into several sections: Cold Mounting techniques includes several techniques and materials that require no heat or expensive equipment; Heat Mounting illustrates and discusses some rather unique approaches to mounting and preserving instructional materials with heat mounting materials and equipment; Laminating covers a variety of techniques and materials designed especially for preserving and protecting flat instructional materials with special acetates; Passe-partout Mounting is a rather comprehensive treatment of mounting materials under glass or plastic for instructional or display purposes; Display Easels is a section devoted to the preparation of an assortment of attractive and useful display easels; and, finally, Mounting Aids briefly describes several types of mounting aids not included in the other five sections of this chapter.

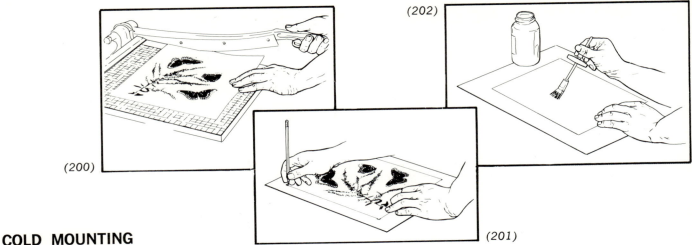

(202)

(200)

(201)

COLD MOUNTING

RUBBER CEMENT MOUNTING

Rubber cement mounting is a quick, easy, and clean technique. It is ideal for mounting many flat instructional materials such as prints, photographs, drawings, and precut letters. Rubber cement is an easy-spreading adhesive for joining paper to paper, cloth, leather, glass, metal, wood, and other surfaces. Good-quality cement is nonwrinkling, noncurling, and easily removed from nonporous surfaces by rolling it off with fingers or a rubber cement eraser. To assure good adhesive quality, the cement should be stored in brown bottles and kept away from high temperatures. It should be thinned with rubber cement thinner (solvent) if the cement does not flow freely from the brush used to apply it. Special plastic or glass dispensers

with a built-in brush are available.

Before starting the mounting, trim the visual to the desired size (200). The trimmed visual is then positioned on the mounting board, and a small, light pencil guideline is placed at each corner (201). A thin, even coat of rubber cement is applied (202) to the back of the visual. This should be done with smooth, even brush strokes, making sure the entire surface is covered. Going back over rubber cement which is not thoroughly dry will cause scuffing and produce a rough surface; the result will be an imperfect mounting.

Apply a coat of rubber cement to the mounting board, extending it slightly beyond the guide marks (203). Better adhesion will be assured if the brush strokes are at a 90° angle to those used on the back of the visual. Allow the

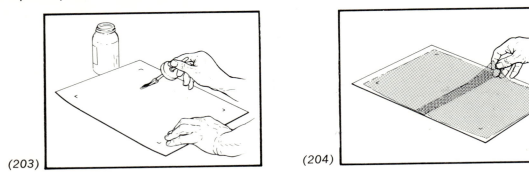

(203)

(204)

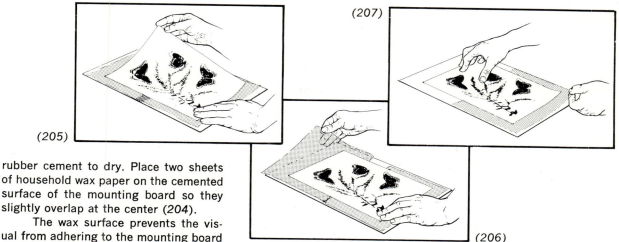

(205)

(207)

(206)

rubber cement to dry. Place two sheets of household wax paper on the cemented surface of the mounting board so they slightly overlap at the center (204).

The wax surface prevents the visual from adhering to the mounting board during positioning. Place the visual on the wax paper with corners registered on the guide marks (205). Firmly hold the lower half of the picture in place as the top sheet of wax paper is withdrawn (206). This permits the two rubber-cemented surfaces to come into direct contact with each other. Next, remove the bottom wax sheet (207).

Finally, smooth down the surface of the visual, starting in the center and working in an outward direction (208). It is advisable to use a protective sheet

of clean paper over the visual to prevent damage to the surface (209). Often a small rubber roller is used for this purpose. When the visual is firmly mounted, remove excess rubber cement by gently rubbing with a finger along the edges of the visual. A rubber cement eraser can also be used to remove excess cement. Erase the guide marks, and the mounting is completed (210).

The technique of mounting just described is often referred to as a permanent method. It is not truly a permanent mounting, however. The quality of the rubber cement used, the mounting technique used, and the storage conditions will determine to a great extent how long the mount will last.

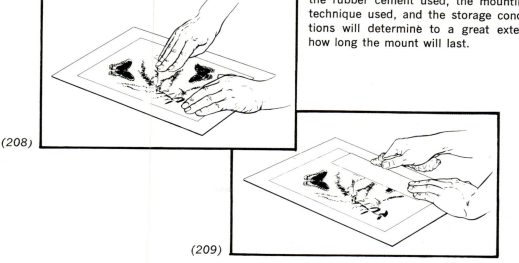

(208)

(209)

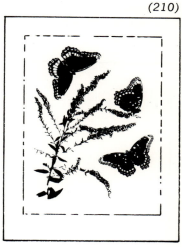

(210)

WAX MOUNTING

Wax adhesives have become a very popular mounting substance, especially for people involved in the process of assembling paste-up art materials or creating displays involving three-dimensional objects. This family of adhesives may be found in several forms.

For the person interested in creating displays, including both two- and three-dimensional materials, there is a wax adhesive stick often referred to as bulletin-board wax. To use, take a small portion of this wax, roll it into a small ball, and place it on the contact point of the material to be mounted. Then position the material on the surface it is to be mounted on and press it firmly into place. This method can be used to suspend flat materials and lightweight three-dimensional objects. When the material is removed from the display, the small lump of wax may be scraped off and used again.

Another form in which wax adhesive material may be procured is that of wax discs. These are small plastic discs coated on both sides with adhesive wax. They may be obtained in a variety of sizes depending upon the size of material to be mounted. The disc is placed at the contact point of the material to be mounted and pressed against the mounting surface.

Spray wax adhesive in an aerosol can is excellent for coating materials with a pressure-sensitive coating of wax. It is waterproof, wrinkleproof, colorless, and fast drying. It is used primarily on two-dimensional materials. One of its most important characteristics is that it will permit repositioning of material on the mounting surface. When the final position is decided upon, burnish the material down with a hard, smooth instrument. Spray wax adhesive is easy to use. Place the material to be coated face down on a large, clean piece of paper. Spray evenly over the back of the material (211) in a smooth back-and-forth motion, being sure to coat the edges thoroughly. Allow a short time for drying. The material is then ready to press in place. For removing unwanted adhesive, follow the directions on the can.

The wax coating machine has been designed for people needing to coat quantities of material with wax adhesive. It is an electrical device for heating and applying adhesive wax. These wax coaters range from small hand-held spreaders to automatic paper-fed machines capable of handling large sheets. As the material passes through the machine (212), it is coated with a layer of pressure-sensitive wax. Material coated by this method may be adhered to surfaces such as paper, plastic, foil, film, tissue, and fabrics. As with spray wax adhesive, this material may be repositioned. When the final position is set, the material is then burnished into place.

(211)

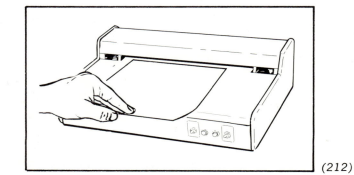

(212)

DOUBLE-COATED ADHESIVE ACETATE

Double-coated adhesive acetate is a mounting acetate with pressure-sensitive adhesive on both sides (*213*). Bourges Cold Mount acetate sheets are 20 by 25 inches and can be cut into smaller sheets. This technique is ideal for mounting such things as photographs, overhead projection transparencies, newspaper clippings, illustrations, and paste-up art. No heat, machine, or additional adhesives are required. Double-coated adhesive tape is also available and used much like the acetate sheet (*214*).

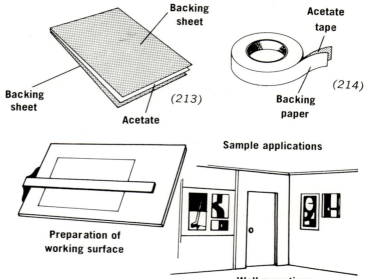

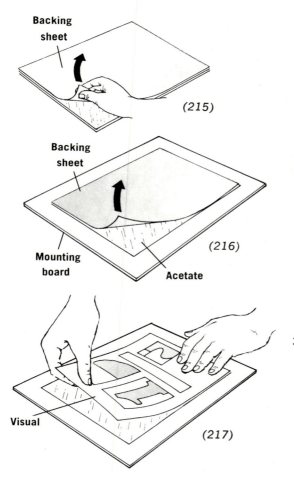

Instructions

1. Separate one of the backing sheets from the acetate at one of the corners with the point of a knife or razor blade or by "flicking" a corner with a finger. Peel the sheet off, exposing the first "sticky" side of the acetate (*215*).

2. Attach sticky side of acetate to mounting surface (cardboard, paper, wood, glass, etc.), contacting the leading edge of the acetate to the upper contact point of the mounting surface; then lower the acetate in place. Rub down the surface with the hand to ensure perfect adhesion. Do not test the adhesive qualities of the acetate by lifting, since it will come off readily when first applied. The adhesive has been designed to work slowly.

3. Repeat step 1 (remove second backing sheet) (*216*). Attach material to be mounted to the sticky side of acetate by contacting leading edge of material to the top edge of acetate; then slowly lower the material at an angle until it is completely flat. Place a protective paper on top and rub down material with the hand to ensure perfect adhesion (*217*).

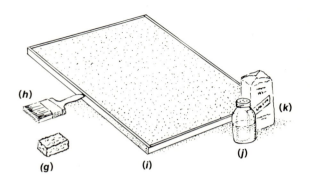

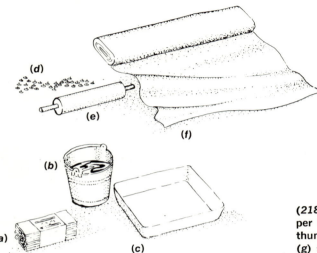

(218) Materials and equipment: (a) paper towels; (b) pail of water; (c) pan; (d) thumbtacks; (e) rolling pin; (f) muslin; (g) sponge; (h) paint brush; (i) mounting board; (j) flour sieve; (k) wallpaper wheat-paste flour.

WET MOUNTING

Wet mounting is a simple technique of backing paper instructional material with cloth, usually unbleached muslin. It is an age-old process and was, in fact, used centuries ago in the Far Eastern countries to protect and preserve paintings and scrolls. The preservation of these ancient works of art in museums today is evidence of the durability of this form of mounting. This mounting technique is ideal for preserving large visual material such as charts, maps, and posters. One of the advantages of this technique of preservation is that all materials and equipment are readily available (218). The mounting surface may be any flat, waterproof surface sufficiently large to accommodate the material to be mounted, or, in cases where there is repeated demand for this method of mounting, it may be a specially prepared board.

A special mounting board (219) is relatively easy to construct. First, size must be determined by the material that will be mounted. It is always desirable to have the board 2 to 3 inches larger than the material to be mounted. Two sizes which have proved quite adequate for a great number of charts, maps, posters, etc., are 33 by 43 inches and 34 by 48 inches. The board should be as moistureproof as possible. There are a number of ways the mounting board may be constructed. However, a heavy sheet of ¾-inch plywood covered by ⅛-inch tempered hardboard has proved to be quite successful. Glue the hardboard to the plywood, using a waterproof glue. Then nail soft pine strips ½ by 1 inch along the edges to frame the board. These strips must be of soft wood to permit the easy insertion and extraction of the thumbtacks. It is not desirable to glue these strips to the main body of the board since they will need to be replaced after long periods of use. After the board is completed,

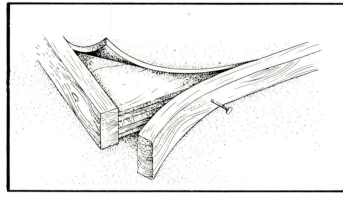

(219)

(220)

it is best to cover it with a good-quality hard-surface varnish.

The mixing of the wheat paste is greatly facilitated by the use of a flour sieve. A combination sieve and storage bottle (220) may be made from a canning jar. Puncture holes in the metal lid so that the paste flour can be shaken out easily during the mixing of the paste. A circular piece of cardboard placed under the perforated lid will keep the flour clean during storage.

First, place the mounting cloth in water (221) so that it will be completely saturated by the time it is to be used. Next, mix the paste (222). Use the bristles of the brush to get an even, smooth, lump-free paste mixture. If the paste thickens after standing, add additional water. (For additional strength, add a small amount of glue size to the paste mixture.)

(221)

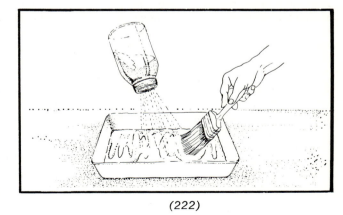

(222)

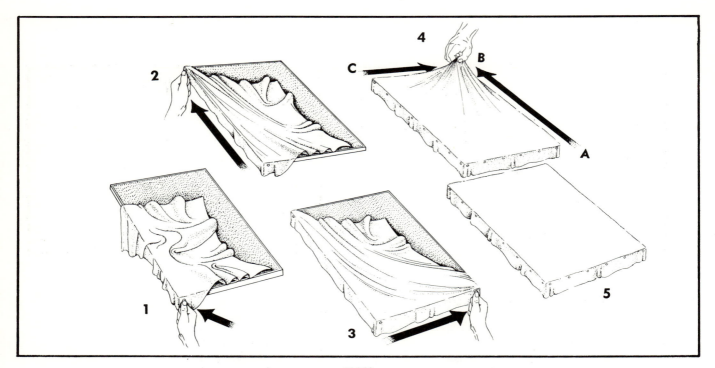

(223)

Stretching the cloth properly is important. A definite attempt should be made to square the thread pattern with the surface on which the cloth is being stretched. One method of stretching the cloth is shown in (223) above. After the cloth is thoroughly soaked in water, wring out the excess moisture and proceed with the following steps in the stretching process. (Before beginning the procedure, be sure that the mounting surface is clean and free of all foreign matter.)

1. Establish one corner and either staple (using staple gun) or thumbtack corner of cloth to corner of mounting board.
2.. Allowing a little excess of the cloth to extend over the edge of the board, stretch edge of cloth to the second corner. Try to keep the thread pattern parallel to the edge of the board.
3. In a similar manner, stretch the second edge of cloth to the third corner.
4. Thumbtack these two established edges at intervals of 3 to 4 inches. Draw the final corner of cloth to the fourth corner and tack it in place temporarily. Starting on the long remaining side AB on corner A adjacent to the already-adhered edge, draw cloth tightly and staple it at intervals of 3 to 4 inches. Do the same to the remaining side BC, always keeping in mind that the thread pattern should be parallel to edges of the board.
5. The stretched cloth is now ready for use.

(224)

(225)

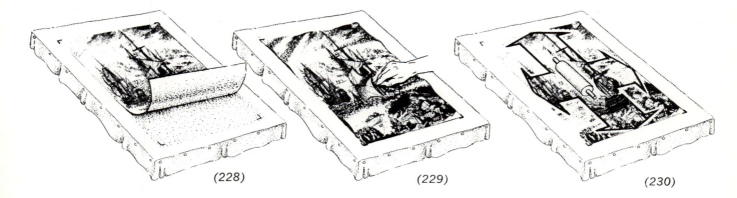

(226)

(227)

Before beginning the wet mounting process, make sure that the printed material is colorfast. If it is not, thoroughly spray (224) the visual material with a clear, plastic spray to set the ink surface and protect it from moisture. Next, place the visual on the stretched cloth, positioning it as desired and with light pencil marks to indicate the corner (225). Now lay the visual face down on a clean, dry surface and thoroughly moisten (226) the paper surface until it lies absolutely flat with no wrinkles or folds in evidence. At this time there will be some evidence of a slight expansion of the paper material.

Apply the paste evenly on the muslin over the entire area indicated by pencil marks (227). It is best to go slightly beyond the area to be used.

Sponge off all excess moisture from the back of the paper material and place it "face" up (228) positioned according to the original marks indicating the corners. Working from the center of the visual, gently rub out (229) wrinkles so that the material will lie smooth and flat against the muslin surface.

Place the rolling pin in the center parallel to the longest dimension of the visual. With light pressure, roll from the center to the two nearest edges (230). Next, roll from the center to the two

(228)

(229)

(230)

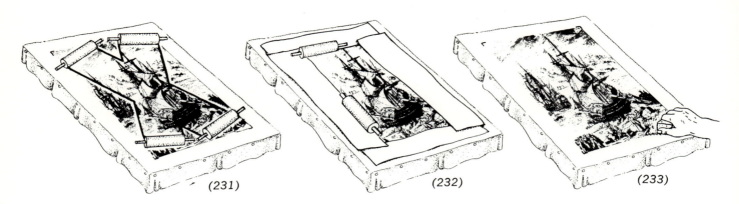

(231)　　　　　(232)　　　　　(233)

remaining edges. This forms a + shape. Again, place the rolling pin in the center and roll to each corner as indicated (231). This forms an X shape.

To complete the mounting process, cover the edges of the visual with strips of newsprint. Start with the rolling pin in the center and roll in an outward direction (232) all along the edges. This squeezes out any excess paste onto the newsprint which can then be discarded.

Next, check to see that there are no folds or wrinkles. If there is evidence of excess paste under any section of the visual, reroll that area. Finally, with a damp sponge, wipe off any excess paste from the surface of the visual (233) as well as from the marginal cloth areas. Let the material dry. When it is completely dry, remove carefully from the mounting board and finish the edges as desired.

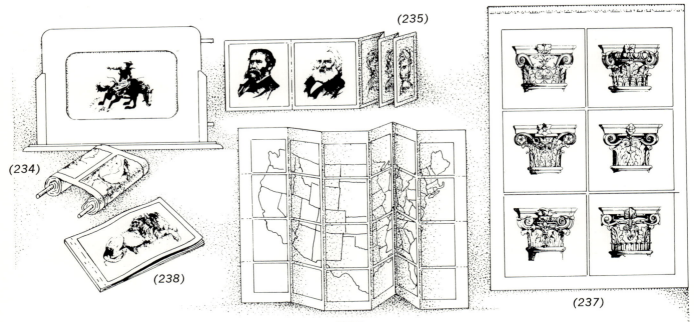

(235)

(234)

(238)

(236)

(237)

There are many variations in the forms that wet-mounted visual materials may take. One of the most valuable characteristics of the wet mounting process is that it gives the material extra durability. Paper materials used in a scroll (234) box may be easily torn by constant use, but cloth backing will add extra durability. The extra strength of the cloth hinge gives accordion-folded materials longer life [(235) to (237)] and permits constant folding. Pictures mounted on cloth and bound together in book form (238) are very durable and resist the wear from constant handling. Not only does the cloth backing add strength to the visual, but it simplifies displaying and storage especially when a series of pictures must be kept in a certain sequence and displayed at one time.

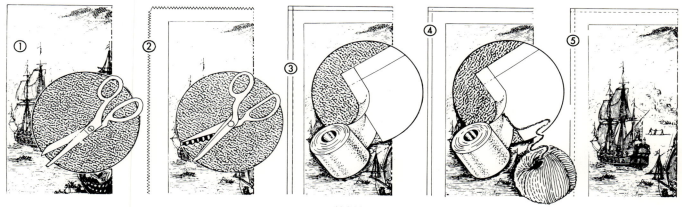

(239)

There are a number of ways to finish the edges on a wet mounting (239). Cutting the cloth flush with the edge of the visual is the easiest method (1). However, if pinking shears (2) are used there will be less danger of the cloth unraveling. Taping the edge (3) prevents raveling and gives added strength. In cases where the material will be handled very roughly, as would be the case with a poster or chart used outdoors in the wind, additional strength may be added by placing a string along the edge of the visual as it is taped (4). Hemming the edge (5) of the cloth material by hand or with a sewing machine makes a neat, strong edge that will be very durable.

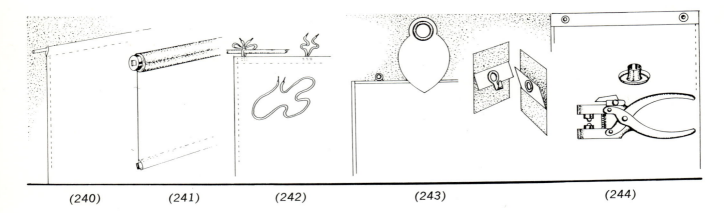

(240)   (241)   (242)   (243)   (244)

There is a variety of methods of displaying a wet mounting. One of the most common ways is to suspend the visual on a rod (240). For lightweight materials the window-shade roller makes an excellent support and permits the rolling up of the visual when it is not in use (241). Shoe strings fastened to the top of a wet mounting permit ease in suspending materials from a variety of supports (242). A variety of gummed-back picture hangers is available to fasten to the mounted visual (243). Eyelets (grommets) may be placed directly in the mounted material with the use of an eyelet punch (244).

HEAT MOUNTING

One of the most important basic areas in the production of visual materials is the mounting and preserving of flat pictorial and graphic imagery. Of all the methods of mounting and laminating, the heat processes have gained tremendous popularity in recent years. These methods of mounting involve the use of heat and pressure. The visual, backed by a dry adhesive sheet and placed on an appropriate mounting surface, is put into a specially designed mounting press. The application of heat and pressure forms a fast, clean mounting within seconds. Lamination is a process by which a special protective film is adhered to the image surface of the visual, and it may be accomplished by using the same equipment as for mounting or by using a machine so designed that heat and pressure are applied with rollers to effect excellent lamination of the picture surface. There are many variations of these processes, as well as a variety of ways in which straight mounting may be combined with lamination. A knowledge of all the possible variables expands the potential of the heat mounting methods and leads to greater flexibility in the mounting area.

The adhesives used may be of a permanent or of a removable nature. They may be purchased in dry sheets or in liquid form applied either by brush or from a pressurized can. The liquid adhesive should be dry before being used in a heat mounting machine. Some adhesives work best on rough surfaces, others on slick or highly polished finishes. It is important to know how the various adhesives adapt to the individual characteristics of printed materials and their supports, including a wide variety of paper, cardboard, cloth, and plastic, all of different weights, textures, and surfaces. Heat may damage some materials. It can affect a limited number of printed surfaces and their support through darkening, changing color, warping, melting. Imagery produced by the thermographic process may not be exposed to the heat of this type of mounting process. Special plastic and wax surfaces on photographic prints may melt when exposed to heat. Humidity is another factor in the heat mounting process. It may be extremely damaging, but if its characteristics are understood, it can be of great value in solving certain mounting problems.

The creative person may use heat lamination in a great variety of ways from the purely decorative to the utilitarian. Lamination film may be purchased in standard or matte surface depending on the effect desired. It may be wrinkled and folded for special effects. Transparent watercolor, crayon, and ink applied to the adhesive side of lamination film before it is mounted can lead to a great variety of interesting and colorful effects.

The heat mounting methods lend themselves to so many variations that their extent of use is limited only by the imagination.

DRY MOUNTING TISSUE

The dry mounting technique is ideal for mounting many flat instructional materials without the use of liquid adhesives. Dry mounting tissue is a thin sheet of paper which is covered on both sides with a coating of high-grade thermoplastic or wax-type adhesive. By applying heat and pressure with a dry mounting press or hand iron, a strong bond is formed between the materials to which the dry mounting tissue has been attached. Materials can be mounted in a matter of a few seconds. When the thermoplastic type of tissue is used, a permanent bond will be made. When the wax-type adhesive is used, it is possible to remove the visual at a later date. Dry mounting tissue is available in sheets of various sizes and in rolls. The effect of heat on the visual being mounted must always be taken into consideration; for example, care must be taken with materials coated with plastic sprays or varnishes, visuals made by the thermographic process, and drawings made with crayon.

Permanent Tissue

SEAL MT5 and KODAK Dry Mounting Tissue are permanent tissues.

The visual (245) should be dry and

(245)

(246)

(247)

(248)

free of wrinkles; if it is not, insert it in the heated press (246) with a protective sheet on top for about ten seconds. It is always important to turn the press on and set the temperature control at the proper temperature setting some time before putting it to use. Heating the press up to temperature will dry out any moisture that may have accumulated in the press because of humidity. Choose a piece of dry mounting tissue which is exactly the same size as the visual or a bit larger so that it can be trimmed with the visual after it has been "tacked" in place. Place the tissue on the back of the visual. Then tack it in two or three places near the center (247) with a heated tacking iron or the tip of a hand iron.

(249)

(250)

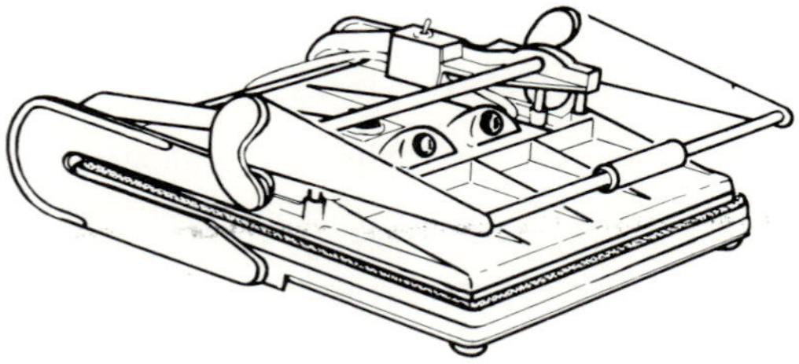

(251)

Dry mounting metal weights

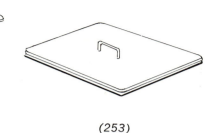

(252)

(253)

(254)

After the dry mounting tissue is securely tacked to the back of the visual, carefully trim (248) it to the desired size, making sure that no mounting tissue extends beyond the margins of the picture. Next, prepare to attach the visual and tissue to the mounting board. Since the tissue is not sticky, it can be positioned as desired on the board. Tack it onto the board by lifting any two opposite corners (249) and by touching the tip of the tacking iron or hand iron to the tissue. This will keep the visual in place during the actual mounting.

Check to see that the press is up to desired temperature (225°F). Insert the visual into the press (250) with a clean sheet of paper on top to protect the surface. Any foreign matter on the picture surface, such as grit or slivers of mounting tissue will cause blemishes. Close the press for the recommended time (251). Thicker visuals will require additional time.

After the visual is removed from the press, it is best to allow it to cool under pressure. Metal weights are available for this purpose. Place the weight on top of the visual (252) with a sheet of paper to protect its surface. Allowing the mounted visual to cool under the weight ensures good adhesion and prevents some warping of the cardboard

(253). When the picture has become cool, it is ready for use (254).

An ordinary hand (255) iron may serve as a substitute for the dry mounting press. The surface of the iron should be just hot enough to "sizzle" when touched with a moistened finger. Use a heat-absorbing paper as a protective sheet over the visual. Keep the iron in motion during the mounting process. To ensure a good adhesion, it is best to start with the iron in the center of the visual and move in an expanding spiral to the outer edges. Always keep the iron in motion to prevent overheating. Additional heat may be applied at any later time if complete adhesion has not taken place.

(255)

Removable Tissue

SEAL Fotoflat is a removable-type tissue.

In contrast to the thermoplastic-type dry mounting tissue used for permanent dry mounting, the removable tissue has a "waxy" appearance. It may be applied with the dry mounting press or hand iron. The fact that it is used at a lower temperature (180°F) makes it especially appropriate for mounting photographic color prints or other delicate materials. It should not be used for mounting visuals that are to be exposed to heat for any prolonged period of time, such as visuals to be placed over heaters or in warm window-display areas. In general, this type of tissue is used in the same way the permanent type is used. This tissue, however, does have the advantage of being removable. To remove a visual from its backing, simply place it in the heated press (200°F) for about one minute. Do not lock the press down. Quickly open the press and lift one corner (256) and gently peel the material from the base. If the material is large, it may require reheating to complete the process. This type of dry mounting ad-

hesive will adhere to extremely slick surfaces, such as glossy photographs, metal, and plastics (257). The "waxy" adhesive will adhere to rough surfaces very well and holds well to wood or cloth surfaces. One valuable use is in the making of flannel-board materials. Visuals are mounted on pieces of flannel or felt and then cut out (258). Even small flannel boards can be made by dry-mounting felt onto surfaces such as hardboard or plywood (259).

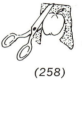

(258)

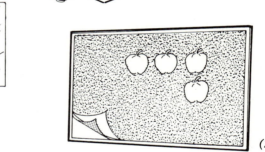

(256)

(257)

(259)

DRY MOUNTING CEMENT

A variation in the use of the dry mounting method is achieved through the use of liquid dry mounting cement (260). The cement is applied by brush directly to the back of the material to be

mounted. It is allowed to dry and then may be mounted at a later date by using either a hand iron or the dry mounting press in the usual manner.

(260)

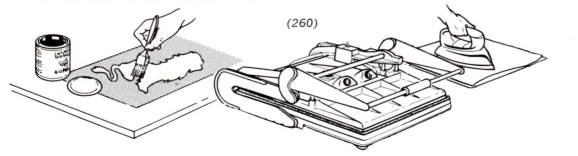

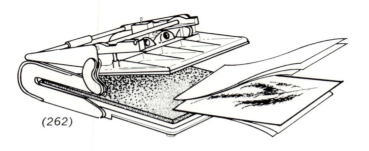

(262)

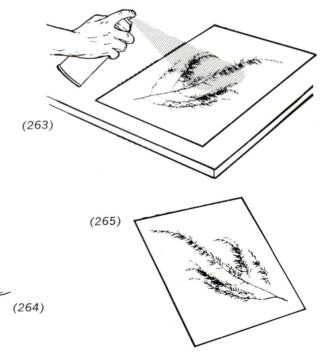

(261)

PLASTIC SPRAY (AEROSOL CAN)

The use of plastic spray adds another dimension to the dry mounting process. At times, it may be desirable to mount delicate materials that are too intricate in form to back with dry mounting tissue. Examples of such materials might be detailed, cut-out silhouettes, lace, or fern leaves. When care is exercised, the finest detailed image that will tolerate the heat necessary can be preserved.

In the example shown here a section of asparagus foliage (261) is mounted on cardboard. It is essential that all material be free of moisture. Place the foliage in the mounting press between several sheets of very absorbent paper, such as newsprint or blotter paper (262). In some cases it may be necessary to change the paper a couple of times because of excessive moisture. When the visual is completely dry, lay the foliage face down on a clean piece of scrap paper and spray a light coat of plastic over it (263). Allow it to dry and then repeat spraying and again allow to dry. Do this three or four times. Next, position the visual onto the cardboard with sprayed side down. Place a protec-

tive sheet of paper over the image, and place it in the press, which should be set at about 180 to 200°F. Leave it in the press for fifteen seconds and remove (264). Quickly remove the protective sheet so that any small seepage of plastic does not stick to it. The mounting is now complete (265). For additional protection, the finished visual may be given a coating of plastic spray.

(263)

(265)

(264)

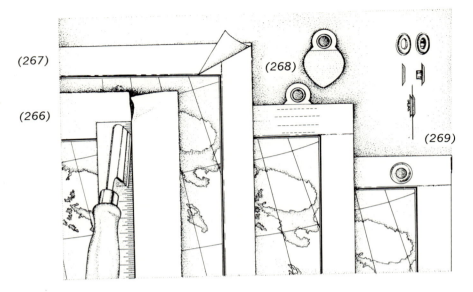

DRY BACKING CLOTH

Similar to the wet mounting technique is the use of dry backing cloth. This cloth is a high-quality cotton fabric with a thermoplastic adhesive coating on one side and is ideal for backing maps, charts, photographs, illustrations, and other flat materials. It adds durability and strength to the material to which it is mounted. Dry backing cloth is unaffected by moisture and will not shrink, buckle, or curl. When one uses this type of cloth, it is important to take into consideration the effect heat will have on the material to which the cloth is mounted. Sheets and rolls up to 42 inches wide are available; when mounting materials wider than 42 inches, the cloth may be spliced by overlapping the edges slightly.

Mounting on cloth is quite simple. Place the visual face down on a clean sheet of paper. Next, lay a sheet of dry backing cloth down over the visual with the adhesive (slick) side down. At this point a decision must be made concerning how the edges of the mounting are to be finished. The cloth may be flush (even) with the material being mounted (266), or the edges may be folded back over as illustrated (267), and ironed down. The latter method requires that an extra portion of cloth be left along the edges. Methods of hanging a mount should also be considered. There are ribbon and eyelets which can be sewed on (268) or grommets (269) which may be inserted into the border material. When sufficient cloth is left at the top and bottom of the mount, fitted sleeves may be made to accept rods for support. The cloth-backed material may be attached to a strong window-shade roller so that it can be rolled up when not in use.

Use a heated tacking iron (270) or a hand iron to "tack" the cloth to the map. To protect the cloth from any foreign matter which may be on the tacking device, put a scrap of clean paper under the device used. The tacking should be done at a center spot on the cloth. If this is done, any wrinkles near the edge will be free to flatten out when the final mounting takes place.

There are three ways to mount the cloth. First, it can be ironed on with a hand iron (271). A clean sheet of paper over the cloth backing will protect it from any foreign matter that may come off the iron. With the iron set at low

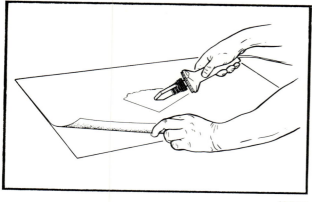

(270)

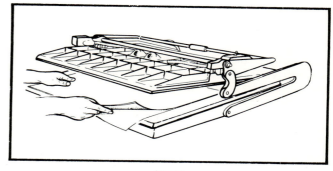

(271)

heat, keep it in constant circular motion. Start at the center of the mount and work to the outer edges. This is the best method to use when special treatment of the edges is desired. If adhesive edges of the cloth are exposed, make certain not to iron all the way to the edge until the special folds, already discussed, have been made.

A second method is the use of the dry mounting press. For flush mounting, where the backing is to be the same size as the visual, the dry mounting press works best. Set the press temperature at about 225°F and insert the material for about five seconds (272). Be sure to cover the visual, before inserting it into the press, with a protective sheet of paper.

Third, photographic print dryers (273) can be used to produce flush mounts. Simply tack cloth to back of the visual as instructed and pass through the dryer set at the recommended temperature (the same as for photographic prints). Allow the mount to cool before flexing or bending it.

Because dry backing cloth is so strong, it makes excellent hinges for notebook covers, displays, and accordion folded materials. Cloth backing may be used in combination with heat laminating films. The film laminations with their high temperature requirements should take place first. The cloth backing should be put on last.

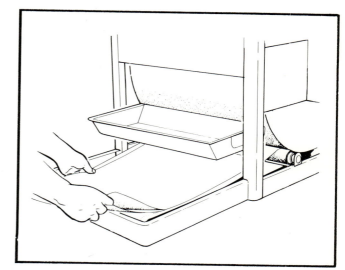

(272)

(273)

LAMINATING

To laminate is to lay a thin layer or coating over another material. In recent years the lamination process has become extremely popular and important in the production of visual materials. The process of adhering a thin coating of transparent film as a protective surface over visual materials has not only contributed to the preservation of the visual but has also given it greater flexibility in use. As the lamination process has become more common, the number of uses for the film has increased. The creativity and imagination of the producer has developed many variations, such as creating flat and three-dimensional texture patterns, using the film as a tracing media, using it as a method of splitting a printed page in half so that both sides of the page can be mounted separately, using it as a means of making picture transfers, and many other techniques too numerous to mention. The process usually involves some type of acetate, vinyl, or mylar film which has a transparent adhesive coating on one side. The film may be obtained in a dull (matte, frosted) finish and in a standard high-gloss surface. For some situations where low reflection is important or where it is desirable to draw on the surface of the film with pen or pencil, the frosted finish may be chosen. It is argued by some people that laminating a printed illustration gives it a glossy surface and tends to brighten the image, making it a more desirable master from which to make a photographic copy.

Laminating film, depending on the type being used, may be applied by either a cold process or a heat process. Laminating film of the cold variety may be applied by hand or in a specially designed machine having pressure rollers. Heat laminating film may be applied by using a flat iron or by a specially designed laminating machine having a heat and roller system to ensure good adherence of the film to the base material.

In some cases thermocopy machines function as laminators. The dry mounting press, because of its heat and pressure system, may also be used to laminate flat materials.

Each method of lamination has its strengths and weaknesses when cost, speed, and flexibility are considered. It is up to the producer to familiarize himself with the various laminating processes and choose the one that best fits his needs.

COLD LAMINATING ACETATE

Cold laminating acetate is a transparent film with a pressure-sensitive adhesive backing that permanently bonds on contact to most dry surfaces. This technique is ideal for preserving photographs, maps, charts, graphs, signs, instruction sheets, and valuable documents and requires no heat, machine, or additional adhesives. High-quality transparencies for projection or display can be made with this type of acetate (see pages 204 to 206).

Acetate can be attached to both sides of the material to be laminated if additional protection is desired.

Instructions

1. Cut the acetate to the desired size. If material is to be laminated on both sides, and a transparent margin is desired, cut the acetate large enough to allow for such a margin. Separate the backing sheet from the acetate at one of the corners with the point of a cutting knife or by "flicking" a corner with a finger as illustrated (274).
2. Lay the acetate face down and peel off the protective paper. This will expose the "sticky" side of the acetate (275).
3. Apply the material to be laminated face down on the sticky side of the

"Flicking" action helps remove backing sheet

(274)

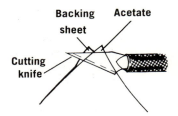

Backing sheet · Acetate

Cutting knife

acetate, contacting the leading edge of the material first, then lower at an angle until it is completely flat (276). Rub down with your hand to ensure perfect adhesion. Do not test the adhesive qualities of the acetate by lifting, because it will come off readily when first applied. The adhesive has been designed to work slowly. If the other side of the material is to be laminated, repeat steps 1, 2, and 3.

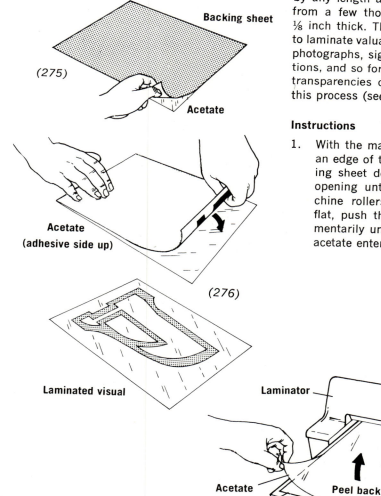

(275)

Backing sheet

Acetate

Acetate
(adhesive side up)

(276)

Laminated visual

LAMINATING MACHINE (COLD PROCESS)

Equipment: film laminator (cold process)
Acetate: cold laminating acetate

Here is a technique for laminating a variety of materials. This laminating process involves a pressure-sensitive acetate and a cold-type laminating machine. Machines are available which can laminate materials up to 20 inches wide by any length and will accept materials from a few thousandths of an inch to ⅛ inch thick. This process can be used to laminate valuable documents, records, photographs, signs, flash cards, illustrations, and so forth. Projection or display transparencies can also be made using this process (see pages 207 to 209).

Instructions

1. With the machine turned off, insert an edge of the acetate paper (backing sheet down) through the front opening until stopped by the machine rollers. Holding the acetate flat, push the switch to "nip" momentarily until about ¼ inch of the acetate enters the rollers (277).

Acetate

Backing sheet

(277)

Laminator

Acetate

Peel back

Backing sheet

Controls

2. Separate the paper backing sheet from the acetate as illustrated and peel back to rest on the machine. Insert the material to be laminated on top of the backing paper, face side up, and slide gently into the nip at rollers (278).

3. Hold the acetate with the left hand as nearly vertical as practical, and flip the switch to start the rollers moving. The machine will pull acetate, material, and backing sheet through to the discharge shelf at the rear (279).

4. Trim laminated material to size, and remove backing paper.

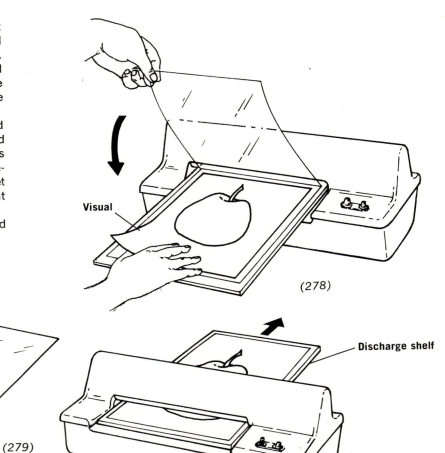

Visual

(278)

Discharge shelf

Laminated visual

(279)

LAMINATING MACHINE (HEAT PROCESS)

Equipment: film laminator (heat process)
Film: heat laminating acetate

The heat laminating machine laminates film to one or both sides of paper, cardboard, film, certain flat specimens, etc. (280). The laminating film usually consists of mylar and polyethylene inseparably welded together to form a tough transparent protective coating. Machines will accommodate many gauges of laminating film from the thinnest, .0015 inch for protecting paper, to .014 for laminating identification cards and other similar materials. The laminating film, combined with the machine that provides heat and pressure, makes up the laminating process.

Among the many types of materials that can be heat-laminated are valuable documents, printed literature, flash cards, posters, signs, illustrations, photographs, and flat specimens. Projection or display transparencies can be made with this process (see pages 210 to 212).

Machines are available to laminate materials from 3 to 60 inches wide, any length.

Laminating Paper or Cardboard Sheets (281)

1. Simply push a button or switch to set the heating unit of the machine in operation. A light will indicate when the machine is ready for lamination.
2. Push the control that starts the roller moving and insert the material to be laminated. It will be discharged at the back of machine sealed between two layers of transparent plastic film. Use the machine's cutter to cut the laminated material where desired. Material can be run through a second time if additional protection is required.

Laminating Flat Specimens or Small Sheets (282)

When laminating flat specimens or small printed sheets, thread the bottom laminating roll as illustrated. This will permit the film to serve as a conveyer. Or, if preferred, the material to be laminated can be fed directly into the machine without changing the threading of the film as suggested. Specimens such as leaves and insects should be dried out before lamination.

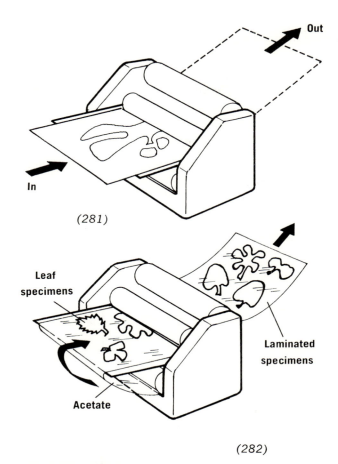

(281)

Leaf specimens

Acetate

Laminated specimens

(282)

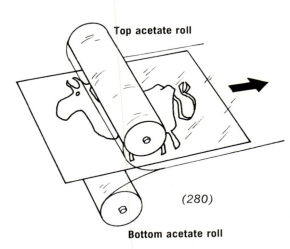

Top acetate roll

(280)

Bottom acetate roll

DRY MOUNTING PRESS LAMINATING

Equipment: dry mounting press
Film: Seal-Lamin and Harco Dura-Lam

The dry mounting press designed to mount flat pictorial material and using both heat and pressure will also serve as a laminating press. Having thermostatic controls, the press can be adjusted in temperature to satisfy the needs of the laminating film. A stiff sheet of cardboard or pressed wood used in the press will ensure better-quality lamination by not only adding pressure but also furnishing a more rigid base for even contact of film to heated surface.

Both matte and glossy-surfaced laminating films are available for the mounting press. The film may be purchased in a variety of sizes in the form of rolls, sheets, and envelopes (Harco "Lami-Pouche" is one type of envelope). The envelopes are designed so that both sides of a visual may be laminated at one time. The envelope is heat-sealed on three edges. The material is slipped into the appropriate-size envelope and placed in the dry mounting press. In a matter of seconds the laminating is completed. The roll and sheet film permit the laminating of one side of a visual or one side at a time. Usually visual materials mounted on cardboard will be laminated only on the face side.

It is possible to laminate materials other than paper such as wood, metal, and cloth. It must be remembered, however, that this process is limited to materials not affected by the heat. Pressure adjustments have to be made to accommodate the various thicknesses of these materials.

When you are dry-mounting visual materials to be laminated, it is best to use the high-temperature dry mounting tissue because the lamination process requires a rather high temperature. It is possible to have some difficulties arise from melting or buckling if high-temperature laminating film is placed over low-temperature mounting tissue.

The process is relatively simple. Cut a piece of laminating film the size of the material to be laminated. If both sides are to be laminated, use a prepared envelope or cut the sheet two times the size of the visual and fold it over so that both sides are covered. Carefully place the material over the visual, being sure all dirt and dust have been removed from the surface (283). To hold the film in place while putting it in the press, wipe over the film surface with a soft rag so that the static electricity will hold the film in place. Place a sheet of clean newsprint over the laminating film (284) and insert it into

the press for the required length of time. Always check the time and temperature instructions as given by the manufacturer. Remove the lamination from the press. The appearance of frosty areas indicates incomplete adherence, and it must be placed back in the press for an added length of time. Rough and irregular edges can be trimmed after the lamination is completed. When laminated material must be mounted with low-temperature mounting tissue or is to be mounted on low-temperature dry backing cloth, do the high-temperature laminating process first and then do the low-temperature mounting as the last step.

(283)

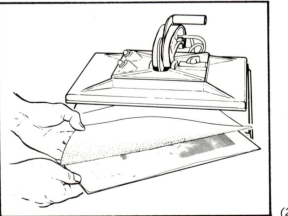

(284)

Laminating Variations
(Leaf Mounting)

With increased use of the dry mounting press as a laminating device, the use of laminating film to protect and preserve a variety of materials has developed. Examples of only a few uses might include the preservation of iron filings formed by a magnetic field, thread designs and mathematical patterns, delicate cutouts from tear sheets, delicate designs formed from flower petals or butterfly wings and other natural objects, finely woven cloth or lace patterns, feathers, and leaves of plants. The possibilities are limited only by the imagination. In most cases the procedure is simply a matter of pressing the object as flat as possible and applying the laminating film in the normal manner. It must be remembered, however, that any material or object affected by heat cannot be laminated in this manner, because the temperature may reach nearly 300°F. In some cases, as with plants and leaves, it is wise to press and dry the material before lamination.

The preservation of leaves by the lamination method is extremely popular (285). First, carefully choose the leaf to be mounted. Although the color of the leaf changes in the process, older leaves tend to hold their color better than younger ones. In the case of autumn colors, some leaves remain very true to their original color patterns. Stems and veins that are extremely heavy may be shaved down with a sharp knife from the back side of the leaf. This will prevent large raised areas in the final lamination. To proceed with the drying process, place the leaves between several layers of clean newsprint (286). Make sure the leaves are lying flat. Place this "sandwich" in the heated press (287). As the leaves are heated, the moisture will be absorbed by the newsprint. When working with leaves having high moisture content, it is wise to check them several times during dry-

(285)

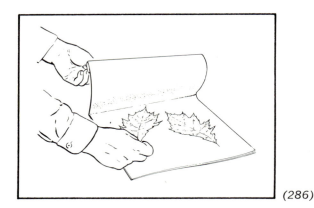

(286)

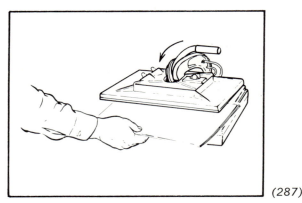

(287)

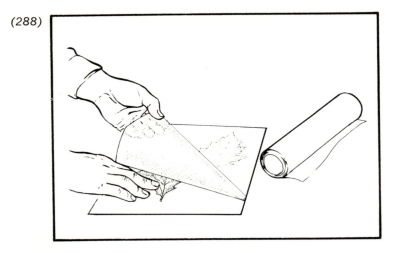

(288)

ing to prevent their sticking to the news-print. This can be prevented by chang-ing their position each time they are checked. For very "lacy" (leaf) material this is extremely important. Drying the leaves at low temperatures helps pre-serve the color. When the leaves are dry, arrange them on the mounting sur-face and cover them with a sheet of laminating film (288). Rub over the film surface with a soft cloth so the static electricity will draw the film tight to the mount. Be sure there are no serious wrinkles or folds. Cover the surface of the film with a clean sheet of newsprint and place in the press for the specified time. Always check to see that the press temperature is up to the temperature required. After the specified time, re-move the lamination from the press. If there are indications of incomplete ad-herence, return to the press for added time. Bridges of film formed near thick sections of the leaf such as the stem may often be tacked down using the tip of the tacking iron. If there is evidence of air trapped in these areas, a small pin prick will allow the air to escape and make adherence easier. If desired, diagrams, lettering, etc., can be added to the base mounting material prior to laminating.

Other variations in the use of lami-nating film made for the dry mounting press involve the manipulation of the film itself. The adhesive side of the film will accept ink quite well. Consequently it can serve as a tracing material. Since the tracing is made on the adhesive side of the film, the image being reproduced must be backwards. If the original is on relatively thin paper, this can be accom-plished by placing it face side down on a light box. Place the film over it with adhesive side up and proceed to trace the image. When the tracing is com-pleted the film may be adhered to what-ever base material is desired. The draw-ing will appear right side up and will be protected by the film itself from any damage. When care is exercised, air-brushing in transparent or opaque color is possible on the adhesive surface. It must be remembered, however, that ex-cessive amounts of ink or paint on the adhesive surface will affect its adhesive quality.

The laminating film is a tough ma-terial which will take a great amount of stress. This characteristic extends its potentials. If the film is wrinkled by crushing it into a ball and then flattened out before mounting, it will give a tex-ture effect to the surface over which it is mounted. For instance, clear wrinkled film mounted over a snow scene gives a feeling of sparkling icing. Color wax crayon chips may be placed beneath

(289)

(290)

(291)

wrinkled or smooth film for brilliant texture patterns. As the heat of the mounting press activates the film, the crayons melt and form interesting color patterns beneath the film (289). The designs may be controlled to a limited degree by the placement of the color crayon chips.

For another example of how laminating film may be manipulated for a special effect, take a sheet and wrinkle it into a ball. Flatten it out and repeat the process. The more times this is done the finer will be the detail of the resulting texture pattern. Spread the wrinkled film out on a clean piece of scrap cardboard or newsprint with the adhesive side up. Do not flatten it completely but allow the wrinkles to form a three-dimensional pattern.

Using transparent or opaque dye or watercolor in an aerosol spray can or airbrush, spray the adhesive surface of the film at a low angle (290). The paint will strike only the surface facing the spray. Allow the color to dry. Then drymount the film onto a backing material. This may be white or tinted cardboard or paper, textured paper, wallpaper, aluminum, wood, or a variety of other materials. After mounting, the texture design created this way will still have a strong three-dimensional appearance (291).

Materials created in the aforementioned ways can contribute to the creation of displays, notebook covers, and special effects for many purposes. The effect shown in (291) may be used to represent a mountain range on a large wall map. For the creative person the possibilities are unlimited.

THERMOCOPY MACHINE LAMINATING

Many flat printed materials, such as valuable documents, photographs, and printed instructions, can have a special acetate laminated to their surfaces through use of a thermocopy machine. The acetate is designed to provide a protective covering and a surface to be written on, erased, and reused.

3M Laminating Instructions

The 3M Company manufactures a laminating film that is designed to be used in thermocopy machines as illustrated here.

1. Assemble materials as illustrated in (292). Make certain the original to be laminated is not folded, creased, or crumpled. All the necessary materials are in the box containing the film.

2. Set the speed control of the thermocopy machine at the slowest speed (darkest setting) and insert materials into the machine. When laminating several sheets without interruption, gradually turn the dial to a slower (lighter) setting.

Viewlex (Viewfax) Instructions

Viewlex manufactures a laminating sheet for use in their thermocopy machines. Here are the instructions:

1. Assemble materials as illustrated and place in a carrier screen. Insert assembled materials into the machine (293).
2. Follow step 2 of the 3M instructions.

Laminating Both Sides of Original

If lamination is required for both sides of the original, simply repeat the aforementioned steps on the reverse side of the original using a second sheet of film.

Laminating Materials Smaller than Laminating Film (Viewlex)

If the original is smaller than the sheet of laminating film (i.e., business or membership card, photograph) the interleaf sheet must be placed underneath the original. Failure to do this will cause the film to laminate to the carrier screen.

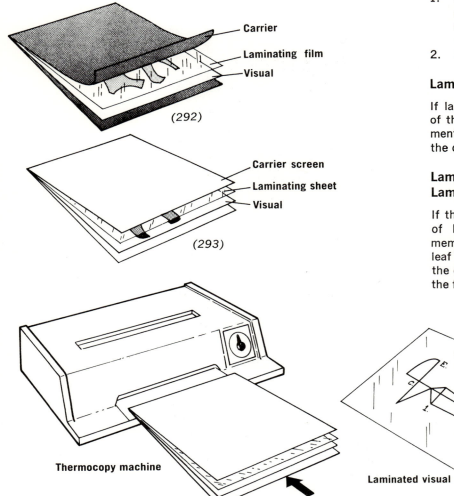

Carrier

Laminating film

Visual

(292)

Carrier screen

Laminating sheet

Visual

(293)

Thermocopy machine

Laminated visual

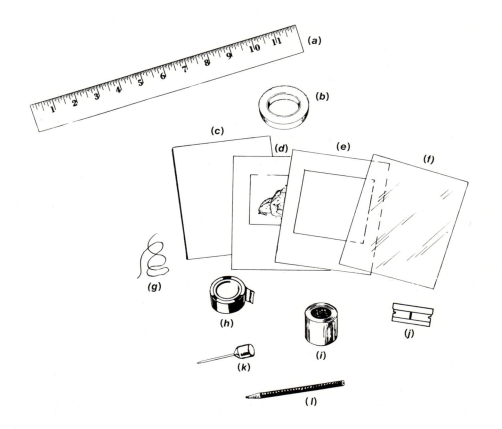

(294) Materials required: (a) ruler; (b) masking tape; (c) mounting board; (d) mounted visual; (e) mat; (f) glass or plastic; (g) string or picture wire; (h) cloth or plastic tape; (i) passe-partout tape (paper); (j) razor blade; (k) awl; (l) marking pencil.

PASSE-PARTOUT MOUNTING

For mounting
 Awards and certificates
 Photographs
 Tear sheets
 Specimens
 Paintings

Passe-partout mounting is a simple, inexpensive framing method for preserving flat and three-dimensional instructional materials under glass or plastic. Colored cloth, paper, or plastic-base tapes, along with a sheet of glass or plastic and a piece of thick mounting board, are all that is required to produce an attractive mounting.

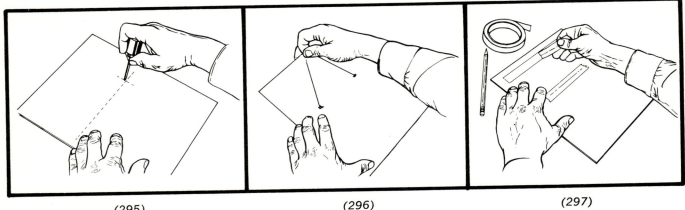

(295)　　　　　　　　(296)　　　　　　　　(297)

When a picture is to be suspended by a string or wire, two holes must be punched in the mounting cardboard. These holes should be on a line about two-fifths of the distance from the top of the cardboard and well in from the right and left edges. The holes may be made by using an awl (295). Through these holes thread a strong string or picture wire. Tie it so it will stretch just short of the top of the picture.

(296). Pull the knot to one of the holes so that it will not interfere with proper hanging. With the string drawn taut, turn the cardboard over and cover the exposed string with a piece of masking tape. This prevents the string from slipping and causing bulges. Next, place a piece of double-coated adhesive tape, mucilage, or rubber cement near the top of the mounting board to hold the visual in place (297).

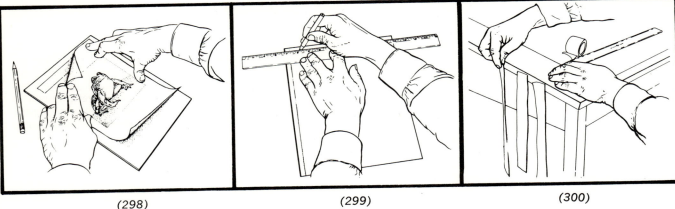

(298)　　　　　　　　(299)　　　　　　　　(300)

Position the visual on the mounting board and adhere it only along the top edge. This permits it to lie loosely over the slight bulge formed by the string (298). To get a uniform width of tape along the edge of the glass, use guidelines made with a marking pencil (299). Cut four strips of framing tape.

Two strips should be 2 inches longer than the vertical height of the glass, and two should be 2 inches longer than the horizontal width. If the adhesive side of the tape is sticky, suspend it from the edge of the table or desk for ease in handling (300).

(301)

(302)

(303)

Next, adhere the tape to the glass. For extra strength, place the tape on the vertical side first. In a horizontal position in front of you, place a strip of tape with adhesive side up. With marking-pencil lines facing up, slowly lower the glass down on the tape making sure its edge coincides with the guideline (301).

Do this on all four sides. When this is completed, press tape tight against glass for good adhesion and wipe off guide-lines from the glass surface (302). Next, place the glass face down in front of you in its correct position and prepare to cut the corners of tape extending beyond the glass (303).

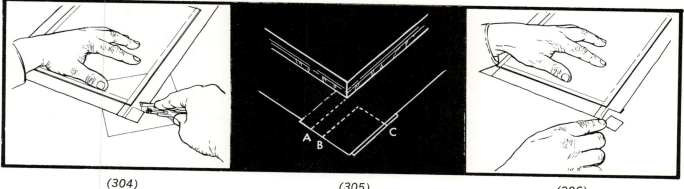

(304)

(305)

(306)

Cut the tape in the lower right corner (304) as indicated by lines A, B, and C in the diagram (305). The width of strip AB should equal the thickness of the mounting (i.e. cardboard, glass, visual, and mat). Remove the free piece of tape (306).

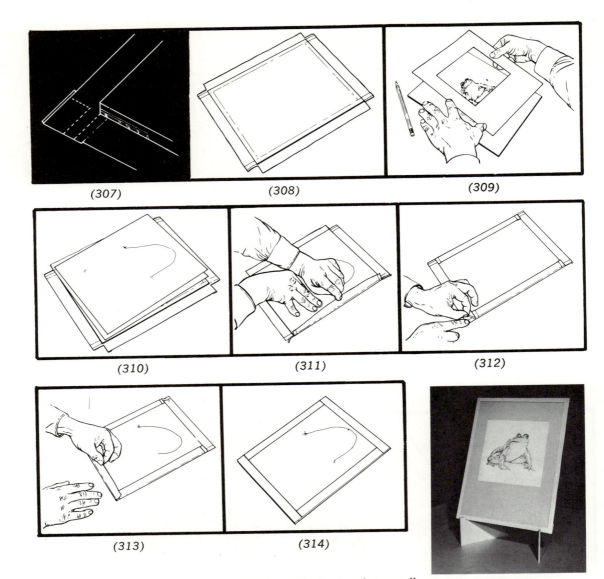

(307)

(308)

(309)

(310)

(311)

(312)

(313)

(314)

(315)

Cut the left corner in a similar manner to the right as indicated in the diagram (307). Turn the taped glass 180° and repeat the procedure with the two remaining corners (308). Now place the mat over the mounted visual, checking to see that any smudges and dirt have been removed (309).

Place the mat and mounted visual face down on the inside surface of the glass (310). Be sure that all edges of the assembled mounting are flush. While holding all parts firmly in place, pull over the vertical tape edges, pressing them firmly down on the mounting board (311). Next, turn the small flaps of tape around the corners and press them in place (312).

The two remaining tape edges are pulled over the mounting cardboard (313) and pressed in place (314). The passe-partout framing of this visual is now completed (315).

(316)

The passe-partout method of framing may be adapted to the mounting of three-dimensional specimens (316). A simple balsa-wood frame is glued to a heavy cardboard. The frame is made of strips with a dimensional height slightly greater than the thickness of the specimens to be mounted (1). A sheet of cotton is placed in the frame as a soft support (2). In cases where insects might damage the specimens, moth crystals or other insecticides may be placed under the cotton layer. A small perforated paper tube or soda straw may serve as a container for the crystals and be placed along one edge of the frame beneath the cotton blanket (3). The specimens being mounted are then positioned on the cotton (4). Small indentations can be made in the cotton blanket for objects of maximum thickness. After all specimens are in place, a cutout mat and cover glass are placed over them (5). The glass has been taped with a wide cloth, plastic, or paper tape as described in the conventional method of passe-partout mounting (6). Carefully pick up the entire assembly and turn it face down on a clean, smooth surface. If the picture is to be hung, a cardboard with string attached may be added (7). The cutting of the corners and drawing of the tape over onto the backing cardboard involves the same procedure as described in the conventional passe-partout mounting method. The visual is now ready for display.

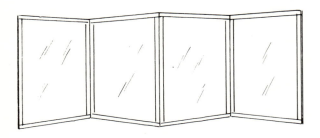

(317)   Passe-partout mounted pictures in an accordion fold.

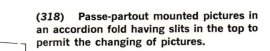

(318)   Passe-partout mounted pictures in an accordion fold having slits in the top to permit the changing of pictures.

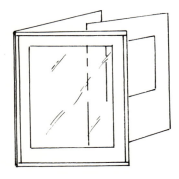

(319)   Single-hinge passe-partout frame permitting quick change of pictorial material.

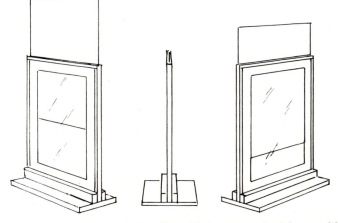

(320)   Two-sided passe-partout frame with slit in top to permit change of visual.

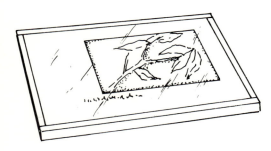

(321)   Three-dimensional passe-partout mounting for the display of specimen.

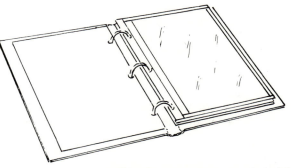

(322)   Passe-partout mounted pictures in a three-ring notebook.

DISPLAY EASELS

ATTACHED EASEL (SIMPLE WING)

For the more permanent type of display materials—those that have repeated use and are displayed on shelves or tables—the simple wing easel may be best to use. It is simple to make and folds flat when not in use, making mailing or storage easy. This support is permanently mounted to the display. By using the grid drawing (323), you may make any size pattern to accommodate any size display. The pattern is next transferred to a sturdy cardboard sufficiently strong to support the display. An easy method to transfer a simple pattern of this type is to lay the pattern onto the cardboard and then with a sharp pointed cutting needle puncture small holes through each corner of the drawn pattern. Remove the original drawing, and with pencil and ruler connect each one of the small pinholes. The pattern is now ready to cut. Because all sides of the wing support are straight, it may be cut out by using a straightedge and razor blade or a straightedge paper cutter (324). Next, a light pencil line is drawn down the middle of the back of the display (325).The wing support is laid along this pencil line, and sturdy paper or cloth tape is applied to the full length of the support (326). The wing support is folded over in the opposite direction, and a second piece of tape is applied (327). Be sure to press the tape firmly in the crease along the edge of the support. The simple wing easel is now ready to use (328).

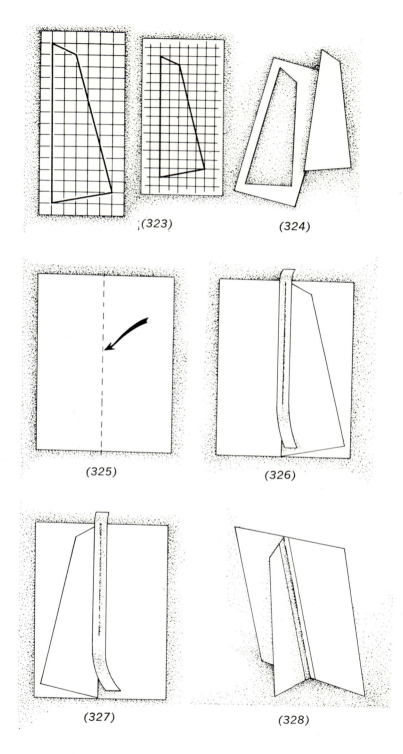

¡(323)

(324)

(325)

(326)

(327)

(328)

ATTACHED EASEL (LOCK WING)

The lock wing easel is more complicated to construct than the simple wing. It is permanently mounted to the display, lies flat, and can be easily stored. The squared diagram (329) gives the basic outline of this type of easel. From this original, any size pattern can be made by enlarging or reducing through the grid drawing method (see pages 46 to 49). Care must be taken in making the original that the locking device is accurately drawn (330) and cut out. If it is inaccurately shaped, it may not lock the easel in place properly. Transfer the pattern onto a cardboard of sufficient weight to support the particular display. First, cut out the basic outline of the easel. This can be done by using a straightedge and mat knife or razor blade. Next, cut along the solid lines of the locking device (331). The dotted lines indicate where the easel must be folded (332). Next, carefully make a slight cut along the dotted lines just sufficiently deep to permit folding. If the cardboard is rather lightweight, scoring or pressing along the line with a blunt pointed instrument may be sufficient to permit ease in folding. Check to see that the easel will fold properly along the vertical dimension (333) and that the lock will fold into place (334). Slight adjustment may have to be made by trimming the edges of the lock. The final step is to glue the vertical

folded edge along a center line drawn on the back of the display (335). Place some heavy weight on the glued flap and allow it to dry. When the glue is dry, the easel is ready for use (336).

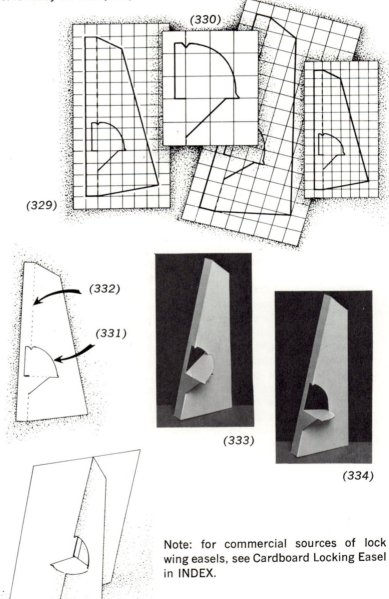

(330)

(329)

(332)

(331)

(333)

(334)

Note: for commercial sources of lock wing easels, see Cardboard Locking Easel in INDEX.

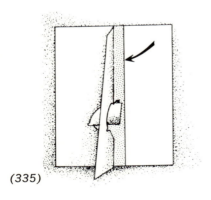

(335)

(336)

FOLDING EASEL

A simple method for displaying mounted pictures, passe-partout mountings, flannel boards, bulletin boards, and other flat materials is through the use of the folding easel (337, 338). It is extremely simple, sturdy in construction, and easy to store. By using the grid drawing (339) a variety of different-sized patterns can be made (340).

After a pattern of the desired size is made and traced onto a piece of cardboard, two sides are cut out (341). These pieces are laid about ¼ inch apart (342) depending upon the weight of the cardboard used.

A strong cloth tape is applied to both sides of the easel (343, 344). The excess tape is trimmed off. The hinge is then finger-pressed together to form a simple sturdy center fold (345). Check to see that the easel will fold (346). The easel is then ready for use (347). To support extra-large materials, more than one easel can be employed (348).

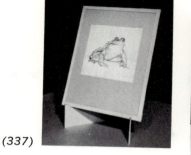

(337)

(338)

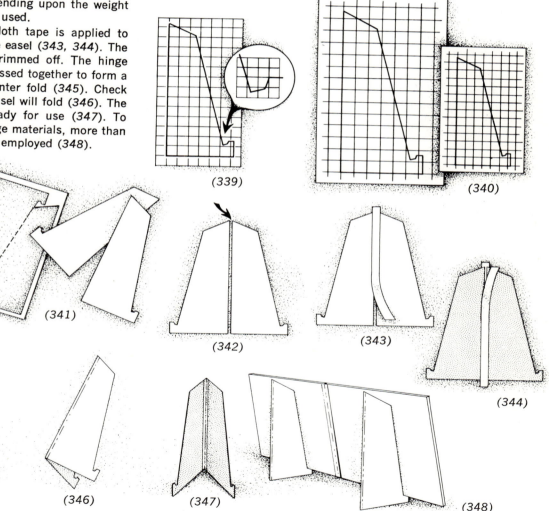

(339)

(340)

(341)

(342)

(343)

(344)

(345)

(346)

(347)

(348)

MOUNTING AIDS

There are a number of good-quality and unusual mounting aids available to help simplify mounting problems. Illustrated and briefly discussed are several recommended mounting aids. Additional information can be obtained from the sources listed in Chapter 6.

Adhesive Pen

A pen-type refillable liquid-adhesive dispensing device (349) using the ball-point principle to dispense dots of adhesive for mounting purposes. Most pens, when filled, will dispense about five thousand adhesive dots.

Liquid Plastic Adhesive

A fast-setting white or transparent all-purpose adhesive (350) that holds on wood, paper, cloth, glass, and all porous and semiporous materials. Can be used in an adhesive pen.

Pliable Plastic Adhesive

A reusable pliable plastic adhesive (351) for attaching materials such as papers, maps, charts, and photographs to most dry surfaces. This adhesive can also be used to attach cardboard or molded plastic letters to most dry surfaces. To use, pull like taffy until warm. Tear off a small piece and attach to the back of material to be mounted.

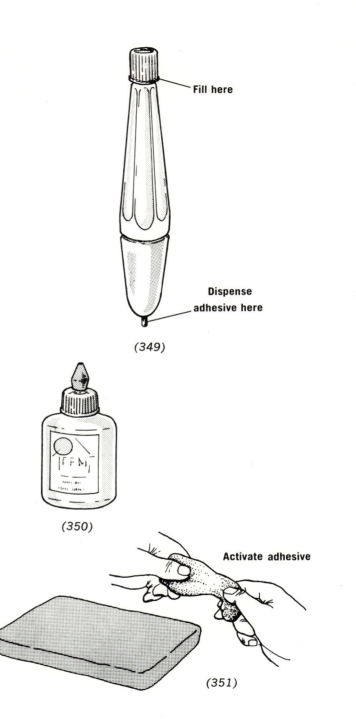

Fill here

Dispense adhesive here

(349)

(350)

Activate adhesive

(351)

LETTERING AND PRINTING TECHNIQUES

Scott Letter-engraving Machine

Mechanical Tracing Lettering Systems
    LeRoy Lettering System
    Letterguide Lettering System
    Varigraph Lettering System
    Panto-Varigraph Lettering System

Letters by Projection

Composition Adhesive Type

Composition Paper Type

Kinder Composition Plastic Type

Phototype Composing Machine

Dry Transfer Lettering

LETTERING AND PRINTING TECHNIQUES

With few exceptions, practically every kind of visual instructional media requires lettering or printing of one type or another. In view of the importance of lettering to the preparation of instructional media, this chapter of the book illustrates and discusses what is believed to be a rather comprehensive assortment of lettering and printing techniques.

Available on the market today is an unlimited variety of letters, lettering guides, mechanical tracing lettering systems, printing machines, tape and plastic embossers, phototype composing machines, paste-up type, and so forth. Such a multitude of techniques and aids might frustrate the novice producer of visual media. However, a quick glance at the Lettering and Printing Selection Chart on page 100 is a suggested starting point for the selection of the technique recommended for a particular lettering problem. To assist with problems of letter layout, spacing, and design, one can refer to page 101.

This chapter has been written mainly for the nonprofessional producer of visual media. However, it is hoped that the most demanding commercial artist can refer to the pages that follow to help solve production problems involving lettering. Should any of the lettering or printing techniques included in this chapter be removed from the market, the selection chart on page 100 lists alternate techniques.

Finally, it should be kept in mind that there are no hard-and-fast rules governing the selection of lettering or printing techniques. The selection should be made only after an analysis of the lettering requirements of a particular job. The choice may depend upon what is available or the ability of one to use a particular technique. In any event, it is hoped that from among the techniques included in this chapter an answer can be found for the lettering problem at hand.

LETTERING AND PRINTING SELECTION CHART

LETTERING AND PRINTING TECHNIQUES

This chart is designed to assist in the selection of lettering and printing techniques best suited for an item being produced. In some emergency situations, lettering techniques not recommended for a particular item can be substituted for use. *First,* locate the item requiring lettering or printing in the column below. The **X**'s to the right of each item indicate the techniques which are recommended for use. The **X**'s with superior numbers should be referred to in the KEY at the bottom of the chart. *Next,* refer to the pages indicated for instructions on the technique.

ITEMS REQUIRING LETTERING OR PRINTING	Bulletin (Primary) Typewriter	Cardboard and Metal Stencil Lettering Guides	Composition Adhesive Type	Composition Paper Type	Dry Transfer Lettering	Dymo-Form Plastic Forming System	Econasign Lettering System	Embosograf Sign-making System	Flatbed Printing Machine	Hallmark Vinyl Plastic Letters	Hot-Press Printing	Kinder Composition Plastic Type	LeRoy Lettering System	Letterguide Lettering System	Lettering Guides for Stencil and Spirit Duplication	Letters by Projection	Panto-Varigraph Lettering System	Phototype Composing Machine	Planotype Letters	Precut Letters	Reynolds Printasign Printing Machine	Rubber Stamp Printing	Scott Letter Engraving Machine	Spray-on Lettering	Tape Embossing Machine	Varigraph Lettering System	Wrico Sign-Maker System
PAGE	120	102	136	138	142	123	108	122	118	112	120	140	124	128	107	134	132	141	113	110	119	116	124	114	122	130	105
Bulletin Boards	X	X	X[1]	X[1]	X	X	X	X	X	X	X[1]	X	X			X[19]	X[19]	X	X[20]	X	X	X			X	X	X
Captions (for Photographs, Illustrations)	X		X[1]	X[1]	X		X	X			X	X[1,2]	X	X				X[2]			X					X	X
Certificates and Awards	X		X[2]	X[2]	X		X									X				X[7]						X	X
Chalkboards	X	X	X[2]	X[2]	X		X			X	X[1,2]	X	X			X[19]	X[19]	X[2]	X[20]	X		X[3]				X[3]	X[3]
Charts, Graphs, Diagrams, and Maps	X[4]			X				X[3]		X[3]	X[3]		X[3,19]	X		X[3]										X[3]	X[3]
Clear Acetate Overlays (for Charts, Transparencies)	X[6]		X		X[9]		X[5,17]	X[5]		*	X[5]	X[5]				X[22]				X[5]						X[5]	X[5]
Diazo Masters	X[6]		X		X			X		X[1,2]	X	X				X										X	X
Electronic Stencil Artwork	X[6]		X[2]	X[2]	X		X		X		X[1,2]	X	X			X[2]				X						X	X
Filmstrip Artwork (for Captions, Titles)		X[8]		X[8]	X[8]	X[8]	X[8]	X[8]				X[8]	X[8]	X[8,19]	X[8,19]	X[8]			X[8]	X[8]	X[8]					X[8]	X[8]
Flannel (Felt) Boards	X[6]		X	X	X[9]		X[5]	X[5]		X[1]	X[5]	X[5]				X[5]			X[9]							X[5]	X[5]
High-contrast Photographic Artwork	X		X[1]	X[1]	X		X	X	X	X	X[1]	X	X			X			X	X	X	X	X	X	X		
Labels (for Files, Containers)	X						X						X	X		X			X			X			X		
Letters, Large Display		X[10]		X[10]	X[10]	X[10]	X[10]	X[10]				X[10]	X[10]	X[10,19]	X[10,19]	X[10]			X[10]	X[10]	X[10]					X[10]	X[10]
Magnetic Boards	X[16]	X[12]										X[13]	X[13]	X			X[12]										
Mimeograph Stencils	X		X[2]	X[2]	X		X	X	X	X	X[1,2]	X	X			X[19]	X[19]	X[2]	X	X	X	X				X	X
Motion-picture Artwork (for Titles, Captions)	X		X[1]	X[1]	X		X	X		X	X[1]	X	X			X[19]	X[19]	X	X[20]	X	X	X	X			X	X
Nameplates								X		X						X[19]	X									X	X
Offset Duplication Artwork (for Photographic Processing)	X[6]	X	X	X	X								X	X		X[19]	X									X[14]	X[14]
Offset Duplication Master (Direct Image)	X[15]			X[9]									X[14]	X[14]						X[7,14]						X[14]	X[14]
Overhead Projection Transparencies																											
Acetate Spirit Master Transparency	X[16]												X[13]	X[13]	X			X[12]									
Carbon-coated Projection Acetate	X[16]												X[13]	X[13]				X[12]									
Clear Acetate (Base and Overlays)	X[4]			X				X[3]		X	X[3]	X[3]				X				X[5,7]	X[5]				X[5]	X[5]
Diazo (Master)	X[6]		X	X[9,17]	X[5]		X[5]			X[1]	X[5]	X[5]		X[5]		X			X[9]				X[5]	X[5]		X[5]	X[5]
High-contrast Photographic (Artwork Only)	X[6]	X	X	X[9]	X[5]		X[5]		X[1]	X[5]	X[5]	X[5]	X			X[11]			X[11]							X[11]	X[5,11]
Matte (Frosted) Acetate	X[4,11]			X[11]				X[3,11]		X[5]	X[5]	X[5]				X[5,7]										X[5]	X[5]
Thermocopy (Artwork Only)	X[6]	X[17]		X[9,17]	X[5]		X[5]			X[3]	X[3]		X			X[3]										X[3]	X[3]
Thermocopy Transparency Film (Processed)	X[4]			X				X	X	X[1]	X	X				X	X[20]		X						X	X	X
Place Cards	X	X	X[1]	X[1]	X	X	X	X	X	X	X[1,2]	X	X			X[19]	X[19]	X[2]	X[20]	X	X	X		X		X	X
Posters	X	X	X[1,2]	X[1,2]	X	X	X	X	X		X[1]	X	X			X[19]	X[19]	X	X[20]	X	X	X	X	X	X	X	X
Signs			X	X[1]	X[1]	X	X	X	X	X	X	X[1]	X	X		X[18]	X[18]	X[19]	X[19,21]	X						X	X
Silk-screen Artwork (Stencil Cutting)	X		X[2]	X[2]	X		X	X		X	X[1,2]	X	X			X[2]	X[20]	X		X						X	X
Slide Artwork (for Captions, Titles)												X[13]	X[13]	X			X[12]										
Spirit (Hectographic) Duplication Masters	X[16]	X[12]																								X	X
Television Artwork (for Captions, Titles)			X[2]	X[2]	X	X	X	X		X	X[1,2]	X	X			X[19]	X[19]	X[2]	X[20]	X	X	X				X	X

KEY

1. Requires photographic processing
2. For paste-up artwork only
3. Requires acetate (plastic) ink
4. Requires overhead transparency typewriter ribbon or carbon sheet
5. Requires black ink
6. Typed character must be dense, opaque
7. Must be traced
8. Finished letter(s) must be backed with flannel, felt, sandpaper, etc.
9. Black letters only
10. Finished letter(s) must be backed with metal or rubber magnet
11. For projection, dull side of acetate must be sprayed with clear plastic spray
12. Must be traced with metal stylus or ball-point pen
13. Mechanical scriber ball-point pen-stylus must be used in scriber
14. Requires offset master (direct image) ink
15. Requires offset master typewriter ribbon
16. Set typewriter on "stencil"
17. Heat-resistant black type only
18. Mechanical scriber silk-screen or swivel knife must be used in scriber
19. When extra large letters are required
20. Opaque letters only
21. Panto-Varigraph silk-screen knife required
22. Positive character (letter) on film

LETTER LAYOUT, SPACING, AND DESIGNS

Letter Layout

The arrangement and form given to letters contributes a great deal to the preparation of a visual material where lettering is involved. Basic to lettering layout is alignment. Here are two suggested approaches to the alignment of letters and words:

Individual-type letters
(precut, dry transfer, etc.)

1. Write down the words intended for one line of lettering (352a).
2. Count up the letters and spaces between the words. Mark the center letter.
3. Assuming that the line of lettering is to be centered on the working surface, make a light pencil mark at the center point as illustrated (352b).
4. Make a light pencil guideline on the working surface for letters that require such a line.
5. Position the middle letter at the center point on the working surface. First, work to the left of the middle letter, as shown in (354). Then work to the right of the middle letter until all letters are in place.

Mechanical-type letters
(stencil or mechanical tracing, etc.)

1. Letter the intended line of letters, with the lettering device selected for the job, on a scrap sheet of paper. Make a mark at the center letter. Make certain to count all letters and spaces when picking out the center letter (353).
2. If the lettering is to be centered on the working surface, make a light pencil mark at the center point. Match up the center mark on the scrap sheet of paper with the mark on the working surface. Repeat the lettering on the working surface, using the scrap sheet as a guide for letter and word spacing. If the line of lettering is not to be centered, position the scrap sheet containing the first lettering where desired and repeat the lettering on the working surface.

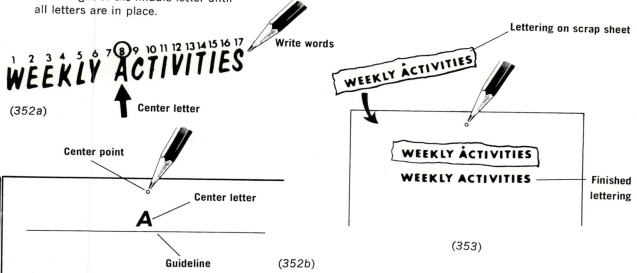

Write words

1 2 3 4 5 6 7 8 9 10 11 12 13 14 15 16 17

WEEKLY ACTIVITIES

(352a)

Center letter

Center point

Center letter

A

Guideline

(352b)

Lettering on scrap sheet

WEEKLY ACTIVITIES

WEEKLY ACTIVITIES

WEEKLY ACTIVITIES — Finished lettering

(353)

(a)　　　　　(b)

(354)

Letter Spacing (354)

Good letter spacing is the arrangement of letters in a line so that they will appear to have equal or uniform distances between them. To achieve this effect, it is often necessary to position the letters at varying distances from one another, depending on the style, size, and combination of letters involved. One way of assuring correct letter spacing is to envisage the areas between letters as being irregular containers of liquid, the objective being to space the letters so that no matter how irregular the shape of these "liquid containers," they will each hold the same amount of liquid. This technique of spacing is also known as optical spacing. Note that although the letters in (a) are equally spaced, the "containers" between them are unequal. Part (b) illustrates the results of spacing letters so that the "containers" are nearly equal.

Designs (355)

Being creative when it comes to visual design is not always easy, especially for the nonprofessional designer of visual media. On this page are examples of designs, made up mainly of lettering, which were the results of ideas taken from magazines, newspapers, and brochures, and combined with many of the lettering techniques included in this chapter. These designs can be used as a starting point for the creation of posters, bulletin-board materials, and projection titles.

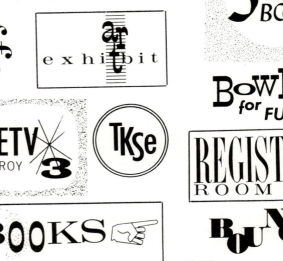

(355)

CARDBOARD AND METAL STENCIL LETTERING GUIDES

Cardboard and metal stencil lettering guides provide a fast, economical way for lettering on opaque surfaces easily and accurately with perfect spacing. The cardboard guides are made up of cleanly cut letters on a durable treated stencil board. A variety of letter styles and sizes are available. Letters range in height from ½ to 8 inches.

Sample letter styles

Individual Cardboard Stencil Letters for Paint Application (356, 357)

Individual stencil letters are unique in that they can be arranged to form complete words for spraying or tracing.

1. To align letters, use a straightedge as illustrated. For best results, overlap stencils. Spacing may be varied by changing the amount of overlap.
2. Fasten letters together with pressure-sensitive tape along the top and bottom edges of the stencils.
3. Tape assembled letters to area to be stenciled. If required, use protective paper to mask the area around the stencils. Spray over stencils with an aerosol spray-can color or apply color with a stencil brush.

Individual Cardboard Stencil Letters as Lettering Guides (358)

1. Follow steps 1 and 2 above.
2. Place assembled letters where lettering is desired and trace outline of letters, or
3. Draw a light pencil guideline where lettering is desired and trace each letter as illustrated. Erase guideline when lettering has been completed.

Stencil Letter Cutting Machine (359a)

A hand-operated stencil-cutting machine for cutting stencil letters out of stencil oil board. Models available for cutting letters from ¼ to 1 inch in height.

Metal Interlocking Stencil Guides (359b)

Metal interlocking guides are letters and numerals that interlock to form a complete word. The completed word can be traced, sprayed with paint or ink, or printed with a stencil brush and ink.

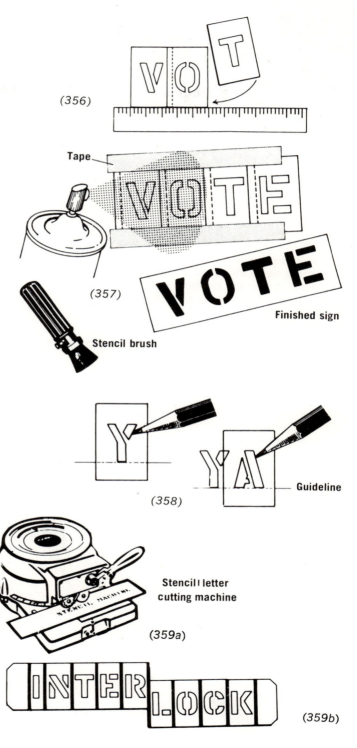

(356)

Tape

(357)

Stencil brush

Finished sign

(358)

Guideline

Stencil letter cutting machine

(359a)

(359b)

Cardboard Stencil Lettering Guides

1. Draw a light pencil guideline on the lettering surface above which letters are to be traced. If guide holes are at the bottom of stencil letter, draw the guideline below where the letters are to be traced. Before each letter is traced, position guide so that the guideline appears through the guide holes below each letter.

2. Position the first letter and trace the outline with a pencil or ballpoint pen. Letter can be filled in with crayon. Before moving guide to next letter, make a pencil dot in the guide hole at the lower right of the letter just completed (361).

3. Position the next letter so that the dot just made shows through the guide hole at the lower left of the letter to be traced. Trace letter and repeat the foregoing steps until the word has been completed. Erase guideline (362).

4. Finished letters can be filled in with color crayons, inks, paints (363).

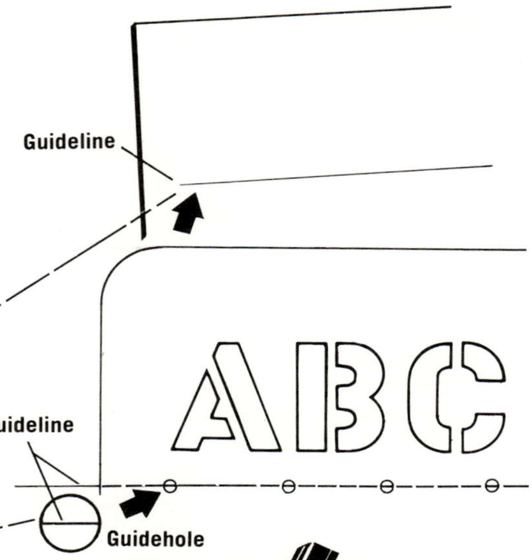

Guideline

Guideline

(360)

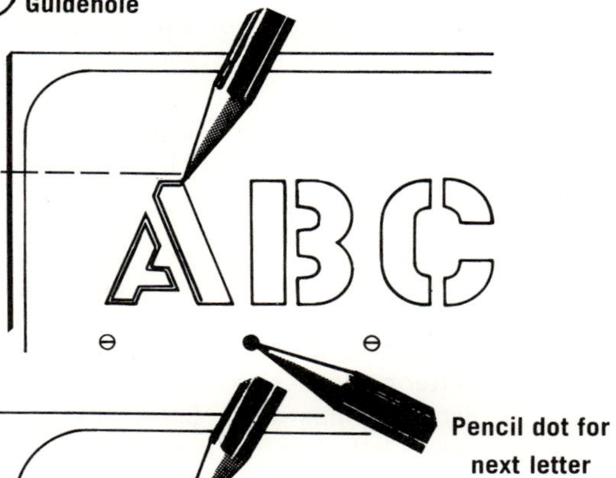

Guidehole

(361)

Pencil dot for next letter

(362)

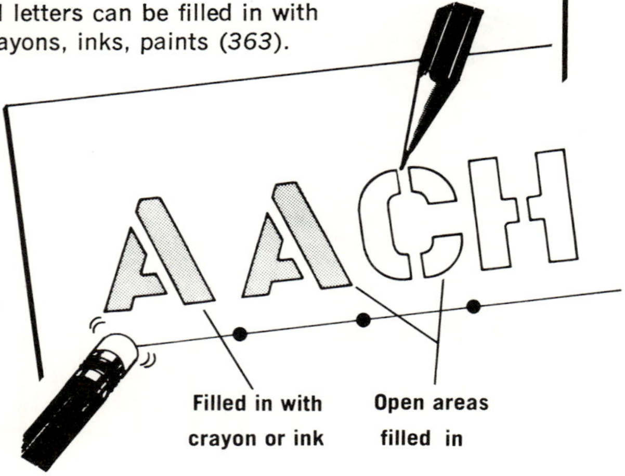

(363)

Erase guideline

Filled in with crayon or ink

Open areas filled in

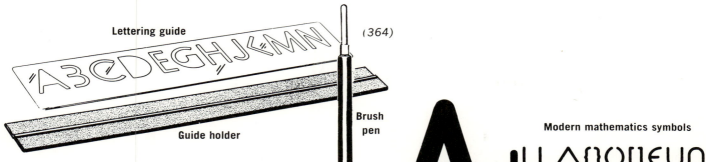

Lettering guide

(364)

Guide holder

Brush pen

WRICO SIGN-MAKER SYSTEM

The Wrico Sign-Maker system (364) consists of transparent plastic lettering guides, a metal guide holder, and a brush or felt-point pen. Letters range in height from ⅜ to 4 inches. There are a number of letter styles to choose from, including modern mathematics symbols. The Sign-Maker is an ideal lettering system for preparing posters; signs; charts; graphs; maps; television, filmstrip, motion picture, and slide titles; flash cards.

Instructions

1. To fill the pen (365a), press plunger down and insert only the brush portion of the pen in ink, and without raising the pen, release the plunger slowly. The pen is now ready for use. To adjust the pen properly for use, twist the adjustment nut until the end of the brush is even with the end of the tip of the pen. If the brush is not out far enough, turn the nut to the right. If the brush is out too far, turn the nut to the left. Finally, turn the adjustment nut a quarter of the way to the left so that the brush is recessed slightly; this will permit the ink to flow freely under the brush and allow for well-inked lines (365b).

2. Place the metal guide holder on the surface to be lettered so that the rubber strips on the bottom of the holder set firmly upon the surface (366). Then rest the lettering guide

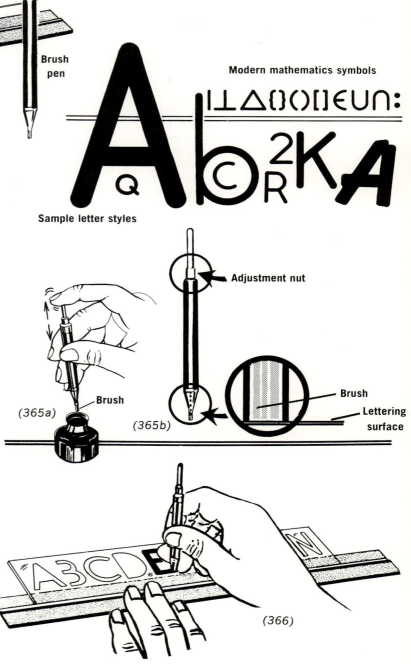

Modern mathematics symbols

Sample letter styles

Adjustment nut

Brush

(365a)

(365b)

Brush

Lettering surface

(366)

105

in the channel of the guide holder. This permits the guide to be moved smoothly to the right or-left without touching the surface to be lettered, thus preventing ink smudges. The guide holder stays securely in position wherever it is placed. This eliminates the necessity for such accessories as straightedges, weights, thumbtacks, or tape.

3. Move the lettering guide so as to position the first letter where desired on the lettering surface. Insert the pen in the first letter. Hold the pen vertically, and glide it through the letter form. Best results are obtained with very light pressure on the point. Many of the characters, both letters and numbers, are made complete with a single opening. Some require two openings. For example, when making the letter B (367), use any vertical line and then move the guide until the curved portion of the B is in position to complete the letter.

4. Slide the guide to the next letter and repeat the process (368).
The lowercase letters c, f, i, j, l, m, n, o, r, s, t, u, v, x, y, and z are made by simply following the proper openings (369). The other letters require two openings. Part of the letter is made with one opening and completed with the other. The openings used for these letters are also indicated.

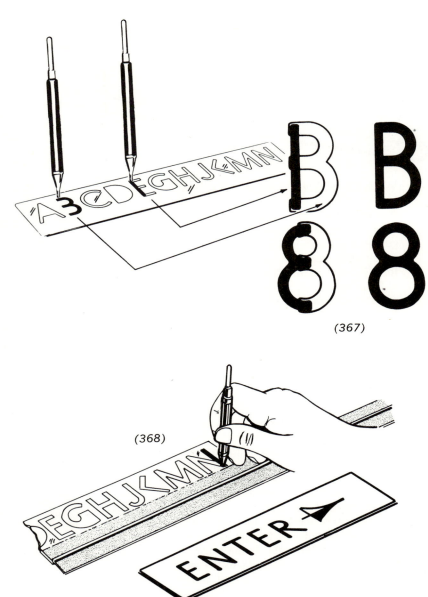

(367)

(368)

(369)

LETTERING GUIDES FOR STENCIL AND SPIRIT DUPLICATION

Lettering guides for stencil and spirit duplication (370a) are made of plastic and have openings in the shape of letters and numerals. There are usually two styles for lettering, one for smaller letters and one for the larger letters. Assorted letter styles and sizes are available.

Stencil lettering guides work equally well on both stencils (mimeograph) and spirit masters. The use of a plastic writing plate (sheet) is recommended when using lettering guides.

Instructions—Stencils

1. Where possible, a glass surface with a light source behind it should be used (370b) (Mimeoscope and Tracing Scope are two brand-name units for use with stencils). Place the plastic sheet directly behind the stencil as illustrated. Position and lock T square in place (371).

2. Choose the lettering guide and the correct stylus (372). The proper stylus to use is indicated on the lettering guide. Make a very light line in the correct letter first. Then go back and forth over the line just drawn several times until sufficient stencil coating is pushed aside from the base tissue to make a clear white line.

3. Always draw toward a point formed by the junction of two lines. For example, when drawing the letter F, draw the long line first, then start at the outer points of the two short lines and draw toward the long line —never away from it.

   Spacing is achieved by estimating the proper distance between each letter with the eye. See Letter Layout, Spacing, and Designs (pages 101 to 102).

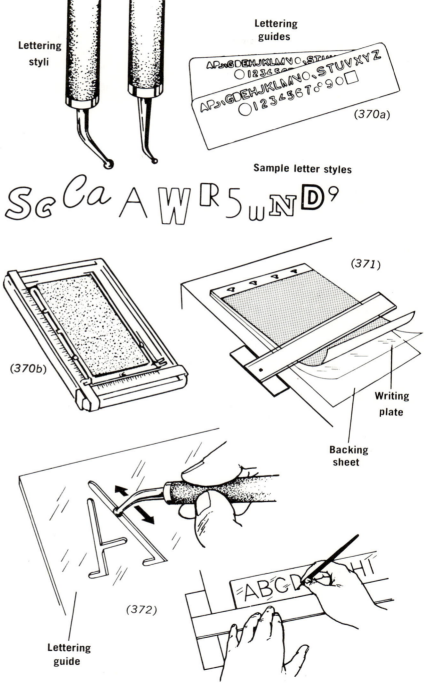

Lettering styli

Lettering guides

(370a)

Sample letter styles

(370b)

(371)

Writing plate

Backing sheet

(372)

Lettering guide

Instructions—Spirit masters (373)

Lettering on a spirit master with stencil lettering guides and lettering on stencils are almost identical. Refer to Preparation of Working Surface (page 23) for instructions on how to prepare master for use.

1. Place a plastic writing plate under the spirit master as illustrated, or if a writing plate is not available, place the master on a hard, smooth surface. Remove the interleaf sheet so that the carbon sheet is next to the master.

2. Choose the lettering guide and correct stylus. Some ball-point pens with a fine point will sometimes work just as well as a stylus. Trace the letter with a firm, steady pressure. Check the master to make certain the carbon is transferring a solid-line letter.
To change color of letter, change the carbon sheet for another color

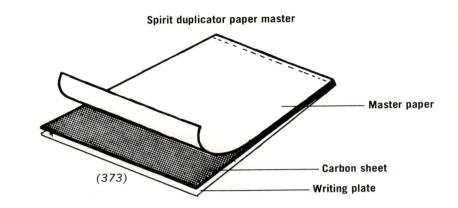

Spirit duplicator paper master

Master paper

(373)

Carbon sheet

Writing plate

carbon. Corrections can be made by carefully scraping carbon transfer off the master and erasing with a correction pencil. Tear off a small section of the carbon sheet, position it under the correction, and retrace the letter.

ECONASIGN LETTERING SYSTEM

For preparing

Charts	Signs
Graphs	Posters
Maps	Certificates
Displays	Flash cards
Exhibits	Diagrams
Television titles	Notices
Television slides	

The Econasign system of lettering (374) is unique in that the letters, numbers, and symbols have the appearance of printed type and can easily be mastered with very little practice. The system consists of stencil, alignment bar, paint box, stencil brush, pushpins, and a cleaning brush. Fourteen ink colors including gold and silver are available.

Econasign stencils are made from thin, hard plastic which is tinted and

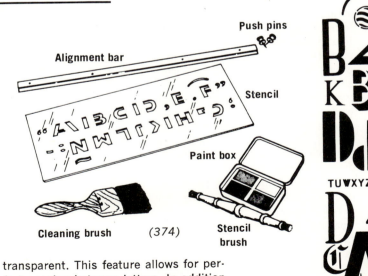

Push pins

Alignment bar

Stencil

Paint box

Cleaning brush   (374)   Stencil brush

Letter styles and designs

transparent. This feature allows for perfect spacing between letters. In addition to letter and number stencils, logotype, ornamental, and harlequin stencils in many styles and sizes are available. Letters range in size from ½ to 6 inches.

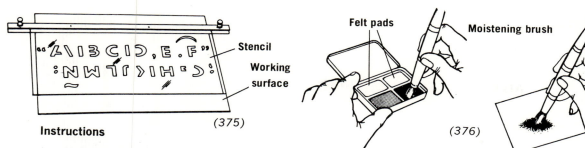

Stencil

Working surface

(375)

Felt pads   *Moistening brush*

(376)

Testing brush

Instructions

1. Moisten felt pad opposite color to be used with a few drops of water. Press moisture well into pad. Additional water may be necessary if doing quantity lettering.

2. See Preparation of Working Surface for instructions on how to prepare lettering surface. Position the alignment bar with the aid of a T square so that the small shelf faces the user. Place the selected stencil on the shelf of alignment bar so that the row of stencil letters is in the desired position on the lettering surface. Insert pushpins in the holes of the alignment bar (375). If the working surface does not permit the use of pushpins, see Preparation of Working Surface for tips on attaching such devices.

3. To moisten the stencil brush, merely touch it to the felt pad. It will soak up sufficient moisture. Do not wet the brush or rub it on the wet pad. Next, rub the brush on the color until it is well charged and nearly dry. Test the brush on a piece of paper to determine if it is properly charged (376).

4. To letter, move the stencil along the shelf of the alignment bar so that the first letter is in position. While pressing the stencil firmly against the lettering surface with the left hand, brush over the letter with a circular motion, holding the brush in a perfectly upright position (377). Make certain the color is dark and evenly distributed. Graduation of color can be obtained by making portions of the letter lighter or darker in color. For additional let-

ters, repeat the procedures used for making the first letter. See Letter Layout, Spacing, and Designs for tips on spacing and layout. When changing from one color to another and when the same stencil is used, wash the stencil as instructed in step 5 before using the second color. This will prevent the first color from mixing with the second color.

5. To clean stencil after use, place it in a flat container such as a pan or dish. Cover with cold water and brush over lightly with the cleaning brush. If using waterproof ink, it is advisable to wash the stencil immediately after use. Rinse it with cold, clean water and place between paper towels or blotting paper and dry. This cleaning procedure lessens damage to the stencil. Do not, on any account, use a sponge or cloth for cleaning (378).

6. When the stencil brush has not been used for several weeks, washing is recommended merely to soften the bristles. The stencil brush can stand a considerable amount of neglect.

Washing brush

(378)

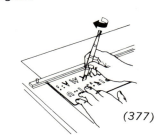

(377)

EXIT

Finished sign

PRECUT LETTERS

Precut letters are available in assorted materials, styles, sizes, and colors. Where three-dimensional and cutout letters are desired, the letters presented here should provide an answer. Additional information on the types discussed can be obtained by writing to the sources listed in Chapter 6.

PLASTIC OR TILE LETTERS

Die-cut or molded plastic or tile letters (379) designed for displays, exhibits, posters, projected titles, and a variety of presentation boards.

Sanded-back Letters (380)

For attaching to hard surfaces with glue for permanent attachment or rubber cement for interchangeable use.

Pin-back Letters (381)

Steel pins in back for attaching to soft surfaces. Can be used over and over again.

Track Letters (382)

Designed with bottom lug to fit into special channels. Ideal for stand-up signs, desk markers, displays, etc.

Magnetic Letters (383)

Molded plastic letter with small metal or rubber magnet attached to the back for use on magnetic boards or steel surfaces.

Velcro-backed Letters (384)

Dimensional plastic letters backed with velcro (hook) tape. Designed for use on velcro (Hook n' Loop) boards. Letters range in height from 1 to 3 inches.

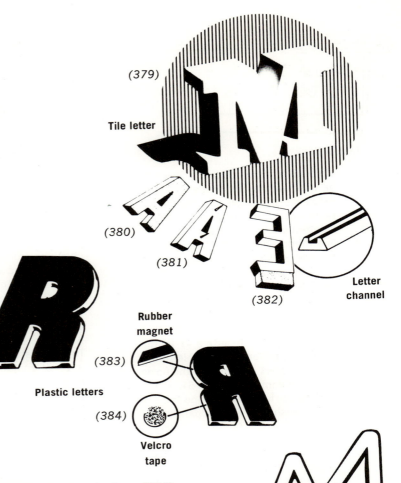

(379)

Tile letter

(380)

(381)

(382)

Letter channel

Rubber magnet

(383)

Plastic letters

(384)

Velcro tape

Molded Magnetic Letters (385)

A semiflexible molded plastic letter that will stick to any steel or magnetic-treated surface. The magnetism is permanent. Letters range in height from ½ to 2 inches and come in several colors.

Vinyl Plastic Pressure-sensitive Letters (386)

Die-cut vinyl plastic letters with a pressure-sensitive adhesive back that will stick to most surfaces. Height sizes range from ½ to 6 inches. Assorted styles and colors are available.

(385)

(386)

CARDBOARD LETTERS (387)

Die-cut from heavy cardboard. Available in colored or uncolored stock and in a wide range of sizes and styles. Ideal for preparing displays; signs; posters; television, motion picture, and slide titles; etc. Letters can also be used for tracing and spray-on lettering (see pages 114 to 115). Magnets can be attached to the back of letters for use on a magnetic board. Sandpaper, felt, or velour can be attached to the back of letters for use on the feltboard.

GUMMED PAPER OR CARDBOARD LETTERS (388)

Die-cut paper or cardboard letters with a gummed back. A pair of tweezers, a straightedge, a moist cellulose sponge, and a blotter are the only tools necessary to produce professional-looking lettering.

PAPER PRESSURE-SENSITIVE LETTERS (389)

Paper letters with a pressure-sensitive back. Simply peel off the protective paper backing and stick letter or number on almost any surface—cardboard, chalkboard, wood, glass, paper. Mere finger pressure will keep the letter firmly in place. Letters usually range in size from 1 to 3 inches in assorted styles and colors.

WOOD OR METAL DISPLAY LETTERS (390)

Precision-cut wood or metal letters are available in heights up to 30 inches and are designed mainly for signs and displays.

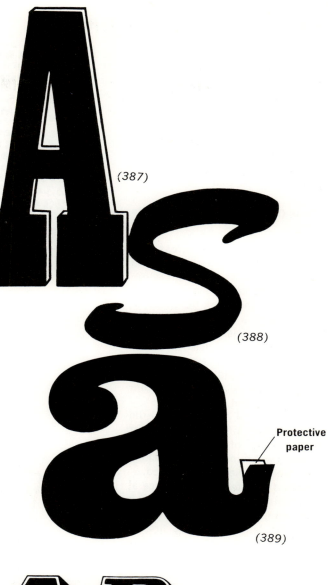

(387)

(388)

Protective paper

(389)

(390)

HALLMARK VINYL PLASTIC LETTERS

The Hallmark pressure-sensitive vinyl plastic letters are weatherproof, washable, permanent, and can be used indoors or outdoors. They can also be cleaned and waxed. These letters are ideal for posters, charts, graphs, signs, television and film titles, and similar uses. Assorted styles are available in white, red, gold, and black. Three sizes are available—⁵⁄₁₆, ½, and 1 inch.

Instructions (for centering a word or line of lettering)

1. Draw a level pencil line across surface on which letters are to be mounted, or a strip of pressure-sensitive tape can be used in place of the pencil line. Mark the center of the line with a light pencil mark. Count up the letters in the word or line of letters to be used including all spaces between words. Determine what the middle letter is. This will be the first letter removed from the backing sheet.

2. Use the point of a knife to peel the center letter off backing sheet (391). Centers of letters such as A, B, and D will remain on the backing sheet when the letter is removed.

3. Position the letter on the surface at center mark and press in place; it will bond immediately (392). Mount remaining letters, working first to the left of the center letter then work to the right of the center until all letters are in place.

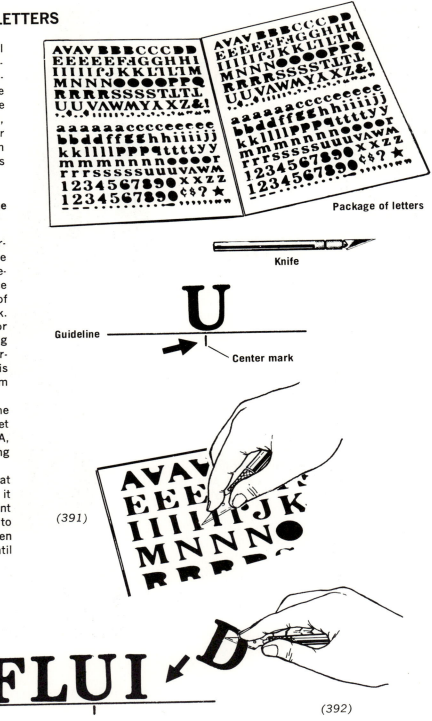

Package of letters

Knife

Guideline — Center mark

(391)

Erase guideline

FLUI D

(392)

112

PLANOTYPE LETTERS

Planotype is a pliable plastic pressure-sensitive letter available in assorted styles and sizes. Opaque letters come in white, black, and red. Transparent letters come in red, blue, green, and yellow. Height sizes range from 5/32 to 1½ inches. Letters will adhere to most surfaces and can be reused many times. Planotype letters are arranged in frequency distribution on aluminum sheets 12 by 15 inches. Transparent letters, designed primarily for projection, will adhere only on glossy surfaces, such as plastic, glass, or film. Opaque letters will adhere on contact to any reasonably smooth surface such as paper, cardboard, plastic, or glass. Planotype is ideal for commercial art, charts, graphs, television and film titling, etc.

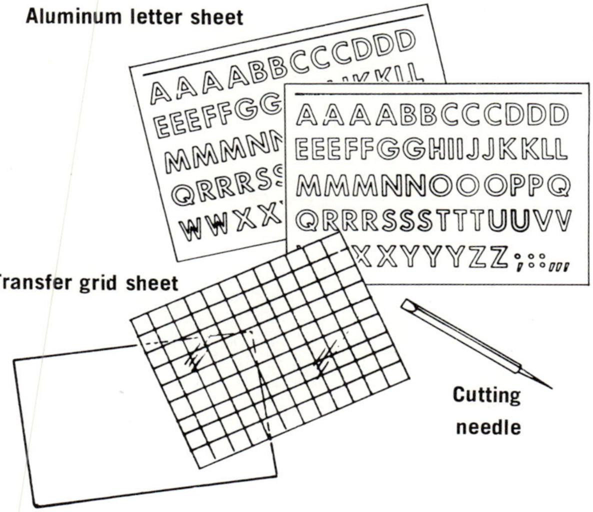

Instructions

1. To remove a letter, insert a sharp-pointed instrument between letter and aluminum sheet (*393*). Press index finger against part of the letter already lifted. Peel letter off sheet. Follow same procedure with all letters intended for immediate use.
2. Place removed letters *face up* on blank side of layout sheet, preferably in desired sequence and lined up (*394*). Do not use reverse side of layout sheet with printed matter on it since letters will stick to it.
3. Position the transparent transfer grid sheet over the first letter to be picked up (*395*). Press the letter against the grid sheet; this will lift the letter from the layout sheet. Follow the same procedure for the remaining letters.
4. To place completed lettering on artwork or other surface, position the grid sheet on the surface where desired and press the sheet with the letter against the surface (*396*). The letters will transfer. Carefully peel the grid sheet off the lettered surface.

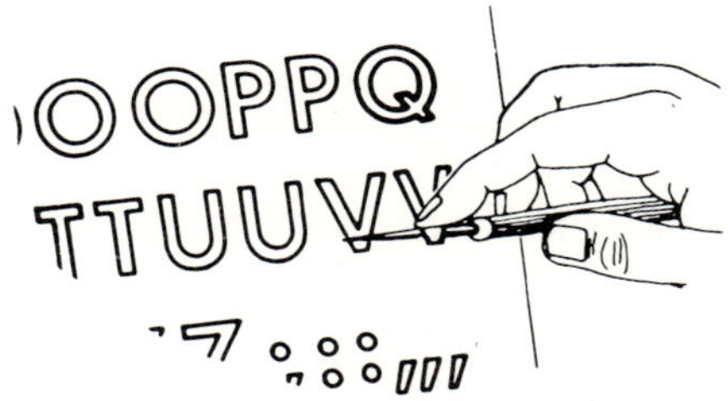

(393)

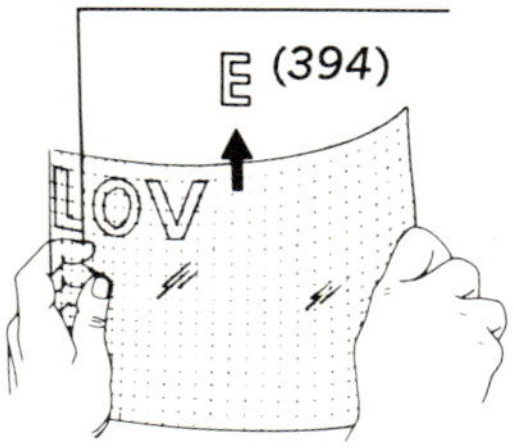

(394)

(395)

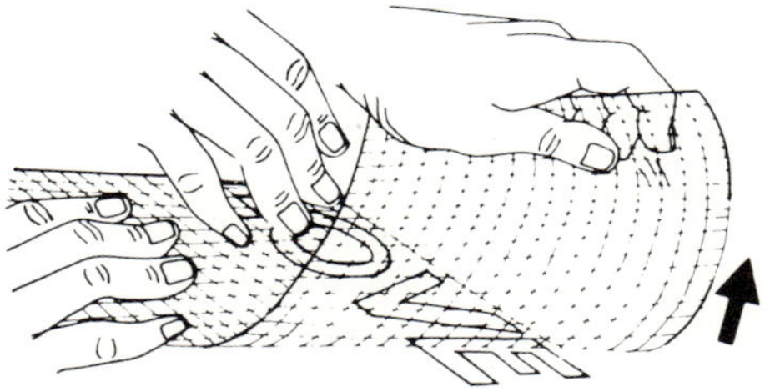

(396)

Commercial spray-on letters

Precut letters

Spray paints

(397)

SPRAY-ON LETTERING

Attractive signs and posters can be made quickly with precut and special spray-on letters (397). Commercial spray-on letters are the best type for this technique in that they are usually made of die-cut thick sponge rubber and will not shift or move when sprayed. American Jet Spray Industries and W. W. Holes Manufacturing Company sell spray sign kits. Letters range in height from ¾ to 12 inches. A variety of aerosol spray-can paints provide excellent colors for this technique.

Instructions for a two-color sign or poster

1. Place surface upon which lettering is to be done on a flat protected surface. Use a piece of cardboard or thick paper to cover one section of the lettering surface (398).
2. Select the letters and numbers desired and arrange them on the lettering surface. A T square or straightedge can be used to align the letters (399). See Letter Layout, Spacing, and Designs for helpful tips.
3. Select color or colors and spray lightly over and around the letters, holding the spray can about 12 inches away at right angles (400). The resulting letter will be sharp and clearly defined. If a three-dimensional effect is desired, hold the spray can at about a 45° angle and

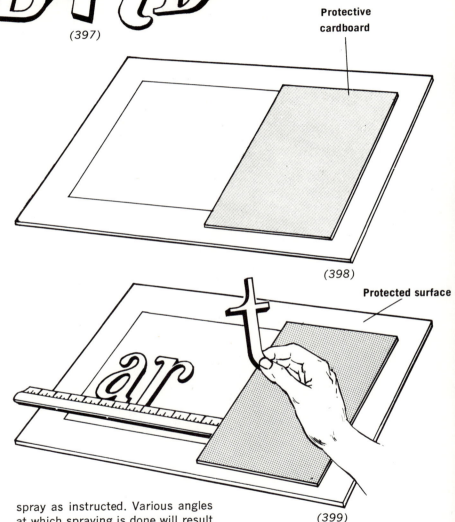

Protective cardboard

(398)

Protected surface

(399)

spray as instructed. Various angles at which spraying is done will result in a variety of effects. Allow paint to dry; this usually takes about ten minutes, depending on the type of paint used. Carefully remove letters from the surface.

NOTE: protect working surface with newspaper, old cardboard, etc.

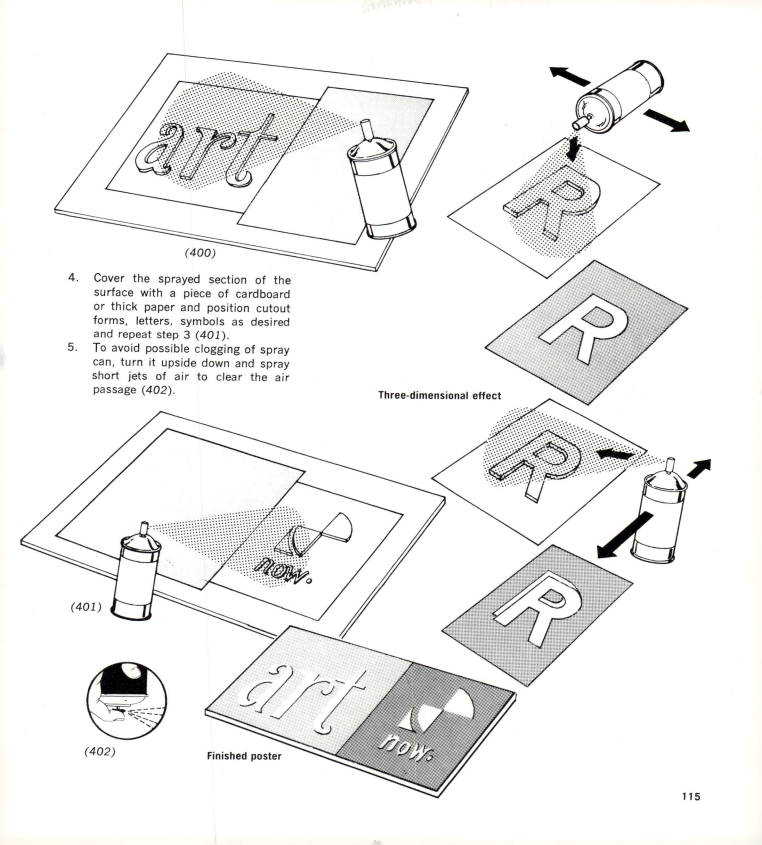

(400)

4. Cover the sprayed section of the surface with a piece of cardboard or thick paper and position cutout forms, letters, symbols as desired and repeat step 3 (401).

5. To avoid possible clogging of spray can, turn it upside down and spray short jets of air to clear the air passage (402).

Three-dimensional effect

(401)

(402)

Finished poster

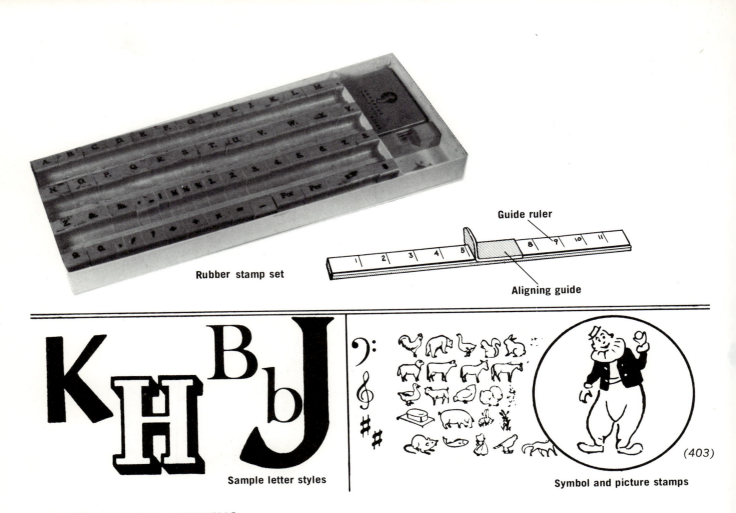

Rubber stamp set

Guide ruler

Aligning guide

Sample letter styles

Symbol and picture stamps

(403)

RUBBER STAMP PRINTING

Rubber stamp printing provides a neat, inexpensive method for printing such things as charts, graphs, maps, flash cards, name plates, posters, and signs. A complete printing set, such as the one illustrated, includes rubber stamp type, guide ruler, aligning guide, stamp pad, and a bottle of black ink and applicator. Miscellaneous type characters like &, !, ?, $, ¢ may also be included in the set. Some typical type faces are shown in (403). Some sources carry picture and symbol stamps as illustrated. The rubber type (letter) is securely cemented to an indexed wooden molding made to rigid specifications.

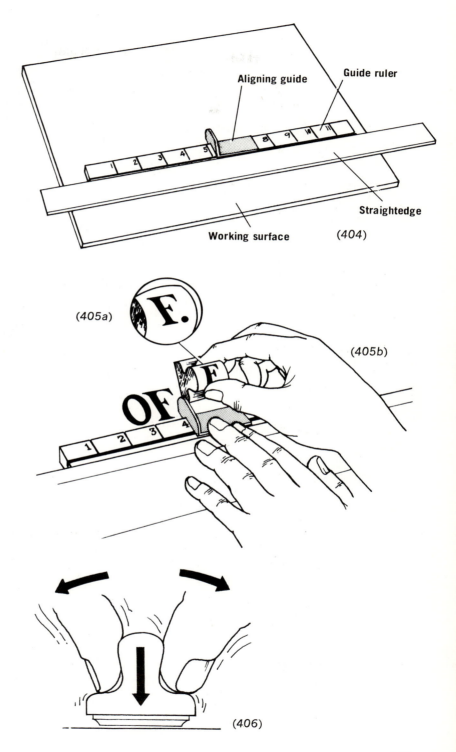

Aligning guide

Guide ruler

Straightedge

Working surface

(404)

(405a)

(405b)

(406)

Instructions

See Preparation of Working Surface for instructions on how to prepare the surface upon which the printing is to go.

1. Position guide ruler and aligning guide against T square or straightedge as illustrated *(404)*.

2. Ink the first letter stamp on the stamp pad and position the bottom portion next to the guide ruler and against the metal aligning guide; this will assure a straight letter impression. Make certain the dot on the stamp is at the lower right of the letter *(405a)*. Move the letter stamp and aligning guide along the ruler to the place on the surface where the impression is to be made. Make certain the stamp is tilted away from the surface to prevent the letter from making an impression before properly located. Hold the ruler and aligning guide in place with the left hand *(405b)*.

3. Press the stamp down on the surface with a firm "rocking" motion. This will ensure a complete letter impression *(406)*.

4. Print the second letter and remaining letters by moving the stamp and aligning guide to the next letter position and repeating steps 2 and 3. See Letter Layout, Spacing, and Designs for tips on spacing, layout, and so forth.

FLATBED PRINTING MACHINE

The flatbed printing machine (407) provides a fast, flexible, economical, and simple method for printing posters, signs, and the like in many sizes and does not require expensive special type or special materials to print on. Generally, it takes less than five minutes to pick and set type, ink and print an average four-line 7- by 11-inch poster. There are models available for producing posters up to 44 by 30 inches. Letters up to 4 inches high in assorted styles add to the versatility of this printing method.

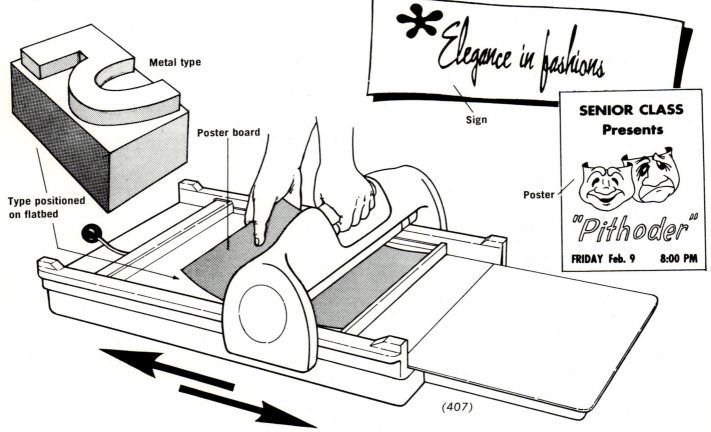

Metal type

Type positioned on flatbed

Poster board

Sign

Elegance in fashions

SENIOR CLASS
Presents

"Pithoder"

FRIDAY Feb. 9   8:00 PM

Poster

(407)

REYNOLDS PRINTASIGN PRINTING MACHINE

This machine (408) is a high-speed graphic typewriter for printing such things as posters; signs; showcards; television, motion picture, slide, and filmstrip graphics. The printing can be done on virtually any surface that will accept ink. Each type character is mounted on a spring-loaded stem in the typecase. To print, the operator selects the character and lowers the operating handle, thus depressing the type onto the printing surface. When the type character retraces, the spacing trigger automatically advances the printing surface into position for the next character. Each character is automatically spaced according to its width. Letter spacing may be varied by merely turning a dial. Typecases are interchangeable, and type is available in any style, including foreign alphabets. Type sizes range from ¼ to 2 inches.

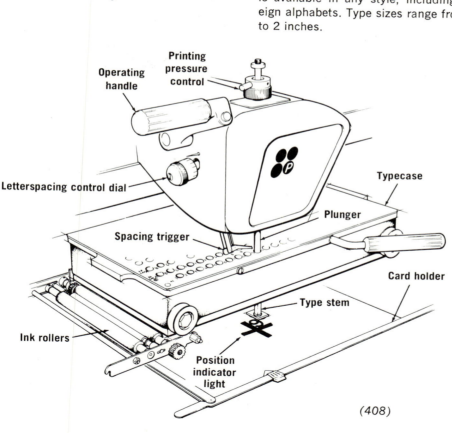

(408)

HOT-PRESS PRINTING

The hot-press printing machine (409) is specially designed for motion-picture producers, special-effects laboratories, animators, television stations, advertising agencies, art departments, and the like. The machine uses a heated metal type to make an impression on paper, cardboard, acetate, and plastic surfaces. Type sizes range from 6 point to 120 point. In place of ink, a roll leaf color foil is used to print letters in color.

The Veach Development Company manufactures an inexpensive heat stamping machine that is ideal for personalizing small items, such as slide mounts, greeting cards, pencils, brochures, photographs, transparencies, etc.

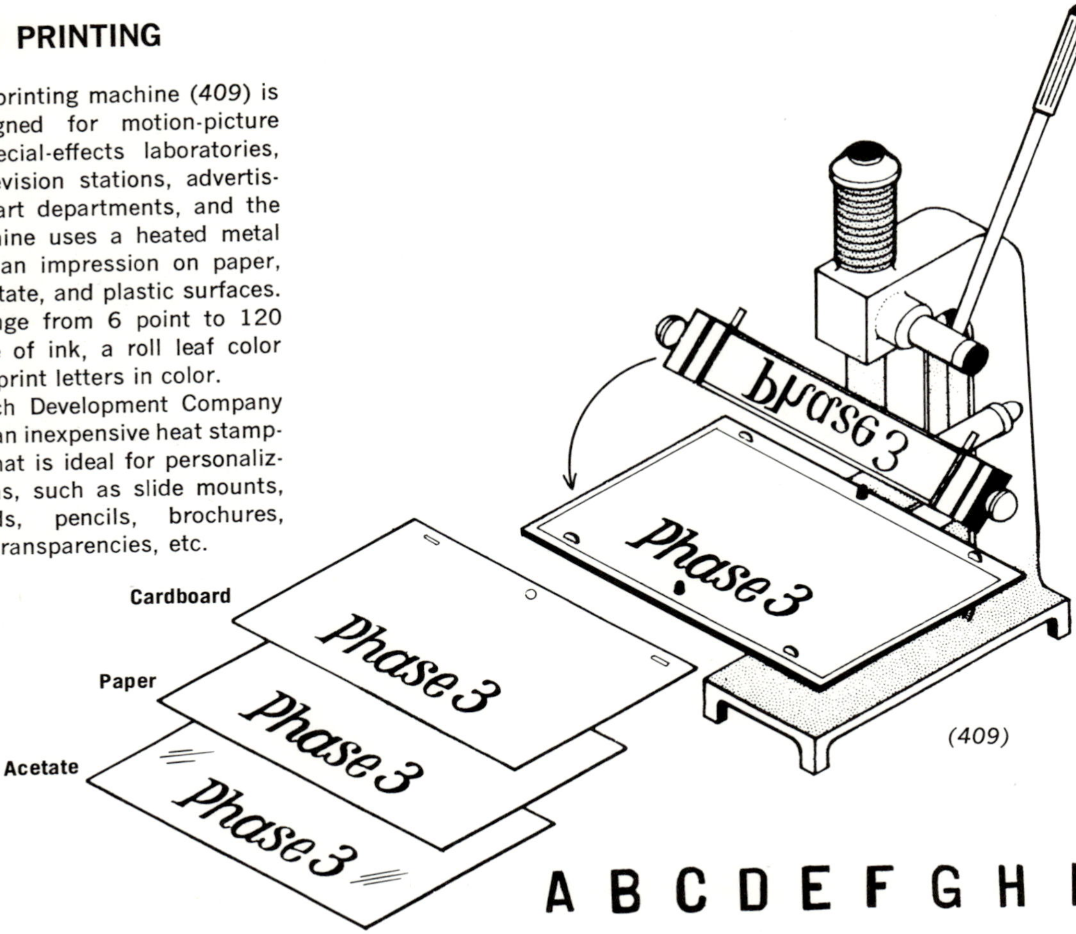

Cardboard

Paper

Acetate

Phase 3

Phase 3

Phase 3

Phase 3

(409)

BULLETIN (Primary) TYPEWRITER

The bulletin typewriter (410) produces letters up to ¼ inch high and is ideal for the preparation of overhead projection transparencies. It is also very well suited for teacher use in preparing classroom worksheets and homework assignments. Manual and electric models are available. The Royal Typewriter Company has developed an Elementary Primer typewriter specifically for use in the primary grades. The type style corresponds exactly to the approved style of lettering and numerals taught to children in the first, second, and third school years.

A B C D E F G H I J
1 2 3 4 5 6 7 8 9 0

SCM TYPE STYLE

Sample letter styles
(actual size)

(410)

Applications

Thermocopy originals

Typing can be done directly on white paper for copying on thermocopy film for projection (411).

Diazo masters

Place a black carbon sheet with the carbon side next to the back of a sheet of good-quality tracing paper and roll into the typewriter and type (412).

Carbon-coated projection acetate

A lightweight acetate film coated with a black opaque carbon material (413). It can be used to produce white letters (or color letters when a color acetate is used behind the transparency) on a black screen when projected. Place a paper backup sheet behind the sheet and type on the shiny side of the acetate. (Set typewriter on "stencil" position for sharpest image.) The carbon coating will transfer to the backup paper, leaving clear letters on the carbon side of the acetate. A sheet of clear acetate can be attached to the carbon side to protect the surface for reuse.

Transmate film

A thermocopy film which can be typed on directly. Roll a sheet of Transmate (414), with a white backing sheet, into the typewriter and type. The purpose of the white sheet is to allow the typist to see what is being typed.

Overhead transparency carbon sheet

A special carbon sheet, usually orange, for typing or drawing directly on clear acetate or plastic sheets (415). When projected, the typed image appears black on the screen. Place the carbon sheet face down on the acetate and type on the back of the carbon sheet. (Set

typewriter on "stencil" position for sharpest image.) Carbon will transfer to the acetate. For permanence, the transferred typing should be sprayed with plastic spray or covered with a clear acetate sheet.

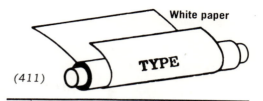

(411) White paper

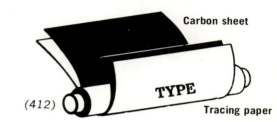

(412) Carbon sheet / Tracing paper

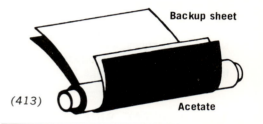

(413) Backup sheet / Acetate

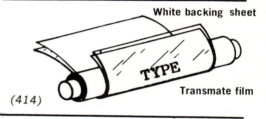

(414) White backing sheet / Transmate film

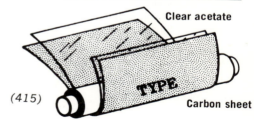

(415) Clear acetate / Carbon sheet

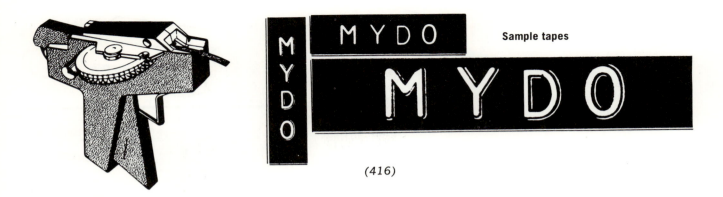

Sample tapes

(416)

TAPE EMBOSSING MACHINE

A hand-operated machine for producing embossed lettered labels on pressure-sensitive plastic or metal tape (416). Assorted letter styles, sizes, and colors are available. Tape widths range from ¼ to ¾ inch. Letter heights range from ⅛ to ½ inch. Standard spacing, optimum spacing, vertical reverse image, and special character embossing wheels are available for some makes and models of embossing machines.

EMBOSOGRAF SIGN-MAKING SYSTEM

The Embosograf sign-making machine (417) embosses letters, numerals, and special characters on cardboard, plastic, aluminum, and plastic-coated stock. No special skill is required for operating this machine. The Embosograf machine will produce, without ink, permanent interior/exterior plastic and aluminum signs, as well as multicolor cardboard signs up to a size as large as 8 by 22 inches.

Instructions

1. Select and set metal type on setup plate of machine.
2. Place color "top paper" over the type with the color side down. This is a special paper for producing letters in color.
3. Lay the sign cardboard face down over the type and top paper, and push the setup plate under the pressure area. Pull down the side lever causing the type to emboss the top paper into the cardboard.

(417)

Embosograf machine

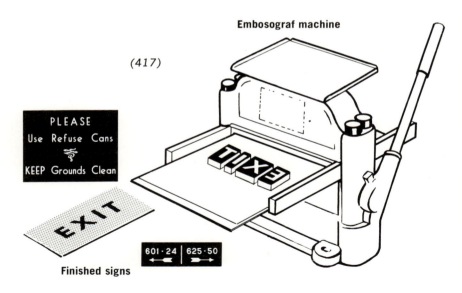

Finished signs

4. Pull the setup plate out and pick up the cardboard. Remove any excess top paper. Repeat steps 2, 3, and 4 for duplicate signs.

DYMO-FORM PLASTIC-FORMING SYSTEM

Here is a heat-forming system that produces three-dimensional letters, signs, displays, craft molds, prototype products, shipping inserts in sturdy 20-mil plastic. No special skill is required for its operation. The unit uses standard 110-volt electric current. A plastic sheet up to 14 by 20 inches can be molded in the Dymo-Form (418, 419).

INSTRUCTIONS

1. Place letters, numerals, or objects to be formed on the forming platen as desired (418).
2. Insert selected plastic sheet in the loading frame. Close frame and latch.
3. Move the frame back over heater. The heating cycle is ready to begin. Adjust controls as instructed. A timer bell will indicate when the plastic is ready for forming.
4. Move the frame, containing the heated plastic, swiftly and firmly down onto the forming platen, while at the same time turning the control lever down to the vacuum position to start the pump. Hold the switch down for five seconds so that the plastic can cool into its new shape. Open the frame and remove molded plastic sign. The finished product is now ready to be painted, mounted, or framed as desired. The instruction booklet that is included with the Dymo-Form should be carefully read before using the unit.

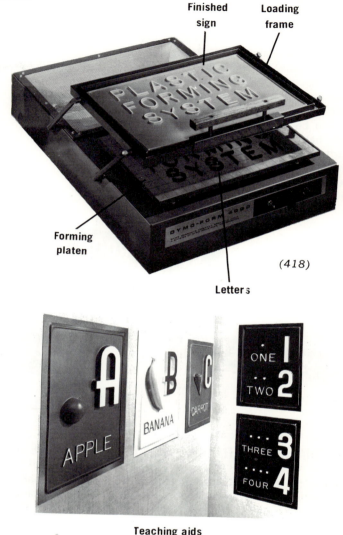

Finished sign

Loading frame

Forming platen

Letters

(418)

Teaching aids

(419)

Art piece

Plastic molded copy of art piece

SCOTT LETTER-ENGRAVING MACHINE

The Scott pantograph engraving machine (420) is designed for letter-engraving plastic, wood, aluminum, brass, and steel materials. The model illustrated engraves flat plates up to 2 inches wide. Master letters are locked in place on the lower portion of the machine, and the plate to be engraved is inserted in the upper half as illustrated. Badges, signs, award plaques, nameplates, identification, outdoor signs, and jewelry are just a few of the many items that can be engraved with the Scott machines.

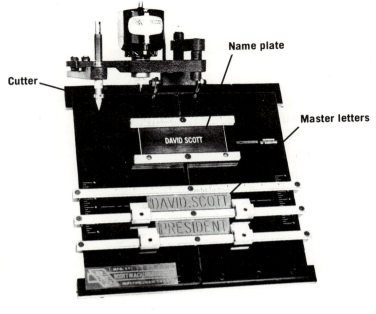

(420)

MECHANICAL TRACING LETTERING SYSTEMS

Mechanical tracing lettering systems are among the most versatile lettering techniques. They consist of a template made up of engraved letters and a mechanical scriber which can be equipped with a pen, pencil attachment, stylus, or special cutting knife. The built-in stylus of the scriber traces around the engraved letter on the template and reproduces a letter on the desired surface. Some of the more complex systems have adjustable settings or controls to make enlargements, reductions, italics, and various special effects from a single template. A variety of type faces and sizes is available, each equally versatile.

Mechanical tracing lettering systems can be used to produce letters on almost any flat surface that will accept ink, pencil, or a cutting knife. Four lettering systems, LeRoy, Letterguide, Varigraph, and Panto-Varigraph, have been chosen for inclusion in this section; each having features distinctive enough to receive special attention.

LEROY LETTERING SYSTEM

The LeRoy lettering system is one of several similar mechanical tracing lettering systems. The basic equipment includes a template (made up of three layers of special plastic material), scriber (421) (lettering instrument), and pen. Complete sets are available with standard templates in many sizes of graphic symbols and alphabets.

No special skill or technique is required to produce professional-looking work. Lettering can be done directly on paper, cardboard, prepared acetate, spirit and stencil duplicating masters (with a ball-point pen-stylus), and many other surfaces. Special templates can be custom-made upon request.

LeRoy Lettering Chart
(Actual Size) (422)

This chart shows the wide range of LeRoy lettering effects that can be produced by combining various LeRoy templates and pens. The asterisks indicate the combination of template and pen recommended for a good proportion between the thickness of stroke and the size of letter.

(421)

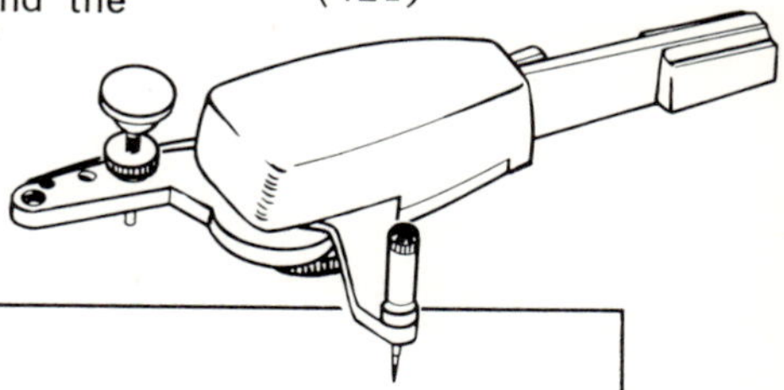

TEMPLATE SIZE	PEN SIZE												
	0000	000	00	0	1	2	3	4	5	6	7	8
50	A*											
60	A*	A	B	C								
80	A	A*	B	C								
100		A	A*	B	C	D						
120		A	B	C*	D	E						
140		A	B	C	D*	E	F					
175		A	B	C	D	E*	F	G				
200		A	B	C	D	E	F*	G	H			
240		A	B	C	D	E	F*	G	H			
290			B	C	D	E	F	G*	H	K		
350			B	C	D	E	F	G*	H	K		
425			B	C	D	E	F	G	H*	K	L	
500			B	C	D	E	F	G	H	K*	L	M

(422)

Accessories

Fixed scriber (423)

For use with all LeRoy pens up to size 8 and pencils and with all LeRoy templates up to size 650 and 60 point. Vertical lettering only. Furnished with double-ended tracer pin.

Adjustable scriber (424)

For use with all LeRoy pens up to size 8 and pencils and with all LeRoy templates up to size 650 and 60 point (vertical or slanting letter). Furnished with double-ended tracer pin. Example letter variations are shown.

Height and slant control scriber (425)

An adjustable scriber to form characters either vertical or slanting at any angle up to 45° forward, and any height from 60 to 150 percent of the size of characters on the template used. The width of the characters is not changed. Adjustment is simple: By loosening the knob, move the arm so that the small red circle of the arm lies directly under the intersection of the "degree slope" and "% height" lines desired. Knob is then retightened. Example letter variations are shown.

Adjustable scriber (426)

For use with LeRoy templates size 700 and larger, and templates 72 point and larger, for vertical or slanting lettering. Adapters furnished for use with pens 0000 to 8, and 9 to 14.

Letter size adapter (427)

For extending or condensing LeRoy lettering. With the adapter, used with first two scribers described, the height of letters or numerals drawn with any LeRoy template can be increased or decreased by amounts up to one-third of their normal height. The width of letters and numerals is not changed.

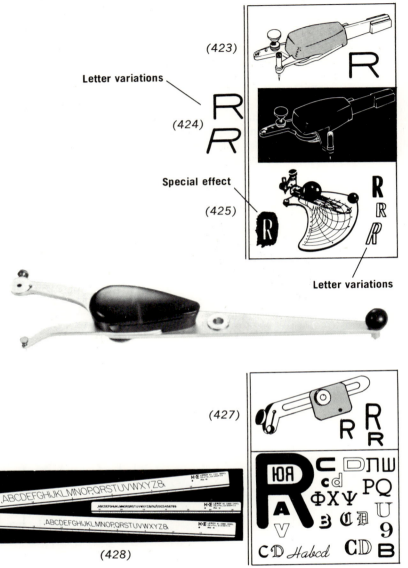

(423)

Letter variations

(424)

Special effect

(425)

Letter variations

(427)

Sample letter styles

(428)

Lettering templates (428)

Templates range in letter size from ⅟₁₆ to 2 inches and are available in many foreign languages such as Russian and Greek. Many letter styles are available. A few letter styles are shown at the bottom of (427).

LeRoy pencil (429)

A precise mechanical pencil with a .020-inch lead. Ideal for pencil lettering work. Insert in any of the LeRoy scribers.

Reservoir pen (430)

A fountain-type pen holding a large supply of ink which will last for several weeks. Pens 000 to 5 are designed to be used in the small fixed and adjustable scribers, and in the large adjustable scriber with a pen adapter. Pens 6, 8, 10, 12, and 14 are designed for use in the large adjustable scriber.

Standard pen (431)

Sizes 0000 to 8 are for use in small fixed and adjustable scribers, and in large adjustable scriber with a pen adapter. Sizes 9 to 14 are for use in large adjustable scriber.

Instructions

See Preparation of Working Surface for instructions on how to prepare the lettering surface.

1. Select the template with the size and style of letter desired. Position it next to the T square or straightedge.
2. Insert and tighten a standard pen in the scriber, or any one of the LeRoy accessories may be inserted (432). Fill standard pen as illustrated (433). To start ink flowing, gently work cleaning pin up and down.
3. Insert the tail pin of the scriber in the straight guideline of the template, and the tracing pin in the left side of the first letter (434). Tilt the scriber away from the lettering surface and move scriber and template so as to position the first letter on the surface.
4. While holding the template in place with the left hand, gently lower the standard pen on the lettering sur-

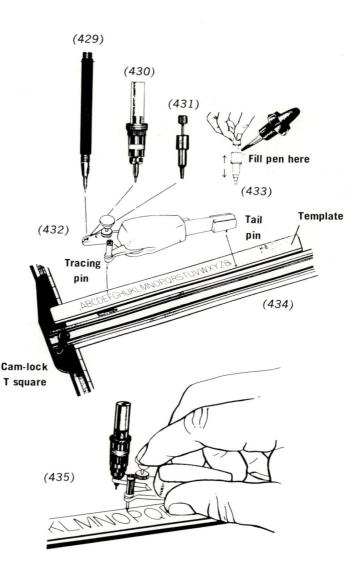

(429)

(430)

(431)

Fill pen here

(433)

(432)

Tracing pin

Tail pin

Template

Cam-lock T square

(434)

(435)

face and trace the first letter (435). One operation forms each letter completely, no combinations are needed. Capitals, lower case, and numbers may be lettered from most templates.

5. Repeat steps 3 and 4 for the remaining letters. See pages 101 to 102 for tips on letter layout, spacing, and sample designs.

127

Sample letter styles

A

Letter variations from adjustments made on scriber

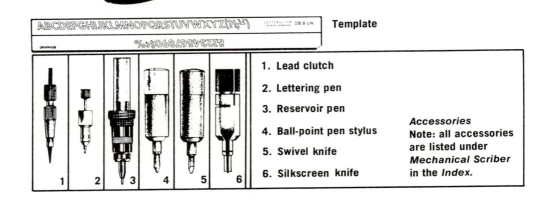

(436)

Mechanical scriber

LETTERGUIDE LETTERING SYSTEM

The Letterguide system (436) consists of a precision engineered mechanical lettering scriber, lettering templates with typographical faces and alphabets engraved in plastic and a variety of lettering accessories. Over 400 different templates are available in a variety of type faces. Sizes range from ³⁄₁₆ up to ¾ inch in most styles, and up to 2 full inches in several styles. Accessories such as ball-point pen-stylus and silk-screen knife add to the versatility of this system. The scriber is calibrated so that with a single adjustment letters can be enlarged (height), reduced, and slanted from just one template. The templates are designed to align horizontally with a T square or straightedge.

ABCDEFGHIJKLMNOPQRSTUVWXYZ[+!¿]
8I234567890$¢%

Template

1. Lead clutch

2. Lettering pen

3. Reservoir pen

4. Ball-point pen stylus

5. Swivel knife

6. Silkscreen knife

Accessories
Note: all accessories are listed under *Mechanical Scriber* in the *Index.*

(437)

Instructions

See Preparation of Working Surface for instructions on how to prepare lettering surface for use (page 23).

1. Position template on artwork and next to straightedge or T square. A Cam-lock T square is illustrated (437).
2. Insert desired point in scriber and adjust scriber for letter size and slant (438). If a pen is used, fill with ink as illustrated. Position scriber on template by placing the tail pin in the center slot of template. Place tracing pin in the first letter to be traced and move both template and scriber along the T square to position the letter on artwork.
3. To letter, hold template in place with left hand and trace letter with right hand (439). For next and remaining letters, slightly raise the scriber (leaving the tail pin in the center slot), slide template to position the next letter, and repeat instructions for first letter.

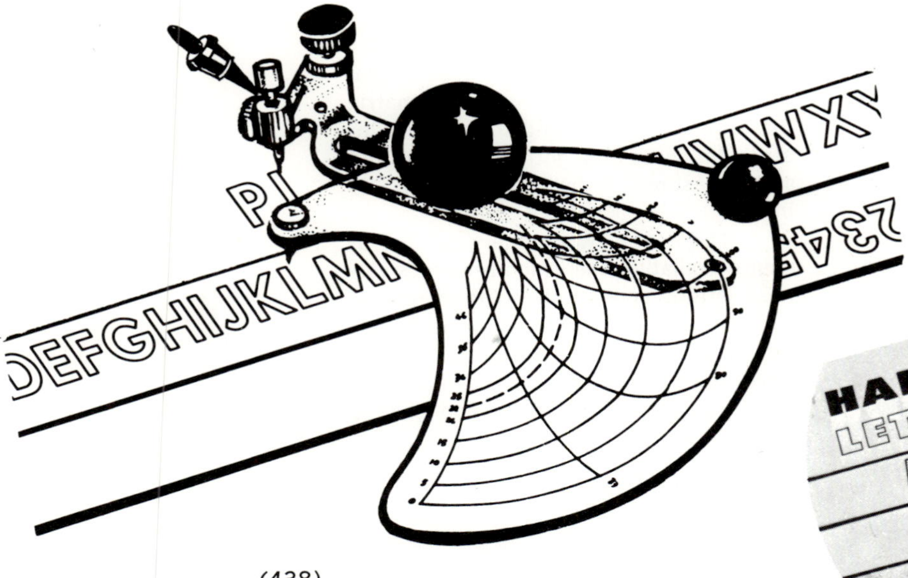

(438)

(439)

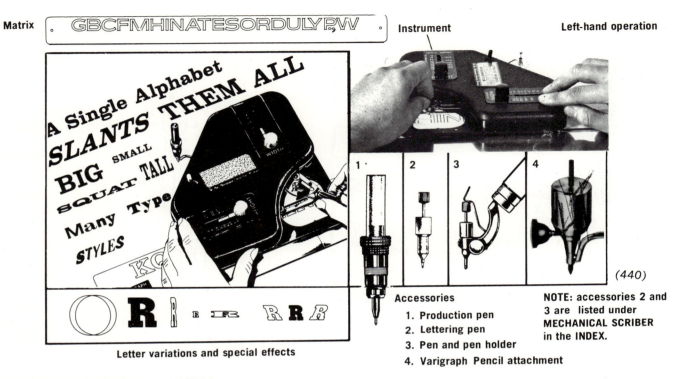

Letter variations and special effects

Accessories

1. Production pen
2. Lettering pen
3. Pen and pen holder
4. Varigraph Pencil attachment

(440)

NOTE: accessories 2 and 3 are listed under **MECHANICAL SCRIBER** in the **INDEX**.

VARIGRAPH LETTERING SYSTEM

The Varigraph lettering system (440) was developed primarily for the production of display typography for photographic reproduction processes such as offset printing and letterpress. However, because of its versatility and increased popularity, it is now used for many additional applications such as silk-screen printing; chart, graph, map and diagram work; posters; overhead projection transparencies; television, motion-picture, filmstrip, and slide titles; certificates; diploma and related engrossing work; displays; and exhibits.

The Varigraph system is made up of a compact precision-built mechanical type-setting instrument, a metal matrix (lettering template), and a pen. The instrument weighs slightly over 1 pound and measures 7 by 7 inches by 1½ inch.

There are two models of instruments available, one which produces vertical letters and another (italic model) which produces back-slant or italic letters from a standard Varigraph matrix. There are over 200 matrices which make possible hundreds of sizes and shapes of type from 14 to 72 points.

CBADCBAEFBC

Sample letter styles

Instructions

Refer to Preparation of Working Surface for instructions on how to prepare the lettering surface for use. A good T square or straightedge is most essential in that the Varigraph instrument has to move from letter to letter; it is also used for achieving parallel lines of lettering. The Boardlock T square has been designed especially for the Varigraph instrument and similar lettering systems.

1. For right-hand operation (tracing stylus in lower right corner), slide the matrix under the instrument from the left side, being certain that it goes between the supporting feet which receive the matrix, and retain it with the instrument. For left-hand operation (tracing stylus in lower left corner) slide the matrix in the instrument the same as for right-hand operation (440).

    While holding the instrument stationary with the left hand, slide the matrix with the right hand to position the desired letter in front of the pointer on the base of the instrument. With the right hand, position the tracing stylus in the groove at a point in the extreme left side of the letter. Apply only a very slight pressure on the tracing stylus, but do not allow it to come out of the letter groove before completing all the remaining instructions.

2. Observe position of the pen and slide the instrument with the left hand until the pen hovers over the point at which the left side of the letter is to begin. The tracing stylus must be held lightly in the groove so that the matrix will move along with the instrument and the desired letter will remain in the proper tracing position.

3. With the index finger of the left hand, push the pen lift fully forward to lower the pen. Begin tracing immediately after the pen touches the paper. Trace around the letter just

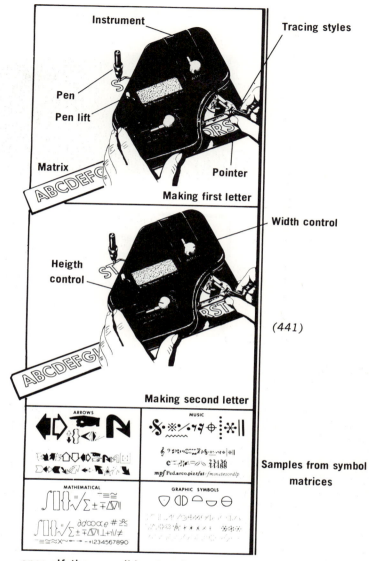

once. If the pen did not write, retract the pen and raise the cleaning pin slightly up and down once or twice to start the ink flowing. Retrace the letter according to the foregoing instructions. Repeat these steps for each of the remaining letters (441).

The best printed instructions for using the Varigraph system are found in the *Instruction Manual for the Varigraph.*

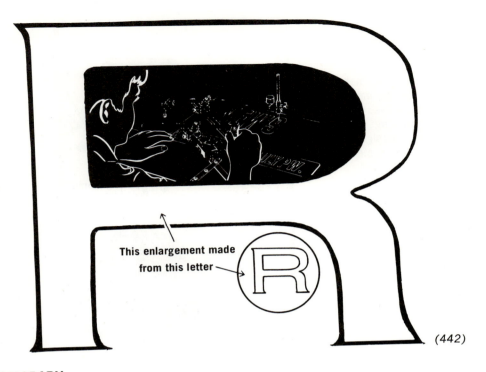

This enlargement made from this letter

(442)

PANTO-VARIGRAPH LETTERING SYSTEM

The Panto-Varigraph is a compact, precision lettering instrument which accurately renders letters up to 8 inches high in any of 100 type faces (442). In addition to the Panto-Varigraph, a Varigraph matrix, a large drawing board (not smaller than 30 by 42 inches) with a T square or straightedge, and means to secure the straightedge or T square firmly to the drawing board complete the system. Where extra-large precision lettering is required, the Panto-Varigraph will provide an answer. The instrument can also reproduce a letter smaller than the size of the letter on the matrix used.

Instructions (443)

1. Refer to Preparation of Working Surface for instructions on how to prepare letter surface for the Panto-Varigraph. Set up the instrument as illustrated.

2. Slip the desired Varigraph matrix (lettering guide) under the Panto-Varigraph linkage, resting it against top edge of the large aluminum base. For positioning of matrix when tracing, consult the instructions on adjacent decal.

3. Set the graduated bars after referring to the numerals on each bar. These numerals refer to reproduced letter height when enlarging from matrix letters approximately 2 inches in height. When using any one of the other three size matrices available, namely 1½ inch, 1 inch, and ¾ inch, a conversion chart for enlarging and reducing will indicate what numerals to set the graduate bars on to get the size letter desired.

4. Select and insert the desired writing or cutting accessory.

5. Position drawing surface.

6. Position letter for scribing.

In that instructions for properly using the Panto-Varigraph are much more detailed than those we have outlined, it is suggested that the *Panto-Varigraph Manual* be obtained and read before attempting to use the instrument.

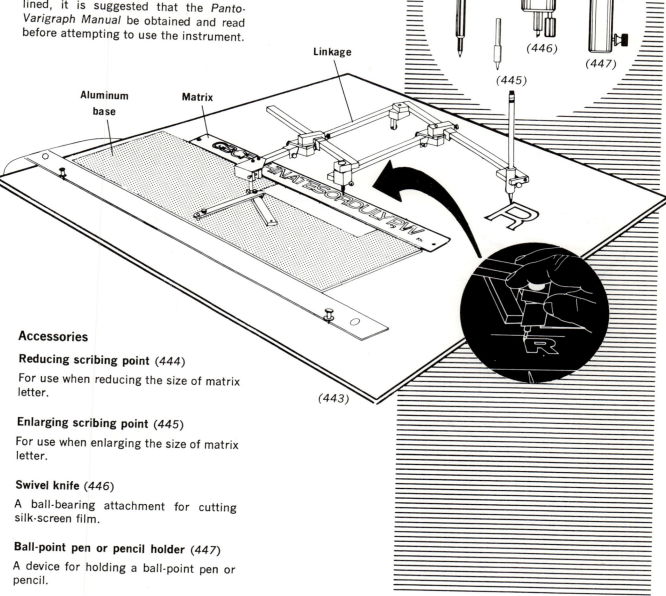

(444)

(445)

(446)

(447)

Linkage

Aluminum base

Matrix

(443)

Accessories

Reducing scribing point (444)

For use when reducing the size of matrix letter.

Enlarging scribing point (445)

For use when enlarging the size of matrix letter.

Swivel knife (446)

A ball-bearing attachment for cutting silk-screen film.

Ball-point pen or pencil holder (447)

A device for holding a ball-point pen or pencil.

133

LETTERS BY PROJECTION

Where large display-type letters are desired, one of a variety of projection devices can be used very effectively. With any one of these devices, it is possible to produce large letters of any size on a variety of materials such as paper, cardboard, wood, cloth, and metal. The letter to be reproduced is inserted in the device used and projected onto the drawing surface. Precut letters are ideal for this technique. However, any printed letter that can be inserted in the projection device can be used.

Instructions

1. Insert letter in projection device. It may be necessary to anchor the letter to a sheet of paper or clear acetate to prevent movement while reproducing larger letters.

2. Fasten surface on which letter is to be reproduced to the wall, floor, or wherever a projected image would normally appear.

3. Position or adjust projection device to give the letter size desired.

4. Trace the outline of the projected letter with a pencil. For straight lines of the letters, use a ruler or yardstick as a tracing guide. Remove finished work and ink or complete as desired.

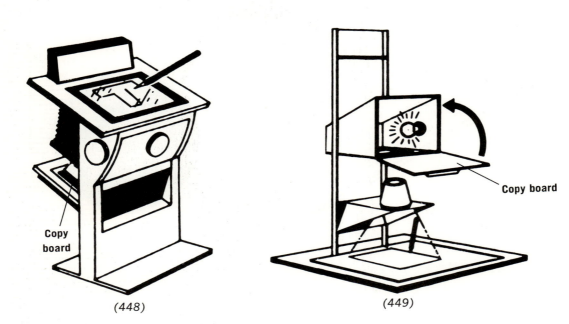

(448)

(449)

Art Aid Camera (448)

Attach letter to be reproduced to copy board of camera, and a sheet of tracing paper to top of camera as illustrated. Follow steps 3 and 4.

Art Aid Projector (449)

Attach letter to be reproduced to the copy board located at the top of the projector. Follow steps 2, 3, and 4.

Photographic Enlarger (450)

Only a precut paper or thin cardboard letter can be used, and it must be a size that can fit into the negative carrier. If the carrier is glass, simply sandwich the letter between the two pieces of glass and insert in the enlarger. If the carrier is glassless, cut two pieces of clear acetate to fit the carrier and sandwich the letter between them and fit into carrier. Insert in enlarger. Follow steps 2, 3, and 4.

Overhead Projector (451)

Place a precut letter on the stage of projector. It may be necessary to place a sheet of glass or clear acetate on top of the letter to hold it in place. Follow steps 2, 3, and 4.

Opaque Projector (452)

Insert precut or printed letter in projector as illustrated. It may be necessary to attach the letter to a sheet of contrasting paper or cardboard to hold the letter in place and to increase the visibility of the letter for tracing. It may be necessary to turn off the room lights while tracing the enlarged letters. Follow steps 2, 3, and 4.

Lantern Slide Projector (453)

Insert precut letter between two pieces of lantern slide glass (3¼ by 4 inches) and insert in projector. Follow steps 2, 3, and 4.

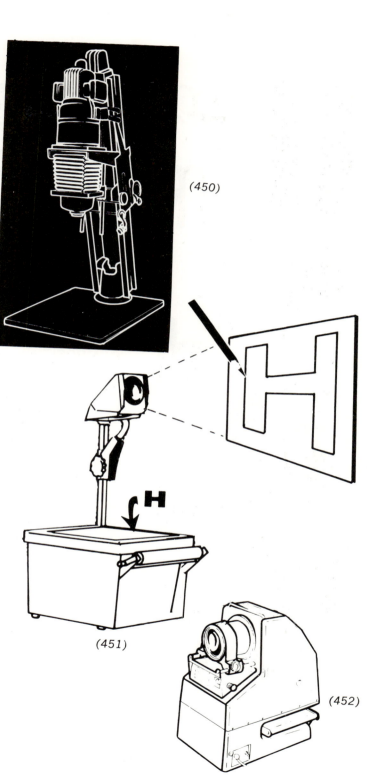

(450)

(451)

(452)

(453)

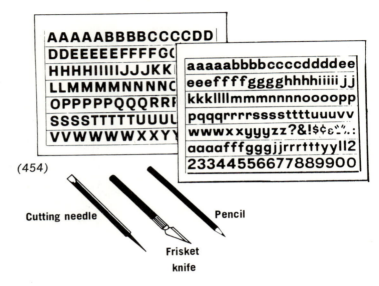

(454)

Cutting needle

Frisket knife

Pencil

COMPOSITION ADHESIVE TYPE

Composition adhesive type (454) is another form of paste-up letter consisting of multiple alphabets printed on a thin acetate sheet with a pressure-sensitive adhesive or wax backing. The printing is usually on the adhesive side. Each letter is carefully cut with a razor blade or similar cutting tool, aligned on the artwork, and then burnished down to form the word desired. The printed lines between and underneath individual letters provide for ease of alignment and standard letter spacing of copy. Guidelines are removed when word composition is completed. For diazo or other heat-generating copying systems, the adhesive-backed rather than the wax-backed type should be used in that the wax-backed type will melt at high temperatures. A "heat-resistant" type is available from a number of manufacturers.

In addition to alphabets in a wide variety of sizes and styles, common phrases, borders, symbols, etc., are also available.

Instructions

1. Lay lettering sheet face down and carefully draw backing sheet away from lettering sheet, then loosely replace and turn sheet over (455).

2. Draw a light pencil guideline on the artwork just below where the word is to appear. This distance should be the same as the distance between the bottom of the letters and the printed guideline below the letters on the lettering sheet. If lettering is to be done on an acetate surface, draw guideline with a marking pencil (456).

3. With a cutting knife, cut lightly around the desired letter. Include printed guideline or lines, being careful not to cut through backing sheet. Lift the letter from the sheet with the point of a knife (457).

4. Position letter with printed guideline in register with guideline on artwork and press into place. Burnish lightly with a burnisher so that changes can be made before final burnishing. Repeat this step for each letter until the assembly is complete. Letters or words can be carefully lifted and repositioned as desired (458).

5. When assembly is complete and corrections have been made, burnish firmly upper portion of letters. Cut away guidelines and complete burnishing. Erase pencil guideline. Finished assembly is now ready for sharp, clear reproduction (459).

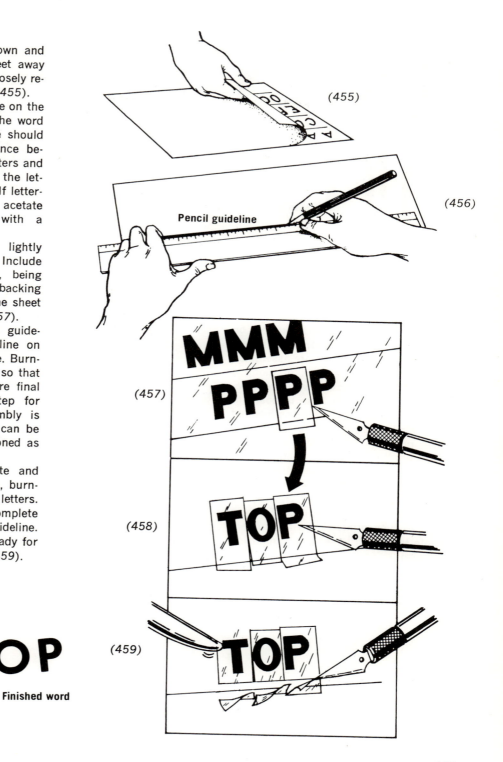

(455)

(456)

Pencil guideline

(457)

(458)

(459)

TOP

Finished word

137

DC N ER GOTHIC SM ER LeTR A R

COMPOSITION PAPER TYPE

Composition paper type (460) is a form of paste-up lettering consisting of individual, self-aligning letters printed on card-weight paper strips or tabs and assembled in a pad. Letters are assembled in a type composing stick or along a straightedge and backed with pressure-sensitive tape to keep them in position. Composition paper type is recommended where reproduction copy is needed for offset printing, zinc engravings, silkscreen printing, gravure, ozalid, verifax, diazo, blueprint, posters, television titles, visual aids and presentations.

Some manufacturers produce reverse-color fonts. In addition, Fototype produces type printed on a transparent acetate tab which is set in a composing stick also.

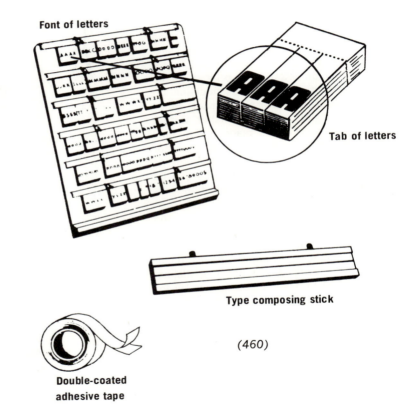

Font of letters

Tab of letters

Type composing stick

(460)

Double-coated adhesive tape

138

(461)

Instructions

1. Assemble letters and blank spaces in left hand as the right hand detaches characters from the pad (461).

2. Snap each letter in place if a composing stick is used. This device aligns and spaces letters automatically. Blue side of letter should be facing up (462).

3. Apply tape to the assembled line of type. Use double-coated adhesive tape if the use of rubber cement is not desired. Lift assembled line of type from composing stick (463).

4. If composing stick is not available, a straightedge can be used. Place a strip of tape on the back of the straightedge. Use double-coated adhesive tape if the use of rubber cement is not desired in the paste-up. Anchor each letter against the straightedge and next to the adhesive side of the tape. Lift assembled line of type off the straightedge (464). See pages 32 to 34 for paste-up instructions.)

5. Position the assembled line of type on artwork. If Fototype is used, position the line of type with the black type facing up. When using double-coated adhesive tape, simply press the type into place on the artwork. Rubber cement is recommended when double-coated tape is not used (465).

Copy is now ready for photographic reproduction. Instructions that come with the composition paper type used are more comprehensive and should be consulted before the extensive use of this technique.

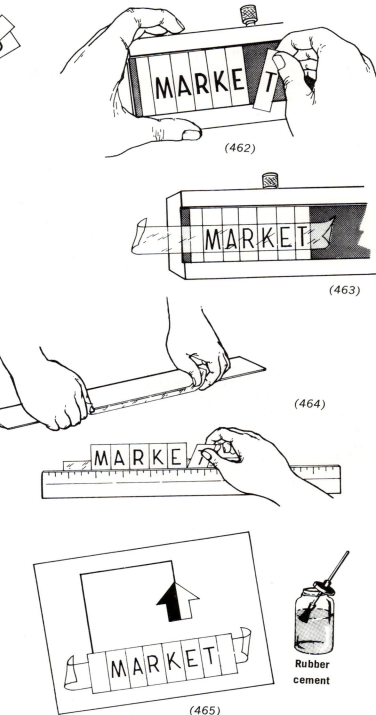

(462)

(463)

(464)

Rubber cement

(465)

KINDER COMPOSITION PLASTIC TYPE

Kinder composition plastic type (466) is a low-cost photocomposition method. No expensive machines are required with this method of setting type for photo-copy. Only one step is required from setting the type to producing a photographic paper or film positive.

Instructions

1. Kameratype is easily set by placing each character in the channel guide. A wire stop is used at either end to hold the line in position. Words and letters may be visually separated, or Kameratype spacers may be used. Since letters are laterally reversed like lead type, they are set from right to left. Proofreading is made easier when a mirror is used to read the type. Channels for each line are placed in position on the copy board or on the floor, using a black background.

2. Composed type is photographed with a camera loaded with photographic film or paper.

3. Normal processing, following procedures recommended by film or paper manufacturer, results in positive typography ready for use. Photo-stabilization machines add even greater efficiency to Kameratype use.

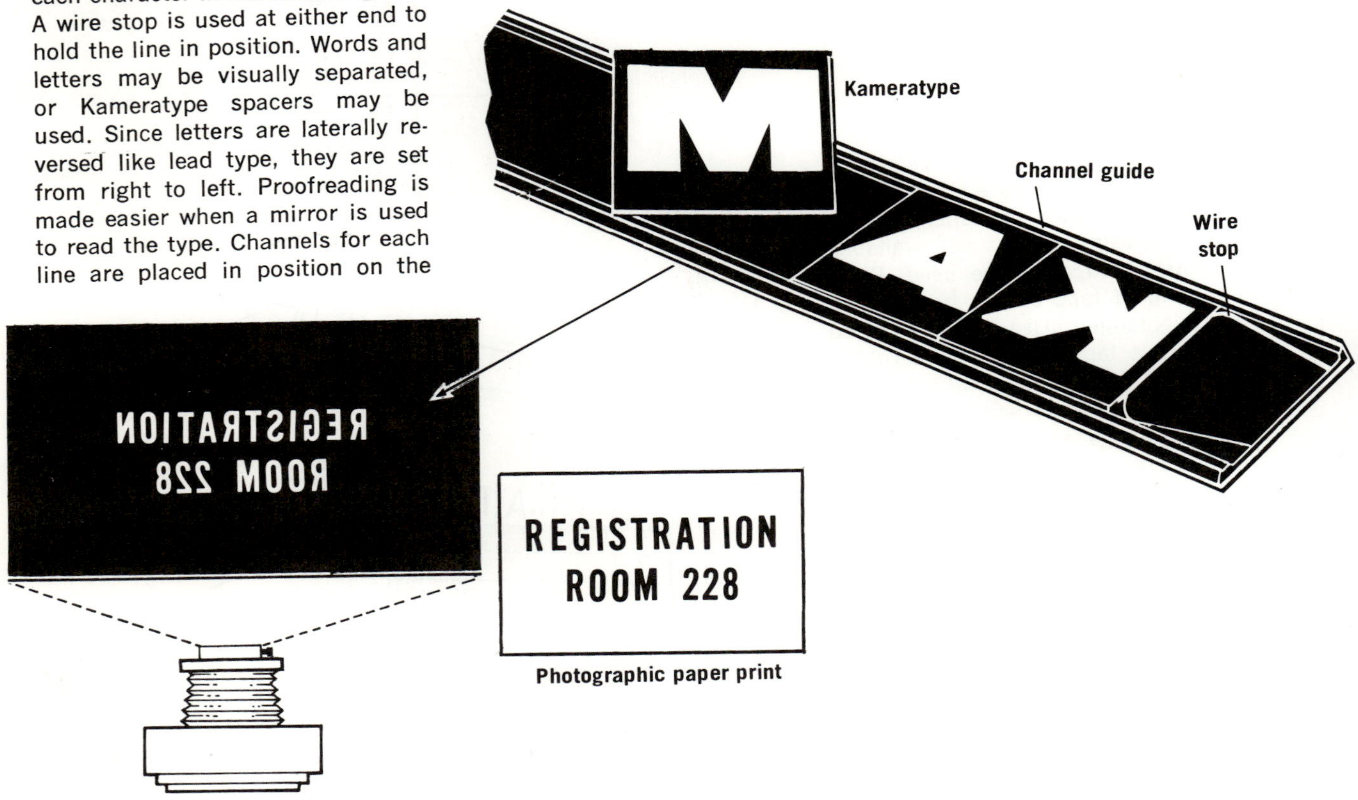

Kameratype

Channel guide

Wire stop

REGISTRATION
ROOM 228

REGISTRATION ROOM 228

Photographic paper print

(466)

PHOTOTYPE COMPOSING MACHINE

There are a number of machines (467) available which use the photographic process to produce display type and type matter for mechanicals, that is, paste-ups which are subsequently copied with a process or copy camera to produce negatives for offset printing and visual media. Some units produce letters up to 3¾ inches high.

Phototype composing is considered to be one of the most sophisticated of the "cold type" techniques. The phototype composing machine makes use of letter fonts, some of which are laminated in plastic or glass for greater life. These fonts are used to compose type, photographically, on sensitized paper or film. The sensitized paper or film is either processed in the machine, in photo-

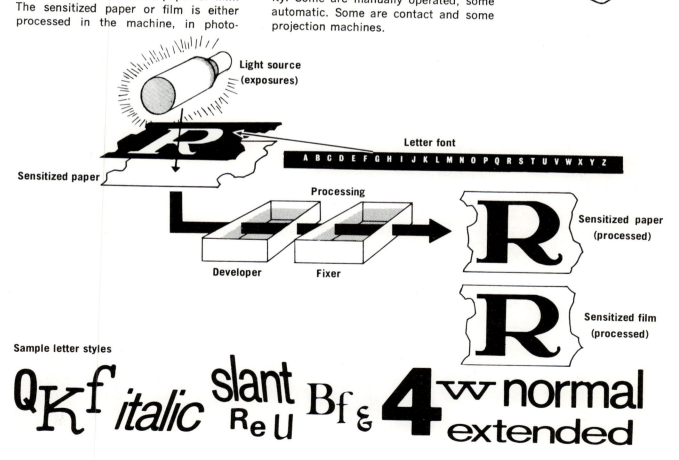

Letter font

(467)

graphic trays, or in a special processing unit. Many of the machines produce phototype on strips of 35mm film or paper which can be pasted up on artwork for copying.

Phototype composing machines vary in price depending on their flexibility. Some are manually operated, some automatic. Some are contact and some projection machines.

Light source (exposures)

Letter font

A B C D E F G H I J K L M N O P Q R S T U V W X Y Z

Sensitized paper

Processing

Developer   Fixer

Sensitized paper (processed)

Sensitized film (processed)

Sample letter styles

DRY TRANSFER LETTERING

Dry transfer lettering (468), known also as *press-on*, *rub-on* and *transfer type* is considered to be one of the most modern lettering techniques available today. The letters, made up of carbon and wax, are printed on a plastic, acetate, or polyethelene carrier sheet. Letters transfer to virtually any dry surface such as paper, wood, metal, or glass by rubbing over the letter with a dull-point pencil or ball-point pen. Dry transfer letters are available in black, white, and a variety of colors. They are also available in transparent colors.

Dry transfer letters, while similar to composition adhesive type, are somewhat more exacting to apply in that once the letters have been burnished into position, they cannot be relocated. They can be removed with pressure-sensitive adhesive tape, razor blade, dry transfer letter eraser, or a rubber cement eraser.

Since only the letter comes off the carrier sheet, there are no edges to

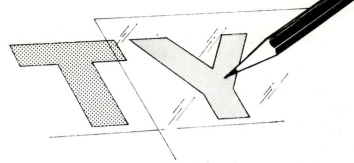

create unwanted lines on the surface to which the letter is applied.

Dry transfer letters are ideal for charts; graphs; maps; diagrams; posters; exhibits; displays; signs; bulletin boards; captions for photographs; television title cards; filmstrips; slide and motion-picture titles; overhead projection transparencies; diazo masters; logos; silk-screen artwork; publications.

For artwork intended to be used in heat-producing reproduction equipment, heat-resistant dry transfer letters are recommended.

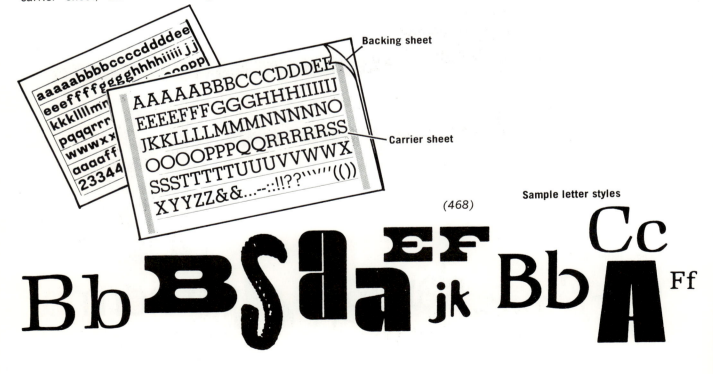

Backing sheet

Carrier sheet

(468)

Sample letter styles

Instructions

1. Draw a light pencil line on the surface to which lettering is to be transferred. *If lettering is to be done on clear or matte acetate, draw the line on a sheet of white paper and place under acetate as a guide (469).*

2. Line up the guideline on the transfer sheet and move letter to desired position. Rub a finger over the letter to form contact between the carrier sheet and the surface *(470)*.

3. Rub the first letter to be transferred with a dull-point pencil, ball-point pen, or similar blunt instrument until the burnished letter changes color. Do not "scrub" or grind the point of the burnishing instrument into the carrier sheet. Burnish all thin lines and edges, if any *(471)*.

4. Carefully peel or lift the carrier sheet away from the artwork *(472)*. Transfer occurs because the adherence of the letter to the artwork is stronger than the adherence to the carrier sheet. Repeat process for remaining letters. To ensure permanence and secure placement, place the backing sheet over transferred letters and burnish the entire area with the burnishing instrument. To remove guideline, place the edge of a sheet of paper over the letters and erase the guideline with a soft pencil eraser.

Making Corrections

Pressure-sensitive tape (such as masking or drafting tape) can be used to remove unwanted letters by lightly pressing adhesive side of tape to letter and carefully peeling it off the artwork. Corrections can also be made with a dry transfer letter or rubber cement eraser, pressure sensitive adhesive tape, or a razor blade *(473)*.

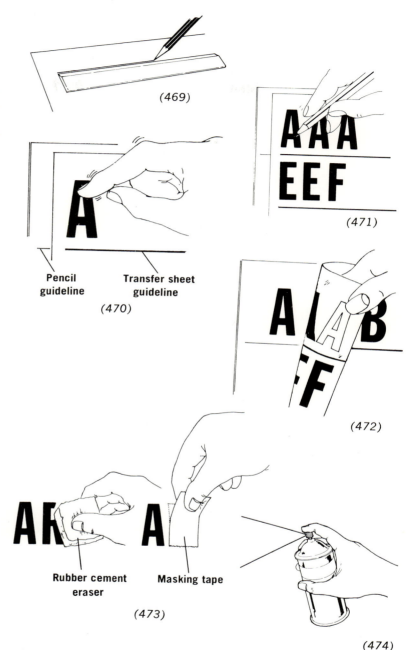

(469)

Pencil guideline   Transfer sheet guideline

(470)

(471)

(472)

Rubber cement eraser   Masking tape

(473)

(474)

Added Protection

When additional protection is desired, spray letters with several light coats of any clear polyester-base plastic spray *(474)*.

COLORING TECHNIQUES

Transparent Liquid Colors
Watercolors
Aerosol-can Colors
Airbrush Techniques

Transparent Color Adhesive-backed Sheets and Tapes

Gold Image Transfer Technique

COLORING TECHNIQUES

The application of coloring or shading, in one form or another, adds an exciting dimension to visual instructional media. Although no attempt will be made in this chapter to relate the psychological effect of certain colors upon the learning process, the tested coloring and shading techniques which make possible the application of coloring or shading to practically all types of instructional media will be discussed and illustrated. Visual instructional media which may require color or shading, or whose visual effectiveness may be enhanced by these techniques include charts; graphs; maps; diagrams; posters; illustrations; photographs; television, motion-picture, filmstrip, and slide titles; overhead projection transparencies; duplication materials.

Each of the coloring and shading techniques included in this chapter has certain characteristics which may limit its application to specific types of instructional media. These characteristics will be brought out in the treatment of each technique. It cannot be overemphasized that color or shading should not be used mainly for the sake of adding color or shading to an instructional material. Moreover, color or shading can be overused and, therefore, can lower the quality of the instructional material.

For the novice lacking the know-how of applying colors, color and shading ideas taken from magazines, newspapers, brochures, posters, commercial transparencies, and other printed materials can provide answers to coloring and shading problems.

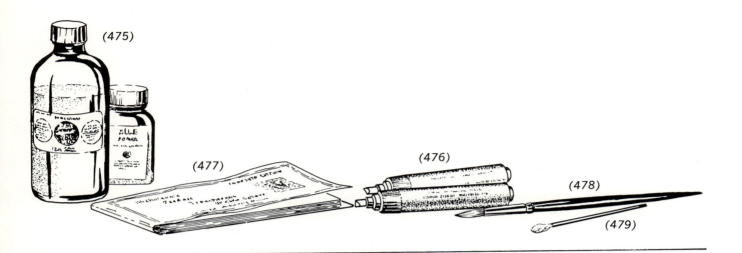

(475) (476) (477) (478) (479)

TRANSPARENT LIQUID COLORS

WATERCOLORS

Transparent watercolors in their many brilliant hues have a variety of uses in the production of visual media. They may be purchased in both liquid and dry state. Liquid watercolors may be obtained in concentrated and diluted form in a number of sizes (475). Felt-point markers containing transparent watercolor are available (476). The colors are brilliant but somewhat limited in shade selection. The feature of the felt point is its ease in use and storage. Food colors available at the local supermarket, although very limited in range of color, are also excellent transparent colors.

Dry transparent watercolors may be obtained in booklet form (477). A high concentration of dry color is adhered to paper pages. When the paper is placed in water, a clear, brilliant liquid color is produced. The depth of this color is determined by the amount of water used. Transparent watercolors are also available in dry cake form to be dissolved in water. They work well on paper surfaces; however, in many cases they are not desirable for use on transparent projected material.

The fine art of watercoloring demands extensive instruction and practice. However, by following a few simple instructions, the novice can make excellent use of transparent watercolors in the preparation of materials. This is especially true when one is working on treated surfaces such as the emulsion found on photographic films and papers. The color may be applied with either a regular watercolor brush (478) or a cotton applicator (479). If large areas on transparent or opaque surfaces have to be tinted in solid or graduated color, the use of the airbrush or transparent color in aerosol cans will greatly facilitate the process.

Tinting Photographic Materials

Although the hand tinting of photographic paper prints and slides with transparent watercolor is an extremely old technique, it is still very popular. Color may be added to continuous-tone and high-contrast photographic images on both film and paper. It will be easier, however, for the novice to tint high-contrast images where solid areas of color are desired, because tinting continuous-tone materials demands more knowledge of the application of transparent watercolor. The tinting technique is based on the principle that the photographic emulsion surface will absorb liquid watercolor. The resulting colors are brilliant, transparent, and quite permanent.

When tinting a photographic print or transparency, you must sometimes do masking to prevent the color from spreading beyond the desired area. A number of different kinds of liquid masking materials can be used. However, rubber cement can be adapted easily for this use. In a clean container (480) place a small amount of pure, clear rubber cement (481). To this add sufficient rubber cement thinner (482) so that the cement will run freely from the stirring stick. Because the cement is quite transparent and consequently difficult to see when applying, some color must be added. A small amount of oil wood stain or mimeograph ink (483) will furnish the necessary tinting. Be sure to mix well before using. This mixture may be stored in an airtight brown bottle for future use. Thinning may be necessary at a later date.

This masking material may be used on either transparent or opaque photographic materials. The photographic-paper print or the transparency may be tinted in either the positive (484) or negative form (485). Although there are exceptions, the positive image tends to be a bit more difficult to tint because of the problem of masking, which is often required. Many negative

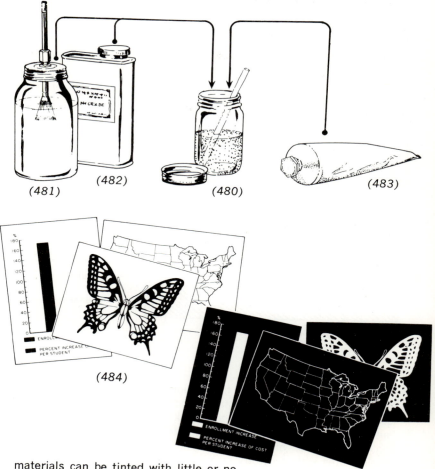

(481) (482) (480) (483)

(484)

(485)

materials can be tinted with little or no use of masking. It must be remembered in this regard that transparent watercolor placed on the black areas of a negative will not project on the screen because the black areas are opaque. Consequently only the color placed on the clear areas of the film will project or be visible to the eye.

The tinting of a positive transparent photographic film will be used as an example of this transparent watercolor tinting technique. Be sure to work on the emulsion or dull side of the film. The emulsion surface must be free of all foreign matter such as wax or oil. Abrasions will also be detrimental to the tinting process, preventing proper absorption of the watercolor.

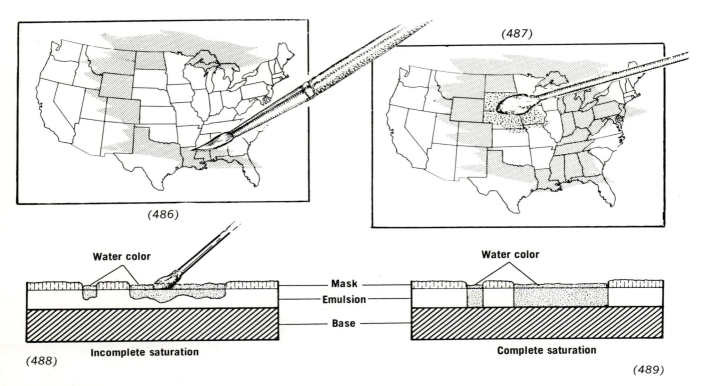

(487)

Water color — Mask
— Emulsion
— Base

Incomplete saturation

(488)

Water color — Mask
— Emulsion
— Base

Complete saturation

(489)

Instructions

First, mask the areas around the section of the film to be tinted with the rubber cement mixture (486). Allow the masking liquid to dry thoroughly. With a cotton applicator or brush flood the unmasked area with generous amounts of liquid watercolor (487).

It is important to permit plenty of time for the watercolor to completely penetrate the emulsion. The color must be kept constantly moving to prevent dry spots from forming (488). When drying takes place, absorption is stopped and irregular tinting results. Complete

(490)

(491)

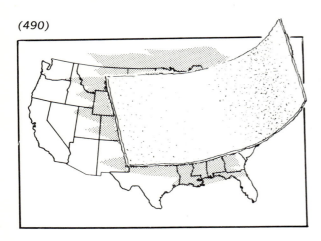

saturation of the emulsion ensures an even tint over the entire area (489).

After three or four minutes, blot the film with a clean blotter to absorb any excess color that may be on the surface (490). This excess color if allowed to dry will appear opaque when projected. Wiping over the color area with a piece of damp cotton will ensure removal of all excess liquid and dry color. If the color area appears uneven at this time, it may be because there was foreign matter such as oily fingerprints or wax on the film surface. This foreign matter will prevent complete absorption of the color, but the problem can often be solved by rewashing the photographic film and repeating the process. After the color is dry on the film, rub off the rubber cement mask (491). As many additional colors may be added as desired by using the same procedure. When this transparency is used for projection, it may be desirable to place a clear piece

of acetate over the color surface for protection. Plastic spray may also be used to seal in the colors. Another common practice is to wipe the surface of the film with a very weak (3 percent) solution of acetic acid (vinegar). This will help set the colors in the emulsion surface, and the transparency will be ready for use (492).

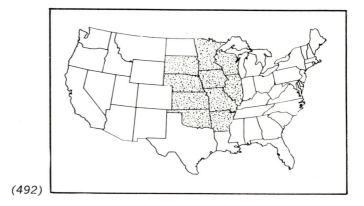

(492)

AEROSOL-CAN COLORS

Along with the development of the aerosol spray can has come a new technique of applying coloring of all descriptions. Brilliant fluorescent colors, enamels, plastics, metallic finishes, dyes, and many other types of color are now available for application to a variety of surfaces. Even synthetic snow flakes in white and colors are available for special effects.

The aerosol can, with its fine spray, approximates the effects one can obtain with an airbrush. There are special handles that fit on any aerosol can that can be used to assist in the control of the spray. Replaceable aerosol cans fitted with a special control lever, spray tip, and bottle may be used to spray any paint that can be thinned enough for spraying. By combining these techniques of color application with the careful use of frisket and masking techniques, pro-

fessional-looking effects can be obtained in the creation of attractive visuals in opaque or transparent form.

Transparent Liquid Color (Aerosol Can)

For general or special use, the aerosol cans containing vivid transparent colors can be used to apply high-quality color to a variety of surfaces including acetate, paper, wood, glass, and metal. The color, when sprayed on a transparency, leaves little to be desired in the way of quality. Preparation for applying color to transparent or opaque materials is quite similar to the preparation for using an airbrush. Frisket paper may be used to protect those areas not to be colored. It is very important to be sure that the edges of the frisket are down extremely well since this rather thin dye may tend

151

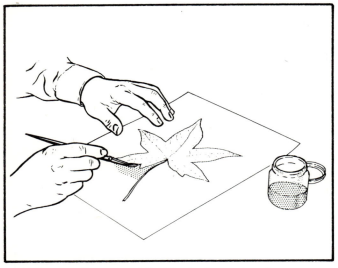

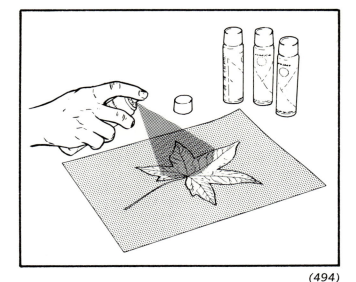

(493)   **Transparent liquid color (aerosol can)**

(494)

to run under small creases and folds in the frisket. As an alternative, a tinted rubber cement mask may be applied around the image to be colored (493) and over all other areas to be protected from the spray. Rubber cement thinned to flow easily from a brush and tinted with a small amount of mimeograph ink or oil stain can be used as this masking material. When the rubber cement has thoroughly dried; spray on an even coating of the desired dye (494). If a smooth, solid area of color is desired, be sure to flood the area slightly with color. Be sure no wax or oil spots are on the area being tinted. Place the sprayed image on a dry, clean, level surface. In a short time the color will have dried. Remove the rubber cement by gently rolling it off with the tip of the finger. The dye may be removed with water, or it may be made permanent by spraying over it with plastic spray to complete the process (495). It is removable from hard, slick surfaces but not from porous surfaces.

(495)

152

AIRBRUSH TECHNIQUES

The airbrush is one of the most valuable tools for the commercial artist; it is equally valuable to those interested in the local production of visual instructional media. We might define the airbrush as a precision, penlike spraying device about the size of a fountain pen (496) connected by a hose to a controllable air supply which forces light-bodied ink, liquid colors, and paint from a small reservoir cup or bottle. There is a variety of models covering a broad range of prices. The more expensive brushes are more precise, having very fine color and air-pressure control. These are designed to be used where fine, delicate detail is important. The less expensive airbrushes are good for the more general application of color. They have less complicated controls and tend to be easier to operate. Airbrushes are a valuable part of the producer's equipment. Airbrushing is simply another way of applying color to almost any surface whether opaque or transparent in nature. Often it is difficult to apply a smooth, even layer of color when using the more common methods of brush, swab, or felt marker. One of the advantages of the airbrush over these other methods of color application is that it *can* apply a smooth, even color over a broad area. Shading and blending of various colors can be done with ease. It may be used in combination with other drawing media for special effects. When internal and/or external stencils are used, complicated forms can be precisely tinted with color. Both opaque and transparent colors can be used in many forms such as inks, watercolors, alcohol colors, oil, and lacquer paints. Colors having impurities or abrasive qualities should not be used. The passing of fine grit or other abrasive material through the delicate tip of the airbrush will cause serious damage. Always check to see that the color is recommended for use in the airbrush. Colors that tend to coagulate

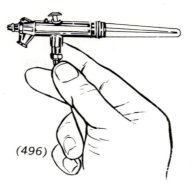

(496)

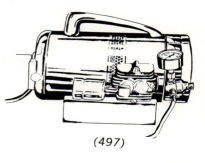

(497)

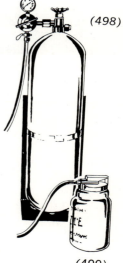

(498)

(499)

or become lumpy will block the passage of paint through the tip of the brush causing great difficulty. This problem can sometimes be overcome by carefully straining the paint through a fine cloth or filter before use.

The air supply needed to operate the airbrush may originate from any of a number of sources. The sources chosen will depend to a great extent upon cost, amount of use, and availability. One of the most common sources of air pressure is the air compressor (497). This is often a relatively small, portable electric unit so designed that it will give a steady, dependable flow of air to the brush. The flow of air must remain at a constant pressure with no fluctations. Variations in air pressure will produce an uneven flow of color from the brush causing difficulty for the operator. Special controls and gauges set the desired pressure from the air compressor. The air compressor costs more to purchase; however, it will operate for extended periods of time with little or no upkeep. A second source of air is the carbonic tank (498). It may be purchased in small

153

sizes or in some cases rented from companies that service soda fountains. In many locations these tanks, if owned by the operator, will be refilled by the same companies at a nominal fee. They furnish an excellent source of pressure and, in cases where the airbrush is not used extensively, they are, economically speaking, a very practical source of pressure. A special gauge is attached to control the amount of pressure at all times. A third source of pressure is a small aerosol pressure tank (499). It is a 16-ounce aerosol can of propellant gas with a pressure-regulating valve. It contains enough pressure to operate an airbrush for one to three hours, depending on the size of the airbrush and the type of work to be done.

(500)

(501)

(502)

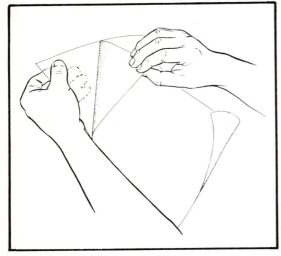

(503)

As with any technique of drawing or painting, learning to use the airbrush demands practice. It is, however, a technique which will permit the novice to create some simple, interesting effects (500, 501, 502). The use of stencils enables the operator to control the spread of the fine spray from the airbrush and permits the formation of intricate forms. A thin frisket paper or film with a special rubber-base adhesive on the back will serve to block out areas while the airbrush is in use. Simply peel the frisket from its backing sheet (503) and place it carefully over the image to be shaded or tinted (504). Be sure to leave plenty of protection around the area to be airbrushed so that any fine color mist will not tint the area of the drawing beyond the frisket. With a sharp tool cut along the outline of the area of the drawing that is to be tinted (505).

After the cutting is completed, remove the frisket from this area (506). Wipe the area free of any foreign matter.

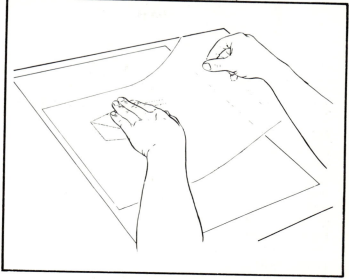

(504)

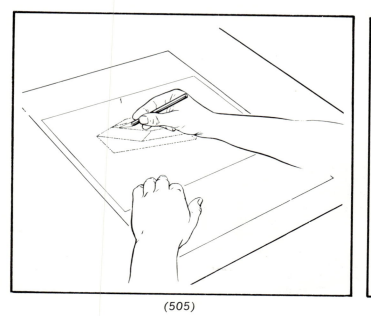

(505)

(506)

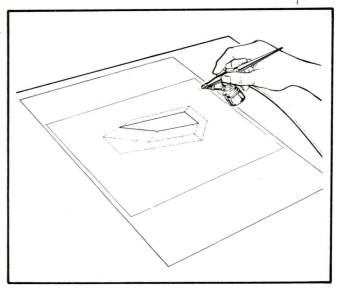

The area is now ready to be sprayed with the airbrush (507). When the desired effect is achieved, the piece of frisket can be replaced and another section removed, following the same procedure. This process can continue until all sections of the drawing are completed. Remove all frisket material and the shading or tinting process is completed (508). It is always advisable to work on good-quality cardboard during this process to ensure the least possible damage to the surface from the frisket adhesive and the cutting process. This procedure may be used for tinting or coloring photographic-paper prints as well as transparencies.

(507)

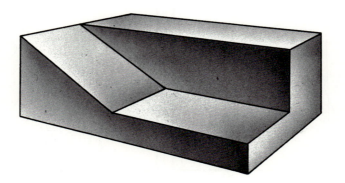

(508)

TRANSPARENT COLOR ADHESIVE-BACKED SHEETS AND TAPES

Vivid colors can be added to either side of either positive- or negative-image transparencies and to the surface of opaque paper-surfaced materials by applying transparent color adhesive-backed sheets and tapes. These coloring materials are made up of vivid transparent color printed on the underside of a thin film with a pressure-sensitive adhesive back. They come in assorted colors, and some sheets and tapes even contain a texture pattern to add still another effect to color.

Instructions

1. With a cutting instrument (frisket knife, razor blade, etc.) score (cutting just through the color sheet) a section slightly larger than required for the area or image on which color is to go (509). Gently slide the point of the knife under the color sheet and peel off the cut section.
2. Position the cut section (adhesive side down) on the area or image (510). Care should be taken to position the color right the first time, since the adhesive of some color sheets will leave an adhesive residue when lifted and repositioned. It may be necessary to slightly burnish the color sheet in place to hold for cutting (511).
3. With the cutting knife, trace (cutting just through the color sheet)

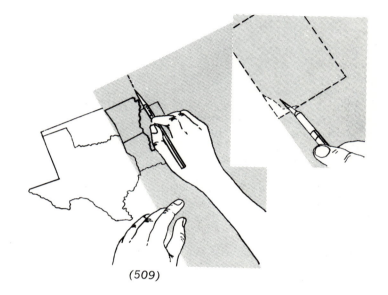

(509)

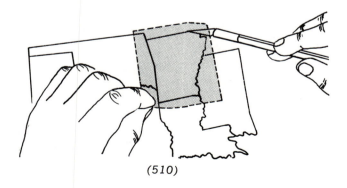

(510)

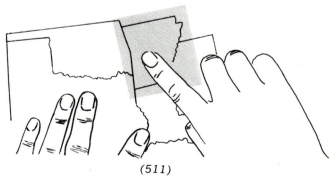

(511)

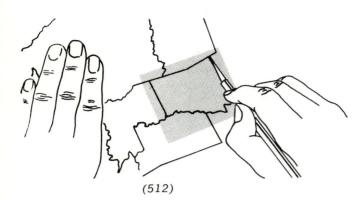

(512)

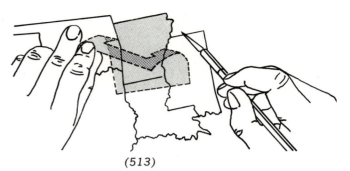

(513)

around the image area (512). Peel away the unwanted color (513).

4. Smooth the color over the image area with the hand or a finger so that it lies evenly. It is recommended that you use a clean sheet of white paper on top of the color during the smoothing; this will help protect the applied color from possible scratches and will also assist in assuring perfect adhesion. Should bubbles appear in the color, make a pinhole and smooth down once more.

Transparent color tapes work much like the sheets. See pages 26 to 27 for instructions related to the use of shading (texture) tapes. These same instructions apply to the color tapes.

Helpful Tips

Two or more colors can be applied to the same area or image for different color effects.

If writing or marking is to be done on a transparency during projection, place the color on the reverse side of the film. This will prevent the writing or marking from damaging the color.

For materials requiring opaque color, opaque color sheets and tapes are available.

GOLD IMAGE TRANSFER TECHNIQUE (Gold Transfer Foil)

Writing, drawing, and lettering can be transferred in genuine gold (usually 23 karat) to surfaces such as paint, paper, plastic, metal, glass, leather (514). A special gold transfer foil (sheet or tape) is used much like an ordinary carbon sheet. The gold sheet or tape is placed over the working surface (dull side down). Writing, drawing, or lettering is done directly on the shiny surface of the sheet. A pencil, ball-point pen, or stylus can be used to transfer the gold. This technique is ideal for lettering on certificates, nameplates, greeting cards, etc.

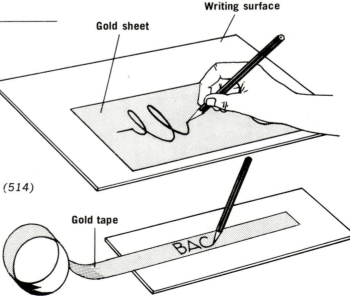

Writing surface

Gold sheet

(514)

Gold tape

BAC

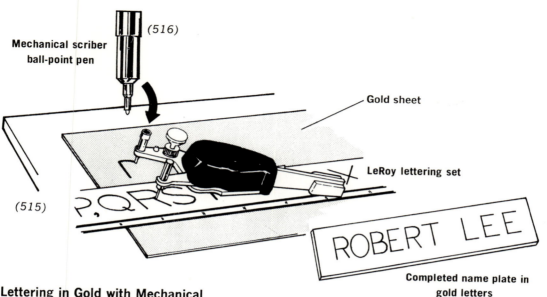

Mechanical scriber ball-point pen *(516)*

Gold sheet

LeRoy lettering set

(515)

ROBERT LEE

Completed name plate in
gold letters

Lettering in Gold with Mechanical Tracing Lettering Systems *(515)*

Gold letters can be made with several of the mechanical tracing lettering systems (Varigraph system not included). A mechanical scriber ball-point pen must be inserted in the scriber for this type of lettering. The ball-point unit out of a regular ball-point pen can be substituted for the mechanical scriber ball-point pen *(516)*. The gold sheet or tape should be taped to the working surface (dull side down) to prevent movement while lettering.

Lettering in Gold with Stencil Duplicator Lettering Guides *(517)*

Stencil duplicator lettering guides and lettering styli can be used to produce letters in gold on any of the surfaces already mentioned. The gold sheet or tape should be taped to the working surface (dull side down) to prevent movement while lettering. See pages 107 to 108 for lettering instructions.

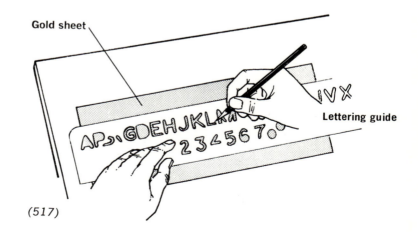

Gold sheet

Lettering guide

(517)

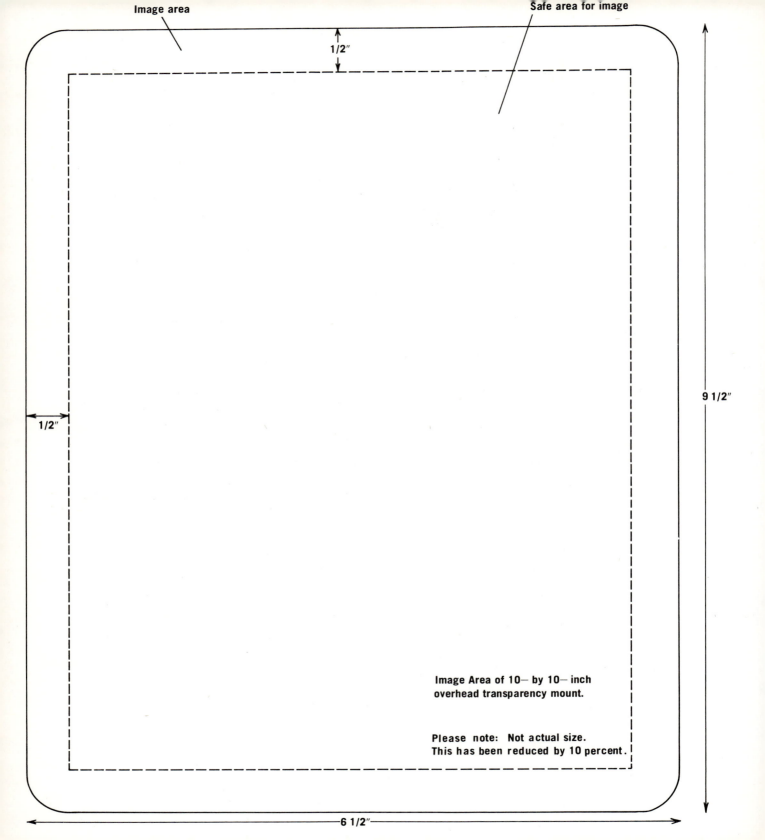

Image area

Safe area for image

1/2"

1/2"

9 1/2"

Image Area of 10— by 10— inch
overhead transparency mount.

Please note: Not actual size.
This has been reduced by 10 percent.

6 1/2"

PRODUCING TRANSPARENCIES FOR PROJECTION AND DISPLAY

Planning and Creating Transparencies

Image Area of Overhead Transparency Mounts

Direct Image on Acetate Transparencies

Clear or Prepared Acetate Transparency
Matte (Frosted) Acetate Transparency
Carbon-coated Projection Acetate Transparency

Spirit Duplicator Transparencies

Paper Spirit Master and Matte or Prepared Acetate Transparency
Acetate Spirit Master Transparency
Thermocopy Acetate Spirit Master Transparency

Hectographic Transparency

Thermocopy Transparencies

Positive- and Negative-image Transparencies
Selfkote Thermocopy Transparency
Parlab Multicolor Thermocopy Transparencies
Transmate Thermocopy Transparency
Stencil Duplicator Thermocopy Transparency

Diazo Transparencies

Single-color Positive- and Negative-image Diazo Transparencies
VariTyper System Diazo Transparencies

Photographic Transparencies

Diffusion Transfer Transparency
Photostabilization Transparencies
Canon/Kalvar Slide System
Polaroid Land Projection Transparencies

Picture Transfer Transparencies

Rubber Cement Picture Transfer Transparency
Cold Laminating Acetate Picture Transfer Transparency
Cold Laminating Machine Picture Transfer Transparency
Heat Laminating Machine Picture Transfer Transparency
Dry Mounting Press Picture Transfer Transparency

Electronic Stencil Cutter Transparency

Polarized Transparencies

Xerographic Transparencies

Large Transparency Mounting Techniques

Transparency Mounts
Mounting Base Transparency
Attaching Overlays
Progressive Disclosure Techniques
Filing and Storing Large Transparencies

Slide Mounting and Binding Techniques

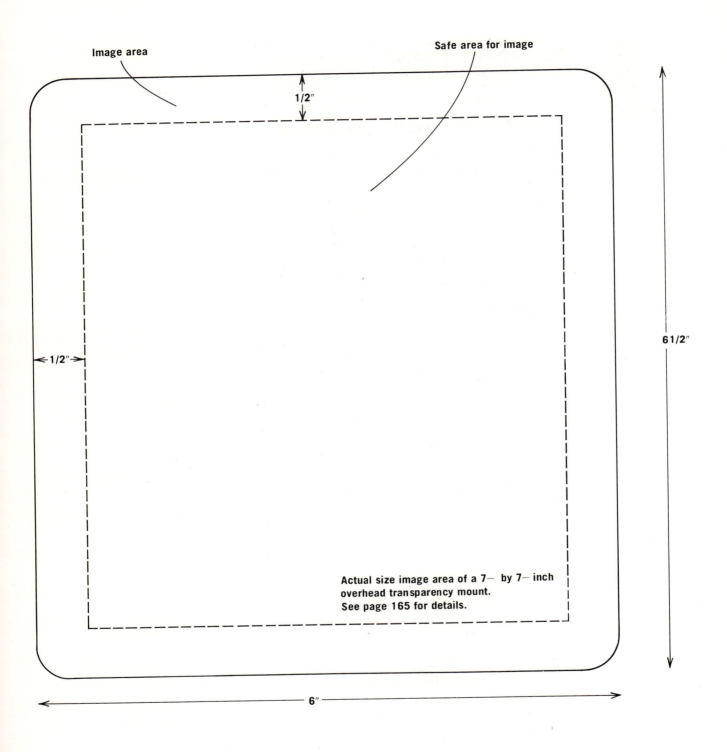

Image area

Safe area for image

1/2″

1/2″

61/2″

6″

Actual size image area of a 7— by 7— inch
overhead transparency mount.
See page 165 for details.

PRODUCING TRANSPARENCIES FOR PROJECTION AND DISPLAY

An almost unlimited variety of techniques, methods, and processes is available today that can be used to produce transparencies for projection and display. In view of this, an extensive investigation was conducted to determine which of the techniques should be included in a book of this type. Recognizing that this book is concerned mainly with the nonprofessional, some of the techniques were automatically eliminated. On the other hand, techniques requiring some professional know-how and greater capital outlay have been included for the professional producer.

Some authorities in graphic communications will argue that a book of this type should more or less direct the intended audience to a few specific techniques for producing transparencies. Although this point of view may have some merit, there are those who feel that this type of book should offer a number of good and practical solutions to a particular production problem, especially when many schools, industrial systems, religious organizations, etc., already have production equipment and materials about whose production capabilities they know little or nothing.

This chapter on producing transparencies includes a number of what the authors feel to be techniques and processes worthy of special attention. Each has its own unique contributions to local production. Those who desire additional technical or nontechnical information can refer to the Annotated Bibliography in Chapter 6. Listed there are publications and projectable visual media related to local production. Moreover, one can write directly to the suppliers, manufacturers, or producers of equipment and materials related to a particular technique. Complete addresses also can be found in Chapter 6.

PLANNING AND CREATING TRANSPARENCIES

Many users of instructional media, especially those using the overhead projector, have expressed a desire to use projectables with visual and written content more closely related to their own method of communication. Until recently this has been a most difficult task in that a large percentage of instructional media users lack the creativeness and artistic skill necessary for planning and creating such items as overhead transparencies. This book is just one of the many attempts to assist the user in producing his own materials. At present there are a variety of materials, equipment, drawing aids, lettering devices that require very little skill to use.

Planning the Transparency

Often the artwork of an intended transparency may already be completed, such as that found in magazines, books, published reports, printed originals (for thermocopy), commercial diazo masters, and so forth. When such is not available, here are a few basic suggestions to follow in planning a transparency.

1. Keep the visual simple. Too much detail or information can be confusing to the audience (518a). It is recommended that you limit, where possible, each visual to one main point or comparison (518b).
2. Avoid masses of black areas, especially when the artwork is to be used in any heat-processing equipment, such as thermocopy. Various shading materials can be used to break up solid areas of a visual (see pages 157–158 for shading instructions).

Too much detail (518a)

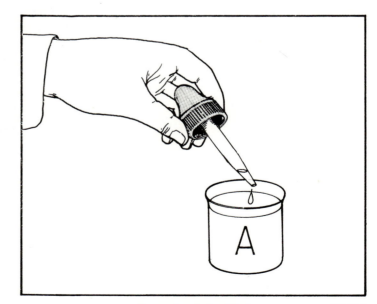

Same visual simplified (518b)

3. Be conservative with lettering (519). Letters should be no smaller than one-twentieth the total height of the image area. Limit each transparency to six or seven words per line. Where possible, limit the number of lines to under seven.

4. Use color with a specific purpose in mind. Do not overuse color, for overuse will take away from the value of the transparency.

For suggested sources of visuals, see pages 24, 25.
For illustrating techniques, see Chapter 1.
For lettering, refer first to the chart on page 100.
To add color, see Chapter 4.

IMAGE AREA OF OVERHEAD TRANSPARENCY MOUNTS

Sizes of overhead transparency mounts (520) or sizes of their image area have not yet been standardized. However, there are two sizes of mounts most frequently used today: the 10- by 10-inch with a 7½- by 9½-inch image area, and the 7- by 7-inch with a 6- by 6½-inch image area (see pages 160 and 162 for actual size image areas).

The image area represents the total area that will be projected on the screen. It is true that all the image area could be used when preparing art or drawing directly on the transparency film. However, it is recommended that you not use the full area, but allow from ¼ to ½ inch of space between transparency content (lettering, visual, etc.) and the border of the image area.

In that a majority of projection screens are rectangular, it is recommended that, where possible, the artwork (on paper, acetate, or whatever) be prepared to fit into the image area so that it can be projected horizontally on the screen.

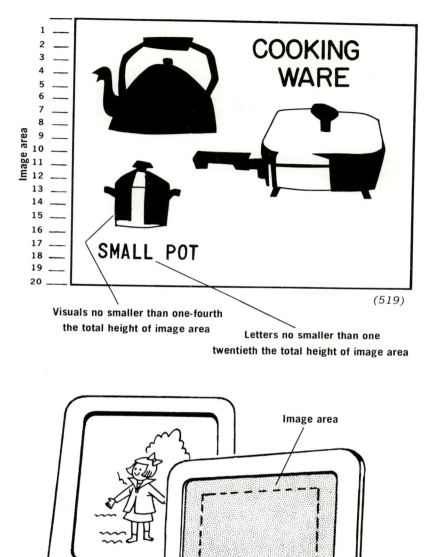

(519)

Visuals no smaller than one-fourth the total height of image area

Letters no smaller than one twentieth the total height of image area

(520)

Image area

Safe area for image

Mount

DIRECT IMAGE ON ACETATE TRANSPARENCIES

Several types of acetate can be used to produce excellent projection slides and overhead transparencies. Visual images, lettering, writing, and so forth, can be done directly on the surface of the acetate. Many of the illustrating, lettering, and coloring techniques included in this book can be combined with various acetates to produce a variety of direct-image transparencies.

Three different types of acetate have been selected for inclusion in this chapter because their surfaces are ideal for quick, easy-to-make transparencies. They include clear or prepared, matte (frosted), and carbon-coated projection acetates. Each will be treated separately in the pages to follow.

CLEAR OR PREPARED ACETATE TRANSPARENCY

When visuals cannot be removed from their original source (book, magazine, newspaper, etc.) and when copying equipment is not available, tracings of visuals can be made directly on clear or prepared acetate, on matte (frosted) acetate, or on tracing paper. The desired final product (whether transparency, diazo master, or whatever) will determine the type of material on which the tracing is to be made.

If the original visual to be traced is the approximate size desired, then the instructions that follow will be sufficient. If the original is too small, see pages 41, 44, 46 for instructions on enlarging visuals. If the original is too large, see pages 43, 44 for instructions on reducing visuals.

Images in black or color line can be projected on the screen by drawing directly on clear or prepared acetate with an opaque or transparent color marking pencil, nylon- or felt-point pen, or drawing ink and pen.

The instructions that follow are for the preparation of transparencies on clear or prepared acetate.

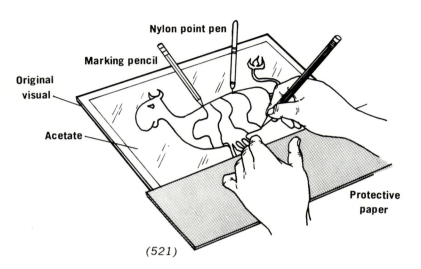

(521)

Instructions

Clear acetate is one of several types of transparent plastics or acetates (reprocessed x-ray film and color acetate are other examples). Prepared acetate (specially surfaced) is recommended when ink is used, because it has a special coating on both sides that will accept inks, watercolors, poster paint, and dyes without crawling.

1. Attach, where possible, a sheet of acetate (clear or prepared) to the surface of the visual to be traced (521). See Planning and Creating Transparencies for tips on how to plan for visuals and lettering when preparing transparencies. Place a sheet of protective paper (any clean sheet of paper will do) over the portion of the acetate where the hands or fingers might come in

contact with the acetate. Oil residue from hands and fingers may be deposited on the surface of the acetate; this may prevent the surface from accepting the ink. In that all clear acetates will not accept ink, talcum powder or pumice can be rubbed over the surface. This will provide a "tooth" necessary to accept and hold the ink line.

2. If a quick, temporary image is desired, draw on the acetate with an opaque or transparent color marking pencil (transparent color pencil will project in color), or with a nylon- or felt-point pen containing a water-base ink.

   If a more permanent image is desired, draw on the acetate with india or acetate ink and pen. Technical fountain, reservoir, and Hunt Bowl Pointed pens are recommended for drawing on clear or prepared acetate.

3. To add color (522), use nylon-point pens for fine-line color and felt-point pens for broad-line color. See pages 148–158 for other coloring techniques.

4. Mount, if desired, for projection (523). See pages 221–226 for tips on mounting techniques.

5. To remove unwanted marking pencil or water-base image lines, use a damp cloth (524).

   If lettering is desired, consult the chart on page 100 for recommended lettering techniques.

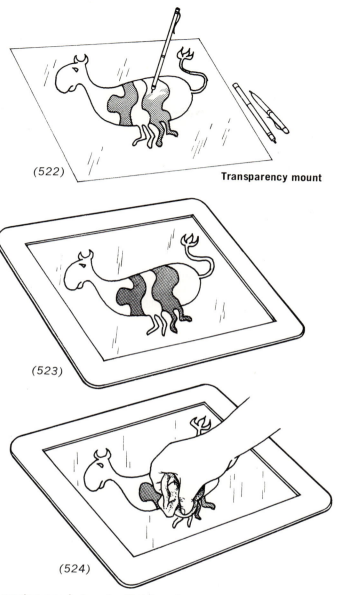

(522)

Transparency mount

(523)

(524)

MATTE (FROSTED) ACETATE TRANSPARENCY

When visuals cannot be removed from their original source (book, magazine, newspaper, etc.) and when copying equipment is not available, tracings of visuals can be made directly on clear or prepared acetate, on matte (frosted) acetate, or on tracing paper. The desired final product (whether transparency,

diazo master, or whatever) will determine the type of material on which the tracing is to be made.

   If the original visual to be traced is the approximate size desired, then the instructions that follow will be sufficient. If the original is too small, see pages 41, 44, 46 for instructions on enlarging visuals. If the original is too large, see pages 43, 44 for instructions on reducing visuals.

Instructions

Matte (frosted) acetate has a finely etched surface which is ideal for accepting india ink, color drawing, and lead pencil lines. Only the matte (dull) side of the acetate will accept the drawing.

1. Attach, where possible, a sheet of acetate to the surface of the visual to be traced (525). See Planning and Creating Transparencies for tips on how to plan for visuals and lettering when preparing transparencies. Place a sheet of protective paper (any clean sheet of paper will do) over the portion of the acetate where the hands and fingers might come in contact with the acetate. Oil residue from hands and fingers may be deposited on the surface of the acetate; this may prevent the surface from accepting the ink or pencil line.

2. If an ink line is desired, draw directly on the acetate with india ink and pen, technical fountain, reservoir, or Hunt Bowl Pointed pen. (526).
    If a pencil line (black or color) is desired, use a soft lead or color drawing pencil. See pages 9 and 10 for recommended pencils (526).

3. Spray matte side of film with clear plastic spray (527). Hold spray can about 10 inches above the acetate and spray back and forth to apply an even coat of plastic.
    or
    Pass acetate through a heat laminating machine (528); this will seal in the image while making it more transparent. See page 210 for use of the laminator.

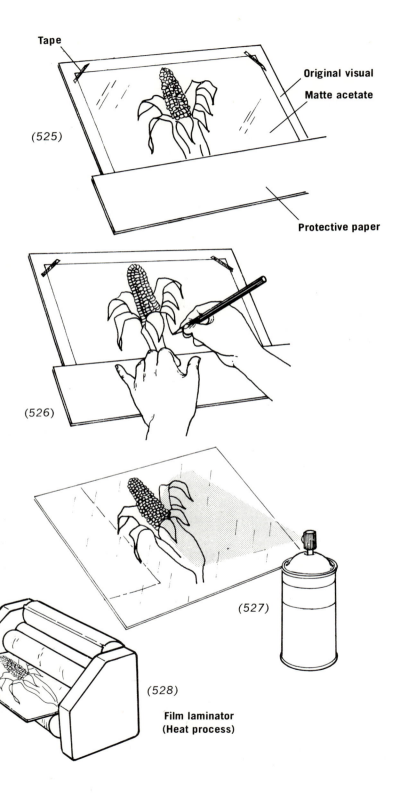

Tape

Original visual

Matte acetate

(525)

Protective paper

(526)

(527)

(528)

Film laminator
(Heat process)

CARBON-COATED PROJECTION ACETATE TRANSPARENCY

A dramatic application of overhead projection is the use of carbon-coated projection acetate. The acetate has a specially formulated coating on an acetate base which when written on (dull side) with a ball-point pen, stylus, pencil, or typewriter (shiny side) produces white lines on a black screen when projected. If a color acetate sheet is placed under the transparency, a color line will be projected. This type of acetate can also be used as a negative for preparing diazo duplicate negatives and photographic positives.

The use of carbon-coated acetate is recommended when a change of pace in presentation is desired and when animated white or color lines are desired in projection.

Applications

Carbon-coated acetate is mounted (dull side up) to the underside of a transparency mount (529). See pages 221–226 for tips on mounting techniques. Draw, write, or letter on the dull side while projecting; use a ball-point pen, stylus, or pencil.

Use the pounce pattern technique (see page 50) to prepare a transparency presentation in advance (530). During projection, simply trace around the chalk-dusted outline with one of the drawing devices mentioned.

Place a sheet of transparent color acetate behind the transparency during projection (531); the result will be a vivid color line when projected. Draw or write with any of the devices mentioned.

Carbon-coated projection acetate can be used to produce white letters (or color letters when a color acetate is used behind the transparency) on a black screen when projected (532). Place a paper backup sheet behind the sheet and type on the shiny side of the acetate (set typewriter on "stencil" position for sharpest image). The carbon coating will

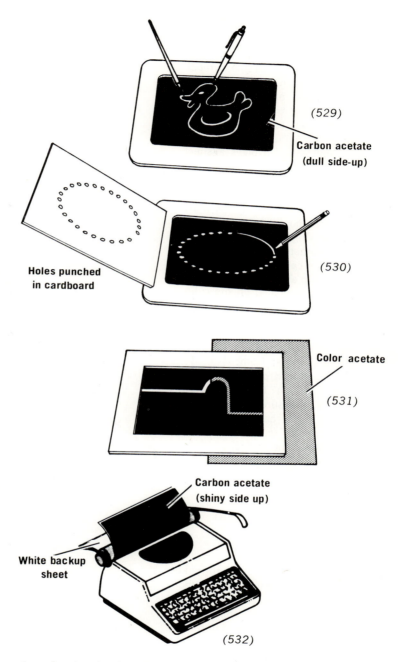

Carbon acetate
(dull side-up)
(529)

Holes punched
in cardboard

(530)

Color acetate
(531)

Carbon acetate
(shiny side up)

White backup
sheet

(532)

transfer to the backup paper, leaving clear letters on the carbon side of the acetate. A sheet of clear acetate can be attached to the carbon side to prevent abrasions and to preserve it for reuse.

SPIRIT DUPLICATOR TRANSPARENCIES

Spirit, sometimes referred to as fluid, duplicating is the fastest, simplest, most economical way to produce 5 to 300 paper copies. There are several techniques for producing transparencies for overhead projection and display with this process.

Spirit duplicating involves a sheet of white master paper or transparent acetate master which is attached to a sheet of paper coated with a waxlike dye or dye-forming substance known more commonly as a carbon sheet.

By handwriting, typing, drawing, or lettering on the master paper or acetate, one transfers the carbon to the back of the master to form a duplicating master.

The master is placed on the cylinder of a spirit duplicator (carbon side up). The copy paper or matte acetate (dull side up) is moistened with an alcohol-like fluid. This is where the term *spirit* duplicating comes from.

As the moistened paper or acetate is forwarded through the duplicating machine, it is pressured against the master, causing the carbon image to dissolve and transfer to the copy paper or acetate, creating the image.

The techniques which follow relate only to the preparation of transparencies with the spirit duplicator.

PAPER SPIRIT MASTER AND MATTE OR PREPARED ACETATE TRANSPARENCY

A spirit duplicator can be used to make excellent color transparencies for projection and display. The process is similar to that used in making paper copies from a regular spirit master, the difference being that the image from the master transfers to a sheet of matte or prepared acetate rather than to paper.

Instructions

1. On a regular paper spirit master, after the interleaf sheet has been removed, write, draw, or letter directly, using a firm, even pressure (533). For best results, use a ball-point pen, 4H pencil or mimeograph drawing stylus. For good, sharp, unbroken lines, work on a piece of plate glass or linoleum. An ordinary

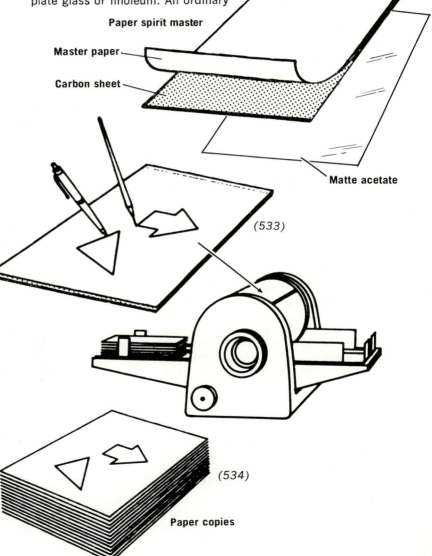

Paper spirit master

Master paper

Carbon sheet

Matte acetate

(533)

(534)

Paper copies

desk top is usually not hard enough. Refer to pages 39–40 for the use of various drawing aids designed for spirit masters. Several lettering aids can be used directly on spirit masters. Refer to the chart on page 100 for such aids.

To add color to the master, simply remove the initial carbon sheet and replace it with the color carbon sheet desired. The color carbon sheet must be the type designed for spirit duplication.

2. Remove the carbon sheet from the master and place the master on the spirit duplicator in the usual way (534). Run several sheets of paper through the duplicator first. Hand-feed a sheet of matte acetate (dull side up) into the duplicator (when prepared acetate is used, either side can be run through the machine); the image from the master sheet will transfer to the acetate. If the image is not the quality desired, dampen a cloth or piece of cotton with some of the spirit fluid and remove the image from the acetate and run through the machine once more.

3. Spray the dull side of the matte acetate with clear plastic spray (535). Lay the acetate on a flat, protected surface and spray back and forth to place an even coating of plastic on the acetate. Hold the spray can about 10 inches from

the surface of acetate while spraying. The plastic spray will make the background more transparent and will seal in the image. The prepared acetate requires no spraying.

For mounting instructions, see pages 221–226.
To add lettering, see the chart on page 100.

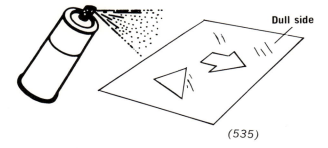

Dull side

(535)

Note: see SPIRIT DUPLICATOR PAPER MASTER in the Index for sources.

ACETATE SPIRIT MASTER TRANSPARENCY

No transparency-making equipment or chemicals are required to make a combination spirit master and transparency for the overhead projector. This type of master transparency enables one to project the same material that has been duplicated and distributed to the audi-

ence. This special unit consists of a sheet of tracing paper—which can be used to trace a visual from almost any source—a clear plastic sheet, and a base carbon sheet. After the master has been prepared, up to 150 paper copies can be run off on any spirit duplicating machine. The master can then be mounted and projected on the overhead projector.

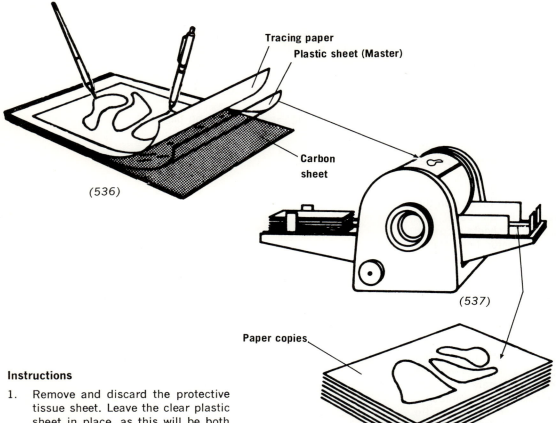

Tracing paper
Plastic sheet (Master)

Carbon sheet

(536)

(537)

Paper copies

Instructions

1. Remove and discard the protective tissue sheet. Leave the clear plastic sheet in place, as this will be both the spirit master and transparency for the overhead projector (536).

2. Write, draw, or type directly on the top tracing paper, the same as on a regular spirit master. Use a stylus or ball-point pen. If a typewriter is used, set it on "stencil" position for sharpest image.

3. Remove the clear plastic sheet and run on any spirit duplicating machine (537). Copies will print in black, or the color of the carbon used.

4. Carefully remove the master from the machine and mount for projection (see pages 221—226) (538). For permanence, spray the master with clear plastic spray or attach a sheet of clear acetate to the carbon side of the master.

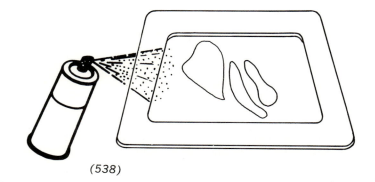

(538)

Note: see SPIRIT DUPLICATOR ACETATE MASTER in the Index for sources.

THERMOCOPY ACETATE SPIRIT MASTER TRANSPARENCY

A dual-purpose thermocopy acetate spirit master (539) produces up to 150 paper copies and a transparency for overhead projector. The unit consists of a clear plastic sheet (master) combined with a special carbon sheet. Some units also include a backing sheet. A unique feature of the process is that the instructor is able to project the same material that has been duplicated and distributed to the audience. The original (material to be copied) must be made up of drawings, lettering, etc., that are reproducible in a thermocopy machine. Generally, these machines will reproduce most impressions made of printing inks, lead pencil, and typewriter ribbon. For more detailed instruction on the preparation of originals for thermocopying see pages 180–188.

Instructions

1. Insert the original (face up) under the carbon sheet, or if the unit includes a backing sheet, place the original between the backing sheet and the carbon sheet (540). Place the assembled materials in a clear plastic carrier (if recommended by the manufacturer). If the unit has no backing sheet, and since good contact is important, place two or three plain sheets of paper under the original before inserting in the machine.

2. Insert the assembled materials in the machine and expose at the recommended setting. It is recommended that a unit be cut into sample test strips. Make exposure test on these strips. Generally the exposure is set at a somewhat lighter setting than for regular thermocopy transparencies. An overexposed unit will show fill-in of the image and excessive background pickup of carbon. An underexposed unit will show the

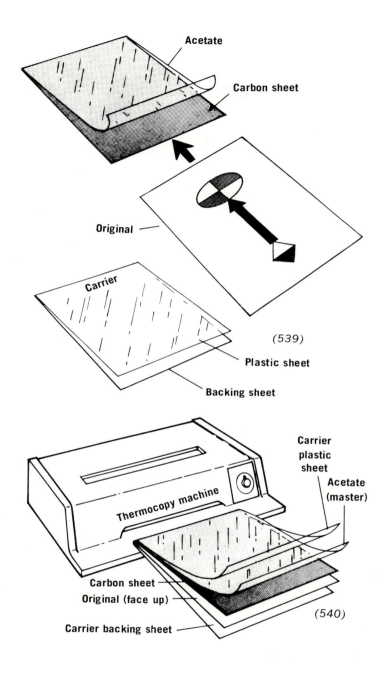

Acetate

Carbon sheet

Original

Carrier

(539)

Plastic sheet

Backing sheet

Carrier plastic sheet

Acetate (master)

Thermocopy machine

Carbon sheet

Original (face up)

Carrier backing sheet

(540)

Note: see SPIRIT DUPLICATOR THERMOCOPY ACETATE MASTER in the Index for sources.

lack of complete carbon coverage of the image.

3. After exposure, gently peel the carbon sheet from the acetate, not the acetate from the carbon sheet. Discard the carbon sheet since it has no additional use.

4. If paper copies are desired from the acetate master, attach it to the duplicator the same as with a regular paper master (carbon image side up) *(541)*. Run off the desired number of copies (limit to 100 copies if possible).

5. Project the acetate master on any overhead projector. The carbon image side of the acetate can be sprayed with clear plastic spray to seal in the image for future projection. See page 168 for spraying instructions.

6. Mount for projection if desired *(542)*. See instructions on page 221 for mounting techniques.

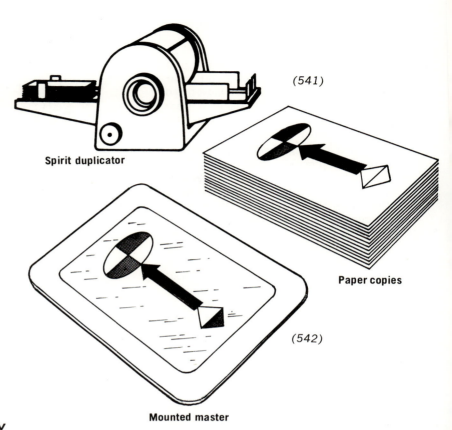

(541)

Spirit duplicator

Paper copies

(542)

Mounted master

HECTOGRAPHIC TRANSPARENCY

The hectograph process is an old duplicating method used in the reproduction of small quantities of paper prints. It is now also used to make multicolor transparencies. Not only can the instructor make a transparency, but he may also make a limited number of additional paper prints to pass out to the students. The process is simple, fast, and inexpensive. The equipment and supplies are readily available and can be purchased from stationery stores, business supply and mail-order houses. If desirable, the gelatin printing surface may be made at home with a little expenditure of time and money.

The master paper copy for this process may be produced in a number of ways. Specially prepared hectograph pencils, ink, carbon paper, and type-writer ribbons may be used alone or in combination to form the carbon image on the master paper copy (on which the success of the whole process depends). These various materials come in a limited number of colors. When copies are being reproduced on paper, the number of prints obtainable by this system of reproduction is limited by the method by which the master is made and by the colors used. Masters made with hectograph pencils tend to give fewer copies than those made by using the special carbon paper. The color purple will be found to be the strongest of the colors and will give the greatest number of copies. When making transparencies by this method, only three or four copies—at the most—can be made. However, it may be assumed in

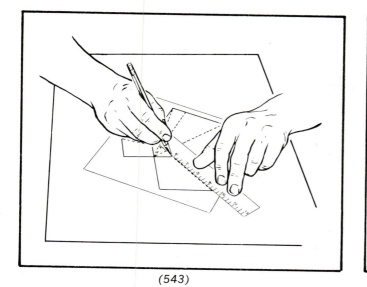

(543)

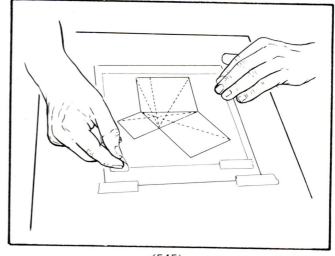

(544)

(545)

most cases that one transparency will be all that is required for a particular teaching situation. Of course after one transparency is made a number of paper prints may be made.

One method, and probably the most common in preparing the artwork, is to make a drawing with ink or pencil on very lightweight paper or tracing tissue (543). A carefully done line drawing will ensure a better end product. This visual may be made by tracing from tear sheets, clip art, or original drawings, or it may be a compilation of these various sources of imagery. Next, tape down a sheet of good-quality hard-surfaced paper, which will be known as the master, onto a surface of glass, formica, plastic, or any other smooth, hard surface (544).

Over this fasten the drawing to be reproduced. Tape it down along the top edge so that it can be lifted without changing its relationship to the master sheet (545). Choose the color of hectograph carbon paper desired and insert it with carbon side down between the

(546)

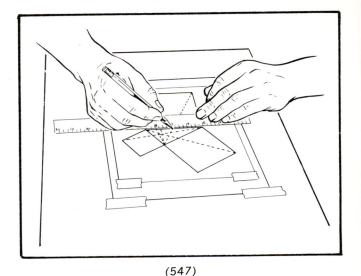

(547)

drawing tissue and the master sheet (546). To prevent movement, use small bits of tape.

Now trace along those lines to be in the color of the carbon now in use (547). Any smooth-tipped instrument can be used to do the tracing, such as a ball-point pen, a stylus, or a pencil. Ball-point pens have proved to be the best. Care must be taken to apply smooth, even pressure to ensure good transfer of the carbon onto the master sheet. When all lines of this color are

completed, a second color carbon is inserted (548) in the same manner, and the drawing process is continued until all lines are drawn with their respective color carbons.

Any area of a carbon that has been used once cannot be used the second time because that area will lack sufficient carbon for a second transfer. If hectograph pencil or ink is used, the drawing is made directly on the master sheet using the colors of pencils or ink appropriate to the desired end result.

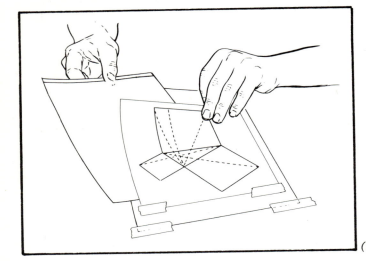

(548)

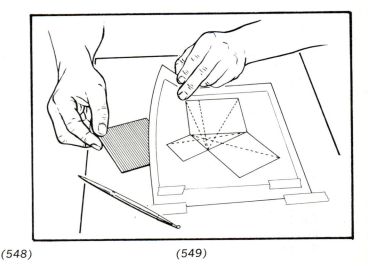

(549)

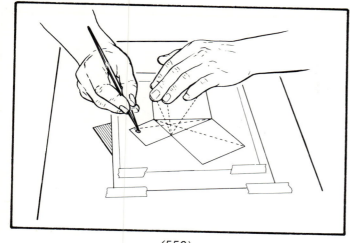

(550)

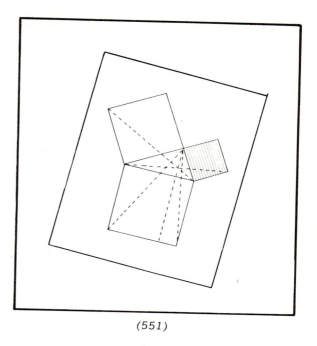

(551)

Special shading and texture effects can be obtained by inserting a shading plate beneath the master sheet (549) and rubbing over the area to be shaded with a blunt stylus (550). The rough-patterned surface of the shading plate causes a like pattern to transfer from the carbon to the master sheet. Other effects of stippling and crosshatch drawing can be very effective when appropriately used. The carbon image on the master sheet should now be checked (551). If any errors are found, the carbon may be scraped off with a razor blade, or cellophane tape may be used to cover the carbon image so that reproduction will be prevented.

Now prepare the gelatin surface of the hectograph by sponging it with cool water (552). When the gelatin is well

(552)

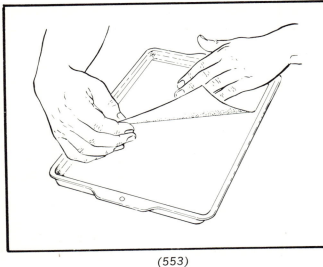

(553)

(554)

saturated, blot off the excess moisture using absorbent paper (553).

Next, place the carbon image of the master sheet in contact with the hectograph's gelatin surface (554). Be sure that the entire image is in contact with the gelatin by rubbing over the back of the master sheet with even, firm pressure. After a period of from thirty to sixty seconds remove the master sheet (555). The gelatin surface of the dupli-

cator has now absorbed a large amount of the carbon from the master sheet.

To make a transparency, a sheet of gelatin-coated film is now placed in contact with this image (556). The gelatin surface of photographic film which has had its image removed by bleaching and also the gelatin surface of diffusion transfer film work well in making this type of transparency. Slight moistening of the photographic film will ensure a

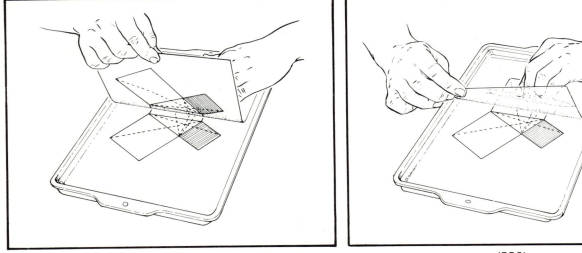

(555)

(556)

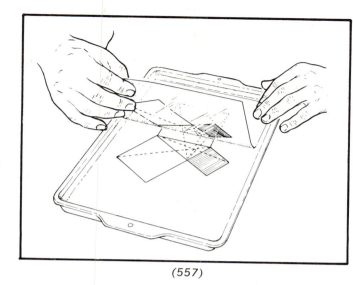

(557)

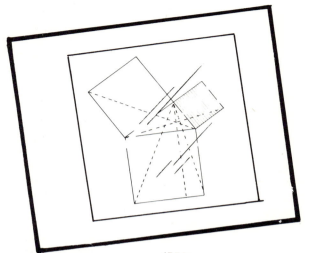

(558)

stronger, brighter image transfer. Care must be taken to be sure that no air blisters form under the film, preventing complete contact with the duplicator image. After thirty to sixty seconds, pull the film off (557). If a little gelatin from the duplicator should stick to the film surface, sponge the surface with water and blot quickly with absorbent paper. Allow time to dry.

Place a protective sheet of acetate over the printed surface and bind in the appropriate type of mask for projection (558). If only one transparency is made in this manner, enough carbon will remain in the gelatin surface to permit the reproduction of a number of paper copies (559). Immediately after using the hectograph, wash off the gelatin surface with cool water to help remove the remaining carbon image and any paper fiber that may have remained on the surface. Blot off the excess moisture, cover, and put away for future use.

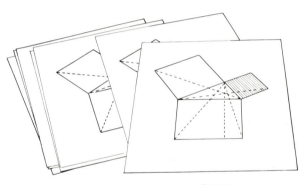

(559)

Preparing the Hectograph Duplicator

To make this simple duplicator, purchase at the local hardware store two shallow baking pans (560) slightly larger than a sheet of paper. One pan will be used to hold the gelatin compound, and

(560)

the other will be used as a cover (561) to protect the printing surface. Try to find pans with lip-shaped handles on each end as illustrated. Two wing-nut bolts through these handles will hold the pans tightly in place.

The gelatin compound may be purchased from duplicator supply houses or made from materials purchased from the local drug store or supermarket. Mix 8 teaspoons of plain dry gelatin (562) into 1¼ cups (563) of cold water in a double boiler. Allow the gelatin to soften. Next, place the pan over hot water on a slow fire until the gelatin is completely dissolved. Warm a pint of glycerin (564) in another pan. When the gelatin has dissolved, add the glycerin and allow it to cook over boiling water for at least twenty minutes. Carefully pour the gelatin mixture into one of the pans. Try to avoid causing bubbles on the surface. If bubbles do appear, scrape them to one side, using a piece of cardboard. Place the pan on a level surface and

(561)

(562)

(563)

(564)

allow the mixture to cool for twenty-four hours. The gelatin hectograph duplicator is now ready to use.

To produce quality lettering on the master, consult the chart on page 100 for recommended lettering techniques.

THERMOCOPY TRANSPARENCIES

POSITIVE- AND NEGATIVE-IMAGE TRANSPARENCIES

The thermocopy process, also known as thermal transfer, thermal copy, dry heat, and infrared, is the only copying process in which exposure and development are simultaneous. It is one of the simplest in both construction and operation. Only one step is involved: the insertion of a specially coated film and the original together into the exposure opening of the copying machine. The image is transferred from the original to the film in about four seconds. What actually takes place during this process is this: When the original (fully opaque or translucent)

is passed through the machine, the heat from the light source (infrared) penetrates through the thermocopy film to the original, which is made up of images containing some metallic substance and whose colors are visible to infrared light. The image areas absorb the heat from the infrared light; thus the "hot" image of the original forms an image on the film at the point of image contact.

Several types of transparencies can be produced with the thermocopy machine. Here is a brief description of each.

Positive-image Transparencies (565)

These transparencies produce an etched, black, or positive image on a clear or transparent color background.

Negative-image Transparencies (566)

These transparencies produce a white or color image on an opaque background when projected on the screen and are recommended where a change of pace is desired in a presentation.

Spirit Duplicator Thermocopy Acetate Master Transparency (567)

A specially coated transparent acetate spirit master for producing a projection transparency and also a master for reproducing paper copies on a spirit duplicator. The master must be processed with a thermocopy machine. Illustrations and instructions for this type of transparency can be found on pages 173–174.

Multicolor Transparencies (568)

Parlab Line and Tone films produce, on a single transparency, images in several colors. Illustrations and instructions for Parlab transparencies can be found on page 184.

Thermocopy Machines (569)

There are basically two types of thermocopy machines—one designed to reproduce an original made up of images, letters, and so forth, containing some metallic substance visible to infrared light, and one designed to reproduce originals not accepted by the infrared machine just mentioned. The 3M Company manufactures such a machine called a dry photo copier. Some models of thermocopy machines will accept bound documents, magazines, books, and other bulky printed materials.

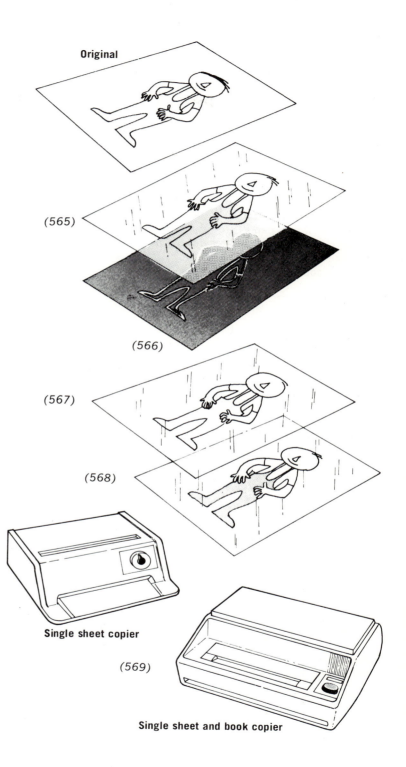

Original

(565)

(566)

(567)

(568)

Single sheet copier

(569)

Single sheet and book copier

181

Handmade Originals

The original from which a transparency is to be made may already be complete, such as a typewritten or mimeographed sheet, a page from a magazine, or a book illustration. When such an original is not available or when modifications of an original are desired, a number of techniques and aids can be used to produce an original. Pages 164–165 illustrate and discuss steps for planning and creating transparencies. Handmade originals can be made on drawing paper (or just plain white paper) (570) or on tracing paper (571), the latter making it possible to trace visuals easily from a variety of sources.

WHAT WILL COPY	WHAT WILL NOT COPY
Carbon-base inks	Most ball-point inks
Most printing inks	Most stamp-pad
Lead pencil	inks
Liquid writing	Color pencils
inks	Blue and violet
Typewriter ribbon	printing inks

Thermocopy Printed Originals

These are packets of original artwork (572) created and produced for making thermocopy transparencies. All that one must do to use them is to select the desired thermocopy film and pass both film and original through the copying machine; the result is a finished transparency ready for immediate projection. Printed originals are available in more than twenty subject areas at present. These areas include health, foreign languages, religion, mathematics, science, and social studies.

Magazines Containing Printed Originals Inserts

Magazines like *News Focus*, prepared by the editors of *Newsweek* magazine, and *Education Age*, published by the 3M Company, contain printed originals that

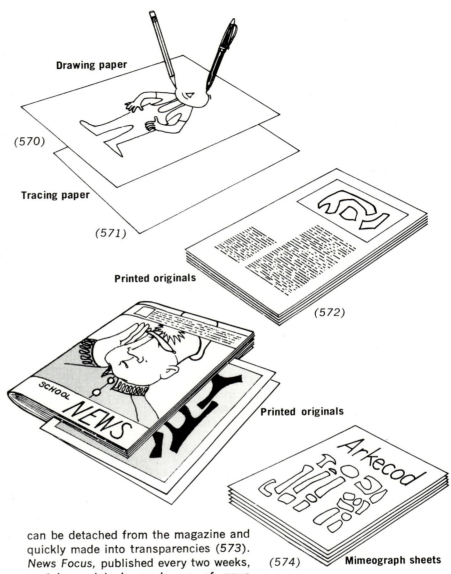

Drawing paper

(570)

Tracing paper

(571)

Printed originals

(572)

Printed originals

(574) **Mimeograph sheets**

can be detached from the magazine and quickly made into transparencies (573). *News Focus*, published every two weeks, contains originals made up of news photos, maps, tables, and charts of current events. In the event these publications are terminated, back issues may be requested from the publishers.

Mimeograph Sheets

Mimeograph (ink printing) sheets can be used as originals (574). Sheets with clear, dark images work best.

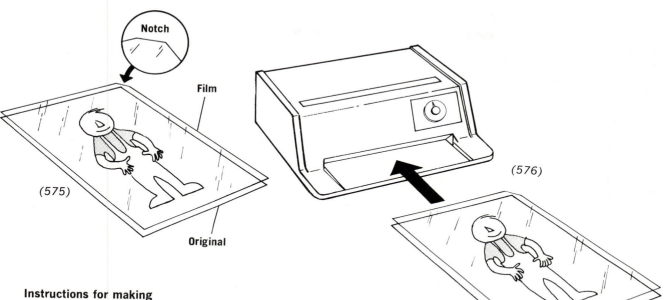

Notch

Film

(575)

Original

(576)

Instructions for making transparencies

1. Place a sheet of thermocopy film, with notch in upper right-hand corner (away from the operator) on top of the original (printed side up). Parlab films require an intermediate step (575).

2. Set the exposure dial midway between the setting for buff and the one for white (these settings apply to thermocopy papers). Some materials have greater latitude in exposure, and the midway point is therefore less critical. Refer to the instructions that come with each box of film for recommended exposure. Feed the film and original into the machine (576).

3. Retrieve film and original and separate them. Mount transparency if desired. Refer to pages 221–226 for mounting instructions (577).

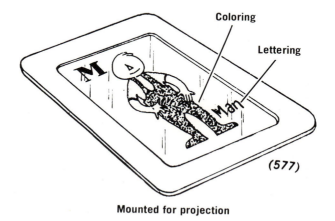

Coloring

Lettering

(577)

Mounted for projection

To add color, see pages 148–158.
To add lettering, see chart on page 100.
To add overlays, see page 224.

SELFKOTE THERMOCOPY
TRANSPARENCY

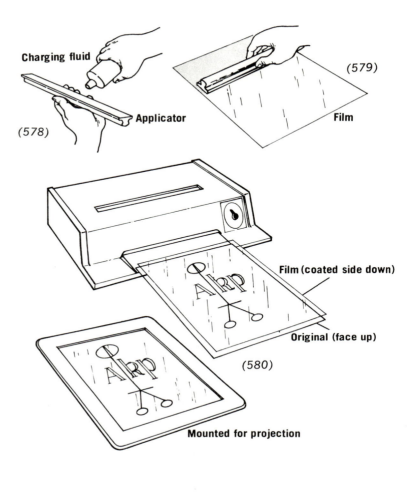

Charging fluid

(578)

Applicator

(579)

Film

ABM Business Automation, Inc., manufactures a thermocopy film that is treated for the thermocopy process by the user. A special charging fluid is applied to 5- or 7½-mil film and then used the same way as any other thermocopy film. Selfkote is considered by many to be superior in projection quality and clarity to many of the other types of thermocopy films. Moreover, this process is unique in that extra-heavy base transparencies (7½ mil) can now be made.

The result is a sharp, deep, black image on a clear background that is projected on the screen without halos.

Film (coated side down)

Original (face up)

(580)

Instructions

1. The bottle spout of the charging fluid is placed over the applicator pad and moved to its opposite end. This is sufficient charging for six to eight sheets of film. A bottle of charging fluid is sufficient for soaking the applicator pad about one hundred times (578).
2. Slide the fluid-soaked applicator pad from top to bottom over the film inside the opened box (579).
3. Place the coated side of the film on top of the original and insert in the thermocopy machine (try medium speed). Mount, if desired, for projection (580).

Mounted for projection

PARLAB MULTICOLOR
THERMOCOPY TRANSPARENCIES

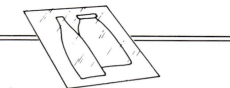

Parlab Line and Tone films produce, when color is applied, multicolor thermocopy transparencies for overhead projection. The Line film is used for making transparencies from high-contrast originals such as printed text, typewritten material, and ink or pencil line drawings. The Tone film provides a full range of intermediate tone values. It makes excellent copies of illustrations clipped from magazines and newspapers. See page 182 for information on types and preparation of originals for thermocopy processing.

A completed Parlab multicolor transparency passes through three stages: charging the original, exposing charged original with film, and applying color.

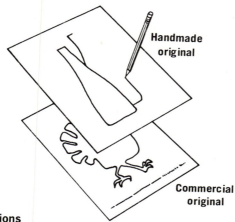

Handmade original

Commercial original

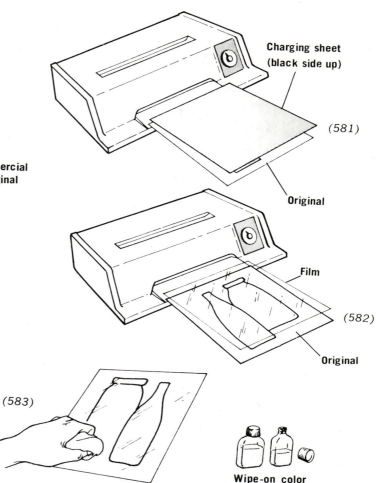

Charging sheet (black side up)

(581)

Original

Film

(582)

Original

(583)

Wipe-on color

Instructions

Set speed-control dial at a medium speed or at the setting for good copy on thermocopy "buff" paper.

1. *To charge the original,* place the charging sheet (black side up) on top of the original and pass through the thermocopy machines. Discard the charging sheet after use (581).

2. *To expose original with film,* place either side of Line or Tone film, depending on the type of original used, on top of the charged original. Pass through the machine. The exposed film will show a pale frosted image on a clear background. Both sides of the film accept images. Consult Parlab timing guide printed on the sheet of instructions with the film (582).

3. *To apply color* to Line film pour a small pool (about the size of a nickel) of Parlab wipe-on color directly on the film where color is desired and spread it with a soft pad of semiabsorbent material or a soft flat brush about an inch wide.

To apply color to Tone film, first apply color to the material used as the applicator. *Do not* pour the color directly on the film. For both films wipe color over the image repeatedly for fifteen or twenty seconds to secure full color depth in the image area, adding more color if necessary (583).

When different colors are to be used on separate parts of the image, use an artist's brush to color desired sections. Brush the color generously over small areas two or three times and blot off excess with soft paper tissue folded flat.

4. *To remove residual color* from the background use a pad of soft paper tissue soaked with water.

5. *To fix color* use Parlab scuff-coat liquid. Wipe on liquid with a clean cotton or cheesecloth pad. Wipe once over only, and let the film dry flat for fifteen or twenty seconds.

TRANSMATE THERMOCOPY TRANSPARENCY

Transmate film is basically an inexpensive thermocopy film that has several unique features. Either side of the film will accept a thermocopy image. It can be typed on without ribbon change or the use of carbon paper, and the message imprinted on the film may then be clearly projected. Transmate film can be written on with any ball-point and the color of the ink left on its surface will be projected on the screen. The same is true of nylon- and felt-point pens and markers.

Instructions

1. Set the thermocopy machine at a medium-slow speed. Place a sheet of Transmate film (either side) on top of the original and insert in the machine as illustrated. If the film sticks to the original, set the speed control at a slightly faster speed. On the other hand, if the film shows no reproduction (image), the speed was too fast; set the speed control at a slower speed (584).

2. If typing is desired, simply insert the film, with a white sheet of paper as a backing, in a typewriter and type directly on the film. Film can be cut into 2-inch strips for test purposes (585).

3. To write in color, use any ball-point or nylon-point pen. Testing different pens will determine which render the best color (586).

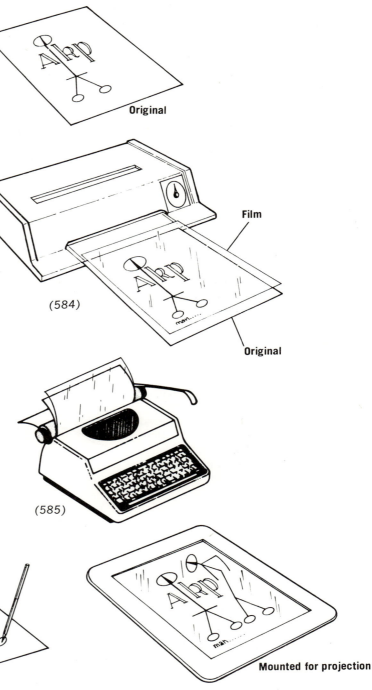

Original

(584)

Film

Original

(585)

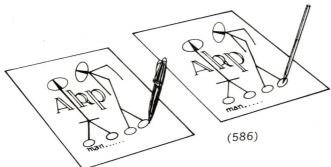

(586)

Mounted for projection

186

STENCIL DUPLICATOR
THERMOCOPY TRANSPARENCY

Stencils (mimeograph) can be made from an original that can reproduce in any standard thermocopy machine. A transparency for the overhead projector is a by-product of this technique. The stencil is a heat-sensitive unit which was designed for stencil (mimeograph) duplication. The copy (text), illustrations, etc., are "cut" into the stencil by running it through a thermocopy machine. The main requirement of the image on the original is that it must contain some metallic substance and colors must be visible to infrared light. Generally thermocopy machines will reproduce most printing inks, liquid writing inks, lead pencil, and typewriter ribbon.

Instructions

Make certain the carrier belt in the machine is clean, because a dirty belt will produce spotty stencils.

1. Preheat thermocopy machine, then set speed-control dial near the slowest speed (medium low). Make a test of original by using regular thermocopy paper. Stencil will reproduce as well as or better than the test paper.

2. Insert the original face up between heavy backing sheet and stencil. Do not remove self-carrier sheet (should there be one) from top of stencil set (587).

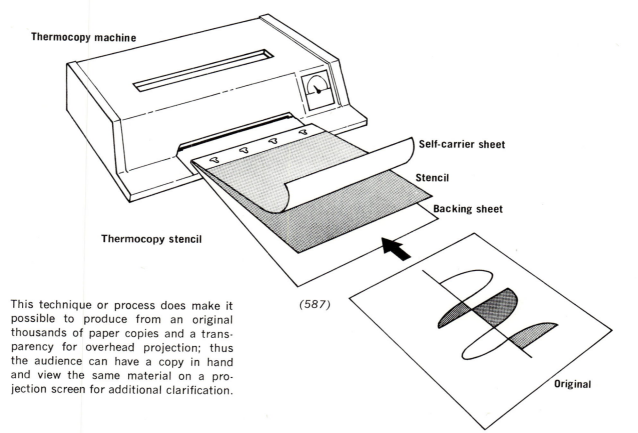

Thermocopy machine

Self-carrier sheet

Stencil

Backing sheet

Thermocopy stencil

(587)

Original

This technique or process does make it possible to produce from an original thousands of paper copies and a transparency for overhead projection; thus the audience can have a copy in hand and view the same material on a projection screen for additional clarification.

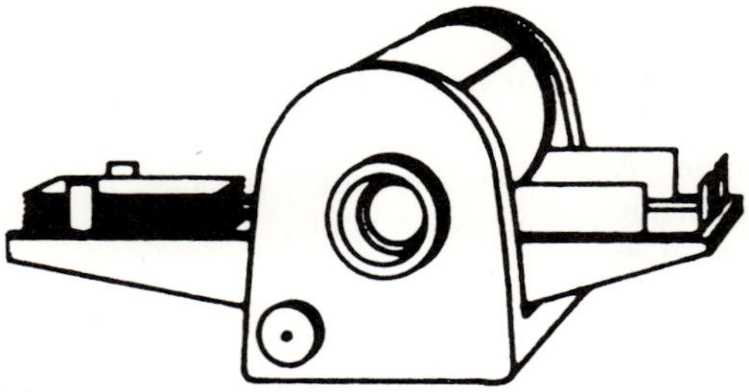

3. Pass the assembled materials through the machine the same as for any other material normally copied in the thermocopy machine. The stencil is now ready for the stencil (mimeograph) duplicator.

4. Run off the desired number of paper copies on the mimeograph duplicating machine (588).

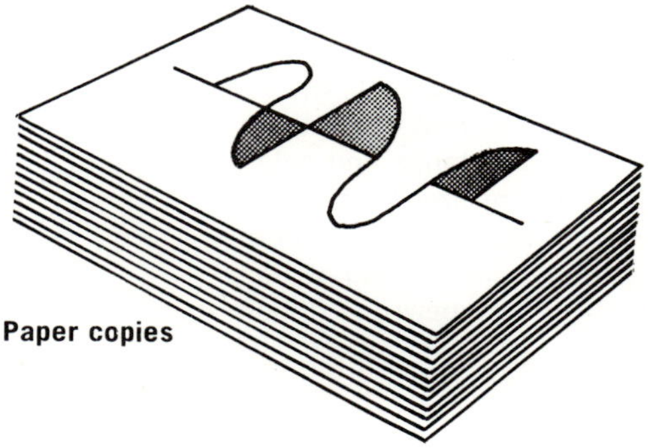

Because instructions may vary from one make of stencil to another, one should first read the instructions sheet that comes with the package of stencils.

To make a transparency for overhead projection, take the original and select the thermocopy film desired and make a copy in the same thermocopy machine (589). See page 183 for instructions.

Note: see THERMOCOPY STENCIL in the Index for sources.

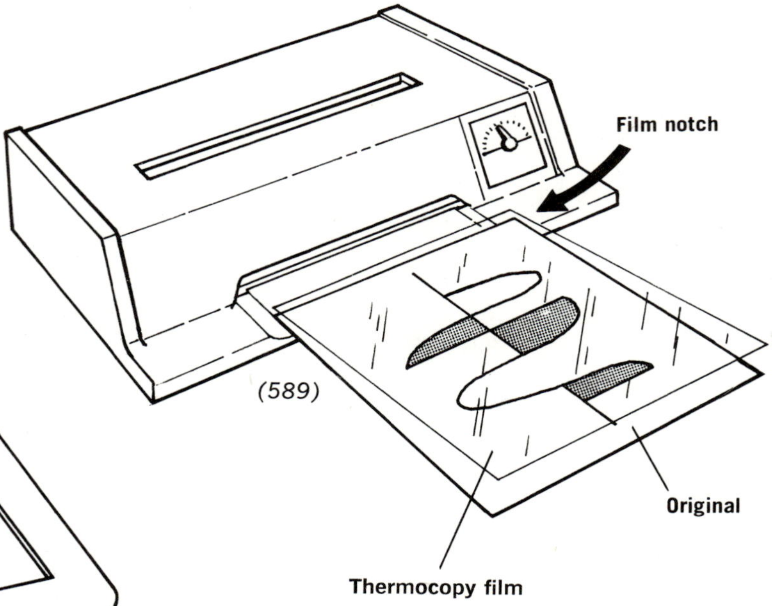

(588)

Paper copies

Film notch

(589)

Original

Thermocopy film

Mounted for projection

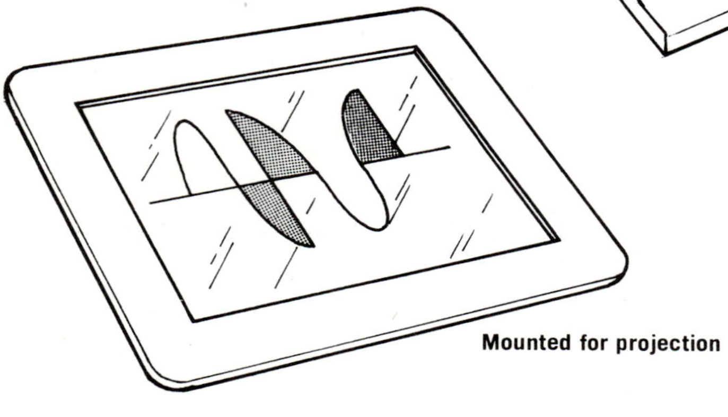

DIAZO TRANSPARENCIES

The diazo process is not new: it dates back to World War I when a serious shortage of photographic papers and films pointed up the need for a substitute reproduction process.

This process works on the principle of ultraviolet light passing through a translucent or transparent original (master), which destroys the chemical coating on the film (foil), except where an opaque image (line, letter, visual, etc.) has blocked the light. The exposed film is then developed, and the remaining chemical is converted into a visible image.

Diazo transparencies project in vivid colors far superior to those of many other techniques for producing projectables. For persons interested, additional history and information on the diazo process can be obtained from manufacturers and suppliers of diazo equipment and materials. These sources are listed in Chapter 6.

SINGLE-COLOR POSITIVE- AND NEGATIVE-IMAGE DIAZO TRANSPARENCIES

Preparation of Master

Several base materials can be used to prepare a master required for making a diazo transparency: tracing paper (590), clear acetate (591), matte acetate, to name a few. The base material must be able to permit light to pass through the area not covered with opaque lines. Affix the selected base material to the surface of the original and trace, or draw (freehand) directly on the surface. Clip-art books provide a good source of visuals that can be traced directly from the printed page. See pages 166–168 for information and instructions on the selection and use of base materials. Drawing should be done in india ink. Technical fountain, reservoir, standard Speedball, Hunt Bowl Pointed and Pel-

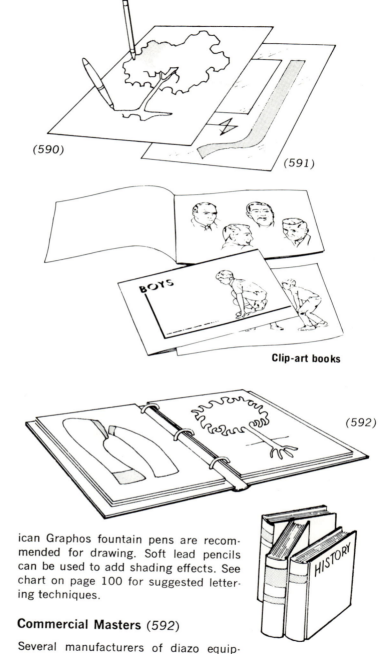

(590)

(591)

Clip-art books

(592)

ican Graphos fountain pens are recommended for drawing. Soft lead pencils can be used to add shading effects. See chart on page 100 for suggested lettering techniques.

Commercial Masters (592)

Several manufacturers of diazo equipment and materials produce printed masters for use in the preparation of diazo transparencies. Keuffel & Esser, for example, produces masters in the areas of history, physics, chemistry, technical graphics, geometry, and others.

Instructions

1. Place the appropriate color diazo film in contact with the handmade or commercial master, face to face. The face side (sensitized) of the diazo film is found by locating the notch in the upper right-hand corner of the film (see illustrations). Use the interleaf sheet, if white or with a white side, as a backup to the master during exposure. Place the white side of the sheet behind the film.

2. To expose (if the light source of the diazo machine is *above* the exposure stage), follow the foregoing instructions; then insert assembled materials in the machine (master on top of film), and expose the recommended time (593).

   To expose (if the light source of the diazo machine is *below* the exposure stage) (594a), follow the foregoing instructions; then insert the assembled materials (film on top of master), and expose the recommended time (594b).

3. After exposure, separate the film from the master and interleaf sheet. Roll the film with the sensitized (emulsion) side in and place in a large-mouth gallon-size jar (595) or insert film in the developing unit of the diazo machine, if it has one. If a large jar is used, soak a sponge or paper towel with strong ammonia water (28 percent is recommended) and place it in the jar. The ammonia can also be placed in a container as illustrated.

4. Mount, if desired, for projection. See pages 221–226 for tips on mounting.

Diazo Enlarger (596)

A specially designed enlarger for producing 8½- by 11-inch diazo transparencies from motion-picture film; 35mm filmstrips, 2- by 2-, 2¼- by 2¼- and 3¼- by 4-inch slides.

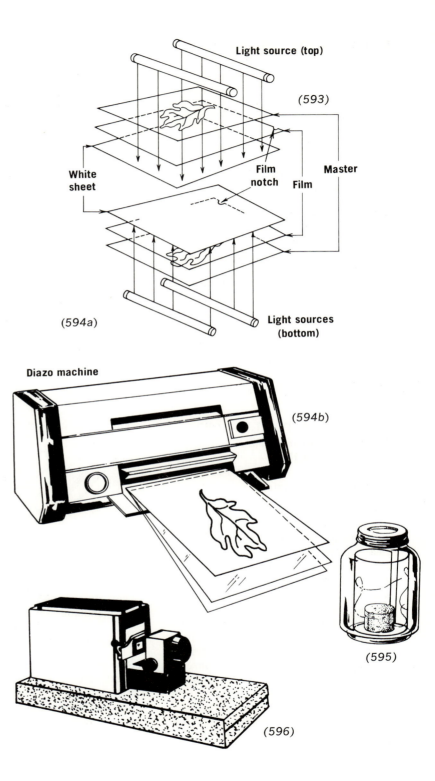

Light source (top)

(593)

White sheet

Film notch   Film   Master

(594a)

Light sources (bottom)

Diazo machine

(594b)

(595)

(596)

VARITYPER SYSTEM
DIAZO TRANSPARENCIES

This is a diazo process system which produces multicolor transparencies for projection by any method, or color visuals on white or aluminum paper for use in signs, charts, displays, etc. There are two types of VariTyper film—single-coated with only one side sensitized for image development and double-coated with two sides sensitized for image development.

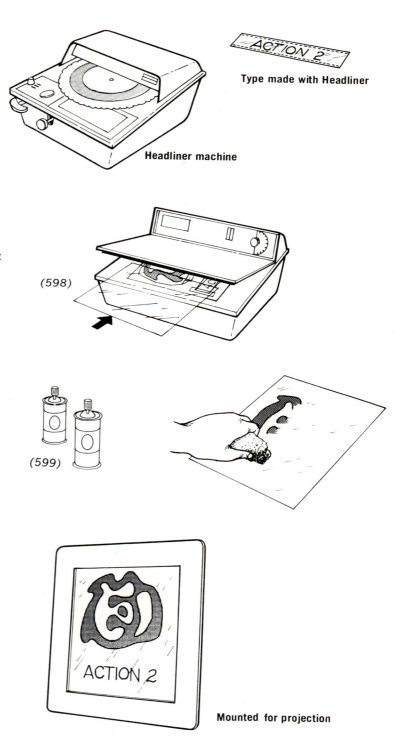

Type made with Headliner

Headliner machine

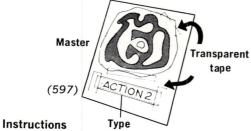

Master

Transparent tape

(597) Type

Instructions

1. Copy (type) can be composed on the VariTyper Headliner machine or by any technique that produces opaque letters on transparent film. Visuals must be drawn, photographically printed, dry transferred on clear acetate, or prepared by any technique which produces an opaque image on transparent acetate or film. Type and visuals are mounted (paste-up) on a clear sheet of acetate; this becomes the master (597).

2. Place a sheet of VariTyper film (sensitized side down) on top of master (face up), insert into printer, close pressure cover. Expose for recommended time (598).

3. Use the special colors contained in the VariTyper multicolor kit to develop the exposed film. The solution, which is in aerosol spray cans, is applied to cotton swabs and wiped on the faintly visible latent image areas; the color appears at once. Since the color is in the developer, it can be applied in any way on single sheets of film or paper for unlimited variety of effects (599).

(598)

(599)

Mounted for projection

ACTION 2

PHOTOGRAPHIC TRANSPARENCIES

There are numerous techniques and processes for producing projection slides and overhead transparencies photographically. Some processes require expensive equipment and professional know-how; they have purposely been eliminated from consideration in this book. From the less expensive processes have been selected several rather distinct approaches to the photographic preparation of projection slides and overhead transparencies.

The Canon/Kalvar slide system produces instant 35mm slides from 35mm negatives and black-and-white negatives from color slides. The equipment is fairly inexpensive and easy to operate. The process used by this system is much like conventional photography with the main difference that heat is used to process the special film.

In recent years the Polaroid Corporation has added a new dimension to the photographic field, a system for producing photographic slides in the camera. At present, two types of slides can be produced with this process: a line (high-contrast) 3¼- by 4-inch slide and a continuous-tone 3¼- by 4-inch slide.

The diffusion transfer process produces line (high-contrast) overhead transparencies from printed or drawn originals in any color within minutes. The equipment and materials are both inexpensive compared to many of the other processes.

The photostabilization process is truly one of the modern "instant" processes in that a line or continuous-tone photographic transparency can be produced in a matter of seconds. After exposing a special photographic film in the conventional way (camera, enlarger, and so forth), it takes about ten seconds to obtain a finished transparency.

The photographic techniques and processes that follow should provide inexpensive and easy-to-use means of producing high-quality photographic slides and overhead projection transparencies.

DIFFUSION TRANSFER TRANSPARENCY

Diffusion transfer is a photo-reflex copying process that produces a line-copy (high-contrast) transparency from printed or drawn original in any color within minutes (600). The original can be a single sheet or a page in a bound book or magazine. The transparency may be projected, displayed, or used as a master for diazo transparencies. The process involves photo-sensitized paper and film and a diffusion transfer machine. To produce a transparency, a negative photographic paper is exposed to a light source in contact with the original from which the transparency is to be made. A "reflex" exposure results (see illustration). The exposed negative paper is passed through a liquid photographic processing solution in contact with a sheet of positive transparent film. The latent image on the negative paper develops and then a positive image also develops and "transfers" onto the surface of the positive film. This is where the term diffusion transfer comes from. The instructions that follow will illustrate and explain this process in more detail.

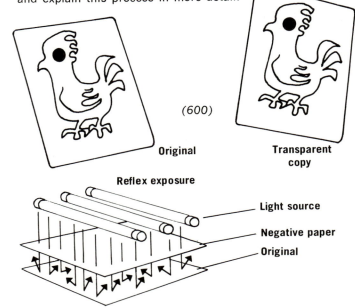

Original

(600)

Transparent copy

Reflex exposure

Light source

Negative paper

Original

**Single sheet and
bound originals**

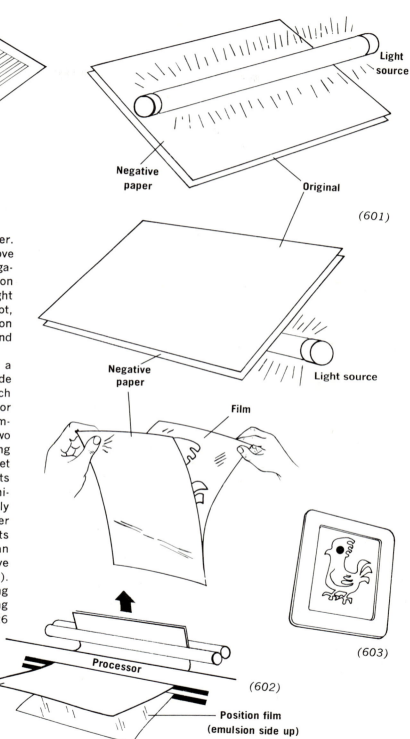

Light
source

Negative
paper

Original

(601)

Negative
paper

Light source

Film

(603)

Processor

(602)

Negative paper
(exposed side down)

Position film
(emulsion side up)

Instructions

1. Expose original with negative paper. If light source of machine is above the exposure slot, place the negative paper (emulsion side down) on top of the original. If the light source is below the exposure slot, place the negative paper (emulsion side up) next to the light source and next to the original *(601)*.

2. The exposed negative paper and a sheet of positive film (emulsion side of paper and film next to each other) are fed into the processor containing the processing chemicals. Twin rollers squeeze the two sheets together, thus transferring the image from the negative sheet to the positive film. The two sheets will emerge from the machine laminated together. Allow approximately twenty-five seconds for the transfer to be completed. Peel the sheets apart. Only one transparency can be made from the exposed negative paper, so discard the negative *(602)*.

3. After about two minutes of drying time, the film is ready for mounting and projection. See pages 221–226 for mounting instructions *(603)*.

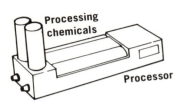

Processing chemicals

Processor

Film

Copy camera

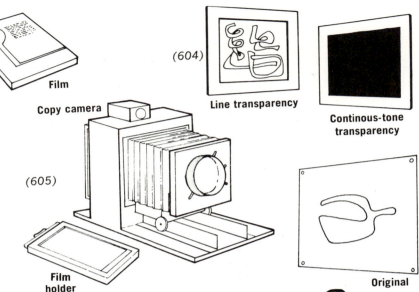

(604)

Line transparency

Continous-tone transparency

(605)

Film holder

Original

PHOTOSTABILIZATION TRANSPARENCIES

The photostabilization process offers a speedy alternative to conventional processing methods for silver halide films and papers which include developing, stopping, fixing, and washing. The photostabilization process reduces the processing steps to two, developing and fixing. After exposure by any of the conventional photographic means, it takes about ten seconds to obtain a stable line or continuous-tone transparency (604). All chemicals required for development of the latent image are contained in the emulsion of the specialized films. When an activator solution is applied to the surface of the film, exposed silver halides are converted to metallic silver. Immersion in a stabilizer solution dissolves the undeveloped halides, arrests development activity, and fixes the film. Processors carry out the processing steps automatically. Units are available to accept film and paper from 5 to 42 inches wide.

Instructions

1. Load photostabilization film (Foto-rite's Foto/Film is one recommended film) into film holder and copy original. Conventional film can be used and processed as instructed. If photostabilization film is used, it can be processed in the processor in seconds. Use this negative for projection or contact print on another piece of film for positive-image projection (605).

2. If a larger transparency is desired, use negative to enlarge image on a larger sheet of photostabilization film and process in processor (606).

3. After brief drying period, the transparency is ready for mounting and projection.

4. Properly stored, the transparency will last for several years without fixing. However, if lasting permanency is desired, immerse transparency, unmounted, in a fixing (hypo) solution for several minutes and then wash and dry (607).

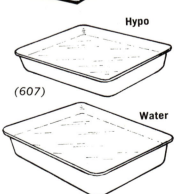

Photographic enlarger

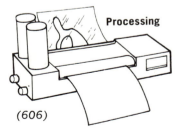

Processing

(606)

Instructions for photostabilization films will vary from brand to brand and should be carefully read before use.

Hypo

(607)

Water

CANON/KALVAR SLIDE SYSTEM

Here is a slide-making system that produces instant 35mm slides from negatives and black-and-white negatives from color slides. The system consists of two units, a printer and a developer. The printer has a magazine that holds over 500 feet of Kalvar film. The developer is a heat-producing processor. This process is much like conventional photography in that a negative is placed in contact with a sensitized film, exposed, and processed. The major difference is in the processing. The Canon/Kalvar system uses heat to process the exposed film. Moreover, Kalvar film is sensitive only to ultraviolet light and can be handled in normal room light.

The Canon/Kalvar system is ideal for duplicating slides and making instant microfilm copies. Detailed instructions and information related to this process can be obtained by writing directly to Canon U.S.A., Inc.

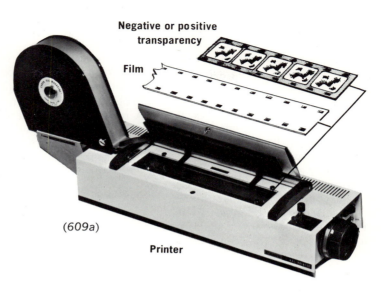

(609a)

Printer

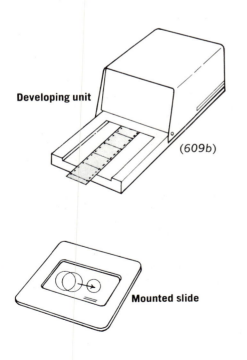

Developing unit

(609b)

Mounted slide

Instructions

1. The original negative (or color transparency or microfilm aperture card) is placed on the printer, emulsion side up (609a).
2. A length of Canon/Kalvar film is drawn from the magazine, cut with the slicing blade on the printer and placed in contact with the original.
3. The cover is closed and the proper exposure (based on the relative density of the original) is dialed.
4. Pressing the exposure button removes a filter from the ultraviolet lamps within the printer and exposes the Canon/Kalvar film for the programmed time (609b).
5. The Canon/Kalvar film is removed from the printer and fed into the developing unit.
6. The developed film is passed out of the developing unit in less than three seconds.

See pages 228–230 for slide-mounting techniques.

POLAROID LAND PROJECTION TRANSPARENCIES

The Polaroid Corporation, makers of the Polaroid Land camera, has developed a transparency (slide)-making system which produces a black-and-white slide on the spot. No darkroom or expensive equipment is required. All that is needed is a Polaroid Land camera and Polaroid Land projection film. This system is ideally suited for displaying information to a large audience, because the transparencies give a projected image of remarkable clarity and brilliance. At present there is a choice of films to make either line-copy or continuous-tone slides. These slides can be projected as large as 20 feet square with a standard lantern slide projector. They can also be shown with overhead projectors or trimmed and mounted for use with 2¼- by 2¼-inch and 35mm projection equipment. Regardless of the projection method, there is no loss of resolution, detail, or tone.

Polaroid Land Projection Films

Type 146-L for line copy (610)

Type 146-L film is very high-contrast material specifically designed to make lantern slides (3¼ by 4 inches) from line originals. This film fits all Polaroid Land roll film cameras using 40-series film, except the J66. As newer-model Polaroid cameras are developed, these specifications may be changed. Slides made with this film can be quickly and easily framed for projection with the Polaroid plastic slide mount 633 (see page 229 for instructions). The framed image area is 2⁷⁄₁₆ by 3¼ inches. Development time is ten seconds; ASA equivalent speed is 120. A roll of film produces eight transparencies. Consult the instructions that accompany film for any recent changes in development time and ASA rating.

Type 46-L for continuous-tone copy (611)

Type 46-L is designed for continuous-tone reproductions. This film produces slides with sharpness, brilliance, and range of tones. Type 46-L produces a horizontal image area 2⁷⁄₁₆ by 3¼ inches when framed in the Polaroid plastic slide mount 633 (see page 229 for instructions). Development time is two minutes; ASA equivalent speed is 800. A roll of film produces eight transparencies. Consult instructions that accompany film for any recent changes in development time and ASA rating.

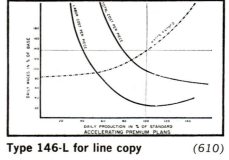

Type 146-L for line copy _(610)_

Type 46-L for continuous-tone copy _(611)_

Instructions

The instructions sheet included in the box of film will contain more detailed instructions than are included here.

EXPOSURE

1. *Snap it* by exposing the film as recommended on the instructions sheet (612). Make certain the camera is held horizontal to the subject matter, because lantern slide projectors always take the slide in a horizontal position.

DEVELOPMENT

2. *Pull tab* slowly but steadily (613); the development will start. A fast pull can create small pinholes in the dark areas of the picture. Hesitation during a slow pull can cause streaks across the image area. Type 146-L film requires about fifteen seconds of development time at 70°F (21°C); Type 46-L film requires two minutes at 60°F and above.

DEVELOPMENT

3. *Lift out* the positive transparency (614); the negative will remain in the camera. When the transparency is removed from the camera, the emulsion is soft and delicate, so care must be exercised. For best results, start removal at the cutout slot in the upper right-hand corner near the cutter bar. Tear out diagonally, from the lower left. Do not allow the transparency to fall back against the negative. Do not touch the image side before hardening.

SNAP IT　　　　(612)　　　**PULL TAB**

(613)　　　**LIFT OUT**　　　(614)

HARDENING

4. *Harden* and stabilize the transparency in the Dippit (615). This should be done within one hour after removal from the camera. For best results, allow the transparency to dry in the air two or three minutes before dipping, or wave the transparency vigorously for ten to fifteen seconds. Here are instructions for using the Dippit:

a. Open the hinged cover of the Dippit and carefully slide in the transparency as far as it will go. Hold the film by the tab.

b. Close cover of Dippit. Make certain the film tab comes out through the slot in the cover. Turn Dippit upside down and agitate for about twenty seconds (rock back and forth).

c. Turn Dippit right side up. With cover still closed, pull the film out with a rapid motion. The lips of the Dippit will squeegee excess liquid from the film.

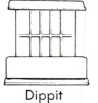

Dippit

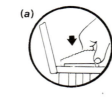

(615)

HARDEN

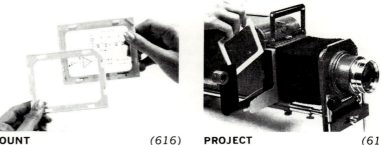

5. *Mount* transparency in a Polaroid plastic slide mount 633 (see page 229) (*616*).
6. *Project* in any standard lantern slide projector (*617*).

MOUNT   (*616*)   **PROJECT**   (*617*)

PICTURE TRANSFER TRANSPARENCIES

The picture transfer process is a method of converting materials printed on an opaque paper surface to transparent or translucent form. Images so converted become valuable as transparencies for light-box displays, as transparent backgrounds for terrariums and aquariums, as transparent lampshades, as diazo masters, and as many other transparent objects.

The process, however, has some limitations. The visual image to be converted should be printed on clay-coated paper. With paper of this type, a white "chalky" surface is coated over the porous absorbent paper fiber (*618*). This coating prevents the ink image from coming in contact with the actual paper. The picture transfer process is possible because the ink image is adhering to this rather unstable water-soluble "chalk" surface. A second limitation is the fact that the size is predetermined by the original printed image. The image cannot be enlarged or reduced by this process. Thirdly, the quality and condition of the original printed image determine the final quality of the transfer. Poor printing, blemishes, or foreign matter on the surface of the printed image will be transferred.

The basic principle of the picture transfer is rather simple. A clear acetate material coated with a transparent non-water-soluble adhesive is adhered to the printed surface (*619*). It is then placed in water. The water dissolves the unstable clay, releasing the ink image to the adhesive acetate surface (*620*).

With careful washing, the remaining clay residue is removed. For better transparency the adhesive side of the picture transfer is transparentized through a variety of methods including spraying with liquid plastic or laminating.

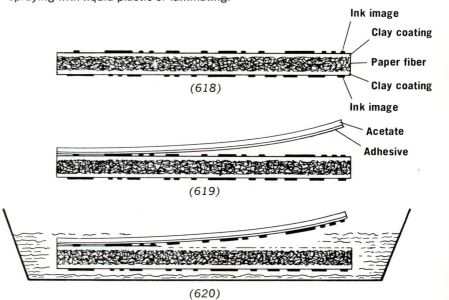

Ink image
Clay coating
Paper fiber
Clay coating
Ink image

(*618*)

Acetate
Adhesive

(*619*)

(*620*)

The various processes for making the picture transfer fall roughly into two categories: those using cold adhesive and those requiring heat to melt the adhesive surface. In a few instances both hot and cold methods are used in combination to form better adhesion. In all methods, pressure is an important element in guaranteeing a successful transfer. The pressure may be applied by hand, in a press, or through rollers to effect good contact and adhesion between the clear acetate and the printed surface.

The several picture transfer processes vary so that it is difficult to say which method is best. Some methods are inexpensive but require more time and ability on the part of the producer; some are easier to do but demand more expensive equipment and materials. The resulting transparencies from some of the methods are permanent, while others can be easily damaged.

Transparencies produced by the heat methods tend to hold more precise detail than those made by using cold adhesives. Audience surveys show, however, that transparencies made by the cold method tend to be slightly more pleasing to view. This difference in appearance is undoubtedly due to the fact that a slight spread of the halftone dot pattern of the printed picture occurs with the cold fluid adhesive, causing a slight blending of colors and tone values. Some of the picture transfer methods permit ease in lifting visual imagery from both sides of the page through the process of splitting the printed page in half. By some methods, dry transfer images and lettering can be added before the transfer process begins. Those interested in the manipulation of picture content where visual elements of one printed picture are added to another will find possibilities in some of the picture transfer processes. If it is done properly, the manipulation that has taken place cannot be detected in the resulting transparency. With a knowledge of the strengths and weaknesses of the various methods of picture transfer, one can produce a great variety of visual materials for projection and display.

RUBBER CEMENT PICTURE TRANSFER TRANSPARENCY

Although there are several methods of making a picture transfer, the use of rubber cement is one of the least expensive methods. This technique does, however, demand a certain amount of skill. If care is taken to choose the proper type of picture, to work under clean conditions, and to apply the rubber cement carefully, excellent results can be expected.

(621) Materials and equipment: cotton; plastic spray; pan of cool water; fine steel wool; mild liquid soap; soft-bristle paint brush; clear genuine rubber cement and rubber cement thinner; razor blades; acetate sheets; overhead transparency mounts; clean newsprint.

INSTRUCTIONS

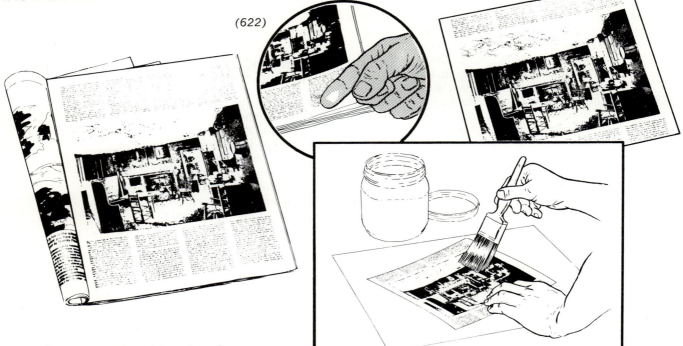

(622)

(623)

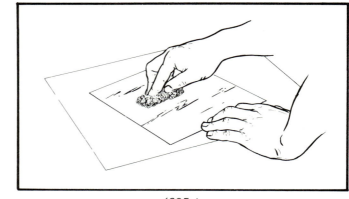

(624)

The success of a picture transfer depends upon whether the paper upon which the picture is printed is clay-coated or not. To check for clay coating, rub an unprinted area with a moistened finger. A white, chalky residue appearing on the finger is a good indication the paper is clay-coated (622). Trim the picture larger than area to be used (623). Apply a thin, even coat of rubber cement to the face of the printed page (624). Care must be taken to avoid getting dirt or dust in the cement.

Cut a sheet of acetate about the size of the picture or slightly larger. Lightly etch one side of the acetate (625a) with fine-grade steel wool, using smooth, even strokes. When etching is completed, remove any resulting dust. Next, apply a thin, even coat of rubber cement to the etched surface of the acetate (625b). To assure better adhesion, it is advisable to brush the rubber cement onto the two surfaces at 90° angles to each other.

(625a)

When both rubber cement surfaces are thoroughly dry, they are ready to adhere together. Lay the picture face up on a smooth, clean surface. Hold the coated acetate with coated side down above the picture. Bend it into a U shape (626). Carefully lower the acetate onto the picture surface, making sure the acetate is centered over the area to be used. Let the two surfaces make contact in the center and then firmly press down on the two edges of acetate until both surfaces are completely in contact. Next, with the finger, press the two surfaces together with a firm pressure going from center out in all directions (627). This should help eliminate air pockets. To assure absolute contact, turn the "sandwich" over on a clean, smooth surface so that the back side of the picture is up. With a new sharp razor blade held at an angle, draw with a firm pressure from the center outward in all directions (628). Be sure the entire surface is pressed into contact by this method.

(625b)

(626)

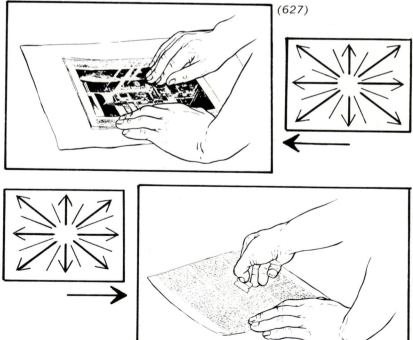

(627)

(628)

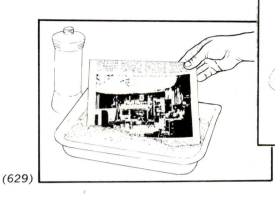

(629)

(630)

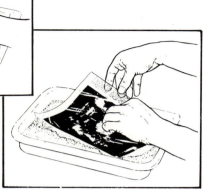

(631)

Place the "sandwich" into a pan of cool soapy water (629). The soap will speed up soaking time. Thicker paper will require longer time in the water. When the paper is completely saturated with water, gently peel the paper from the acetate (630). Care must be taken along the edges of the "sandwich" not to tear any rubber cement that might cling to the paper edge. If any paper fiber remains on the rubber cement surface, rub over it gently with the finger tip. It will generally release and wash off. When the paper has been removed, a milky chalk still remains on the picture transfer. Gently wash this off with a ball of cotton and plenty of soapy water (631). Excess water may be removed from the transparency by blotting with a paper towel.

Hang up the transparency to dry. Allow about thirty minutes for this step

(632). When dry, the rubber cement side of the transparency will have a frosty appearance. The rubber cement will be very easy to damage, so handle it with care. Next, place the picture down on a smooth, dry surface with rubber cement side up. Tape down the four corners. To make this surface more transparent and to protect the surface, spray this side with a clear plastic spray (633). Hold the spray can about 10 inches above the transparency and spray back and forth to apply an even coating of plastic. Allow it to dry thoroughly.

Even though the rubber cement surface has been protected by plastic spray, it is still susceptible to damage. It is best to cover it with a piece of clear

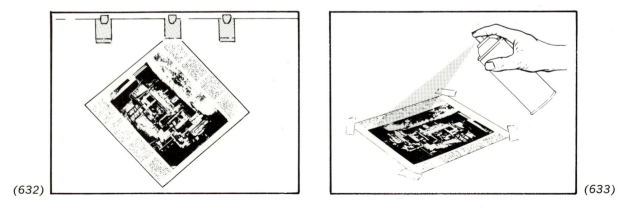

(632)

(633)

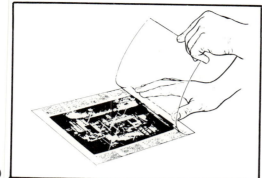

(634)

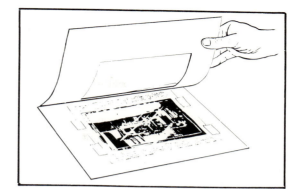

(635)

acetate for protection (634). Bind the transparency between two overhead transparency mounts. If the transparency is of an odd size, it is relatively easy to cut the frames from 8- or 10-ply cardboard. The opening should be slightly smaller than the transparency. Tape the entire "sandwich" firmly to one frame (635). Lay the other frame over the top and tape along the edges (636). A frame constructed in this manner will be very durable. The wide borders afford a handy place to write any pertinent information or instructions concerning the transparency.

(636)

Points to Remember:

Thin rubber cement with rubber cement thinner, so that it will run freely from the brush.

Use a wide, soft-bristle brush for ease of application.

Use commercially frosted acetate when possible to help alleviate problems of dust. Use .005-inch thick acetate for best results.

Work on a clean, smooth, dry surface.

Be sure that both rubber cement surfaces are absolutely dry before placing them in contact.

Be sure to use good-quality pictures that are free of creases or surface flaws.

Always test for a clay-coated printing surface.

Avoid using transparencies smaller than the 3¼- by 4-inch size.

COLD LAMINATING ACETATE PICTURE TRANSFER TRANSPARENCY

Transparencies in full color or black and white can be made with cold laminating acetate used as a base material. This type of acetate is transparent and has a pressure-sensitive adhesive on one side. Printed matter on clay-coated paper, combined with pressure-sensitive acetate, can be processed to produce quality transparencies for projection or light-box display.

To assure a successful picture transfer, a test must be made to determine if the picture has been printed on clay-coated paper. This can easily be determined by gently rubbing a moist finger on an unprinted area of the page (637). A white, chalky residue appearing on the finger is a good indication that the paper is clay-coated. Be sure the picture is free of all creases, abrasions, oily or waxy smudges and is good-quality printing. Carefully remove the picture from the magazine (638), being sure extra margin areas are left around the image area. Next, cut laminating acetate the same size as the picture to be transferred. Peel the glassine paper (639) from the acetate.

MATERIALS AND EQUIPMENT

COLD LAMINATING ACETATE	PAPER TOWELS
COMB OR RAZOR BLADE	PLASTIC SPRAY
PAN OR WATER	TRANSPARENCY MOUNTS
COTTON	TAPE
LIQUID SOAP	CLEAR ACETATE
MAGIZINE VISUAL	

Chalky residue

(637)

(638)

Acetate   Glassine paper

(639)

(640)

(641)

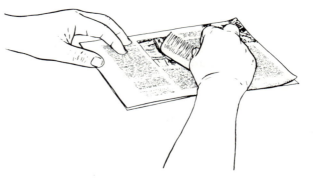

(642)

(643)

With the sticky side of the cold laminating acetate down, bend the acetate in a U shape and gently lower it down onto the face of the visual (640), pressing it in a down and outward direction. Next, gently rub acetate down (641) from center to outer perimeter of the picture. Do this gently so that any air that might be trapped beneath the acetate can escape.

Turn the visual over onto a smooth, clean surface so the acetate face is down. Using a firm pressure, rub the entire surface with the flat, smooth side of a comb or razor blade held at an angle (642). It is best to systematically rub from the center in an outward direction. Avoid cutting or tearing the paper surface. Next, place the visual into a pan of cool soapy water and allow it to soak for a few minutes (643).

Gently peel paper from acetate

(644). If peeling is difficult, return the paper and acetate to water for additional soaking. After paper is removed, return picture transfer to water and gently wash off clay residue (645) from transfer side with cotton or soft tissue.

(645)

(644)

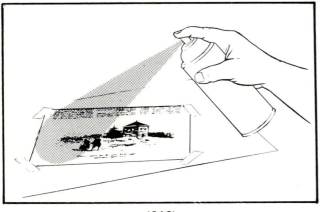

(646)

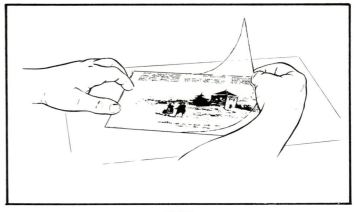

(647)

If care is taken, excessive moisture may be blotted from the picture transfer with paper towels. However, it may also be hung to dry. When dry, the adhesive side will have a dull appearance. Next, spray the dull side of the transparency with clear plastic spray (646). Because of the constant flow of new materials on the market, caution should be taken in the spraying of material of this type. The plastic spray may dissolve the adhesive and cause destruction of the ink transfer. It is wise, therefore, to run a test to see if the spraying process is safe to use. If it is not, it is often possible to use another piece of the same type of acetate to cover the tender image; the acetate will serve as a protection and a transparentizer of the surface.

Hold the spray can about 10 inches above the transparency and spray across the transparency in smooth, horizontal movements from top to bottom. If sprayed properly, the surface of the transparency should have a slick appearance. Be sure to work on a smooth, level surface to avoid "runs." Allow the sprayed transparency to dry. To give the tender sprayed side of the transparency extra protection, place a piece of clear acetate over it (647).

Bind the transparency in a cardboard mount for protection and ease of use (648). The picture transfer is now completed and ready for use (649).

(648)

The First Church in Philadelphia, late 17th Century.

(649)

COLD LAMINATING MACHINE
PICTURE TRANSFER
TRANSPARENCY

Equipment: film laminator (cold process)
Film: cold laminating acetate

In addition to the processes of picture transfer using rubber cement and adhesive-backed acetate is the method of using a film laminator (cold process). A pressure-sensitive adhesive-coated laminating film is pressed onto the ink image by two motor-driven rollers. This assures good, even contact between the ink and the film. By this process some variations in picture transfer are possible that are not easily accomplished by some other methods. The equipment used for this process is a light portable film laminator (cold process) (650). It contains two rollers that rotate in contact with each other at a very high, even pressure. The film used is cold laminating acetate.

As with all other picture transfer processes, the printing must be on clay-coated paper. A simple test for clay coating is to moisten a small unprinted area of the paper. If with slight rubbing a white chalky residue appears, this is a fairly reliable indication that the paper surface is clay-coated. The picture may be printed in color or black and white. Two different weights of laminating film on a special paper support are used for each picture transfer. The lighter-weight film is used first in the process.

Take a sheet of the lighter-weight film. Lay it face up on the bed of the machine. With the special switch, turn the rollers just enough to catch and hold the end of the film and its backing. Now carefully pull the film from its backing and curl it back over the top of the machine (651). Lay the picture to be transferred face up on the backing sheet (652). Be sure the picture is lying flat. Any wrinkles, dirt, or imperfections on the picture surface will prevent the final product from being perfect. Turn on the

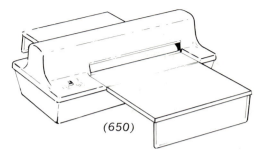

(650)

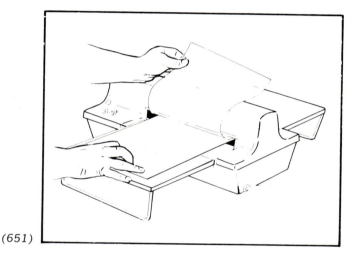

(651)

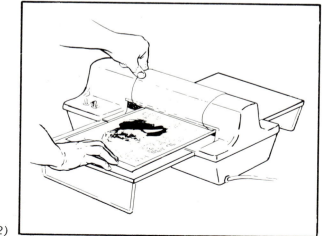

(652)

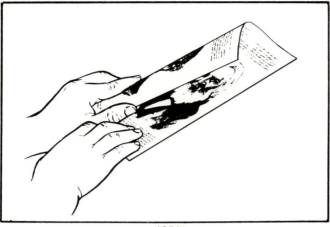

(653)

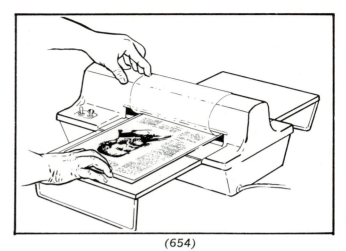

(654)

motor and allow the picture to pass between the rollers. Hold the film firmly so that the rollers press it onto the picture surface. Always be careful to check to see that the rollers are free of dirt or other foreign matter before use.

To show an important feature of this type of picture transfer let us assume that there are visual images on both sides of the page to convert into transparent form (653). At this point we have applied laminating acetate to only one side of the page. By following the same procedure, apply a sheet of cold laminating acetate to the reverse side (654). Both sides of the page will now be covered with a sheet of film. Trim all

excess film from around the page.

The next step is to split the two pages apart. With a razor blade or other sharp instrument, make a slit in one corner between the two laminated surfaces. (A small scrap of paper inserted in the corner first before the second side is laminated will simplify the problem of starting the splitting process). Carefully take hold of each corner of the two sides and pull slowly (655), with an even force. In this manner it is possible to split the printed page in half. The two sides of the page will now be separated and can be made into two separate transparencies (656).

At this point the split pages are

(655)

(656)

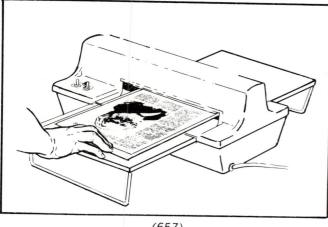

(657)

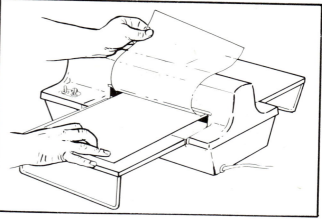

(658)

placed into cool soapy water. After a short period of soaking, the remaining paper fiber is peeled off. With a ball of cotton wash off the excess clay from the adhesive surface. As long as the adhesive is wet, it will not have sticky characteristics.

By placing the wet transfer back onto its backing paper as it was in its original state (adhesive side in contact with backing paper) it may again be run through the rollers to wring out the moisture (657). A couple of paper towels under the machine will absorb any excess moisture that may accumulate. After the transfer has passed through the rollers for drying, remove it from the backing paper. Place a second sheet of laminating acetate (heavier weight) in the press. With the lead edge pinched between the rollers, peel back the adhesive-coated acetate as was done previously (658).

Place the transfer with adhesive side up on the backing sheet (659). Make sure it is lying absolutely flat. Turn on the motor. Pull gently on the adhesive sheet as the material is drawn through the rollers. This prevents the formation of folds or wrinkles. Trim the picture to the desired size and mount (660) in the appropriate frame for projection. See pages 221—226 for mounting instructions.

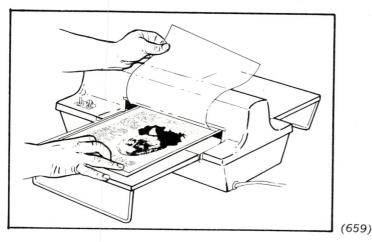

(659)

(660)

HEAT LAMINATING
MACHINE PICTURE TRANSFER
TRANSPARENCY

Equipment: film laminator (heat process)
Film: heat laminating acetate

Although originally designed strictly for lamination, the heat laminating machine is one of the fastest and best methods for making transparencies from printed material. As with all picture transfer methods, the picture must be printed on clay-coated paper stock. A simple test to check whether paper is clay-coated is to moisten the tip of your finger and gently rub an unprinted area of the paper from which you want to make the transfer. If a white, milky, residue forms on your finger, you can be quite certain the paper is clay-coated and the printed image will transfer. Both black-and-white and colored pictures can be used. Colored pictures tend, however, to result in somewhat better-quality transparencies.

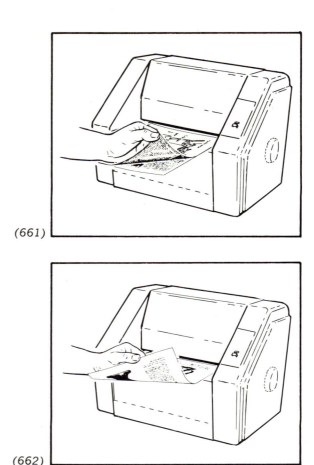

(661)

Since in most cases the heat laminating machine laminates both sides of a page simultaneously, it is possible to make two transparencies at one time. This can be done by placing two printed pictures of the same size back to back as they are fed into the machine (661). As they pass between the two heated rollers, a thin laminating film is applied to both outer surfaces. When the excess film is trimmed off, the two pictures will separate and have only the desired surfaces laminated. A similar situation occurs when you have a page with pictures on both sides (662) from which you want to make transparencies, and you simply pass the page through the laminator. Always make sure that the surface of the picture is free of any foreign matter such as lint or dust before placing it in the machine. At this point it is wise to pass the material through the laminator a second time (663) to give it a double coat of lamination. (With the page doubly laminated on both sides, it

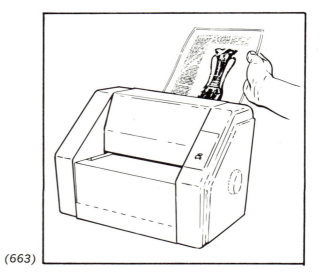

(662)

(663)

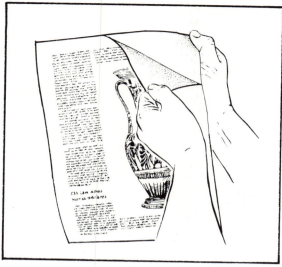

(664)

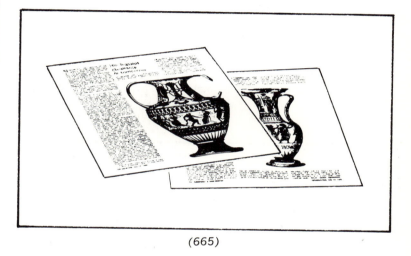

(665)

is possible to split the page in half so that the printing on the two sides will be on two separate sheets. It is difficult, however, to get a start in separating the two laminated sides. If before passing the printed page through the laminator a corner or edge of the page is turned over about ¼ inch, this, when the laminated page is trimmed, will furnish a small separation of the two laminated surfaces, permitting ease in splitting the page.) As the laminated page emerges from the machine the second time, trim off the excess film flush with the page. The corner or edge turned over prior to lamination will now present a place where both surfaces of laminating film can be grasped between the fingers.

With an even, steady pull you can separate the two film layers, thus splitting the paper page in two (664). Now both sides of the page become potential material for transparencies (665).

Place the laminated picture in warm water containing a little liquid soap. This will soften the clay between the paper and the film. When the paper is well saturated with water, strip it off (666). Allow additional soaking time for

(666)

any resistant areas. When the paper has been completely removed, wash off any remaining clay from the ink and film surface with soft cotton (667). Rinse the transparency in clean water. The film may be dried by blotting with paper towels, or it may be air-dried by hanging it up.

When it is dry, pass the transparency through the machine (668), laminating it the third time to protect the ink image and add more rigidity to the transparency. As a final step, mount the transparencies as desired for projection or display (669). See pages 221–226 for mounting instructions.

Very closely related to the method just explained is that used in the thermocopy process. The thermocopy machine, being a heat copying machine, is ideal for use with thermocopy laminating acetate.

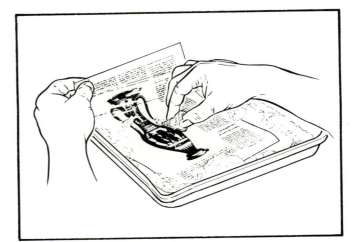

(667)

(668)

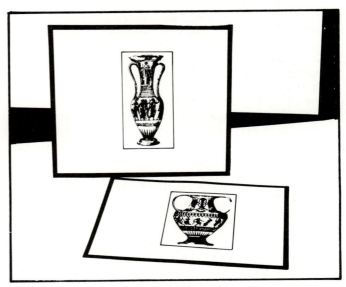

(669)

(670) Equipment and materials: Seal Transpara-Film; paper towels; pan and water; plastic spray; liquid soap; cotton; dry mounting press; felt pad; pressed-wood board; two metal plates.

DRY MOUNTING PRESS PICTURE TRANSFER TRANSPARENCY

By using a dry mounting press with a special transfer film (Seal Transpara-Film), black-and-white and color transparencies of excellent quality can be made. The success of this process depends upon correct use of heat and pressure. A picture transfer transparency produced by the heat process is one of the most durable. As in all picture transfer processes, this form of transparency is an excellent master for reproduction by the diazo process on film or paper.

Because this process depends upon heat and pressure to ensure a good image transfer, a special "sandwich" (671) must be used in the dry mounting press. This "sandwich" is made up of two smooth metal plates (a, c) such as cookies sheets or photographic ferrotype plates. They must be clean and free of any blemishes. These two plates tend to distribute the heat evenly over the entire sandwich area. A felt pad (b) serves to cushion any small blemishes, flaws, or irregularities in the printed paper image or the transfer film. The ¼-inch pressed-wood board (d) furnishes extra even pressure. It must be noted at this point that too much pressure can damage the press. Most presses have provisions for normal pressure adjustment. The press

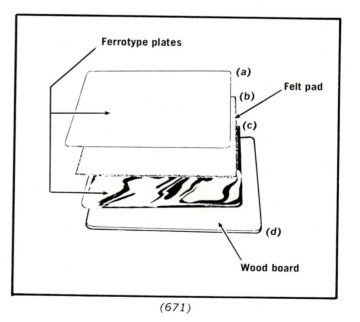

Ferrotype plates

(a)

Felt pad

(b)

(c)

(d)

Wood board

(671)

should close with an even pressure but should not require extra force. Set the temperature of the press at about 275°F to 300°F. To ensure a good picture transfer, the sandwich must be preheated. Insert it into the press for a period before use so that it will be up to temperature. Do not close the press but allow the heating element to rest loosely on the "sandwich" (672).

Choose a picture of good printing quality with no blemishes (673). As with other picture transfer processes, the printing must be on clay-coated paper. To test, rub a moist finger on an unprinted area of the page. If a chalky residue appears on the finger, you can be fairly certain that the paper is coated. After the sandwich is heated up to temperature, insert the picture and special film between the felt and metal plate (674). Have the back of the transfer film down on the metal plate and the image face down on the adhesive side of the film. Be sure the surface of the film does not extend beyond the material to be transferred. If the coated side of the film extends beyond the paper, it will adhere to the felt pad.

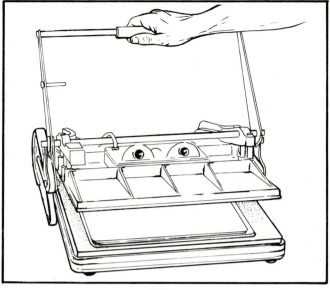

(672)

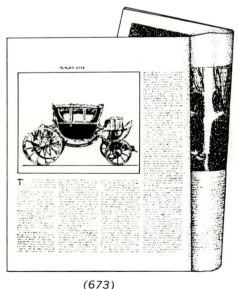

(673)

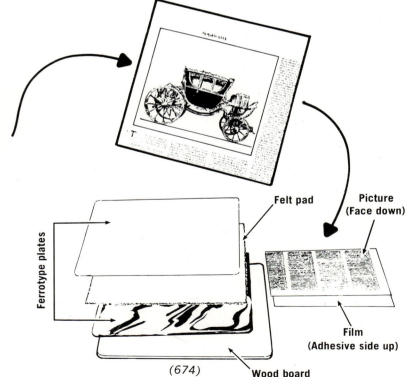

(674)

Ferrotype plates

Felt pad

Picture (Face down)

Film (Adhesive side up)

Wood board

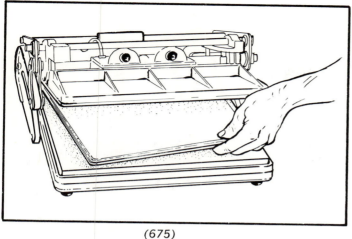

(675)

(676)

Place the sandwich carefully in the press, being sure that there is a good firm pressure (675). After about five to seven minutes carefully remove the picture from the press (676). A quick check of the surface should find it bright and glossy. If frosty areas appear, quickly return the picture to the press as before for further heating. (If the picture transfer cools, it is difficult to return it to the press without damaging the ink surface.) After the picture is removed from the heat, it will tend to curl. Do not force it open.

Place the picture transfer into cool or lukewarm soapy water (677). As the paper becomes wet, it will uncurl. Thicker or heavily inked papers will take longer soaking time than thinner material. When the paper is completely saturated, check to see whether the paper will peel from the film (678). If peeling is difficult, allow a longer soaking period.

(677)

(678)

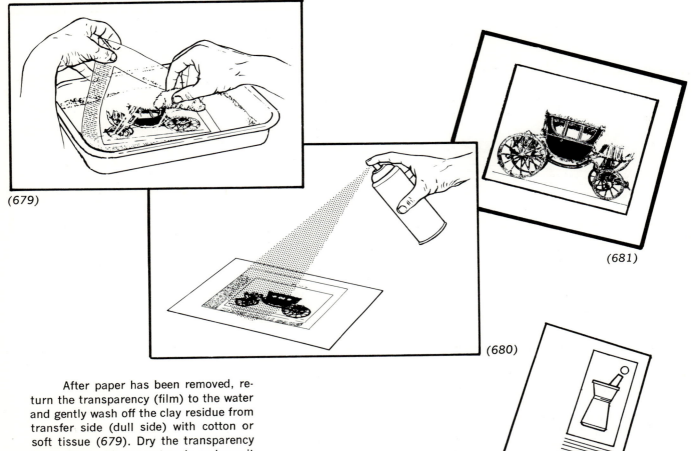

(679)

(680)

(681)

(682)

After paper has been removed, return the transparency (film) to the water and gently wash off the clay residue from transfer side (dull side) with cotton or soft tissue (679). Dry the transparency by blotting with paper towels or hang it up to dry. When the film is completely dry, the dull side will have a slightly ''ashy'' appearance.

Spray the dull side of the film with clear plastic spray (680). This will make the image on the film more transparent and will provide a protective coating for the transfer side. Tape the film down to a flat, clean surface for spraying. Hold spray can about 10 inches above the film surface and spray in a systematic pattern back and forth to apply an even coat of plastic. Allow it to dry thoroughly. For added protection, cover the image side of the film with clear acetate and bind in an overhead transparency mount (681). See pages 221–226 for mounting instructions.

ELECTRONIC STENCIL CUTTER TRANSPARENCY

Here is a technique for producing a high-quality image of printed and visual material on both a stencil and a sheet of transparent film at the same time. The original (682) can be anything from a page from a book to drawings, or even paste-up artwork that includes photographic halftones. The electronic stencil-cutting machine produces a stencil and a finished transparency for immediate projection.

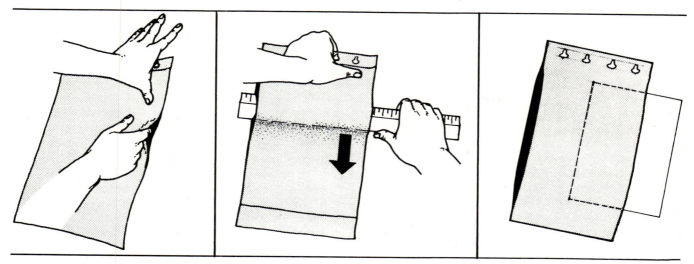

(685a)

Instructions

The Gestetner Corporation has prepared a booklet, *How to Make a Paste-Up Layout for Your Gestefax,* which contains instructions and illustrations for preparing artwork for the electronic stencil cutter. Refer to pages 32–34 for tips on paste-up techniques.

1. Carefully separate the stencil from the backing sheet, starting at a point approximately 3 inches from the top right side of the stencil (*683*). Peel just enough of the stencil to insert a ruler.
2. Insert, with care, a ruler in the opening created between the stencil and the backing sheet (*684*). Gently push the ruler to the opposite side of the stencil, then move the ruler downward about 11 inches. This will create a "pocket" in which the film is inserted.
3. Place a sheet of Gestefax overhead transparency film in the "pocket" (*685a*). Thermocopy and most other clear acetate sheets can be used as substitutes for the Gestefax film.
4. Attach stencil, with film inserted, to the stencil drum in the usual manner (*685b*). Use regular settings required for the type of material reproducing. Start the machine.

Original

Stencil

(685b)

Electronic stencil cutter

5. After the stencil has been cut, detach from stencil drum and remove film (686). It is now ready for immediate use on the overhead projector.

To add color, see pages 147–158.
To mount or mask, see pages 221–226.
To add lettering, see page 100.
To add motion, see section below.

6. The "cut" stencil can be attached to a mimeograph duplicator and hundreds of paper copies can be made from it (687).

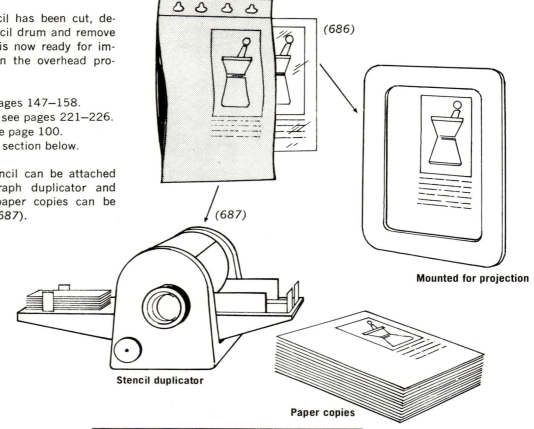

(686)

Mounted for projection

(687)

Stencil duplicator

Paper copies

POLARIZED TRANSPARENCIES

A new dimension can be added to overhead projection transparencies with the use of polarizing (Technamation) materials (688). Almost any existing or new original overhead transparency can be made into an exciting instructional medium. Polarizing is an invaluable technique in conveying concepts of sequence, flow, and cause and effect. Even subject matter that is considered static in content can be made more interesting and exciting with the application of polarized materials. In addition to polarized material applied directly to the surface of the transparency, all that is needed is a manual- or motor-driven polarized spinner; the result is a projected transparency with "motion."

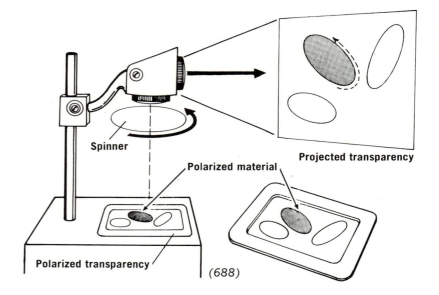

Spinner

Projected transparency

Polarized material

Polarized transparency

(688)

Instructions

1. Place the finished transparency, less the polarizing material, on a viewing light box (light table or tracing board) or on the stage of the overhead projector. This will provide a light source for analyzing the transparency for polarizing and for the actual placement of the material (689).

2. Select the desired polarizing (Technamation) material with the aid of a manual spinner. This can be done by placing the sample sheet (Technamation demonstration plate) on the stage of the projector or by holding it up to a light source and rotating spinner (690).

3. Place the desired motion material over the area to which motion is to be added; and while holding it firmly in place, take a pencil and trace an outline in the desired shape. Use a straightedge where straight cuts are desired. Press hard enough with the pencil to make a clear outline for final cutting (691).

4. Cut out the motion material with a pair of sharp scissors. Before removing the backing sheet, place the material on the transparency area to be animated to check the fit (692).

5. Remove backing sheet and, with the point of cutting knife wrapped with a piece of pressure-sensitive tape (sticky side out), pick up the motion material (knife tip on top) and position on the transparency as desired. Press material firmly in place; it will bond on contact (693).

Detailed instructions and information on this technique can be obtained from manufacturers and distributors of polarizing (Technamation) materials and equipment listed in Chapter 6.

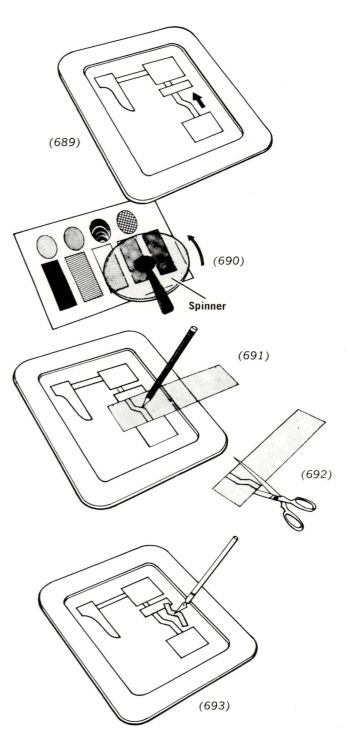

(689)

(690)

Spinner

(691)

(692)

(693)

XEROGRAPHIC TRANSPARENCIES

Transparencies can now be made in any model Xerox copier as easily and simply as making regular paper copies (694). Both Arkwright and Sepsco manufacture special film for Xerox copiers. Clear, matte, and color films are available (695).

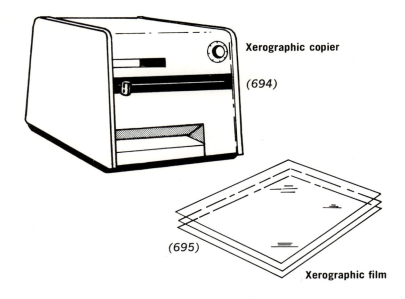

Xerographic copier

(694)

(695)

Xerographic film

Instructions (Arkwright transparency fims)

Arkwright Xerographic film is designed for use only in Xerox office copiers. Do not attempt to run this film through copiers produced by other manufacturers. Operating instructions vary slightly from one model Xerox copier to another.

Xerox models 914, 420, and 720

1. Fan film sheets to allow for easy feeding and handling.
2. Place supply of sheets (approximately ten to fifteen) into the loading tray with white opaque strip facing up and feeding into the machine.
3. Make prints in the normal way with pressure lever and temperature control at same settings as used for paper. If the print is too light, pump up toner to desired darkness level.
4. If fusion is not adequate, go to next higher heat setting (use this setting when making future transparencies).

Xerox models 813, 660, and 330

1. Fan film sheets to allow for easy feeding and handling.
2. Load tray with opaque strip feeding into machine, but with the strip facing down.
3. Put dial setting on 1 after loading tray. Do not set dial for more than one copy at a time.
4. Print one sheet at a time.

Xerox model 2400

1. Fan film sheets to allow for easy feeding and handling.
2. Place as many sheets as required in the loading tray with white opaque strip facing up and at the left-hand side of loading tray.
3. Make prints in the normal way.

Instructions (Zelar transparency films)

Xerox model 2400

All six Zelar films will feed multiple sheets automatically in a single loading on the 2400. Count the number of transparencies desired, being sure each sheet is separated with a sheet of paper. *Important: Do not remove special paper interleafing packed with film (696).* Load on top of existing paper supply pile with the rounded corner in the *upper right-hand* corner of the supply tray (when standing in front of the machine in the operator's position). Proceed as if making regular paper reproductions. Any slight surface oil will usually disappear in twenty-four hours.

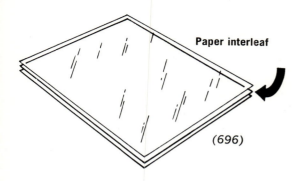

Paper interleaf

(696)

Xerox models 420, 720, and 914

Place single sheet of Zelar film on top of the existing paper supply pile with the rounded corner in the *upper right-hand* corner of the supply tray. Close drawer slowly and proceed as if making paper copies. *Important: Do not load more than one sheet at a time.* Should the toner image tend to rub off or smudge, additional heat may be indicated. This is easily increased by adjusting the heat-control buttons located in the top front console panel to a higher number. Example: If setting is L-2 then reset to H-1 or H-2. The film will not burn or melt even at the highest heat.

Xerox models 330, 660, and 813

Xerox desk-top models 330, 660, and 813 copy images on the reserve side of the sheet. Place a single sheet of film on top of the existing paper supply in the drawer. However, be sure to place the rounded corner in the *upper left-hand* corner of the tray. *Important: Load only one sheet of film at a time.*

Mounted
Xerographic
transparency

LARGE TRANSPARENCY MOUNTING TECHNIQUES

Large transparencies may be projected unmounted if the base (film) is thick enough to lie flat on the stage of the overhead projector. However, there are several good reasons for mounting transparencies. A mount will, for instance, block out light projecting around the edges of the transparency so that only the intended projection image area is seen on the projection screen. A mount also provides a solid base for easy handling, manipulating overlays, and storing. Moreover, the surface of many mounts can be used to write notes related to the transparency.

Careful consideration should be given to size, material, method of securing film to mount, and masking and hinging overlays when mounting large transparencies for projection. Since sizes of mounts and image areas have not yet been standardized, the recommended mount size is one that fits a standard letter-size file or can be carried in a briefcase.

A widely accepted mount size for the 10- by 10-inch overhead projector measures 10½ by 12 inches (outside dimension), with a 7½- by 9½-inch image area opening (see page 160).

Mounted transparencies can be projected horizontally or vertically. However, it is recommended that where possible the transparency should be produced and mounted horizontally so that full advantage can be taken of the most commonly used horizontal projection screens.

TRANSPARENCY MOUNTS

Overhead Transparency Cardboard Mount (697)

A die-cut pressed cardboard mount that will accept transparencies up to 8½ by 11 inches (see page 223 for instructions on mounting base transparency and overlays).

Overhead Transparency Plastic Mount (698)

White high-impact plastic mount that is waterproof, nonwarping, and reusable (see page 223 for instructions on mounting base transparency and overlays).

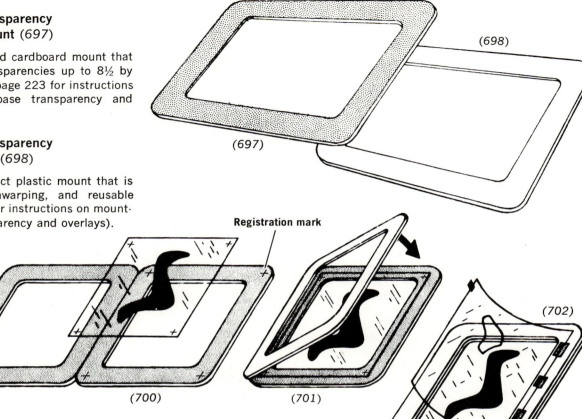

(697)

(698)

Registration mark

(699)

(700)

(701)

(702)

Overhead Transparency Cardboard Mount (Adhesive-backed) (699)

A sandwich-type cardboard mount with pressure-sensitive adhesive to permit the mounting of one or more "cells" inside. Place the mount open on a flat surface. Position the base "cell" on one side of the mount. Some mounts have registration marks to assist in the registration of "cells" (700). Fold the opposite side of the mount over so that it locks the base "cell" in place. Rub, with firm pressure, around the top of the mount to assure good adhesion (701). Position overlays as desired and attach as illustrated in (702).

Overhead Transparency Transparent Plastic Mount (703)

A self-contained transparent plastic mount with an opaque border. No mounting or masking is required, unless overlays are desired. Lettering, writing, coloring, etc., are done directly on the surface of the mount.

(703)

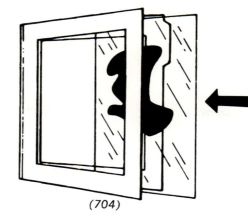

(704)

Handmade Overhead Transparency Mount (704)

Almost any opaque material with a fair degree of thickness can be used to make a mount. Regular manila file folders are ideal for mounts. Openings 7½ by 9½ inches, or the size desired, can be cut in one or both sides of the folder. Other materials such as chipboard and posterboard can be used as long as the material is stiff enough to hold the transparency.

Transparent Plastic Holder (705)

An acetate sleeve-type protector designed for protecting photographs, papers, etc. Ideal for protecting and projecting overhead transparencies. Some holders are punched for insertion in loose-leaf notebooks.

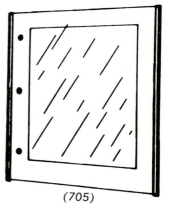

(705)

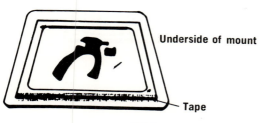

Underside of mount

Tape

(706)

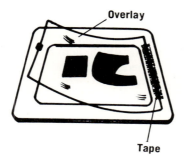

Overlay

Tape

MOUNTING BASE TRANSPARENCY

No matter what type of transparency mount is used, the simplest and easiest way to attach the single or base transparency to the mount is with a pressure-sensitive tape such as masking or drafting, Scotch Magic mending, or overhead transparency tape (706). Double-coated adhesive tape is another good product for attaching the transparency to the mount. An ideal width tape is ½ inch. *To attach transparency* to the mount, tape all four edges of the transparency to the underside of the mount. Using the underside makes for a more attractive mounting and leaves the top of the mount free for attaching overlays and making notations and cues for lecture purposes.

223

ATTACHING OVERLAYS

Overlays can be attached in a variety of ways, including using any of the tapes already mentioned or overhead transparency hinges. These hinges are made of mylar and have a pressure-sensitive backing. If overlays are always to be projected in the same order, they should be hinged on one edge of the mount. However, if the order of presenting each overlay is to vary from time to time, each overlay should be hinged on different edges of the mount. *To tape overlays* to the transparency mount, tape the edge to be hinged to the top side of the mount as illustrated. Check the overlay after hinging to make certain it works as desired. If additional overlays, to be projected in the same order, are desired, attach the same as for a single overlay. *To hinge overlays with overhead transparency hinges* remove the paper backing from the first hinge and follow these instructions:

1. Position hinge, adhesive side up, under the film at the center position on the edge which is to be hinged (*707*). The bottom of the film is pressed onto the adhesive.
2. Then fold the hinge over, pressing it against the top of the film (*708*). The film is now sandwiched firmly between the two adhesive sides of the hinge.
3. Insert two staples through each hinge, or stack of hinges if other sequential overlays are used (*709*). An overhead transparency stapler is recommended since an ordinary stapler with standard staples may not penetrate the overlay and mount. Three hinges are recommended for each overlay.

PROGRESSIVE DISCLOSURE TECHNIQUES

Progressive disclosures add an important and exciting dimension to an already

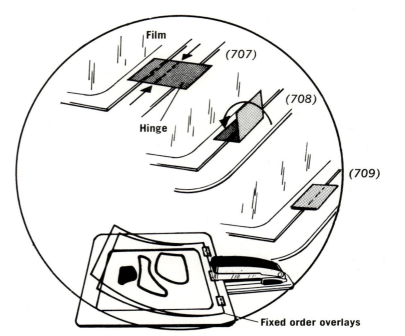

Film
(707)
(708)
Hinge
(709)
Fixed order overlays

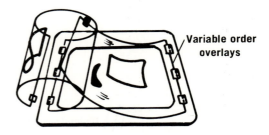

Variable order overlays

high-impact instructional medium. Progressive disclosures allow the presenter to control the rate at which information is presented to the audience on the projection screen. Disclosures may be made in the form of transparent or opaque overlays or masks which add or subtract certain elements of the total image. Illustrated and discussed here are just a few of the more widely used techniques.

Circular Masks (710)

Circular masks are dramatic and effective when information that can fit into a circular design is used. A mask, cut out of cardboard, opaque plastic sheet, etc., is attached to the base transparency with a grommet or thumbtack and pencil eraser. The thumbtack is inserted from the underside of the base transparency and through the mask on top of the transparency. The eraser is attached to the point of the tack and serves as a "locking" device for the mask.

Pivoting Overlays (711)

Overlays that are to be projected in a fixed order can be attached to one corner of the mount in much the same manner as the circular masks. The corner where the grommet or thumbtack is inserted acts as a pivoting point for the overlays. To project each overlay, simply swing it into position over the opening of the mount.

Folding Masks (712)

Folding masks, also known as accordion-pleat masks, are excellent for progressive disclosure of projected material. Strips of cardboard, cut the correct size, can be hinged together with pressure-sensitive tape and hinged to the edge of the mount; or simply fold an opaque sheet of heavy paper in strips the correct width and hinge to the mount. To use the folding mask, lift each fold or section as required to disclose another part of the image area. Notes and cues can be made on each fold.

Hinged Masks (713)

A progressive disclosure can be achieved by masking all or a portion of the transparency with an opaque sheet, such as cardboard or an overhead transparency plastic mask. Instructions for hinging masks and attaching overlays are the same and can be found on page 224.

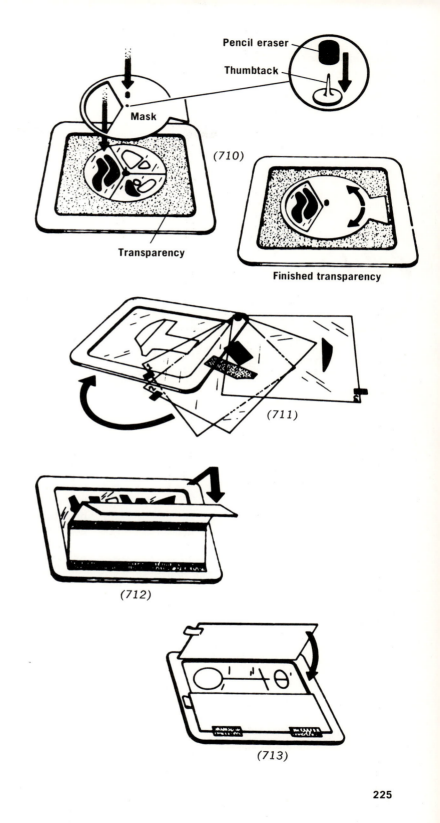

Pencil eraser

Thumbtack

Mask

(710)

Transparency

Finished transparency

(711)

(712)

(713)

Overhead Transparency Plastic Pointer (714)

A device used in place of a finger or pencil to point out portions of an overhead transparency. The pointer is made out of transparent plastic. Handmade pointers can be made out of heavy-gauge transparent plastic.

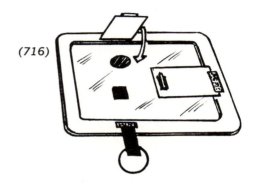

Track

(715)

Sliding Masks (715)

Sliding masks, made of cardboard, overhead transparency plastic mask, or other opaque material, can be used to achieve a controlled-pace presentation. The projection screen at the beginning of the presentation is dark; then as the mask slides off the mount, the image is revealed to the viewers. The track for the mask can be made from two pieces of cardboard and stapled to the mount as illustrated, or commercial overhead transparency plastic tracks can be purchased. An overhead transparency stapler is recommended for attaching tracks to the mount, since an ordinary stapler with standard staples may not penetrate the track and mount.

Spot Masks (716)

Spot masks (or *barn door* masks) are designed to reveal a selected portion of a transparency. Masks can be cut into any shape desired and attached in much the same way as any of the other masks included in this section. Among the materials that can be used for spot masks are cardboard, file folder, overhead transparency plastic mask.

(716)

Mask Lifters (717)

Pressure-sensitive tapes or commercial overhead transparency hinges can be used to make a simple lifter (handle) for overlays and masks. To make, fold the tape or hinge, with adhesive side in, allowing enough of the adhesive side to be attached to the mask or overlay for good holding contact. Lifters serve as a handle for lifting the mask or overlay off the base transparency.

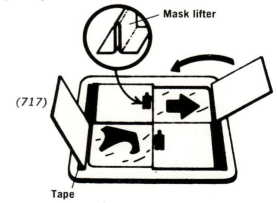

Mask lifter

(717)

Tape

FILING AND STORING LARGE TRANSPARENCIES

Filing and storing large transparencies is much like filing and storing other materials of similar size and thickness, such as photographs, file folders, catalogs. Many existing storage containers and facilities can be adapted for accepting large transparencies.

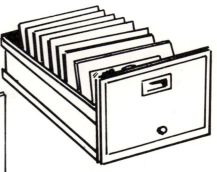

Transparencies stored in standard size files

(718)

(719)

Unmounted Transparencies (718)

Unmounted transparencies can be hole-punched and filed in a large ring binder. A white sheet of paper should be inserted between each transparency to help facilitate quick location of each. Transparencies can also be inserted in transparent plastic protectors and filed in a ring binder.

Mounted Transparencies (719)

The external dimensions of large transparencies allow them to be filed and stored in standard file cabinets. Overhead transparency storage files are steel cabinets specifically designed for large transparencies. Transparencies filed and stored in large ring binders can also be filed in standard or overhead transparency storage files.

Overhead Transparency Carrying Case (720)

A combination carrying and storage case designed especially for large transparencies. The cases are usually made of vinyl or pressboard.

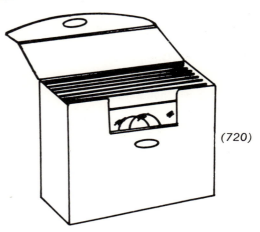

(720)

SLIDE MOUNTING AND BINDING TECHNIQUES

Usually slides which are commercially processed are returned in cardboard mounts. If the slides are not subjected to rough handling or if they are stored in slide magazines or trays, cardboard mounts are satisfactory. For those processing their own slides or wishing to provide a more permanent protection from dust, fingerprints, etc., a brief description of several types of slide mounts and techniques is included in this section.

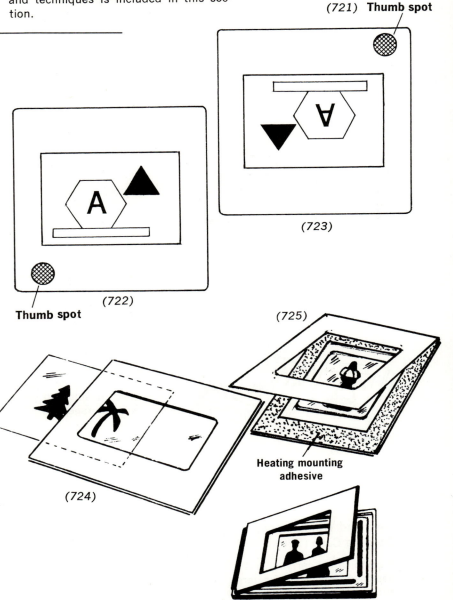

(721) **Thumb spot**

(723)

Thumb spot (722)

(725)

(724)

Heating mounting adhesive

(726)

Slide Thumb Spot (721)

Slide thumb spot is a guide for accurate positioning of slide in the projector. The thumb spot is usually made of gum- or adhesive-backed paper. (See page 230 for examples.)

1. After slide has been mounted, turn so that it reads properly and place the thumb spot in the lower left-hand corner of the mount (722).
2. To project, turn slide so that the thumb spot is in the upper right-hand corner of the mount (722). (723).

Cardboard Slide Mount

A one-piece cardboard mount which may or may not be designed for heat mounting. Some mounts have a slot for inserting the film (724); no adhesive is required. Other mounts (Kodak Ready-Mount is one) are designed for heat mounting and require a slide mounting press (see page 230) (725), tacking iron (see page 72), or the tip of a hand iron for mounting after film has been inserted.

Plastic Slide Mount (One-piece) (726)

A one-piece heat-resistant polypropylene slide mount that will not warp. No adhesive is necessary. Mount has self-locking seams that hold film securely but is easy to open for reuse. The surface of some mounts will accept pencil and ink markings.

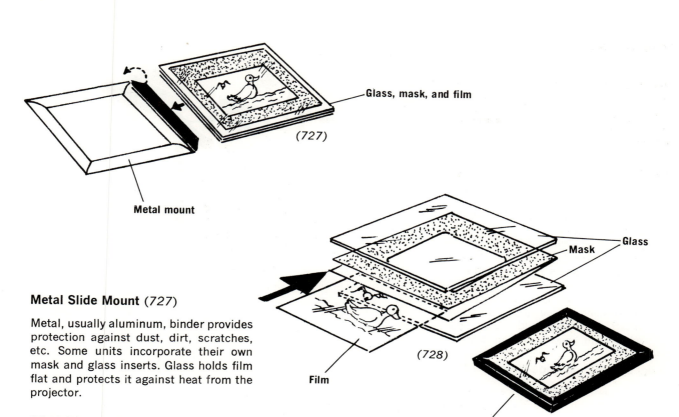

Glass, mask, and film

(727)

Metal mount

Glass

Mask

(728)

Film

Slide binding tape

Metal Slide Mount (727)

Metal, usually aluminum, binder provides protection against dust, dirt, scratches, etc. Some units incorporate their own mask and glass inserts. Glass holds film flat and protects it against heat from the projector.

Slide Glass and Slide Binding Tape Mount (728)

An economical technique for mounting and binding slides of all sizes. Film may be inserted into a mask and sandwiched between two pieces of plain (cover) glass. Slide binding tape is used to bind the film, mask, and glass together.

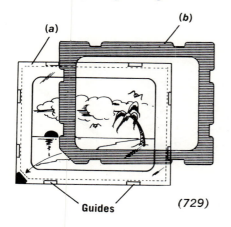

(a)

(b)

Guides

(729)

Polaroid Slide (Transparency) Mount 633 (729)

A snap-in white plastic mount for 3¼- by 4-inch Polaroid Land projection transparency film.

Mounting Instructions

1. Tear off tab along perforation of the transparency (film).
2. Place transparency in position within the eight guides on (a) of the mount. *Note:* One corner of the transparency has a diagonal corner cutout. This should be fitted against the diagonal guide of (a).
3. Snap each of the notches on (b) so that it locks with the matching guides of (a).

Slide Mounting Press (730)

A hand-operated electric press for mounting all popular sizes of slides. Models are available for mounting 2- by 2-inch, 2¼- by 2¼-inch and 3¼- by 4-inch slides in cardboard mounts designed for heat mounting.

Instructions for Seary presses

1. Place film in cardboard mount and fold.
2. Slip folded mount in between heated pressure plates.
3. Squeeze handles together like a pair of pliers. Press locks, freeing operator's hands for preparation of next slide.
4. After two seconds, pull release handle and sealed slide drops out. Insert next slide and close press while right hand is still on handles.

Two- by two-inch Slide Notcher (731)

A hand-operated metal device for notching 2- by 2-inch slides and slide cardboard mounts of other sizes. Notching assures correct positioning in projector.

Adhesive-backed Paper Tabs (Labels) (732)

There are a number of identification products on the market for identifying, numbering, indexing slides. The adhesive-backed paper tab (label) illustrated (photo-slide label) provides space for identification and ownership plus a red dot to ensure correct placement of the slide in projector. Tabs may be used on all sizes of slides and photographic negatives.

Slide markers (Sanders Numbatabs is one) are available in letters, numbers, or blanks. Blanks can be marked on with a ball-point pen. Assorted colors are available.

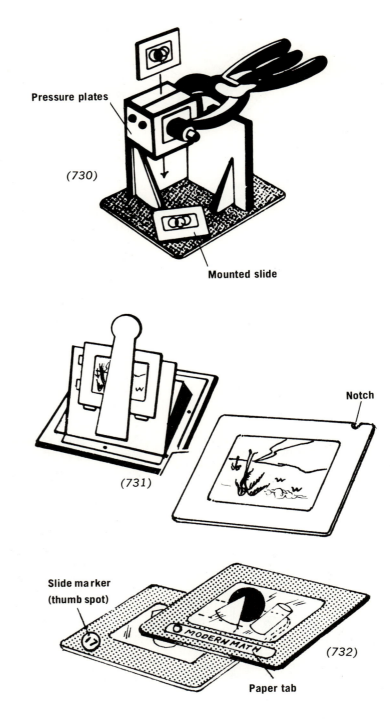

Pressure plates

(730)

Mounted slide

Notch

(731)

Slide marker (thumb spot)

MODERN MATH

(732)

Paper tab

SLIDE MOUNTS

The *actual* sizes of the more commonly used slide mounts are illustrated in (733) to (737). The dotted outline for each illustration indicates the image area that will be projected.

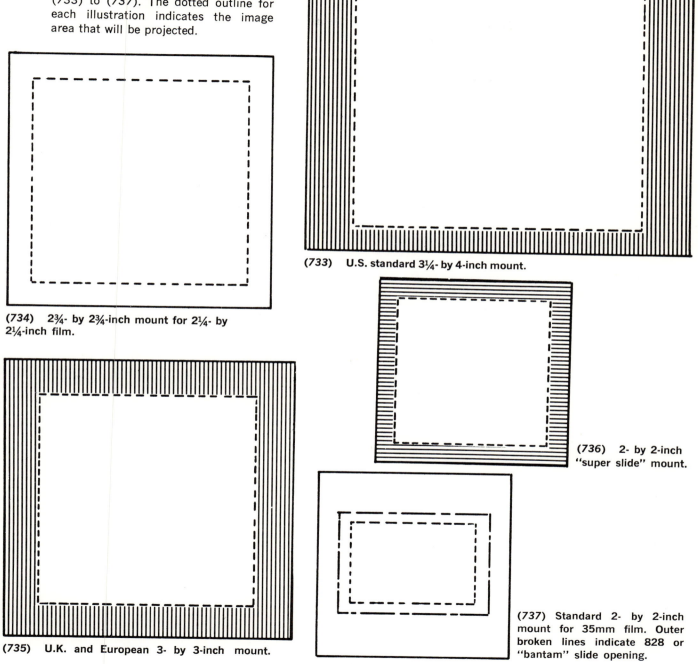

(734) 2¾- by 2¾-inch mount for 2¼- by 2¼-inch film.

(733) U.S. standard 3¼- by 4-inch mount.

(736) 2- by 2-inch "super slide" mount.

(735) U.K. and European 3- by 3-inch mount.

(737) Standard 2- by 2-inch mount for 35mm film. Outer broken lines indicate 828 or "bantam" slide opening.

REFERENCES

Annotated Projectable Visual Media

Address Directory

Glossary

Annotated Bibliography

ANNOTATED PROJECTABLE VISUAL MEDIA

The projectable visual media annotated below and on the following pages have been included in this book to help supplement its contents. Included in the listings are 16mm motion-picture films (16mm film), 8mm cartridge-load single-concept (single idea) motion-picture films (8mm SC film), 35mm filmstrips, 35mm double-frame unmounted slides, 2- by 2-inch slides, 10- by 10-inch overhead transparencies, and diazo masters. The availability of a visual aid in color or black and white (b and w) is also indicated. Chapters which each visual aid supplements are indicated by boldface numbers in parentheses following most entries. Visual media which have no chapter reference indicated are included for their value to a better understanding of the preparation and utilization of instructional media. While a number of the items listed here are somewhat dated, they are still obtainable from many film-rental libraries throughout the country. The names and addresses of producers and distributors can be found in the Address Directory.

ADMINISTRATIVE ORIENTATION, *35mm filmstrip, 50 frames, sound, color, Educational Media, 1967.*
This filmstrip is designed to impress public school administrators with the need to develop the basic educational graphics skills of their faculties. Its use should assist media directors, supervisors, and principals in creating and expanding top-level administrative support for such in-service programs.

ADVANCED PRODUCTION TECHNIQUES, *35mm filmstrip, 51 frames, sound, color, Educational Media, 1968.*
Various color-producing processes; diazo production techniques; "color-lifting," special color-yielding systems. (**4,5**)

AIRBRUSH MANIPULATION, *8mm SC film, three minutes, silent, color, Grafcom.*
Demonstrates, through motion picture, the movement of hand, arm, and fingers during a demonstration by a professional artist. (**4**)

AN INTRODUCTION TO THE AIR-BRUSH, *35mm filmstrip, sound, color, Grafcom.*
Presents an overview of the operation and utilization of the airbrush. An explanation of both alcohol- and water-base paints is included. (**4**)

BETTER BULLETIN BOARDS, *16mm film, thirteen minutes, sound, b and w or color, Indiana University, 1956.*
The creation and use of bulletin boards for various purposes; values of pupil participation in planning and use. Catching and holding the viewer's eye through placement, size, and design. Choices of materials; mounting and lettering devices for integrating materials into effective design patterns. (**1,2,3,4**)

BULLETIN BOARDS: AN EFFECTIVE TEACHING DEVICE, *16mm film, eleven minutes, sound, color, Bailey, 1956.*
Gives suggestions for the planning and organization of creatively designed bulletin boards and presents twelve displays arranged by a class. Shows a class discussing, planning, and arranging a bulletin board. (**1, 2,3,4**)

BULLETIN BOARDS AND DISPLAY, *35mm filmstrips (2), 36 frames each, color, Bailey, 1966.*
Amusing drawings and examples of good bulletin-board design show how the bulletin board can be made to function as an effective educational tool. Examples of various types of background materials and fastening devices, illustrations of layouts and principles of good design and organization, will encourage the design and construction of simple, powerful bulletin-board displays. (**1,2,3,4**)

BULLETIN BOARDS AT WORK, *35mm filmstrip, 42 frames, b and w, Wayne State University, 1950.*
Outlines the use of the bulletin board as a teaching aid. Contains many actual bulletin boards to illustrate various uses. Rules for good layout of different types of bulletin boards are presented. (**1,3,4**)

BULLETIN BOARDS FOR EFFECTIVE TEACHING, *16mm film, eleven minutes, sound, color, University of Iowa, 1953.*
Deals with the elements of effective classroom bulletin-board display in detail. Shows selection of a specific topic, selection of materials, planning the arrangement, use of color, use of appropriate lettering, creation of the proper atmosphere, making the arrangement tell a story, use of eye catchers, and the mechanics of assembling the display. (**1,2,3,4**)

CARDBOARD PRINTING, *35mm film-strip, 43 frames, color, Society for Visual Education, 1965.*
Making posters, book covers, programs, greetings cards, and design duplication. (1,3,4)

CHALK AND CHALKBOARDS, *16mm film, seventeen minutes, sound, color, Bailey, 1959.*
This comprehensive film introduces the physical properties of chalk and chalkboards, showing what they are made of and how they should be cared for. It treats at length many techniques which can be used on all grade levels to improve everyday teaching. Laboratory and classroom demonstration sequences show that the chalkboard is a particularly effective teaching aid because it is readily available, allows illustrations showing action, helps develop explanations in logical sequence, can involve student ideas, will focus attention upon specific points, permits group participation, and is adaptable to a wide variety of uses. (1)

CHALKBOARD APPROACH TO TEACHING TYPEWRITING, THE, *16mm film, twenty-three minutes, sound, b and w, University of Iowa, 1962.*
Shows an effective way to present the keyboard using psychological principles of skill development. Shows in detail how to utilize the chalkboard, and how and when to demonstrate. (1)

CHALKBOARDS AND FLANNEL BOARDS, *35mm filmstrips (4), 30 frames each, color, Bailey, 1967.*
This set of four color filmstrips follows the format of the highly successful set *Bulletin Boards and Display* and the motion pictures *Chalk and Chalkboards* and *Flannel Boards and How to Use Them.* The care, use, and construction of these often-overlooked, yet powerful classroom tools are covered in depth. Examples of various types of boards and materials are shown, as well as many types of presentations on the boards. (1,2,3,4)

CHALKBOARD UTILIZATION, *16mm film, fifteen minutes, sound, b and w, McGraw-Hill Text-Films, 1954.*
Demonstrates the many ways a chalkboard can be used more effectively in teaching. Explains the various methods of transferring drawings to the chalkboard. (1)

CHARTS FOR CREATIVE LEARNING, *16mm film, ten minutes, sound, color, Bailey, 1961.*
Actual school situations dramatize the many uses that can be made of charts in primary, elementary, and secondary classrooms. (1,3)

CLOTH MOUNTING (Fold) Parts 1 and 2, *8mm SC films, four minutes each, silent, b and w, McGraw-Hill Text-Films, 1965.*
Dry mounting a large map, separated into sections, on Chartex cloth for folding during storage. (2)

CLOTH MOUNTING (Roll), *8mm SC film, four minutes, silent, b and w, McGraw-Hill Text-Films, 1965.*
Dry mounting a large map in one piece on Chartex cloth for rolling during storage. (2)

COLOR COLLAGE, *16mm film, twenty-two minutes, sound, color, Eastman Kodak, 1961.*
Shows the art director how to increase sales through effective use of color. Also provides a stimulating program for an art class or a camera club. (4)

COLOR LITHOGRAPHY: AN ART MEDIUM, *16mm film, thirty-two minutes, sound, color, University of Mississippi,. 1955.*
Pictures, in detail, how an artist prepares a lithograph. Presents a display of lithographs by world-famous artists. (1,4)

COMPOSITION, *35mm filmstrip, 43 frames, sound, color, Educational Media, 1967.*
Composition is discussed from an instructional point of view rather than an artistic point of view. Layout, use of color, proper letter, style standards and the use of various mattes and background materials are discussed. (1)

COMPOSITION FOR INSTRUCTION, *8mm SC film, two minutes, color, Hester.*
Shows how the eye sees instructional materials and indicates ways to best plan effective displays. (1)

CREATING CARTOONS, *16mm film, eleven minutes, sound, b and w, Bailey, 1956.*
Uses demonstrations in humorous animation to explain the elements of cartooning. (1)

CREATING INSTRUCTIONAL MATERIALS, *16mm film, fifteen minutes, sound, b and w or color, McGraw-Hill Text-Films, 1963.*
Through a series of classroom scenes, the importance and impact of instructional materials is stressed. From the audiovisual series.

DARKROOM TECHNIQUES, *16mm film, thirty minutes, sound, b and w, University of Minnesota, 1961.*
Shows processes and equipment used in developing film, making contact prints, and enlarging pictures. (5)

DESIGN, *16mm film, ten minutes, sound, color, Bailey, 1955.*
Presents a nontechnical formula for basic design through using animated illustrations as examples. Shows how to make flat surfaces appealing through application of basic shapes, combining shapes, repeated shapes, etc. (1)

DEVELOPING THE NEGATIVE, *16mm film, sixteen minutes, sound, b and w, DuArt, 1950.*
Shows procedures in developing still camera film and explains the com-

position of the developing solution. From the fundamentals of photography series. **(5)**

DISCOVERING FORM IN ART, *16mm film, twenty-one minutes, sound, color, Film Associates, 1967.*
This film shows the five basic forms in art: the sphere, cube, cone, cylinder, and pyramid. Each form is a structure of planes or surfaces which join to create a distinctive volume. The artist creates with these forms, combining them and varying the proportions endlessly. The illusion of volume may be suggested, as in drawing and painting, or actual forms may be created from a variety of materials. **(1,4)**

DISCOVERING PERSPECTIVE, *16mm film, fourteen minutes, sound, color, Film Associates, 1967.*
We live in a world of depth, of distance. Some things are close to us, some far away. We can create the appearance of distance on a flat surface by using perspective. Overlapping, vertical position, graying colors, varying detail, varying size, and converging lines are techniques used to create perspective. Any one or more of these methods helps create the appearance of depth. **(1)**

DRAWING AND THE SHOP, *16mm film, fifteen minutes, sound, b and w, McGraw-Hill Text-Films, 1947.*
Shows the relationship between making the drawing and various production operations in the shop and factory. Clarifies the need for certain drafting requirements. Provides a glimpse of organization of modern production methods. **(1)**

DRY MOUNTING, *35mm filmstrip, 51 frames, sound, color, Educational Media, 1967.*
Use of the dry mount press and various types of tissue. Treatment of tear sheets and other materials prior to dry mounting, cover-sheet use, tacking iron, cutter, and matting and framing are discussed and explored. Numerous examples are illustrated. **(2)**

DRY MOUNTING (Hand Iron), *8mm SC film, three minutes, silent, b and w, McGraw-Hill Text-Film, 1965.*
Using a hand iron and dry mounting tissue to mount a magazine picture on cardboard. **(2)**

DRY MOUNTING (Press), *8mm SC film, three minutes, silent, b and w, McGraw-Hill Text-Films, 1965.*
Using a dry mount press and dry mounting tissue to mount a magazine picture on cardboard. **(2)**

DRY MOUNTING AND LAMINATING PICTURES, *16mm film, ten minutes, sound, color, Horn Films.*
The film illustrates dry mounting and plastic lamination methods using a dry mounting press, tacking iron, and household iron. Techniques for applying captions and punching permanent pinholes to create professional-looking study guides are demonstrated. **(2)**

DRY MOUNTING INSTRUCTIONAL MATERIALS: BASIC TECHNIQUES, *16mm film, five minutes, sound, color, also available in 8mm optical or magnetic sound, University of Iowa, 1965.*
Presents the basic dry mounting techniques that involve dry mounting tissue and Fotoflat, shows how these materials are used and the purpose for which each is appropriate, and outlines the techniques of operating dry mounting presses. **(2)**

DRY MOUNTING INSTRUCTIONAL MATERIALS: CLOTH BACKING, *16mm film, five minutes, sound, color, also available in 8mm optical or magnetic sound, University of Iowa, 1965.*
Shows what Chartex backing cloth is, how it is applied with a dry mounting press and some of the ways it can be used in preparing, presenting, and preserving instructional materials. Stresses step-by-step procedures and techniques which will yield good results and long service. **(2)**

DRY MOUNTING INSTRUCTIONAL

MATERIALS: CREATIVE APPLICATIONS, *16mm film, seven minutes, sound, color, also available in 8mm optical or magnetic sound, University of Iowa, 1969.*
This film demonstrates some possibilities for use of the dry mounting press as a creative tool. Useful for basic design courses. **(1,2)**

DRY MOUNTING INSTRUCTIONAL MATERIALS: DISPLAY AND USE, *16mm film, five minutes, sound, color, also available in 8mm optical or magnetic sound, University of Iowa, 1965.*
Illustrates various classroom uses of instructional materials prepared with the dry mounting press. **(2)**

DRY MOUNTING INSTRUCTIONAL MATERIALS: LAMINATING AND LIFTING, *16mm film, six minutes, sound, color, also available in 8mm optical or magnetic sound, University of Iowa, 1965.*
Presents the concept of laminating flat instructional materials with a clear plastic sheet, thereby preserving materials destined for hard use or much handling. A further extension of this technique known as "lifting" (a process whereby full-size transparencies for the overhead projector are made from printed pages) is also demonstrated. Both techniques are illustrated in step-by-step detail. **(2,5)**

DRY MOUNTING INSTRUCTIONAL MATERIALS: SPECIAL TECHNIQUES, *16mm film, five minutes, sound, color, also available in 8mm optical or magnetic sound, University of Iowa, 1965.*
Illustrates special applications and processes utilizing a variety of dry mounting materials and techniques. **(2)**

DRY MOUNTING INSTRUCTIONAL MATERIALS: USING IDEAS, *16mm film, eight minutes, sound, color, also available in 8mm optical or magnetic sound, University of Iowa, 1969.*
Shows ways in which the dry mount-

ing process can be put to use in the classroom, once you have mastered the techniques illustrated in the previous films of the series. Suggests the potential of dry-mounted materials as an instructional aid. (2)

DRY MOUNTING LARGE MATERIALS, *8mm SC film, four minutes, silent, color, Hester.*
Techniques for dry mounting materials as large as an open newspaper, using a standard dry mounting press. (2)

DRY MOUNT YOUR TEACHING PICTURES, *16mm film, ten minutes, sound, b and w, McGraw-Hill Text-Films, 1958.*
Shows the step-by-step procedure for using dry mounting tissues and an ordinary iron in mounting pictures. (2)

DUPLICATING BY THE SPIRIT METHOD, *16mm film, fourteen minutes, sound, color, Bailey, 1961.*
Carbon master sets are shown and the dye transfer process is illustrated in this demonstration of spirit duplicating (also known as liquid or fluid duplicating). Typing the master set, making corrections by various methods, using hand lettering and colored carbons are shown in detail. Close attention is given to each step in operating the machine. Proper care of equipment is stressed. (1, 3,4,5)

EDUCATIONAL MEDIA KIT, *McGraw-Hill Text-Films, 1968.*
A carefully developed and integrated series of audiovisual materials (films, slides, transparencies, and recordings) designed for use in presenting developments in education which involve many types of instructional resources. This media kit is the culmination of many years of work by outstanding media specialists around the nation and was originally developed under contract by San Jose State College with the United States Office of Education (N.D.E.A. Title VIIB). (1,3,4,5)

ELECTRIC BOARDS, *16mm film, six minutes, sound, b and w, University of Iowa, 1965.*
Introduces various types of electric boards, shows their construction, and suggests a variety of uses for these simple but effective teaching devices.

EXCITING BULLETIN BOARDS, *35mm filmstrips (2), 40 frames each, sound, color, McGraw-Hill Text-Films, 1963.*
Shows color, lettering, and three-dimensional bulletin board materials. (1,3,4)

FELTBOARD IN TEACHING, THE, *16mm film, nine minutes, sound, color, Wayne State University, 1951.*
Suggests uses which the classroom teacher may make of the feltboard. The feltboard is also known as the visual board, feltogram, or flannelgraph. (1)

FELT PEN SKETCHING, *16mm film, eleven minutes, sound, b and w, McGraw-Hill Text-Films, 1957.*
Demonstrates how the common felt-point marking pen can be used in a variety of ways for sketching. (1)

FLANNEL BOARDS AND HOW TO USE THEM, *16mm film, fifteen minutes, sound, color, Bailey, 1958.*
Explains what flannel boards are, how they are made, and how they may be used. (1,2,3)

FLANNELGRAPH, ITS APPLICATION IN THE PRIMARY AND ELEMENTARY CLASSROOM, *16mm film, twenty-seven minutes, sound, color, University of Minnesota, 1956.*
Tells how flannelgraphs can be used in first-grade reading, arithmetic, art, health, and music classes. Shows flannelgraphs made by first-grade children. (1,2)

FLAT PICTURES, *16mm film, eighteen minutes, sound, b and w, Pennsylvania State University, 1959.*
Discusses the potentialities and limitations of using flat pictures. Shows

the principles of these aids. (1)

HANDMADE LANTERN SLIDES, *35mm filmstrip, 46 frames, color, Ohio State University, Teaching Aids Lab, 1954.*
Shows simple techniques for preparing 3¼- by 4-inch slides. Includes supplementary information on making and using glass and cellophane slides. (1,3,4,5)

HANDMADE MATERIALS FOR PROJECTION, *16mm film, twenty minutes, sound, b and w or color, Indiana University, 1956.*
The principles of transparency, translucency, and opacity applied to materials for overhead, slide, and opaque projectors. A variety of techniques and materials for inexpensive projected materials: carbon film; dot-dusted stencils; coated acetate; adhesive shading and coloring materials; transfer of magazine pictures to acetate (lifting). (1,3,4,5)

HIGH CONTRAST PHOTOGRAPHY FOR INSTRUCTION, *16mm film, fourteen minutes, sound, b and w or color, Indiana University, 1956.*
Making negatives and prints on high-contrast film; the preparation and duplication of materials for making slides, large transparencies, and paper prints; making a photogram; copying a line drawing from a book; making photocopies of material assembled on a flannel board, menu board, and a paste-up; coloring; combining two negatives; and making multiple copies. (1,3,4,5)

HOW A COMMERCIAL ARTIST WORKS, *16mm film, fifteen minutes, sound, b and w, Modern Talking Pictures.*
Shows a commercial artist working on an advertisement from rough layout through finished artwork. (1,2,3,4)

HOW KODALITH FILM IS MADE, *16mm film, twenty minutes, sound, color, Eastman Kodak.*
Acquaints the graphic art trade, or

those interested in the trade, with the highly sophisticated technology required in the manufacture of Kodalith films. (5)

HOW TO DO CARTOONS, *16mm film, twenty minutes, sound, b and w, Schulman, 1957.*
Artist Russell Patterson demonstrates a simple and direct approach to cartooning. (1)

HOW TO EMBED SPECIMENS IN LIQUID PLASTIC, *35mm filmstrip, 53 frames, b and w, Syracuse University, 1955.*
Shows the process of preserving small specimens in liquid casting plastic. (2)

HOW TO KEEP YOUR BULLETIN BOARD ALIVE, *35mm filmstrip, 32 frames, color, Ohio State University, Teaching Aids Lab, 1950.*
Attempts to diagnose the present faults of most bulletin boards. Some general rules about captions, illustrations, and text. (1,3,4)

HOW TO MAKE AND USE A DIORAMA, *16mm film, twenty minutes, sound, color, McGraw-Hill Text-Films, 1956.*
Demonstrates the construction of the diorama framework and the preparation of its realistic miniature scenes. (1)

HOW TO MAKE A STENCIL PRINT, *16mm film, twelve minutes, sound, color, Bailey, 1961.*
Introduces simple ways to cut and print original stencils as an approach to creative design. Demonstrates the use of tempera paint on different textured paper and printing on cloth with permanent textile paints. (1,4)

HOW TO MAKE BIOLOGICAL DRAWINGS, *16mm film, fifteen minutes, sound, color or b and w, McGraw-Hill Text-Films, 1964.*
Describes the technique for translating a gross specimen into an accurate drawing. (1)

HOW TO MAKE HANDMADE LANTERN SLIDES, *16mm film, twenty-one minutes, sound, b and w or color, Indiana University, 1947.*
The production of seven basic types of 3¼- by 4-inch slides: clear and etched glass, plastic, translucent paper, cellophane, gelatin, and silhouette. The variety of materials for coloring and shading; sources of materials; special production techniques; binding methods. Examples of handmade slides for a variety of learning situations. (1,3,4,5)

HOW TO MAKE PAPER MACHE ANIMALS, *16mm film, twelve minutes, sound, color, Bailey, 1954.*
Demonstrates the steps involved in making paper maché animals. Explains how to decorate the animal forms. (1)

HOW TO PLAN YOUR TRAVEL SHOW, *2- by 2-inch slides (150), sound (tape), color, Eastman Kodak.*
Shows how to produce a sound-slide presentation. Includes instructions on titles, sound, etc. (3,5)

IDEAS FOR PHOTOGRAPHIC CHRISTMAS CARDS, *2- by 2-inch slides, color, Eastman Kodak.*
Gives ideas and instructions for both beginning and experienced picture makers in the planning and making of personalized photographic Christmas cards. (1,3,5)

IMPROVING THE USE OF THE CHALKBOARD, *35mm filmstrip, 44 frames, silent, color, Ohio State University, Teaching Aids Lab, 1956.*
Shows techniques for teachers to improve the use of the chalkboard with artwork and photographs. (1)

INSECT MOUNTING AND PRESERVING, *16mm film, fourteen minutes, sound, color, Bailey, 1961.*
Accurate preservation of insect examples is a vital step in further study of living insects for classroom purposes. Illustrated here are appropriate methods of mounting and

preserving a variety of insects for permanent study. Correct procedures for using such tools as a relaxing jar, spreading board, insect pins, transparent paper, and the proper chemicals are carefully demonstrated. Identification and labelling are shown as important aspects of this activity. (2,3)

INSTRUCTIONAL MEDIA, *diazo master book. (Stanley A. Huffman, Jr., author), Keuffel & Esser Co., 1969.*
The most extensive visual instructional media diazo master book available today. Contains masters created mainly to assist professional personnel to teach potential and experienced teachers functions of and techniques for using various types of media. The masters are designed for quick, easy reproduction with diazo color projection films. Included are masters related to the production of visual instructional media. (1,2,3,4,5)

INTRODUCTION TO CONTOUR DRAWING, *16mm film, twelve minutes, sound, color, Film Associates, 1967.*
Most of us only half see the objects at which we look. This film shows how we can use the technique of contour drawing to develop our powers of observation. Through contour drawing we learn to see details we might otherwise overlook. Contour drawing is also an aid in developing hand and eye coordination. A perfect likeness of the subject being drawn is not the objective. Practice in contour drawing is valuable training in drawing technique. (1)

INTRODUCTION TO DRAWING MATERIALS, *16mm film, nineteen minutes, sound, color, Film Associates, 1966.*
Introduces various drawing materials, such as chalk, crayons, pencils, tempera, watercolor, felt-tip pens, and oil pastels. Stresses the special qualities of each material

and the value of experimentation. (1,4)

INTRODUCTION TO GESTURE DRAWING, *16mm film, twelve minutes, sound, color, Film Associates, 1967.*
This film shows and explains that gesture drawing is an exercise that describes motion. It expresses the direction and rhythm of an action. Practice in this rapid technique will add vigor and life to your other types of artwork. It will also make you aware of the different kinds of motion while helping you to develop skill and spontaneity in expressing those motions. (1)

INTRODUCTION TO GRAPHIC DESIGN, *35mm filmstrips (2), 50 frames each, sound, color, Bailey, 1967.*
A basic introduction to the materials and techniques of the graphic artist, covering the materials and tools used in all phases of work from layout to lettering and the basic techniques from ruling to rubber-cementing. (1,2,3,4)

INSTRUCTIONAL USE OF PREPARED MATERIALS, *35mm filmstrip, 27 frames, sound, color, Educational Media, 1967.*
This filmstrip combines, in models and examples, the various skills covered by the skill filmstrips in the Basic Educational Graphics series. Proper use of chalkboard areas, walls, and bulletin boards, as well as stand-up teaching charts, student-prepared materials, etc. (1)

LAMINATING, *35mm filmstrip, 49 frames, sound, color, Educational Media, 1967.*
Laminating is accomplished with the flat-type dry mount press. This filmstrip covers step-by-step laminating of conventional items and then explains processes for laminating very large items, section by section, and cutting and rehinging. (2)

LAMINATING LARGE MATERIALS,

8mm SC film, four minutes, silent, color, Hester.
Procedures for using Seal-Lamin film in preserving instructional materials. This process makes such materials waterproof and wear-resistant. (2)

LAMINATING LEAVES, *8mm SC film, two minutes, silent, color, Hester.*
Many teachers require permanent leaf collections; here are shown techniques for permanently preserving such collections. (2)

LEARNING TO DRAW, *16mm film, nine minutes, sound, color or b and w, Beseler, 1954.*
A presentation of the fundamentals of perspective as treated in the *Drawing Textbook* by Bruce McIntyre. Illustrates one use of the overhead projector. (1)

LEARNING TO DRAW, *16mm film, eleven minutes, sound, b and w, University of Iowa, 1954.*
Demonstrates the advantages of using the overhead projector and a complete set of transparencies with overlays and other transparent aids in teaching beginning drafting (mechanical drawing). By using these materials, one can present information and procedures quickly and effectively to pupils with high aptitude and ability, or they can be used to drill the slower or younger pupils. (1)

LET'S DRAW WITH CRAYONS, *16mm film, eleven minutes, sound, color, Coronet, 1952.*
How to use, how to care for, and how to store crayons. Shows many interesting effects one can achieve through different crayon techniques. Includes information on creative drawing, poster making, and numerous other crayon crafts. (1,4)

LETTERING, *8mm SC film, four minutes, silent, color, Hester.*
A simple but effective means of teaching lettering principles is presented. Several basic letters are

analyzed. (3)

LETTERING: THE FELT PEN (Applications), *8mm SC film, four minutes, silent, color, McGraw-Hill Text-Films, 1965.*
Results of using felt pens for preparing lettering styles, flash cards, displays, charts, and bulletin boards. (3)

LETTERING: THE FELT PEN (Basic Skills), *8mm SC film, four minutes, silent, color, McGraw-Hill Text-Films, 1965.*
Characteristics of commonly used felt pens; proper finger, wrist, and arm position as pen is used; methods of forming letters; and proper pen speed during use. (3)

LETTERING FOR PROJECTION, *8mm SC film, four minutes, silent, color, Hester.*
Proper size standards for lettering projectables is shown, as well as the use of lettering guides and pens. (3,5)

LETTERING INSTRUCTIONAL MATERIALS, *16mm film, twenty minutes, sound, b and w or color, Indiana University, 1955.*
Easy-to-use lettering equipment for lettering on signs, posters, bulletin boards, displays, and materials for projection. Lettering techniques using rubber stamp letters; cutout letters; stencils; pens and lettering guides; mechanical lettering systems; projection and photographic reproduction. (3,5)

LETTERING: LEROY 500 AND SMALLER, *8mm SC film, three minutes, silent, b and w, McGraw-Hill Text-Films, 1965.*
Using LeRoy template, scriber, and pen for lettering ½ inch and smaller. (3)

LETTERING: LEROY 700 AND LARGER, *8mm SC film, three minutes, silent, b and w, McGraw-Hill Text-Films, 1965.*
Using LeRoy template, scriber, and

pen for lettering ¾ inch and larger. (3)

LETTERING: PREPARED LETTERS, *8mm SC film, four minutes, silent, b and w, McGraw-Hill Text-Films, 1965.*
Shows using construction-paper cutouts, gummed-backed letters, and dry transfer letters. (3)

LETTERING: SKILL DEVELOPMENT, *35mm filmstrip, 52 frames, sound, color, Educational Media, 1967.*
Explains simple lettering techniques. Explores the use of stencils, spray paints and lettering fonts, lettering standards, and other lettering devices. (3)

LETTERING: WIRE BRUSH LETTERING EQUIPMENT, *35mm filmstrip, 38 frames, sound, color, Educational Media, 1967.*
Exhibits applications for and use of pen and guide lettering sets. Simple sets of this type require little time and effort in in-service education and have multiple uses in the classroom. Details such as pen and guide sizes and styles, felt-pen sets and step-by-step processes of use are explained. (3)

LETTERING WITH FELT PENS, *8mm SC film, three minutes, silent, color, Hester.*
Proper methods for professional-quality lettering in color with felt pens. (3,4)

LETTERING WITH GUIDES, *8mm SC film, four minutes, silent, color, Hester.*
Through the use of Wrico lettering set, this film shows the procedures for obtaining professional-quality lettering. (3)

LETTERING: WRICOPRINT, *8mm SC film, two minutes, silent, b and w, McGraw-Hill Text-Films, 1965.*
Using Wricoprint stencil lettering guide and pen for lettering ½ inch and smaller. (3)

LETTERING: WRICO SIGNMAKER, *8mm SC film, four minutes, silent, b and w, McGraw-Hill Text-Films, 1956.*
Using Wrico Sign-maker stencil lettering guide with brush pen and felt pen for lettering ½ inch and larger. (3)

LINE PHOTOGRAPHY, *35mm slides (79), color, Eastman Kodak, 1968.*
Unit includes seventy-nine color slides and typewritten script. The general procedures in line photography, a process important to industry, are discussed in this special program for graphic arts education. Other topics covered include preparation of copy for line photography; and exposure, processing, and preparation of the line negative for lithographic plate making and printing. (1,5)

MAGAZINES TO TRANSPARENCIES, *16mm film, twelve minutes, sound, color, International Film Bureau, 1958.*
Demonstrates the making of transparencies from magazine photographs with common materials— scissors, rubber cement, and sheets of frosted acetate. (1,5)

MAGIC OF THE FLANNEL BOARD, THE, *16mm film, nineteen minutes, sound, color, Association Films, 1964.*
Shows ways creative visual cutouts may be used to stimulate student curiosity and motivations, to drill students in mathematics and reading, and to introduce abstract ideas and difficult concepts. (1)

MAKING A MOVIE WITHOUT A CAMERA, *16mm film, six minutes, sound, color, Bailey.*
Shows a group of students working on their own art film. They are drawing directly on film leader, in the process made popular by Norman McLaren. The finished efforts of the group, set to music, appear at the finale.

MAKING A POSTER COMBINING WRICO LETTERING WITH A PICTURE MOUNTED WITH A SEAL DRY MOUNTING PRESS, *35mm double-frame unmounted slides, color, Training Services, 1968.*
A slide set developed originally for training preservice teachers at the University of Connecticut. This set deals with producing a simple poster combining stencil tracing lettering (Wrico) with a mounted picture. (1,3,4)

MAKING A THERMO-FAX TRANSPARENCY FROM A PENCIL MASTER, *35mm double-frame unmounted slides, color, Training Services, 1968.*
A slide set developed originally for training preservice teachers at the University of Connecticut. This set deals with the basic principles of making a thermocopy transparency from a handmade pencil master (original). (1,5)

MAKING MAPS AND CHARTS, *8mm SC film, three minutes, silent, color, Hester.*
Covers advantages of using movable instructional materials rather than static posters and bulletin boards. (1,3)

MANIPULATIVE DEVICES, *8mm SC film, four minutes, silent, color, Hester.*
Covers advantages of using movable instructional materials rather than static posters and bulletin boards.

MEET PHOTOSCREEN PRINTING, *16mm film, fourteen minutes, sound, color, Eastman Kodak, 1956.*
Traces the progress of screen printing from the hand methods of centuries ago to modern photomechanical technique.

MIMEOGRAPH, THE, *35mm filmstrip, twenty-four minutes, sound, color, A. B. Dick.*
Shows choosing the right ink, inking the machine, operating the

mimeograph, and shortcuts to color work. (1,4)

MIMEOGRAPHING TECHNIQUES, 16mm film, sixteen minutes, sound, color, Bailey, 1958.
Demonstrates the complete process of typing a mimeograph stencil, making corrections, using the mimeoscope for handlettering, and operating a modern electric mimeograph machine. Supplies, equipment, and specialized tools are shown. Handy tips are offered to improve mimeographed copies in both black and white and color. The film also discusses different types of duplicating processes, their purposes and advantages. (1, 3, 4)

MOUNTING: A CUT-OUT PICTURE, 8mm SC film, three minutes, silent, b and w, McGraw-Hill Text-Films, 1965.
Dry mounting a picture that requires removal of advertising or other material from the page around the picture. (2)

MOUNTING AND MASKING PROJECTUALS, 35mm filmstrip, 41 frames, sound, color, Educational Media, 1968.
Identification of various terms associated with special mounting techniques; effective use of single- and multi-overlay projectables and examples of basic masking techniques. (5)

MOUNTING: A TWO-PAGE PICTURE, 8mm, SC film, four minutes, silent, color, McGraw-Hill Text-Films, 1965. Dry mounting a picture that extends across two separate pages in a magazine. (2)

MOUNTING: OVERCOMING DRY MOUNTING PROBLEMS, 8mm SC film, three minutes, silent, b and w, McGraw-Hill Text-Films, 1965.
Preventing the formation of bubbles when dry mounting and what to do if they appear after mounting. (2)

MOUNTING PICTURES, 35mm filmstrip, 58 frames, color, University of Texas at Austin, 1957.
Presents methods of mounting pictures for a variety of purposes. Describes materials used, steps in mounting, and ways of protecting pictures. Shows basic steps in mounting with rubber cement and dry mounting tissue. (2)

MOUNTING: SETTING GROMMETS, 8mm SC film, two minutes, silent, b and w, McGraw-Hill Text-Films, 1965.
Setting metal grommets (rings) in a cloth-backed map for ease in displaying. (2)

MOUNTING: USING LAMINATING FILM, 8mm SC film, four minutes, silent, b and w, McGraw-Hill Text-Films, 1965.
Dry mounting a mylar film, for protection, over the surface of a mounted picture. Shows other uses for laminating film. (2)

MURAL MAKING, 16mm film, six minutes, sound, color, International Film Bureau, 1956.
Explains that the urge to draw and paint can be encouraged along constructive lines in the classroom. Shows the making of a mural as a class project with everyone participating. (1)

OPAQUE PROJECTOR, THE, 35mm filmstrip, 46 frames, color, Ohio State University, Teaching Aids Lab, 1957.
Presents a pictorial analysis of the instructional use of the opaque projector together with suggestions on operation and the preparation of materials to be projected. (1)

OPAQUE PROJECTOR: ITS PURPOSE AND USE, THE, 16mm film, 6 minutes, sound, b and w, University of Iowa, 1958.
Shows how to adjust the projector for screen size, how to clean the lenses, how to focus, and how to

handle other details of preparation of the projector for use in the classroom. (1)

OUTLINE MAPS: OVERHEAD PROJECTION TRANSPARENCIES, 10- by 10-inch overhead transparencies, G. A. F. Corp.
Fully processed and mounted 10- by 10-inch transparencies of outline maps of all major countries of the world. Maps can be projected on a projection screen or on any other drawing surface for tracing. (1,5)

OVERHEAD PROJECTOR, THE, 16mm film, twenty-seven minutes, sound, b and w, 3M Company, 1967.
Details and demonstrated effective classroom use and reinforcement techniques as related to the overhead projector. (1,4,5)

OVERHEAD PROJECTOR, 16mm film, seventeen minutes, sound, b and w, University of Iowa, 1953.
Shows a variety of materials that can be used and different techniques for preparing transparencies, including drawing and writing on transparent materials and using carbon-backed film and cutouts. Demonstrates the preparation of diazo transparencies (diazo process) and the use of autopositive paper. (1,3,5)

OVERHEAD TELEVISION, 16mm film, thirty minutes, sound, color, University of California, Berkeley, 1960.
Suggests ways in which recent innovations in television techniques can be used to meet the expanding needs in classroom communication. (1,5)

PAPER IN ART, 16mm film, seventeen minutes, sound, color, Churchill Films, 1967.
Demonstrates the processes of chalking, painting, crayoning, decorating with objects, folding, cutting, stenciling, weaving, collage, paper sculpture, puppet making, and paper maché. (1,4)

PAPER MACHE, *16mm film, fifteen minutes, sound, color, ACI Productions, 1967.*
Presents the basic processes involved in making three-dimensional forms of paper maché.

PASSE PARTOUT FRAMING, *16mm film, ten minutes, sound, b and w or color, Indiana University, 1957.*
Framing flat and object materials using a transparent cover, a picture, a cardboard backing, and a tape binding; framing three-dimensional materials; the uses of passe-partout materials and the means of displaying and filing them. **(2)**

PERSPECTIVE DRAWING, *16mm film, eight minutes, sound, color, University of California, Department of Theatre Arts, 1951.*
Presents an introduction to mechanical perspective; useful in teaching freehand sketching. **(1)**

PHOTOGRAPHIC DUPLICATION, *16mm film, twenty-one minutes, sound, b and w, Ohio State University Motion Picture Division, 1953.*
Techniques and equipment used in the commercial production of blueprints, ammonia prints, and photostats are discussed. **(5)**

PHOTOGRAPHIC SLIDES FOR INSTRUCTION, *16mm film, eleven minutes, sound, b and w or color, Indiana University, 1957.*
The preparation and use of slides made by the photographic process. The range of materials that can be copied from books and magazines; the use of color and black and white film in indoor and outdoor situations; flash photography, copying, and the use of Polaroid transparency film for making slides in a variety of subject areas. **(1,3,4,5)**

PHOTOGRAPHY: CLOSE-UPS AND COPYING WITH 35MM CAMERAS, *35mm filmstrips (4), sound, color, Bailey, 1964.*
Graphic color photographs and artwork are combined with efficient narration to motivate the audience and explain how to use a 35mm camera in the interesting field of close-up and copying photography. Answers the needs of teachers and students who have 35mm cameras and who want to photograph close-ups and copy slides. Supplementary materials are included in a manual for those who desire further study. **(1,5)**

PLANNING THE PROJECTUAL, *35mm filmstrip, 47 frames, sound, color, Educational Media, 1968.*
Setting objectives and story-boarding; projectual composition; using color and overlays. **(1,3,4,5)**

POSTER MAKING, *8mm SC film, three minutes, silent, color, Hester.*
Various ways of creating posters which are clean-cut, easily read, and effectively designed. Also, consideration is given to the spacing of letters. **(1,3,4)**

POSTER MAKING: DESIGN AND TECHNIQUE, *16mm film, ten minutes, sound, color, Bailey, 1953.*
Stresses the principles of poster making, including layout, lettering, painting, optical spacing, color contrast, and painting. **(1,3,4)**

POSTER MAKING: PRINTING BY SILK SCREEN, *16mm film, fifteen minutes, sound, color, Bailey, 1953.*
A step-by-step presentation of the process involved in silk-screen printing from the design to the mounting. **(1,4)**

POSTERS FOR TEACHING, *35mm filmstrip, 40 frames, silent, b and w, McGraw-Hill Text-Films, 1963.*
Presents arrangement, lettering, and color as they apply to poster making. **(1,3,4)**

PREPARING MATERIALS, *16mm film, twenty-seven minutes, sound, b and w, 3M Company, 1967.*
Explains different functions and use of various transparency-making materials and gives best sources of acquiring visual originals. **(1,3,5)**

PREPARING PROJECTED MATERIALS, *16mm film, fifteen minutes, sound, color, Bailey, 1965.*
Illustrates the growth of the audio-visual field by contrasting the old magic lantern with the modern projection materials. Discusses the use of projectors, 35mm cameras, Polaroid copying stand, and Thermofax copier. **(1,5)**

PRINT-FINISHING TECHNIQUES, *2-by 2-inch slides, twenty-five minutes, sound, color, Eastman Kodak.*
Print-finishing techniques for black-and-white prints. Techniques covered include mounting, spotting, and etching. Slides show what to do and how to do it. **(5)**

PRINTING THE POSITIVE, *16mm film, nineteen minutes, sound, b and w, DuArt, 1950.*
Shows hand and machine methods of making photographic prints. Emphasizes cleanliness, timing, temperature, testing of solutions, and drying. **(5)**

PROJECTING IDEAS, II: DIAZO TRANSPARENCY PRODUCTION, *16mm film, eleven minutes, sound, color, University of Iowa, 1964.*
Provides a source of visualized information concerning the basic aspects of diazo transparency production. Demonstrates elementary concepts of exposing and developing diazo film and the step-by-step procedure for preparing a transparency. Stresses procedures that can be used by persons unfamiliar with diazo materials. **(1,3,4,5)**

PROJECTING IDEAS, III: DIRECT TRANSPARENCY PRODUCTION, *16mm film, five minutes, sound, color, University of Iowa, 1964.*
Introduces production of hand-drawn and -lettered transparencies, primarily on acetate, and illustrates use of various types of pencils, felt-tipped pens, and lettering devices. Discusses types of sheet material

available, and use of printers' ink, watercolors, and colored transparent tapes. **(1,3,4,5)**

PROJECTING IDEAS ON THE OVERHEAD PROJECTOR, *16mm film, seventeen minutes, sound, color, University of Iowa, 1960.*
Outlines the advantage of the overhead projector as a visual aid to learning in classrooms, in business and industry. Shows the great variety of uses of the equipment with opaque, translucent, and transparent materials, and combinations of these, both in contrasting colors and in monochrome. Stresses the ease with which effective presentations can be improvised through the use of movable graphic components, overlays, Polaroid filters, transparent working models, and even chemical reactions in a test tube. **(1,4,5)**

PROJECTO-TRACE CLASSROOM PICTURES, *35mm filmstrips (8), color, Encyclopaedia Britannica Films.*
This series of filmstrips provides teachers with a quick, effective method of preparing chalkboard illustrations. Each filmstrip contains a series of simple, professionally executed, white line drawings which may be projected onto a chalkboard or other drawing surface and then quickly traced. The series include: *Holidays and Special Days, The Farm, Wild Animals, Community Helpers, Plants, Birds, Foods, and Seasons and Weather.* **(1)**

PUT YOUR BEST HAND FORWARD IN LETTERING, *35mm filmstrip, 60 frames, color, Hunt Manufacturing Co., 1960.*
Shows techniques of hand lettering with Speedball pens taught in junior and senior high schools. Illustrates the need of lettering as it fits into the classroom situation and how it can improve your work in school. **(3)**

RESEARCH IN EDUCATIONAL MEDIA, *10- by 10-inch overhead transparencies, University of Iowa, 1968.*

A valuable set of overhead transparencies for preservice and inservice education courses. The set includes such subjects as the importance of size in pictures, display captions, color, type size for overhead transparencies, etc. **(1,3,4,5)**

RUBBER CEMENT MOUNTING, *8mm SC film, four minutes, silent, b and w, McGraw-Hill Text-Films, 1965.*
Using rubber cement on the back of a picture and on cardboard to mount permanently a magazine picture. **(2)**

SCREEN PRINTING, *16mm film, fourteen minutes, sound, b and w, University of Iowa, 1958.*
Shows examples of amateur and professional screen printing and gives suggestions for design and materials. A demonstration makes a screen, transfers a design, and prints a fabric. **(1,4)**

SILK SCREEN PRINTING, *16mm film, ten minutes, sound, color, AV-ED, 1957.*
Demonstrates the technique whereby hand screen printing has been brought up to date. Shows preparation, washing, dyeing, printing, and completion. **(1)**

SILK SCREEN PROCESS, *16mm film, twenty minutes, sound, b and w, Library Films, 1945.*
Shows the techniques of silk-screen printing. Gives a detailed presentation of the steps involved in making screens and in printing. **(1,4)**

SILK SCREEN TEXTILE PRINTING, *16mm film, eleven minutes, sound, color, Bailey, 1952.*
Translates a dress-material design into a silk-screen stencil and textile print. Explains the basic silk-screen process and suggests use of it for printing Christmas cards, place mats, and other gifts. **(1,4)**

SIMPLE LETTERING TECHNIQUE, *8mm SC film, four minutes, silent, color, Hester.*

Simple procedures for using precut letters, spray paint, and stencils for the rapid production of classroom bulletin boards and posters. **(3)**

SIMPLE PROJECTUAL PRODUCTION, *35mm filmstrip, 40 frames, sound, color, Educational Media, 1968.*
Part A: techniques of preparing handmade projectuals which will have professional appearance and effectiveness. Part B: procedure for making heat-transfer masters and production of heat-transfer projectuals. **(1,4)**

STENCIL, THE, *35mm filmstrip, twenty-two minutes, sound, color, A. B. Dick.*
Shows how to type stencils; make corrections; select the right stencil; draw, letter, and shade stencils; and principles of electronic stencil imaging. **(1,3,4)**

SUCCESSFUL EXHIBIT IDEAS, *35mm filmstrip, 81 frames, silent, b and w, Pocket Films, 1958.*
Shows selection of backgrounds, design and color, drawings, cartoons, pictures, captions, and lettering. **(1,3,4)**

TAPES, HINGING AND STORING, *35mm filmstrip, 39 frames, sound, color, Educational Media, 1967.*
Concerned with the multitude of adhesive materials which are now available, and very useful, for classroom use. Covered are edging and binding tapes, plus special polyesters used in hinging. Educational storage problems are discussed. **(2)**

TEACHER EVALUATION, *35mm filmstrip, 26 frames, sound, color, Educational Media, 1967.*
Techniques which can be used by teachers in evaluating their own materials and that of others in the basic graphics area. This filmstrip is designed to be used after lab exercises in skill areas and should be of considerable assistance in the development of critical and analytical thinking where visual materials are concerned.

TEACHER ORIENTATION, *35mm filmstrip, 56 frames, sound color, Educational Media, 1967.*
Designed to familiarize classroom teachers with meaning of such terms as basic educational graphics, local production, and so forth. Also includes an overview of basic classroom skills, the equipment and materials required, and rationale for use.

TEACHING DRAFTING WITH TRANSPARENCIES, *16mm film, nine minutes, sound, b and w, University of Iowa, 1956.*
Presents the idea that, with an understanding of the fundamentals of drawing, and with patience, anyone can learn to draw. Outlines the basic ideas in use of perspective, in treatment of surfaces, sizes, surface lines, overlapping circles, and shadings to achieve the desired effects. **(1,4,5)**

TEACHING WITH VISUAL MATERIALS, *35mm filmstrips (6), 38 frames each, color, McGraw-Hill Text-Films, 1964.*
Six color filmstrips designed to promote teacher interest in visual teaching and to provide practical suggestions for the effective use of the bulletin board, flannel board, poster, and chalkboard as visual teaching devices.

TECHNIQUES OF MODERN OFFSET, *35mm filmstrips (7), sound, color, A. B. Dick Co.*
This series provides teachers and students with a complete course in how to use the offset duplicating process, including preparation of artwork, master and plate imaging, selection and use of inks and papers and machine operation. **(1,3,4)**

TRAINING AIDS: SLIDES, LARGE DRAWING AND TRANSPARENCIES, *16mm film, eighteen minutes, sound, color, United World, 1952.*
Urges instructors to make their own 3¼- by 4-inch lantern slides and large transparencies for use with the overhead projector. Explains the nature of the equipment and materials which are needed and the opportunity for preparing and using such aids. **(1,3,5)**

TRANSPARENCIES: ADDING COLOR, *8mm SC film, three minutes, silent, color, McGraw-Hill Text-Films, 1965.*
Using felt pens, diazo films, and transparent color adhesives for coloring areas on transparencies. **(4,5)**

TRANSPARENCIES: DIAZO PROCESS, *8mm SC film, three minutes, silent, color, McGraw-Hill Text-Films, 1965.*
Exposing a translucent paper master drawing and a diazo film in a Beseler Vugraph ultraviolet printer and developing the film in a jar containing ammonia vapor. **(1,4,5)**

TRANSPARENCIES: HANDMADE METHOD, *8mm SC film, three minutes, silent, color, McGraw-Hill Text-Films, 1965.*
Using felt pens and transparent marking pencils on clear acetate. **(1,4,5)**

TRANSPARENCIES: HEAT PROCESS, *8mm SC film, two minutes, silent, color, McGraw-Hill Text-Films, 1965.*
Using thermocopy (infrared) projection film to prepare a transparency from an original diagram in the "secretary" model copying machine. **(1,5)**

TRANSPARENCIES: MAKING OVERLAYS, *8mm SC film, three minutes, silent, color, McGraw-Hill Text-Films, 1965.*
Preparing translucent paper master drawings as a series of overlays from an original sketch with emphasis on use of corner registration marks to ensure alignment of final transparencies. **(1,4,5)**

TRANSPARENCIES: MOUNTING AND MASKING, *8mm SC film, three minutes, silent, color, McGraw-Hill Text-Films, 1965.*
Using tape to mount a single-sheet transparency and one with overlays to a cardboard frame. Shows results of masking and disclosing information on transparencies with a sliding mask and hinged masks. **(5)**

TRANSPARENCIES: PICTURE TRANSFER 1 and 2, *8mm SC films, three minutes each, silent, color, McGraw-Hill Text-Films, 1965.*
Shows how to use a dry mount press to seal a clay-coated picture to Seal Transpara film; then how to separate, in water, the paper from the picture and film. Shows the resulting transparency after drying and spraying. **(1,5)**

TRANSPARENCIES: PRINCIPLE OF DIAZO PROCESS, *8mm SC film, four minutes, silent, color, McGraw-Hill Text-Films, 1965.*
Results of four experiments to illustrate the principle of diazo process: (1) developing diazo film without exposure, (2) exposing diazo film to sunlight and developing, (3) partially covering diazo film with paper, exposing and developing, (4) covering diazo film with a diagram on tracing paper, exposing and developing. **(1,4,5)**

TRANSPARENCIES: SPIRIT DUPLICATOR, *8mm SC film, three minutes, silent, color, McGraw-Hill Text-Films, 1965.*
Using a spirit duplicator machine to prepare a transparency on frosted acetate from a spirit master in three colors. **(1,4,5)**

USING THE OVERHEAD PROJECTOR, *35mm filmstrip, 43 frames, sound, color, Educational Media, 1968.*
The development of overhead projection as a classroom technique; comparison: overhead projector with opaque projector; flexibility of the overhead projector; some basic rules for use; and some applications. **(1,5)**

WET MOUNTING PICTORIAL MATERIALS, *16mm films, twelve minutes, sound, b and w or color, Indiana University, 1952.*

Selecting a map to be mounted, mixing the paste, preparing the map, tacking the cloth backing to the working surface and applying the paste, rolling to spread the paste evenly, and finishing the edges. Methods of displaying and using the mounted materials including film or turnover charts, opaque projection strips, and wall charts. **(2)**

ADDRESS DIRECTORY

A

A1. ABC SUPPLY, INC., 34 E. Andrews Dr., N.W., Atlanta, Ga. 30305

A2. ABM BUSINESS AUTOMATION, INC. 115 E. 23rd St., New York, N.Y. 10010

A3. ACI PRODUCTIONS, 16 W. 46th St., New York, N.Y. 10036

A4. ACROLITE PRODUCTS, INC., 810 Martin St., Rahway, N.J. 07065

A5. ACS TAPES, INC., 217 California St., Newton, Mass. 02158

A6. ADDO-X, INC., 300 Park Ave., New York, N.Y., 10022

A7. ADDRESSOGRAPH MULTIGRAPH CORP., 1200 Babbit Rd., Cleveland, Ohio 44117

A8. ADHESIVE PRODUCTS CORP., 1660 Boone Ave., Bronx, N.Y. 10460

A9. ADHESIVE TAPE CORP., 58-64 Seabring St., Brooklyn, N.Y. 11231

A10. ADOBE INTERNATIONAL, 4131 El Camino Real, Palo Alto, Calif. 94306

A11. ADVERTISING AIDS CO., 315 Fifth Ave., N., Minneapolis, Minn. 55401

A12. AGFA-GEVAERT, INC., 275 North St., Teterboro, N.J. 07608

A13. AGNEKO, INC., 177 Louis St., Maywood, N.J., 07607

A14. S. B. ALBERTIS, 5 Tudor City Pl., New York, N.Y. 10017

A15. ALLWAY MFG. CO., Dept. AG-68, 1513 Orlmstead Ave., Bronx, N.Y. 10462

A16. THEODORE ALTENEDER & SONS, 1217 Spring Garden St., Philadelphia, Pa. 19123

A17. ALTMAN CAMERA CO., 16 S. Wabash Ave., Chicago, Ill. 60603

A18. ALVIN & CO., INC., 611 Palisado Ave., Windsor, Conn. 06095

A19. AMERICAN BOOK CO., College Division, 450 W. 33rd St., New York, N.Y. 10001

A20. THE AMERICAN CRAYON CO., 1706 Hayes Ave., Sandusky, Ohio 44871

A21. AMERICAN JET SPRAY INDUSTRIES, INC., P.O. Box 14006, Edgewater, Denver, Colo. 80214

A22. AMERICAN LIBRARY COLOR SLIDE CO., INC., 305 E. 45th St., New York, N.Y. 10017

A23. AMERICAN MAP CO., INC., 3 W. 61st St., New York, N.Y. 14215

A24. AMERICAN MARKETING SERVICES, 600 Winter St., Waltham, Mass. 02154

A25. AMERICAN OPTICAL CO., INSTRUMENT DIV., Eggert & Sugar Rd., Buffalo, N.Y. 14215

A26. AMERICAN STENCIL MFG. CO., 4290 Holly St., Denver, Colo. 80216

A27. AMERICAN TYPE FOUNDERS CO., INC., 200 Elmora Ave., Elizabeth, N.J. 07207

A28. ANCHOR CHEMICAL CO., INC., 500 W. John St., Hicksville, N.Y. 11801

A29. ANCO WOOD SPECIALTIES, INC., 81-08 80th St., Glendale, N.Y. 11227

A30. ANKEN CHEMICAL & FILM CORP., Newton, N.J. 07860

A31. APPLETON COATED PAPER CO., 825 E. Wisconsin Ave., Appleton, Wis. 54911

A32. APPLIED GRAPHICS CORP., 58 Shore Rd., Glenwood Landing, L.I., N.Y. 11547

A33. APPLIED SCIENCES, INC., 12435 Euclid Ave., Cleveland, Ohio 44106

A34. A. A. ARCHBOLD, PUBLISHERS, P.O. Box 57985, Los Angeles, Calif. 90057

A35. ARKWRIGHT, Main St., Fiskeville, R.I. 02823

A36. B. ARONSTEIN & CO., 41-02A 162nd St., Flushing, N.Y. 11358

A37. ART DIRECTIONS BOOK CO., 19 W. 44th St., New York, N.Y. 10036

A38. ARTIST SUPPLY CO., 3194 E. 65th St., Cleveland, Ohio 44127

A39. ART-O-GRAPH, INC., 529 S. 7th St., Minneapolis, Minn. 55415

A40. ARTS & CRAFTS MATERIALS CORP., 321 Park Ave., Baltimore, Md. 21201

A41. ARTYPE, INC., 345 E. Terra Cotta Ave. (Rt. 176), Crystal Lake, Ill. 60014

A42. ASSOCIATION FILMS, INC., 600 Madison Ave., New York, N.Y. 10022

A43. AUDIOVISUAL INSTRUCTION, NEA, 1201 16th St., N.W., Washington, D.C. 20036

A44. AUDIO VISUAL SECTION, 43 Ross St., Brooklyn, N.Y. 11211

A45. A-V COMMUNICATIONS, INC., 159 Verdi St., Farmingdale, N.Y. 11735

A46. AV-ED FILMS, 7934 Santa Monica Blvd., Hollywood, Calif. 90046

A47. AVERY LABEL CO., 1616 S. California Ave., Monrovia, Calif. 91016

A48. AZTEC INDUSTRIES, INC., 3137 W. 25th St., Chicago, Ill. 60623

B

B1. BADGER AIRBRUSH CO., 9201 Gage Ave., Franklin Park, Ill. 60131

B2. BAILEY FILMS, 6509 DeLongpre Ave., Hollywood, Calif. 90028

B3. BANTAM BOOKS, INC., 271 Madison Ave., New York, N.Y. 10016

B4. BARNES & NOBLE, INC., 105 Fifth Ave., New York, N.Y. 10003

B5. BASIC CRAFTS CO., 312 E. 23rd St., New York, N.Y. 10010

B6. BAUSCH & LOMB, INC., Rochester, N.Y. 14602

B7. BECKLEY-CARDY CO., 1900 N. Narragansett, Chicago, Ill. 60639

B8. BEE PAPER CO., INC., P.O. Box 1016, Passaic, N.J. 07055

B9. BELL & HOWELL CO., 7100 McCormick Rd., Chicago, Ill. 60645

B10. BEMISS-JASON CORP., 3250 Ash St., Palo Alto, Calif. 94306

B11. CHARLES BESELER CO., 219 S. 18th St., East Orange, N.J. 07018

B12. RICHARD BEST PENCIL CO., INC., Springfield, N.J. 07081

B13. BEST PLASTIC PRODUCTS, INC., 325 W. 25th Pl., Chicago, Ill. 60616

B14. BIENFANG PAPER CO., INC., Amboy Ave. & Linsley Pl., Metuchen, N.J. 08840

B15. BISHOP INDUSTRIES CORP., 11728 Vose St., North Hollywood, Calif. 91605

B16. BLAIN-WHITTED GRAPHICS, INC., 2447 N. Ashland Ave., Chicago, Ill. 60614

B17. BLAIR ART PRODUCTS, INC., 3540 Summer Ave., Memphis, Tenn. 38122

B18. DICK BLICK, P.O. Box 1267, Galesburg, Ill. 61401

B19. BLU-RAY, INC., Essex, Conn. 06426

B20. THE BORDEN CHEMICAL CO., 350 Madison Ave., New York, N.Y. 10017

B21. BOURGES COLOR CORP., 80 Fifth Ave., New York, N.Y. 10011

B22. ROBERT J. BRADY CO., 130 Que St., N.E., Washington, D.C. 20002

B23. W. H. BRADY CO., 727 W. Glendale Ave., Milwaukee, Wis. 53209

B24. BREWSTER CORP., Old Lyme, Conn. 06371

B25. BRO-DART, P.O. Box 1120, Newark, N.J. 07101

B26. BROOKS MFG. CO., P.O. Box 41195G, Cincinnati, Ohio 45241

B27. ARTHUR BROWN & BROTHER, INC., 2 W. 46th St., New York, N.Y. 10036

B28. WILLIAM C. BROWN BOOK CO., PUBL., 135 S. Locust St., Dubuque, Iowa 52001

B29. BRUMBURGER CO., INC., 1948 Troutman St., Brooklyn, N.Y. 11237

B30. CHARLES BRUNING CO., 1800 W. Central Rd., Mount Prospect, Ill. 60058

B31. BUCKINGHAM GRAPHICS, INC., 537 Custer Ave., Evanston, Ill. 60202

B32. BUHL OPTICAL CO., 1009 Beach Ave., Pittsburgh, Pa. 15233

B33. BUHL PROJECTOR CO., INC., 1776 New Highway, Farmingdale, N.Y. 11735

B34. BURKE & JAMES, INC., 333 W. Lake St., Chicago, Ill. 60606

B35. THE BUSINESS PRESS, 288 Park Ave., W., Elmhurst, Ill. 60126

B36. BUSINESS REPORTS, INC., 1 West Ave., Larchmont, N.Y. 10538

C

C1. UNIVERSITY OF CALIFORNIA, Department of Theatre Arts, 405 Hilgard Ave., Los Angeles, Calif. 90024

C2. UNIVERSITY OF CALIFORNIA, Extension Media Center, 2223 Fulton St., Berkeley, Calif., 94720

C3. CALUMET MFG. CO., 6550 N. Clark St., Chicago, Ill. 60626

C4. CANON U. S. A., INC., 554 Fifth Ave., New York, N.Y. 10036

C5. CARDINELL CORP., 15 Label St., Montclair, N.J. 07042

C6. CARTER'S INK CO., Cambridge, Mass. 02142

C7. CELLO-TAK MFG., INC., 35 Alabama Ave., Island Park, L.I., N.Y. 11558

C8. CENCO EDUCATIONAL AIDS, 2600 S. Kostner Ave., Chicago, Ill. 60623

C9. CENTRAL PLASTICS DIST., 527 S. Wells St., Chicago, Ill. 60607

C10. CHANDLER PUBLISHING CO., 124 Spear St., San Francisco, Calif. 94105

C11. CHARTPAK ROTEX, One River Rd., Leeds, Mass. 01053

C12. CHARVOZ-CARSEN CORP., 5 Daniel Rd., Fairfield, N.J. 07006

C13. CHARVOZ-ROOS CORP., 50 Colfax Ave., Clifton, N.J. 07011

C14. CHEMCO PHOTOPRODUCTS CO., INC., P.O. Drawer 151, Glen Cove, N.Y. 11542

C15. CHILTON BOOKS, EDUCATIONAL DIV., 525 Locust St., Philadelphia, Pa. 19106

C16. CHURCHILL FILMS, 662 N. Robertson Blvd., Los Angeles, Calif. 90069

C17. C-LINE PRODUCTS, INC., 1530 E. Birchwood Ave., Des Plaines, Ill. 60018

C18. CODACOLOR, 45 N. Dean St., Englewood, N.J. 07631

C19. JOHN COLBURN ASSOCIATES, INC., 1122 Central Ave., Wilmette, Ill. 60091

C20. COLE STEEL EQUIPMENT CO., INC., 415 Madison Ave., New York, N.Y. 10017

C21. COLIGHT, INC., 123 N. Third St., Minneapolis, Minn. 55401

C22. COLONIAL CARBON CO., 2020 S. Mannheim Rd., Des Plaines, Ill. 60018

C23. COLONIAL FILMS, INC., 71 Walton St., N.W., Atlanta, Ga. 30303

C24. COLUMBIA CEMENT CO., INC., 150 Ingraham St., Brooklyn, N.Y. 11237

C25. COLUMBIA RIBBON-CARBON MFG. CO., INC., Herbhill Rd., Glen Cove, N.Y. 11542

C26. COMARK PLASTIC DIV., 1407 Broadway, New York, N.Y. 10018

C27. COMMERCIAL BALL PEN, 30 W. 32nd St., New York, N.Y. 10001

C28. DAVID C. COOK PUBLISHING CO., 850 N. Grove Ave., Elgin, Ill. 60120

C29. COPY RESEARCH, 875 W. 15th St., Newport Beach, Calif. 92660

C30. COPY-RITE CORP., 1201 Cortland St., Chicago, Ill. 60614

C31. CORONET FILMS, 65 E. Water St., Chicago, Ill. 60601

C32. WEBER COSTELLO, 1900 N. Narragansett, Chicago, Ill. 60639

C33. THE CRAFTINT MFG. CO., 18501 Euclid Ave., Cleveland, Ohio 44112

C34. CREATIVE HANDS BOOK-SHOP, Printers Bldg., Worcester, Mass. 01608

C35. CREATIVE PLAYTHINGS, INC., Princeton, N.J. 08540

C36. CREATIVE VISUALS, INC., Box 310, Big Springs, Texas 79720

C37. CRESCENT CARDBOARD CO., 1240 N. Homan Ave., Chicago, Ill. 60651

C38. THOMAS Y. CROWELL CO., 201 Park Ave., S., New York, N.Y. 10003

C39. THE C-THRU RULER CO., 6 Britton Dr., Bloomfield, Conn. 06002

C40. CUSTOM-BILT MACHINERY, INC., 920 Elm St., York, Pa. 17403

C41. CUSTOM PRINTERS SUPPLY, 406 E. Elm St., Springfield, Mo. 65806

D

D1. C.P.DA CORTA, 5 Hardy St., Boston, Mass. 02154

D2. DAIGE PRODUCTS, INC., 160 Denton Ave., New Hyde Park, L.I., N.Y. 11040

D3. BERT L. DAILY, INC., 120 E. Third St., Dayton, Ohio 45402

D4. THE DATAK CORP., 85 Highland Ave., Passaic, N.J. 07055

D5. DAVIS PUBLICATIONS, Printers Bldg., Worcester, Mass. 01608

D6. DEE-LITE INDUSTRIES, INC., 7016 20th Ave., Brooklyn, N.Y. 11204

D7. DELKOTE, INC., Box 1335, Wilmington, Del. 19899

D8. DEMCO, Box 1488, Madison, Wis. 53701

D9. THE DEMP-NOCK CO., 21433 Mound Rd., Warren, Mich. 48090

D10. T. S. DENISON & CO., INC., 321 Fifth Ave., S., Minneapolis, Minn. 55415

D11. DENNISON MFG. CO., Framingham, Mass. 01702

D12. DIAZO SPECIALTY CO., 6035 Baltimore Ave., Riverdale, Md. 20840

D13. A. B. DICK CO., 5700 W. Touhy Ave., Chicago, Ill. 60648

D14. EUGENE DIETZGEN CO., 2425 N. Sheffield Ave., Chicago, Ill. 60614

D15. DISMAR PRODUCTS, INC., N.W. Corner "A" and Clearfield Sts., Philadelphia, Pa. 19134

D16. DITTO, INC., 6800 McCormick Rd., Chicago, Ill. 60645

D17. JOSEPH DIXON CRUCIBLE CO., Wayne & Monmouth Sts., Jersey City, N.J. 07303

D18. T. J. DONAHUE CO., Kimber-

ton, Pa. 19442

D19. DOVER PUBLICATIONS, INC., 180 Varick St., New York, N.Y. 10014

D20. DRI MARK PRODUCTS, INC., 158 S. 12th Ave., Mt. Vernon, N.Y. 10550

D21. DUART FILM LABS., INC., 245 W. 55th St., New York, N.Y. 10019

D22. DUKANE AUDIOVISUAL DIVISION CORP., St. Charles, Ill. 60174

D23. DURO ART SUPPLY CO., 1832 Juneway Terrace, Chicago, Ill. 60626

D24. DYMO PRODUCTS CO., P.O. Box 1030, Berkeley, Calif. 94701

E

E1. EAGLE PENCIL CO., INC., Eagle Rd., Danbury, Conn. 06810

E2. EASTMAN KODAK CO. (For publications: Audio-Visual Services), Rochester, N.Y. 14650

E3. EBERHARD FABER PEN & PENCIL CO., INC., Crestwood Rd. 3, Wilkes-Barre, Pa. 18703

E4. ECONASIGN CANADA CO., Box 887, Niagara-on-the-Lake, Ontario, Canada

E5. THE ECONASIGN CO., LTD., 19-21 Palace St., Victoria, London, S.W. 1, England

E6. EDMUND SCIENTIFIC CO., Barrington, N.J. 08007

E7. EDUCATIONAL MEDIA LABORATORIES, 4101 S. Congress Ave., Austin, Texas 78745

E8. EDUCATORS PUBLISHING SERVICE, INC., 301 Vassar St., Cambridge, Mass. 02139

E9. EHRENREICH PHOTO-OPTICAL INDUSTRIES, INC., 623 Stewart Ave., Garden City, N.Y. 11533

E10. E & I PRINTING CO., P.O. Box 152, Austin, Texas 78762

E11. ELECTRO-STYLUS MFG. CO., 31 Cheyenne Blvd., Colorado Springs, Colo. 80906

E12. EMBOSOGRAF CORP. OF AMERICA, 38 W. 21st St., New York, N.Y. 10010

E13. EMDE PRODUCTS, INC., 2040 Stoner Ave., Los Angeles, Calif. 90025

E14. ENCYCLOPAEDIA BRITANNICA FILMS, INC., 1150 Wilmette Ave., Wilmette, Ill. 60091

E15. ERIE SCIENTIFIC CORP., 693 Seneca St., Buffalo, N.Y. 14210

E16. THE ESTERBROOK PEN CO., Box 230, Cherry Hill, N.J. 08034

E17. EVANS SPECIALTY CO., INC., P.O. Box 4220, Richmond, Va. 23224

E18. E-Z BUCKLE, INC., 545 N. Arlington Ave., East Orange, N.J. 07017

E19. THE E-Z LETTER STENCIL CO., 1415 Mondawmin Concourse, Baltimore, Md. 21215

F

F1. A. W. FABER-CASTELL-HIGGINS, 41—47 Dickerson St., Newark, N.J. 07103

F2. FAIRCHILD GRAPHIC EQUIPMENT, 221 Fairchild Ave., Plainview, N.Y. 11803

F3. FASSON PRODUCTS, 250 Chester St., Painesville, Ohio 44077

F4. FEARON PUBLISHERS, INC., 2165 Park Blvd., Palo Alto, Calif. 94306

F5. FILM ASSOCIATES OF CALIFORNIA, 11559 Santa Monica Blvd., Los Angeles, Calif. 90025

F6. FILMOTYPE CORP., 7500 McCormick Blvd., Skokie, Ill. 60076

F7. OSCAR FISHER CO., INC., P.O. Box 2305, Newburgh, N.Y. 12550

F8. SAM FLAX, 25 E. 28th St., New York, N.Y. 10016

F9. FLAX'S, 250 Sutter St., San Francisco, Calif. 94108

F10. FLOQUIL PRODUCTS, INC., Cobleskill, N.Y. 12043

F11. FLORIDA STATE UNIVERSITY, Audio-Visual Center, Division of University Relations, Tallahassee, Fla. 32306

F12. FOCAL PRESS, INC., 20 E. 46th St., New York, N.Y. 10017

F13. FOTORITE, INC., 6901 N. Hamlin Ave., Chicago, Ill., 60645

F14. FOTOTYPE, INC., 1414 Roscoe St., Chicago, Ill. 60657

F15. FRANKEL MFG. CO., P.O. Box 597, Denver, Colo. 80201

F16. FREKOTE, INC., P.O. Box

825, Boca Raton, Fla. 33432

F17. FRIDEN, 2352 WASHINGTON AVE., San Leandro, Calif. 94577

F18. A. I. FRIEDMAN, INC., 25 W. 45th St., New York, N.Y. 10036

F19. FUJI-KIDEN MFG. CO., LTD., 5-8, 1-Chome, Matsue, Edogawa-Ku, Tokyo, Japan

G

G1. G. A. F. CORP., 140 W. 51st St., New York, N.Y. 10020

G2. GAKKEN CO., LTD., C.P.O. Box No. 97, Tokyo, Japan

G3. GANE BROS. & LANE, INC., 1335 W. Lake St., Chicago, Ill. 60607

G4. GAYLORD BROS., INC., P.O. Drawer 61, Syracuse, N.Y. 13201

G5. GENERAL AIR BRUSH MFG. INC., 545 Sixth Ave., New York, N.Y. 10011

G6. GENERAL BINDING CORP., 1101 Skokie Blvd., Northbrook, Ill. 60062

G7. GENERAL PENCIL CO., 67 Fleet St., Jersey City, N.J. 07306

G8. GENERAL PHOTO PRODUCTS CO., INC., 10 Paterson Ave., Newton, N.J. 07860

G9. GESTETNER CORP., 216 Lake Ave., Yonkers, N.Y. 10702

G10. GOLDEN PRESS, INC., 850 Third Ave., Educational Division, New York, N.Y. 10022

G11. M. P. GOODKIN CO., 122 Arlington St., Newark, N.J. 07102

G12. GRAFCOM, P.O. Box 2665, Tulsa, Okla. 74114

G13. GRAFLEX, INC., General Precision Equipment Corp., 3750 Monroe Ave., Rochester, N.Y. 14603

G14. GRAND CENTRAL ARTISTS' MATERIALS, INC., 3 E. 40th St., New York, N.Y. 10016

G15. HENRY H. GRANT, P.O. Box 366, Redondo Beach, Calif. 90277

G16. GRAPHIC COMMUNICATIONS CORP., 101 Cedar Lane, Teaneck, N.J. 07666

G17. GRAPHIC PRODUCTS CORP., 3810 Industrial Ave., Rolling Meadows, Ill. 60008

G18. GRAPHIC SYSTEMS, 925 Danville Rd., Yanceyville, N.C. 27379

G19. GREGORY MAGNETIC INDUSTRIES, INC., Box 10196, Ft. Lauderdale, Fla. 33305

G20. M. GRUMBACHER, INC., 460 W. 34th St., New York, N.Y. 10001

G21. GRUNDIG BUSINESS MACHINES, INC., 355 Lexington Ave., New York, N.Y. 10017

H

H1. HALLMARK MONOGRAM CO., INC., 215 Englewood Ave., Englewood, N.J. 07631

H2. HAMMOND, INC., 515 Valley St., Maplewood, N.J. 07042

H3. HARCO INDUSTRIES, INC., 10802 N. 21st Ave., Phoenix, Arizona 85029

H4. HARPER & ROW PUBLISHERS, 49 E. 33rd St., New York, N.Y. 10016

H5. HASTINGS HOUSE PUBLISHERS, INC., 151 E. 50th St., New York, N.Y. 10022

H6. HAYES SCHOOL PUBLISHING CO., INC., 321 Pennwood Ave., Wilkinsburg, Pa. 15221

H7. D. C. HEATH & CO., 280–285 Columbus Ave., Boston, Mass. 02116

H8. KARL HEITZ, INC., 979 Third Ave., New York, N.Y. 10022

H9. JOHN HENSCHEL & CO., INC., 195 Marine St., Farmingdale, L.I., N.Y. 11735

H10. H. T. HERBERT CO., INC., 21–21 41st Ave., Long Island City, N.Y. 11101

H11. HERCULES POWDER CO., INC., Wilmington, Del. 19899

H12. HERNARD MFG. CO., INC., Executive Blvd., Elmsford, N.Y. 10523

H13. HESTER & ASSOCIATES, P.O. Box 20812, Dallas, Texas 75220

H14. HEYER, INC., 1850 S. Kostner Ave., Chicago, Ill. 60623

H15. HIGGINS INK CO., INC., 271 Ninth St., Brooklyn, N.Y. 11215

H16. HILLHOUSE, INC., P.O. Box 727, Sunnyvale, Calif. 94086

H17. W. W. HOLES MFG. CO., St. Cloud, Minn. 56301

H18. THE HOLSON CO., 111 Danbury Rd., Wilton, Conn. 06897

H19. HOLT, RINEHART & WINSTON, INC., 383 Madison Ave., New York, N.Y. 10017

H20. HOPPMANN CORP., 5410 Port Royal Rd., Springfield, Va. 22151

H21. HORDER'S STATIONERY STORES, INC., 231 S. Jefferson St., Chicago, Ill. 60606

H22. T. N. HUBBARD SCIENTIFIC CO., P.O. Box 105, Northbrook, Ill. 60062

H23. HUDSON PHOTOGRAPHIC INDUSTRIES, INC., Educational/Industrial Products Div., Irvington-on-Hudson, N.Y. 10533

H24. HUNT MFG. CO., 1405 Locust St., Philadelphia, Pa. 19102

H25. HUNTER ASSOCIATES, 182 Clairmont Terrace, Orange, N.J. 07050

I

I1. IDEA ART, 30 E. 10th St., New York, N.Y. 10003

I2. IDEAL SCHOOL SUPPLY CO., 11000 Lavergne Ave., Oak Lawn, Ill. 60453

I3. ILFORD, INC., 70 Century Rd., Paramus, N.J.

I4. INDIANA DUPLICATOR CORP., 3642 W. 16th St., Indianapolis, Ind. 46222

I5. INDIANA UNIVERSITY, Audio-Visual Center, Bloomington, Ind. 47401

I6. INSTANTYPE, INC., 7005 Tujunga Ave., North Hollywood, Calif. 91605

I7. INSTRUCTIONAL AIDS, INC., Box 293, Owatonna, Minn. 55060

I8. THE INSTRUCTO CORP., Paoli, Pa. 19301

I9. INTERNATIONAL AEROSOLS, Rahway, N.J.

I10. INTERNATIONAL BALSA CORP., 100 Boyd Ave., Jersey City, N.J. 07304

I11. INTERSTATE PRINTERS & PUBLISHERS, INC., 19–29 N. Jackson St., Danville, Ill. 61832

I12. UNIVERSITY OF IOWA, Audio-visual Center, Iowa City, Iowa 52240

J

J1. J/ART CO., 4565 Artley, Belleville, Mich. 48111

J2. JIFFY ENTERPRISES, INC., 146-48-50 N. 13th St., Philadelphia, Pa. 19107

J3. JOHNSON PLASTICS, INC., 526 Pine St., Elizabeth, N.J. 07206

J4. JOHNS-MANVILLE, Dutch Brand Div., 22 E. 40th St., New York, N.Y. 10016

J5. JUDY CO., 310 N. Second St., Minneapolis, Minn. 55401

K

K1. PHILIP B. KAIL ASSOCIATES, INC., 1601 Eliot St., Denver, Colo. 80204

K2. KAISER PRODUCTS, Box 3101, Colorado Springs, Colo. 80907

K3. THE KALART CO., Plainville, Conn. 06062

K4. KALVAR CORP., 907 S. Broad St., New Orleans, La. 70125

K5. KENRO CORP., Cedar Knolls, N.J. 07927

K6. KENWORTHY EDUCATIONAL SERVICES, INC., P.O. Box 3031, Buffalo, N.Y. 14205

K7. KEUFFEL & ESSER CO., Educational/Audiovisual Division, 20 Whippany Rd., Morristown, N.J. 07960

K8. KEYSTONE VIEW CO., 865 Market St., Meadville, Pa. 16335

K9. THE KIMAC CO., Old Greenwich, Conn. 06870

K10. KINDERMANN, 623 Stewart Ave., Garden City, N.Y. 11533

K11. KINDER PRODUCTS, INC., 1105 Jefferson St., Wilmington, Del. 19801

K12. KLEEN-STIK PRODUCTS, 7300 W. Wilson Ave., Chicago, Ill. 60656

K13. KLING PHOTO CORP., P.O. Box 1060, Woodside, N.Y. 11377

K14. KOH-I-NOOR, INC., 100 North St., Bloomsbury, N.J. 08804

K15. KRYLON, INC., P.O. Box 390, Norristown, Pa. 19404

L

L1. LABELON CORP., 10 Chapin St., Canandaigua, N.Y. 14424

L2. LACEY-LUCI PRODUCTS, INC., 2679 Route 70, Manasquan, N.Y. 08736

L3. LASSCO PRODUCTS, INC., Rochester, N.Y.

L4. LEA A-V SERVICE, 240 Audley Dr., Sun Prairie, Wis. 53590

L5. LECTRO-STIK CORP., 3721 Broadway, Chicago, Ill. 60613

L6. E. LEITZ, INC., 468 Park Ave., New York, N.Y. 10016

L7. LETRASET, INC., 2379 Charleston Rd., Mountain View, Calif. 94040

L8. LETTERGUIDE CO., INC., P.O. Box 30203, Lincoln, Neb. 68503

L9. LEWIS ARTIST SUPPLY CO., 6408 Woodward Ave., Detroit, Mich., 48202

L10. LIBRARY FILMS, INC., 723 Seventh Ave., New York, N.Y. 10019

L11. THE LIETZ CO., 330 Corey Way, South San Francisco, Calif. 94080

L12. LINDY SALES CO., 7250 Laurel Cannon Blvd., North Hollywood, Calif. 91605

L13. JAY G. LISSNER, 3417 W. First St., Los Angeles, Calif. 90004

L14. LITHO-ART PRODUCTS, INC., 3418 N. Janssen, Chicago, Ill. 60657

L15. ANDREW E. LUTZ CO., P.O. Box 5, Syracuse, N.Y. 13211

M

M1. THE MACMILLAN CO., 866 Third Ave., New York, N.Y. 10022

M2. MACO MAGAZINE CORP., 757 Third Ave., New York, N.Y. 10017

M3. MADISON A-V CO., 62 Grand St., New York, N.Y. 10013

M4. MAGIC MARKER CORP., 88 St. and 73rd Ave., Glendale, N.Y. 11227

M5. MAGNA MAGNETICS, 777 Sunset Blvd., Los Angeles, Calif. 90046

M6. MAGNA VISUAL, INC., 1200 N. Rock Hill Rd., St. Louis, Mo. 63124

M7. MAGNET SALES CO., 3955 S. Vermont Ave., Los Angeles, Calif. 90037

M8. MAGNIPHOTO CORP., 84 Fifth Ave., New York, N.Y. 10011

M9. MAIER-HANCOCK SALES, INC., P.O. Box 5135, Sherman Oaks, Calif. 91413

M10. MAJOR SERVICES, 1740 W. Columbia Ave., Chicago, Ill. 60626

M11. MAKER PRODUCTS, INC., Irvington-on-Hudson, N.Y. 10533

M12. MARKETING CORP., Athens Building, Ardmore, Pa. 19003

M13. MARKWELL MFG CO., INC., 424 W. 33rd St., New York, N.Y. 10001

M14. JOHN G. MARSHALL MFG. CO., INC., 167 N. Ninth St., Brooklyn, N.Y. 11211

M15. MARSH STENCIL, 707 E. B St., Belleville, Ill. 62222

M16. MARSIC INDUSTRIES, 1 Saddle Rd., Cedar Knolls, N.J. 07927

M17. MASTER WOODCRAFT, INC., 55—33rd St., Brooklyn, N.Y. 11232

M18. MATH-U-MATIC, INC., 607 W. Sheridan Ave., Oklahoma City, Okla. 73102

M19. CHARLES MAYER STUDIOS, INC., 776 Commins St., Akron, Ohio 44307

M20. McDONALD PHOTO PRODUCTS, INC., P.O. Box 22224, Dallas, Texas 75222

M21. McGRAW COLORGRAPH CO., 175 W. Verdugo Ave., Burbank, Calif. 91503

M22. McGRAW-HILL BOOK CO., 330 W. 42nd St. (For films and filmstrips: Text-Films), New York, N.Y. 10036

M23. McMANUS & MORGAN, INC., 2506 W. Seventh Ave., Los Angeles, Calif. 90057

M24. JOSHUA MEIER CO., INC., 7400 West Side Ave., North Bergen, N.J. 07047

M25. MICHAEL'S ARTIST AND ENGINEERING SUPPLIES, INC., 7005 Tujunga Ave., North Hollywood, Calif. 91605

M26. MICO-TAPE, INC., 7005 Tujunga Ave., North Hollywood, Calif. 91605

M27. MICO-TYPE, INC., 7005 Tujunga Ave., North Hollywood, Calif. 91605

M28. MICROCOPY, INC., 3808 W. 54th St., Los Angeles, Calif. 90043

M29. MICROPOINT, INC., 620 E. Taylor St., Sunnyvale, Calif. 94086

M30. MICRO VU, INC., P.O. Box 150, Burbank, Calif. 91504

M31. MILIKEN PUBLISHING CO., 611 Olive St., St. Louis, Mo. 63101

M32. MILO HARDING CO., 500 Monterey Pass Rd., Monterey Park, Calif. 91755

M33. MIOPLEX PRODUCTS MFG. CO., P.O. Box 79, Brooklyn, N.Y. 11223

M34. UNIVERSITY OF MISSISSIPPI, Extension Division, University, Miss. 38677

M35. MITTEN DESIGNER LETTERS, P.O. Box 351, Redlands, Calif. 92373

M36. MODERN SCHOOL SUPPLIES, P.O. Box 958, Hartford, Conn. 06101

M37. MODERN TALKING PICTURES, 3 E. 54th St., New York, N.Y. 10022

M38. MONTGOMERY WARD, 618 W. Chicago Ave., Chicago, Ill. 60607

M39. MOORE PUSH-PIN CO., 133 Berkley St., Philadelphia, Pa. 19144

M40. MORGAN & MORGAN, INC., 25 Main St., Hastings-on-Hudson, N.Y. 10706

M41. THE MORGAN SIGN MACHINE CO., 4510 N. Ravenswood Ave., Chicago, Ill. 60640

M42. MUTUAL EDUCATION AIDS, 1946 Hillhurst Ave., Los Angeles, Calif. 90027

N

N1. NATIONAL CARD, MAT & BOARD CO., 4318–36 Carroll Ave., Chicago, Ill. 60624

N2. NATIONAL COUNCIL OF TEACHERS OF MATHEMATICS, 1201 16th St., N.W., Washington, D.C. 20036

N3. NATIONWIDE ADHESIVE PRODUCTS, INC., 19600 St. Clair, Cleveland, Ohio 44117

N4. KARL A. NEISE, INC., 56-02 Roosevelt Ave., Woodside, N.Y. 11377

N5. NEWMARK ASSOCIATES, 29 Portsmouth Terrace, Rochester, N.Y. 14607

N6. NEW PRODUCTS DISTRIBUTOR, P.O. Box 422, Danville, Ill. 61832

N7. NEWS FOCUS, 350 Dennison Ave., Dayton, Ohio 45401

N8. JOSEPH NEWSTAT, 8501 Agusta St., Philadelphia, Pa. 19152

N9. NOBEMA PRODUCTS CORP., 91 Broadway, Jersey City, N.J. 07306

N10. nuARC COMPANY, INC., 4110 W. Grand Ave., Chicago, Ill. 60651

O

O1. OHIO FLOCK-COTE CO., INC., 13229 Shaw Ave., East Cleveland, Ohio 44112

O2. OHIO GRAPHIC ARTS SYSTEMS, INC., 1037 Ivanhoe Rd., Cleveland, Ohio 44110

O3. THE OHIO STATE UNIVERSITY, Teaching Aids Laboratory, Lord Hall, 124 W. 17th Ave., Columbus, Ohio 43210

O4. THE OHIO STATE UNIVERSITY, Motion Picture Div., 1885 Neil Ave., Columbus, Ohio 43210

O5. OLIVETTI-UNDERWOOD CORP., 1 Park Ave., New York, N.Y. 10016

O6. ORAVISUAL CO., INC., Box 11150, St. Petersburg, Fla. 33733

O7. OTTENHEIMER, INC., Baltimore, Md. 21208

P

P1. PAASCHE AIRBRUSH CO., 1909 Diversey Parkway, Chicago, Ill. 60614

P2. PANAMA-BEAVER, 188 Third Ave., Brooklyn, N.Y. 11217

P3. PAPER MATE CO., 444 Merchandise Mart, Chicago, Ill. 60654

P4. PARA-TONE, INC., P.O. Box 136, La Grange, Ill. 60525

P5. PARKER PUBLISHING CO., West Nyack, N.Y. 10994

P6. PEERLESS COLOR LABORATORIES, 11 Diamond Pl., Rochester, N.Y. 14609

P7. PEERLESS PHOTO PRODUCTS, Route 25A, Shoreham, L.I., N.Y. 11786

P8. PENN PRODUCTS CO., 963 Newark Ave., Elizabeth, N.J. 07207

P9. PENNTEL OF AMERICA, LTD., 333 Michigan Ave., Chicago, Ill. 60601

P10. PERFEX CORP., P.O. Box 503, Bryn Mawr, Pa. 19010

P11. PERGAMON PRESS, INC. 44-01 21st St., Long Island City, N.Y. 11101

P12. PERRY-SHERWOOD CORP., 257 Park Ave., S., New York, N.Y. 10010

P13. PHOTO GRAPHIC PRODUCTS, INC., 311 N. Fifth Ave., Minneapolis, Minn. 55401

P14. THE PHOTO MART, 2312 E. Michigan Ave., Lansing, Mich. 48912

P15. PHOTO MATERIALS CO., 2450 Estes Ave., Elk Grove Village, Ill. 60007

P16. PICTYPE CO., 885 Seventh Ave., New York, N.Y. 10019

P17. PITMAN PUBLISHING CORP., 20 E. 46th St., New York, N.Y. 10017

P18. POCKET FILMS, 505 Fifth Ave., New York, N.Y. 10017

P19. POLAROID CORP., 549 Technology Square, Cambridge, Mass. 02139

P20. FREDERICK POST CO., Box 803, Chicago, Ill. 60690

P21. POTDEVIN MACHINE CO., INC., 200 North St., Teterboro, N.J. 07608

P22. POTTER'S PHOTOGRAPHIC APPLICATIONS CO., 160 Herricks Rd., Mineola, L.I., N.Y. 11501

P23. PRENTICE-HALL, INC., Englewood Cliffs, N.J. 07632

P24. PRESTAPE, INC., 136 W. 21st St., New York, N.Y. 10011

P25. PRESTO PROCESS CO., 183 St. Paul St., Rochester, N.Y. 14604

P26. PRESTO PRODUCTS CO., 1216 W. Madison St., Chicago, Ill. 60607

P27. PRESTYPE, INC., 194 Veterans Blvd., Carlstadt, N.J.

P28. PRINTING ARTS RESEARCH LABORATORIES, INC., Film Products Division, 273 La Arcada Bldg., Santa Barbara, Calif., 93104

P29. PRODUCT AID SERVICE CLIPS, Box 362, Westbury, L.I., N.Y. 11591

P30. PROFESSIONAL TAPE CO., INC., 355 E. Burlington Rd., Riverside, Ill. 60546

P31. PROJECTION AID DIVISION, 1095 Niagara St., Buffalo, N.Y. 14213

P32. PROJECTION OPTICS CO., INC., 271 11th Ave., East Orange, N.J. 07018

P33. PROTYPE, INC., 323 E. 38th St., New York, N.Y. 10016

P34. P-T TEMPLET CO., INC., P.O. Box 941, Golden, Colo. 80401

Q

Q1. THE QUIK-STIK CO., P.O. Box 3796, Baltimore, Md. 21217

Q2. QUON'S PLASTIC MOUNTS, 18660 S. Figueroa St., Gardena, Calif., 90247

R

R1. RADIANT COLOR CO., 28 Radiant Ave., Richmond, Calif. 94806

R2. REDI-ART, INC., 30 E. 10th St., New York, N.Y. 10003

R3. THE REDIKUT LETTER CO., 12617 S. Prairie Ave., Hawthorne, Calif. 90250

R4. REINHOLD BOOK CORP., 430 Park Ave., New York, N.Y. 10022

R5. REX BUSINESS MACHINES CO., 121 S. Pennsylvania St., Indianapolis, Ind. 46204

R6. REYNOLDS PRINTASIGN CO., 9830 San Fernando Rd., Pacoima, Calif. 91331

R7. RICHARD MFG. CO., P.O. Box 2041, Van Nuys, Calif. 91404

R8. ROCKLAND ASSOCIATES, 333 E. 46th St., New York, N.Y. 10017

R9. ROLATAPE CORP., 1301 Olympic Blvd., Santa Monica, Calif. 90404

R10. THE RONALD PRESS CO., 15 E. 26th St., New York, N.Y. 10010

R11. ROOVERS INC., Randolph Industrial Pk., Randolph, Mass. 02368

R12. CHARLES J. ROSS CO., 1525 Laimount Ave., Philadelphia, Pa. 19138

R13. ROYAL TYPEWRITER CO., INC., School Department, 850 Third Ave., New York, N.Y. 10022

R14. RUSSELL INDUSTRIES, INC., 98 Station Plaza, Lynbrook, L.I., N.Y. 11563

S

S1. SALT LAKE STAMP CO., 380 W. Second South, Salt Lake City, Utah 84101

S2. SAMUEL LAWRENCE SCHULMAN PRODUCTIONS, P.O. Box 1794, Trenton, N.J. 08601

S3. THE SANDERS CO., Box 111, Rochester, N.Y. 14601

S4. GEORGE W. SANDERS CO., 4119 San Fernando Rd., Glendale, Calif. 91204

S5. SANFORD INK CO., 2740 Washington Blvd., Bellwood, Ill. 60104

S6. SAVIN BUSINESS MACHINES CORP., 161 Sixth Ave., New York, N.Y. 10013

S7. SCHAEFER MACHINE CO., INC., Box 462, Clinton, Conn. 06413

S8. SCHOLARLY BOOKS IN AMERICA, 1525 E. 53rd St., Suite 531, Chicago, Ill. 60615

S9. SCHOLASTIC PRODUCTS, 1449 37th St., Brooklyn, N.Y. 11218

S10. SCHOOL PEN CO., P.O. Box 407, Chatman, N.J. 07928

S11. SCHOOL SERVICE CO., 647 S. La Brea Ave., Los Angeles, Calif. 90036

S12. SCM CORP., 299 Park Ave., New York, N.Y. 10017

S13. SCOTT MACHINE DEVELOPMENT CORP., P.O. Box 217, Walton, N.Y. 13856

S14. SCOTT PLASTICS CO., P.O. Box 2840, Sarasota, Fla. 33561

S15. SCRIPTO, INC., P.O. Box 4847, Atlanta, Ga. 30302

S16. SEAL, INC., Roosevelt Dr., Derby, Conn. 06418

S17. SEAL-O-MATIC DISPENSER CORP., 2260 Avenue A, Bethlehem, Pa. 18001

S18. SEARS, ROEBUCK & CO., Mail Order Dept., Chicago, Ill.

S19. SEARY MFG. CO., 19 Nebraska Ave., Endicott, N.Y. 13760

S20. SEPARON CO., INC., 56 W. 22nd St., New York, N.Y. 10010

S21. SEPSCO FILMS DIV., P.O. Box 80545, Chamblee, Ga. 30005

S22. SHEFFIELD BRONZE PAINT CORP., Cleveland, Ohio 44119

S23. SHERBURN GRAPHIC PRODUCTS, INC., P.O. Box 7503, Fort Worth, Texas 76111

S24. SHIVA ARTIST'S COLORS, 10 & Monroe, Paducah, Ky. 42001

S25. SHOWCARD MACHINE CO., 320 Ohio St., Chicago, Ill. 60610

S26. THE SIGNPRESS CO., P.O. Box 1267, Galesburg, Ill. 61401

S27. SIMMON OMEGA, INC., Phototypesetting Div., P.O. Box 1060, Woodside, N.Y. 11377

S28. SIMPLE SPACE-RITE LETTERING SYSTEM, 3442 N. 29th Ave., Phoenix, Ariz. 85017

S29. SLOAN MARKETING CORP., 11 E. Athens Ave., Ardmore, Pa. 19003

S30. SMITH SUPPLY CO., 170 S. Second St., Milwaukee, Wis. 53201

S31. SOCIETY FOR VISUAL EDUCATION, INC., 1345 Diversey Parkway, Chicago, Ill. 60614

S32. SOS PHOTO-CINE-OPTICS, INC., 387 Park Ave. S, New York, N.Y. 10036

S33. SPAULDING-MOSS, INC., 415

Summer St., Boston, Mass. 02210

S34. SPEEDRY CHEMICAL PRODUCTS, INC., 73rd Ave. at 88th St., Glendale, N.Y. 11227

S35. SPIRATONE, INC., 135-06 Northern Blvd., Flushing, N.Y. 11354

S36. SPRAYWAY, INC., 7644 S. Vincennes Ave., Chicago, Ill. 60620

S37. SQUIBB-TAYLOR, INC., P.O. Box 20158, Dallas, Texas 75229

S38. J. S. STAEDTLER, INC., Box 68, Boonton Ave., Montville, N.J. 07045

S39. STANDARD OIL COMPANY OF CALIFORNIA, Public Relations Dept., 225 Bush St., San Francisco, Calif. 94120

S40. STANDARD PROJECTOR & EQUIPMENT CO., INC., 1911 Pickwick Ave., Glenview, Ill. 60025

S41. STANPAT PRODUCTS, INC., Main & Covert Sts., Port Washington, N.Y. 11050

S42. STEINER PAPER CORP., 601 W. 26th St., New York, N.Y. 10001

S43. HENRY STEWART, INC., Bowen Rd., East Aurora, N.Y. 14052

S44. STEWART INDUSTRIES, 6520 N. Hoyne Ave., Chicago, Ill. 60645

S45. STIK-A-LETTER CO., Rt. 2, Box 1400, Escondido, Calif. 92025

S46. STRIP PRINTER, INC., P.O. Box 18-895, Oklahoma City, Okla. 73118

S47. JOSEPH STRUHL CO., INC., 195 Atlantic Ave., Garden City Park, N.Y. 11040

S48. SUMMIT INDUSTRIES, P.O. Box 415, Highland Park, Ill. 60036

S49. SUPRE-PRINT CORP., 1841 Broadway, New York, N.Y. 10023

S50. SUPT. OF DOCUMENTS, U.S. Govt. Printing Office, Washington, D.C. 20402

T

T1. THE TABLET & TICKET CO., 1021 W. Adams St., Chicago, Ill. 60607

T2. TACTYPE, INC., 43 W. 16th St., New York, N.Y. 10011

T3. TALENS & SONS, INC., P.O. Box 453, Union, N.J. 07083

T4. TEACHING AIDS SERVICE, INC., Visual Education Bldg., Floral Park, N.Y. 11001

T5. TECHNAMATION, INC., 30 Sagamore Hill Dr., Port Washington, N.Y. 11050

T6. TECHNICOLOR CORP., Commercial and Educational Div., 1300 Frawley Dr., Costa Mesa, Calif. 92627

T7. TECNIFAX CORP., 195 Appleton St., Holyoke, Mass. 01040

T8. TEPPING STUDIO SUPPLY CO., 3517 Riverside Dr., Dayton, Ohio 45405

T9. TESTRITE INSTRUMENT CO., INC., 135 Monroe St., Newark, N.J. 07105

T10. THE UNIVERSITY OF TEXAS at Austin, Instructional Media Center, Drawer W, University Station, Austin, Texas 78712

T11. THAYER & CHANDLER, INC., 215 W. Ohio St., Chicago, Ill. 60610

T12. 3M CO., Visual Products Div., Box 3100, St. Paul, Minn. 55101

T13. TIME SAVING SPECIALTIES, 2922 Bryant Ave., South Minneapolis, Minn. 55408

T14. TIMELY PRODUCTS CO., Box 416, Baltimore, Ohio 43105

T15. TRAINING SERVICES, 1815 Greenlawn Ave., Kalamazoo, Mich. 49007

T16. TRANSILWARP CO., INC., 4427 N. Clark St., Chicago, Ill. 60640

T17. TRANSPARENT INDUSTRIAL ENVELOPE, INC., 210 Fifth Ave., New York, N.Y. 10010

T18. TUDOR PUBLISHING COMPANY, 221 Park Ave., South, New York, N.Y. 10003

T19. TWEEDY TRANSPARENCIES, 208 Hollywood Ave., East Orange, N.Y., N.Y. 07018

U

U1. UNION RUBBER & ASBESTOS CO., P.O. Box 1040, Trenton, N.J. 08606

U2. UNITED TRANSPARENCIES, INC., P.O. Box 888, Binghamton, N.Y. 13902

U3. UNIVERSAL DYNAMICS, INC., 301 E. Hill, Oklahoma City, Okla. 73105

V

V1. VALDES ASSOCIATES, INC., Box 362, Westbury, L.I., N.Y. 11590

V2. VALIANT INSTRUCTIONAL MATERIALS CORP., 172 Walker Lane, Englewood, N.J. 07631

V3. D. VAN NOSTRAND CO., INC., 120 Alexander St., Princeton, N.J. 08540

V4. VAN SON HOLLAND INK CORP. OF AMERICA, Union & Library Sts., Mineola, N.Y. 11501

V5. VARIGRAPH, INC., P.O. Box 690, Madison, Wis. 53701

V6. VARITYPER CORP., 720 Frelinghuysen Ave., Newark, N.J. 07114

V7. VEACH DEVELOPMENT CO., 8921 Ashcroft Ave., Los Angeles, Calif. 90048

V8. VENUS PEN & PENCIL CORP., 730 Fifth Ave., New York, N.Y. 10019

V9. VIEWLEX, INC., Broadway Ave., Holdbrook, N.Y. 11741

V10. THE VIKING PRESS, 625 Madison Ave., New York, N.Y. 10022

V11. VILLA MFG. CO., 3750 Oakton, Skokie, Ill. 60076

V12. VISUAL ARTS PRESS, 130 Q St., N.E., Washington, D.C. 20002

V13. VISUALCRAFT, INC., 2737 W. Union Ave., Blue Island, Ill. 60406

V14. VISUAL GRAPHICS CORP., 1398 N.E. 125th St., Miami, Fla. 33161

V15. VISUAL MATERIALS, INC., 2549 Middlefield Rd., Redwood City, Calif. 94063

V16. HARRY C. VOLK, JR., ART STUDIO, Pleasantville, N.J. 08232

W

W1. WATSON-GUPTILL PUBLICA-TIONS, 2160 Patterson St., Cincinnati, Ohio 45214

W2. WAYNE STATE UNIVERSITY, AV Utilization Center, Detroit, Mich. 48202

W3. F. WEBER CO., Wayne & Windrim Aves., Philadelphia, Pa. 19144

W4. WEBSTER BROS. LABORATORY, R.R. 3, Box 41, Lake Villa, Ill. 60046

W5. WESTWOOD SALES CO., P.O. Box 295, Westwood, N.J. 07675

W6. JOHN WILEY & SONS, INC., 605 Third Ave., New York, N.Y. 10016

W7. H. WILSON CORP., 546 W. 119th St., Chicago, Ill. 60628

W8. WINSOR & NEWTON, INC., 555 Winsor Dr., Secaucus, N.J. 07094

W9. WOLD AIR BRUSH MFG. CO., 2171 N. California Ave., Chicago, Ill. 60647

W10. WOOD-REGAN INSTRUMENT CO., INC., 184 Franklin Ave., Nutley, N.J. 07110

X

X1. X-ACTO PRECISION TOOLS, INC., 48-41 Van Dam St., Long Island City, N.Y. 11101

X2. XEROX CORP., 1250 Midtown Tower, Rochester, N.Y. 14604

Z

Z1. ZIP MARK CORP., P.O. Box 227, Bordentown, N.J. 08505

GLOSSARY

The following brief definitions and descriptions of terms, materials, and equipment are provided for a better understanding of this book. In many cases the definitions or descriptions given are only outlines for the full meaning of the items. Purchase sources for a large percentage of the items listed here can be found in the Index.

A

Acetate. (See Clear Acetate Sheet and Matte Acetate.)

Acetate Additive. A liquid chemical in a highly concentrated form which may be used to prepare acetates for accepting inks and colors. Prevents inks and colors from creeping and crawling on acetate surface.

Acetate (Film) Cleaner. Specially formulated liquid for cleaning most acetate surfaces. Removes excess residue left by adhesive-backed sheets and dry transfer materials.

Acetate Film. (See Clear Acetate Sheet and Matte Acetate.)

Acetate (Plastic) Ink. Opaque or transparent color ink designed for use on acetate or plastic surfaces.

Acetate Liquid Color. Opaque watercolor expressly developed for drawing on acetate, glass, and plastic sheets. Suitable for pen, brush, and airbrush applications.

Adhesive-backed (Pressure-Sensitive). Broadly, refers to any of a group of adhesives which do not have to be moistened or have heat applied for use. Such adhesives stick to a clean, dry surface on contact. Wax adhesives belong to this group.

Adhesive-backed Acetate. (See Cold Laminating Acetate.)

Adhesive-backed Paper. High-quality paper with pressure-sensitive adhesive back. Available in a variety of colors and surfaces. Uses include displays, signs, labels, nameplates.

Adhesive-backed Paper Tab (Label). Paper tab in assorted sizes and shapes for use as labels, badges, etc. Back of tab is coated with a pressure-sensitive adhesive.

Adhesive-backed (Two Sides) Paper Tab. A special paper tab for mounting paper and cardboard letters on any smooth, dry surface. Tab has pressure-sensitive adhesive on both sides.

Adhesive-backed Shading (Texture) Sheet. Shading, texture, screen, and mosaic patterns printed on the underside of a transparent pressure-sensitive sheet that can be transferred to most surfaces. Available in white and colors.

Adhesive-backed Shading (Texture) Tape. Shading, texture, screen, and mosaic patterns printed on the underside of a transparent pressure-sensitive tape in such a way that they can be transferred to most surfaces.

Adhesive-backed Symbol Sheet. Miscellaneous opaque symbols printed on a clear or matte adhesive-backed acetate sheet. Symbols are roughly cut around and removed from the sheet and positioned on the drawing surface.

Adhesive-backed Symbol Tape. Miscellaneous opaque symbols printed on a clear or matte adhesive-backed acetate tape. Symbols are roughly cut around and removed from the tape and positioned on a drawing surface.

Adhesive Pen. A pen-type refillable liquid adhesive device, using the ball-point principle to dispense dots of liquid adhesive. Most pens when filled will dispense about five thousand adhesive dots.

Adjustable (Flexible) Curve. Plastic or metal curve-drawing aid that is easily bent to any desired curve or shape.

Airbrush. A precision pen-like spraying device about the size of a fountain pen and connected by a hose to a controllable air supply which forces light-bodied ink, liquid colors, and paints from a small reservoir cup or bottle.

Airbrush Aerosol Pressure Tank. A 16-ounce aerosol can of propellant gas with a pressure-regulating valve. Contains enough pressure for one to three hours of airbrush use depending on the size of the airbrush and type of work to be done.

Airbrush Carbonic Tank. A small ready-to-use tank unit with a supply of air to last many hours of airbrush work. Can be refilled by any concern that services soda fountains.

Air Compressor. A portable electric unit that produces a dependable air supply for airbrushes.

Airbrush Liquid Color. Color in liquid form designed especially for airbrush work.

Arkwright Transparency Film. A clear nonsensitized film for making positive-reading overhead projection transparencies with any model Xerox copier (see also Xerographic and Zelar Transparency Film).

Art Aid Camera. A specially designed camera for enlarging or reducing original artwork. Original artwork can be opaque or transparent. Some models will accept photographic film and paper.

Art Aid Projector. A wall- or floor-type projector which projects opaques, transparencies, and three-dimensionals down and upon a drawing-board surface. Provides complete artwork in one operation without transferring from a tracing.

Artype Frisket. A thin matte-surfaced acetate sheet with a heat-resistant adhesive back. For preparing pressure-sensitive art. Surface accepts writing, drawing, or typing.

Artype ModulArt. A product of Artype, Inc., consists of a number of specially designed illustrative figures, costumes, animals, backgrounds, vehicles, and accessories; all in modular form printed on the underside of clear, matte-surfaced pressure-sensitive adhesive acetate.

B

Ball-point Eraser. An elliptical eraser for erasing ball-point ink and ball-point lead.

Ball-point Pen. Special ink-controlled ball-point pen designed for smooth lettering and drawing. Ideal for use with cardboard and plastic stencil lettering guides, die-cut letters, etc. Assorted ink colors available.

Balsa Wood. An exceedingly light wood used for life preservers, rafts, model building, etc. Can be cut with a small knife or razor blade.

Beam Compass. Metal bar-type compass which will accept a variety of drawing and cutting attachments.

Beam Compass Reservoir Pen Attachment. Special attachment for a beam compass which permits the use of a reservoir pen.

Blackboard Ink. A special white ink for use on blackboards; will resist erasing and washing. Ink can be easily removed from blackboard by a cloth dampened with a special solvent.

C

Cam-lock Drawing Board. A drawing board equipped with a calibrated metal Cam-lock T-square channel.

Cam-lock T Square. An all-steel or clear plastic-edge T square designed for use on a drawing board equipped with a Cam-lock channel.

Caption. Properly a leadline or title and especially of an illustration, but more commonly the description accompanying the illustration.

Bleed. Where part of the printing area intentionally runs off one or more edges of the page. Actually most bleeds are accomplished after printing by trimming off part of the printed area.

Brochure. Strictly, any book of eight or more pages and stitched; but generally applied loosely as a term for any pretentious advertising piece stitched or not.

Brush-point Pen. A nonclogging fountain pen that will accept drawing, writing, and acetate inks. The interchangeable points are made of nylon or flexible perlon fibers. Ideal for making wide lines and for filling large and open letters.

Bulletin (Primary) Typewriter. Manual or electric typewriter which produces approximately ¼-inch type. Letter size is ideal for overhead projection transparencies, spirit masters, mimeograph stencils, direct offset masters, and the like.

Burnisher. A small bone, wood, or plastic tool for burnishing down adhesive-backed shading and color sheets, dry transfer letters, etc.

Carbon-coated Projection Acetate (Film). A lightweight acetate film coated with a black opaque carbon material. When used on the overhead projector, a white luminous line will appear on a black background when it is scribed on the coated side with a pencil or other stylus-type instrument.

Cardboard Adhesive-backed Letter. Cardboard die-cut letters with a pressure-sensitive back that will stick to most surfaces. Assorted styles, sizes, and colors available.

Cardboard Gummed-back Letter. Die-cut letters, numbers, and symbols made from gummed paper. Assorted styles, sizes, and colors available.

Cardboard Letter. Die-cut from cardboard. Ideal for tracing and direct use. Available in many styles, sizes, and colors.

Cardboard Locking Easel. Heavy die-cut cardboard easel which can be attached to the back of posters and other similar display materials. Can be folded and put away when not in use.

Cardboard Slide Mount. Pressed die-cut cardboard slide mount. Assorted types and sizes available.

Cardboard Stencil Lettering Guide. Lettering stencil guide, usually made of oiled cardboard, containing cutout letters which can be traced with a variety of lettering and drawing devices.

Chalkboard Compass. Large wood or metal compass which holds chalk, pencil, or crayon in an adjustable holder on one leg. Useful for making large circles on chalkboard, cardboard, etc.

Chalkboard Paint. Special formula light green paint for painting or resurfacing chalkboards. Also available in aerosol spray cans.

Changeable Display Letter. Plastic die-cut letter designed for use on grooved display boards. Assorted styles and sizes available.

Circle (Compass) Cutter. A metal compass device for cutting perfect circles out of paper, acetate, thin cardboard, etc.

Circle Template (Guide). Transparent plastic template for drawing circles on opaque and transparent surfaces.

Circular Proportional Slide Rule. White plastic device for obtaining proportions on reduced or enlarged photographs, artwork, etc. Gives number of times of reduction or enlargement of original size plus all new possible proportions.

Clay-coated (Base) Paper. A smooth-surfaced printing or drawing paper with a clay base coating which will permit the transfer of printed or hand-drawn images to picture transfer film. Most of the popular magazines are printed on clay-coated paper.

Clear Acetate Roll (Overhead Projector). Designed for use on the overhead projector. Surface will accept a number of marking and drawing devices. Requires a roll adapter for use on the projector.

Clear Acetate Sheet. An all-purpose transparent cellulose acetate sheet. Can be used much like an ordinary sheet of paper for drawing, writing, and so forth. Surface will accept a number of marking and drawing devices. (See also Reprocessed X-ray Film.)

Clear Cellophane. An all-purpose clear cellophane for use on the overhead projector as a writing or drawing surface.

Clip Art. Line and tone ready-to-use illustrations covering every practical subject classification from A to

Z. Many clip-art sheets and books contain symbols, decorative borders, etc.

Cloth-base Binding Tape. Has a pressure-sensitive adhesived back that will stick on contact to most clean, dry surfaces.

Cold Laminating Acetate or Mylar (Film). A thin, transparent acetate or mylar with a pressure-sensitive adhesive on one side. It seals itself with hand pressure or with a special applicator.

Coits Lettering Pen. Ball-bearing lettering pen that works like a brush. Produces clean-cut, sharp line. Available in nine widths from $\frac{1}{16}$ to 1 inch.

Color Acetate. Acetate sheet in vivid transparent color. Can be used to add color background for overhead projection transparencies and other visual materials. Available in a variety of colors.

Color Cellophane. Brilliantly colored cellophane in economical rolls for slides, overhead projection transparencies, and general use.

Color Drawing Pencil. Water-soluble or special lead coloring pencil which permits writing, drawing, and coloring on matte (frosted) acetate. Clear plastic spray must be applied to the working surface to make the color transparent for projection.

Color Lift Film (Picture Transfer). Picture transfer film produced by Viewlex, Inc. Will produce transparencies from magazine pictures printed on clay-coated paper. Film requires the use of a thermocopy machine.

Color Masking Tape. General-purpose masking tape in bright colors.

Combination Plate. A photoengraving in which the characteristics of a halftone and a line plate are both

present. Usually obtained by double-printing a negative from line art with one from continuous-tone copy.

Composing Stick (Fototype). A precision aluminum composing device required for setting Fototype in perfect alignment and automatic spacing.

Composition Adhesive Type (Letter). Removable opaque letters, symbols, numerals printed on the back side of a thin, transparent acetate sheet. Will adhere to most surfaces. Available in black, white, and colors.

Composition Paper Type (Letter). Opaque paste-up letters, symbols, numerals printed on paper tabs or sheets of lightweight cardboard paper. Can be used when precision hand typesetting is required. Available in many styles and sizes. (See also Fototype.)

Construction Paper. A wood-pulp paper of sufficient body to accept crayon, chalk, paint, charcoal, or pencil. Its many other uses include cutouts and chart making. Available in assorted colors.

Contact Print. A photograph printed in direct contact with a negative and therefore the same size as the negative.

Con-Tact Transparent Pressure-sensitive Acetate. A thin, transparent acetate with a pressure-sensitive adhesive on one side. It seals itself with hand pressure or with a special applicator. Ideal for making picture transfer transparencies. Most Woolworth stores carry this product.

Contact Print Frame (Photographic). A frame made of sturdy wood or metal, designed for making paper or film contacts from photographic negatives or positives.

Continuous-tone Photographic Film. A photographic film which produces a negative or positive film image exhibiting a complete and continuous tonal range from black, through all the middle tones, to white.

Continuous-tone Photographic Print. Specifically a photographic print, but any print not made with a halftone screen and exhibiting a complete and continuous tonal range from black, through all the middle tones, to white.

Contour Pen. A ruling pen for drawing curves; will follow irregular curves with ease. Can also be used as a regular ruling pen.

Copy. Reading matter as distinct from art or illustration. Any material prepared for camera. All original material for printing. The mechanical, plate, or electro sent a publication. One of an issue of a printed piece.

Copy Camera. Photographic camera designed for copying flat and three-dimensional materials on photographic film, paper, and slide plates.

Cork Letter. Die-cut letter made of thin, natural cork.

Cork Sheet. Natural cork sheet that can be cut with knife or scissors. Ideal for bulletin-board surfaces.

Corner Rounder. Metal cutting device for rounding corners of cardboard, paper, acetate, etc.

Corrugated Cardboard. Made up of two layers of thin cardboard glued together. The base layer is flat, while the top layer consists of a series of corrugations glued to the surface of the base layer. Available in assorted colors.

Corrugated Paper. Made up of two layers of paper glued together. The base layer is flat, while the top layer consists of a series of corrugations glued to the surface of the

base layer. Available in assorted colors.

Cropping. Indicating by tissue overlay, drop-out mask, or pencil lines (which must not cross the photograph) that part of artwork or photograph which it is desired to reproduce.

Crow Quill Pen. A very fine pen that has a flexible point with a tubular shaft that fits a special holder. Ideal for fine-line pen and ink drawing.

Cutting Blade Holder. Metal device for holding single-edge razor blade or special cutting blade.

Cutting Needle (Stylus or Teasing). A small cutting device for color, texture, shading, symbol, letter, and acetate sheets.

D

Decal Letter. Printed letter on an adhesive film mounted on a paper support from which it can be floated onto glass or other smooth surface to which it adheres.

Diazo Enlarger. A photographic enlarging device which produces diazo transparencies from 16mm motion-picture film; 35mm film; 2- by 2-inch, 2¼- by 2¼-inch and 3¼- by 4-inch slides.

Diazo Equipment. Processing equipment necessary for the production of diazo-sensitized materials. Equipment may consist of an exposure unit only, or may include both an exposure and developing unit.

Diazo Master (Commercial). Specially prepared translucent paper diazo masters for producing base transparency and overlays on diazo films (foils). Available in the subject areas of geometry, physics, United States history, biology, and technical graphics.

Diazo Process. A method of mak-

ing positive line reproductions directly from positive line originals without the use of negatives.

Diazo Reproducing Ball-point Pen. Ball-point pen containing a nonfading black opaque ink for preparing diazo masters.

Die-cut. A desired shape or form cut from a metal die or mold.

Diffusion Transfer Equipment. Photographic reproduction equipment used to expose and process diffusion transfer—sensitized materials.

Diffusion Transfer Film. Photosensitized film designed for use with the diffusion transfer process. Produces a black positive image on a clear, transparent background.

Diffusion Transfer Process. A negative-to-positive process which requires no camera or darkroom. Ideal for preparing transparencies from opaque originals.

Double-coated Adhesive Acetate. Clear acetate with a pressure-sensitive adhesive on both sides; useful for mounting whenever a two-sided adhesive material is required.

Double-coated Adhesive Tape. Transparent or opaque mounting tape with a pressure-sensitive adhesive on both sides; useful for mounting whenever a two-sided adhesive tape is required.

Double-coated Adhesive Tape Dispenser. For double-coated adhesive tape. The protective liner of the tape is removed as the tape is dispensed.

Doubletone Drawing Paper. Highquality drawing paper with two invisible shading (texture) patterns brought out with the application of two chemical developers. A variety of shading patterns is available.

Dowel Rod. Round wood rod used to hang maps, charts, etc.

Drafting Tape. Extra-strong heavy-weight paper-base tape with a pressure-sensitive adhesive side that sticks to most surfaces with a slight hand pressure. Holds lightly but firmly, yet removes easily when work is completed. Leaves no adhesive residue.

Drawing Board. A special drawing working surface made of seasoned pine or poplar wood.

Drawing Ink (Color). Color ink that can be applied, with a variety of drawing and lettering devices, to opaque and transparent surfaces.

Drawing Ink Dispenser. Ink-dispensing device for ruling pens and other ink-drawing instruments.

Drawing Paper. High-quality paper for all drawing purposes. A variety of surfaces and weights available.

Drawing Pencil. Pencil with a specially compounded lead for degree uniformity and point retention.

Dry Backing Cloth (Chartex). A high-quality cotton fabric with a thermoplastic adhesive on one side. Ideal for mounting maps, charts, and other flat materials where a cloth backing is desired. Available in rolls and sheets.

Dry Mounting Adhesive, Aerosol Can. A thermoplastic spray-on dry mounting adhesive; requires the use of a dry mounting press or electric hand iron.

Dry Mounting Cement (Adhesive). A thermoplastic adhesive applied to the back of material to be mounted with a brush. Requires the use of a dry mounting press.

Dry Mounting Fotowelder. A hand-mounting electrical device for mounting small photo snapshots and other similar-size materials. Designed to be used with Fotoflat dry mounting tissue and dry backing cloth.

Dry Mounting Metal Weights. Flat-surfaced weights made of cold steel that are perfectly balanced to assure level, steady pressure that makes it easy to flatten materials mounted with dry mounting tissue, dry backing cloth, etc. Available in two sizes —9 by 12 inches and 12 by 15 inches.

Dry Mounting Press. An electrically controlled mounting device which applies heat and pressure necessary for mounting and laminating materials treated with a thermoplastic adhesive.

Dry Mounting Tacking Iron. A small electrical heating device used to "tack" dry mounting tissue and dry backing cloth to mounting surfaces. Some models are equipped with a thermostatic control, and some have a teflon-coated base.

Dry Mounting Tissue, Permanent. A thin tissue coated on both sides with a thermoplastic adhesive which fuses to both the material to be mounted and the mounting surface. It is used with a dry mounting press or an electric hand iron.

Dry Mounting Tissue, Removable. Heavy duty, low temperature, mounting tissue. Ideal for mounting delicate materials such as color prints and fabrics. Can be applied and removed with a dry mounting press, Fotowelder, or an electric hand iron.

Dry Transfer Art Sheet. Professionally prepared black opaque art printed on a translucent plastic carrier. Art transfers to drawing paper, acetate, cardboard, etc., with the aid of a pencil, ball-point pen, or burnisher.

Dry Transfer Color Sheet. Transparent color printed on a plastic carrier. Color transfers to any dry surface by rubbing down with a burnisher.

Dry Transfer Letter, Opaque Color.

Opaque color letter which is printed on a plastic sheet and transfers to any dry surface by rubbing the letter down with a pencil, ball-point pen, or burnisher. Assorted styles, sizes, and colors available.

Dry Transfer Letter, Transparent Color. Transparent color letter which is printed on a plastic carrier and transfers to acetate, cellophane, glass, and other smooth surfaces by rubbing the letter down with a pencil, ball-point pen, or burnisher. Assorted styles, sizes, and colors available.

Dry Transfer Letter Eraser. An eraser designed for clean and quick removal of dry transfer letters, symbols, colors, etc.

Dry Transfer Letter Protective Coating. Aerosol-can plastic spray specifically made for use on dry transfer letters. Several separate applications of the spray will build up a heavy acrylic film that completely encapsulates the transfer in a hard, weatherproof shield.

Dry Transfer Process. A process that allows a preprinted letter, number, symbol, color, etc., to be transferred from a transparent or translucent carrier sheet to any dry surface by rubbing the image down with a pencil, ball-point pen, or burnisher.

Dry Transfer Shading (Texture) Sheet. Black opaque shading, texture, screen, and mosaic patterns printed on a translucent plastic carrier. Patterns transfer to any dry surface by rubbing down the pattern with a pencil, ball-point pen, or burnisher.

Dry Transfer Symbol Sheet. Black opaque symbols printed on a translucent plastic carrier. Symbols transfer to any dry surface by rubbing them down with a pencil, ball-point pen, or burnisher.

Dry Transfer Symbol Tape. Opaque symbols printed on a translucent plastic carrier tape. Symbols transfer to any dry surface by rubbing them down with a pencil, ball-point pen, or burnisher.

Du-All TapePrinter Kit. A rubber-stamp-making kit which contains a dual-purpose device for embossing three-dimensional letters on plastic or rubber tape. Kit contains a set of nine rubber stamp holders. The embossing device is available for ⅜-inch or ½-inch tape.

Dummy. A physically exact representation of a proposed book or publication with or without layout.

Duplicating (Mimeograph) Stencil. A thin waxed paper or plastic sheet on which written or typewritten matter or drawings are made with a typewriter, stylus, or electronic stencil cutter. Stencil is attached to a stencil (mimeograph) duplicator machine when used.

Dymo Plastic-forming System (Dymo-Form). A portable electrical plastic-forming device which permanently reproduces three-dimensional objects in sturdy 20-mil plastic. Produces such objects as letters, signs, display materials, craft molds, and protype products.

E

Econasign Lettering System. A printing stencil system consisting of precision-cut plastic stencil guides, alignment bar (for holding guides in place), paint box, pushpins, and stencil brush.

Edging Tape. Pressure-sensitive paper or transparent tape for use in a tape edger. Available in ½-inch and ⅜-inch width.

Electric Stylus. A compact electrical device that writes like a pencil on such surfaces as acetate, plastic, glass, wood. Engraves lines, letters, visual, etc.

Electric Tape Dispenser. Electric machine for dispensing gummed-back or reinforced tape. Dispenses measured, cut, and moistened tape.

Electronic Stencil Cutter. Electronic stencil-cutting machine which produces stencils and transparencies directly from line or wash illustrations, photographs, etc.

Ellipse Template (Guide). Transparent plastic guide for drawing or cutting perfect forms and shapes.

Embosograf Sign-making Machine. An embossing sign-making machine that produces plastic, aluminum, and cardboard signs up to 14 by 48 inches in one piece. Letters range in size from ¼ to 4 inches high.

Embosograf Sign and Picture Mount. Special mounting material ¹⁄₁₆ and ⅛ inch thick, with pressure-sensitive adhesive on both sides. For mounting signs, posters, pictures, and the like to most wall or display-board surfaces.

Empty Ink Bottle. Clear-glass empty ink bottle with or without dropper-stopper.

Emulsion. A suspension of silver halide crystals in gelatin (or, formerly, collodion) which is coated on an opaque (paper) or transparent (film) base or support to make it light-sensitive.

Enlargement. A copy, usually made by projection printing from a translucent intermediate such as a film negative, which is larger than the intermediate.

Enlarging Projector. A small opaque projector which enlarges any opaque copy, up to 6 by 6 inches, by projection. Size of projection is controlled by distance of projector from projection surface.

Eyelet (Grommet). Round metal or plastic reinforcement for holes

punched in cloth, paper, cardboard, etc. An eyelet tool is usually required for attaching eyelet to the desired material.

Eyelet Punch. An eyelet device that punches holes and sets metal eyelets in paper, leather, plastic, cloth, and cardboard.

F

Felt-board Letter. Die-cut felt letters, numbers, and symbols for use on flannel, felt, and other presentation boards with similar surfaces.

Felt-board Paper. A medium-weight paper with a surface of velvetlike textile fabric; can be cut and used to back materials for the feltboard.

Felt-point Pen (Marker), Permanent Ink. Plastic or metal fountain-type pen with one of a variety of felt points. Contains permanent color ink. Assorted points and ink colors available.

Felt-point Pen (Marker), Water-base Ink. Plastic or metal fountain-type pen with one of a variety of felt points. Contains water-base color ink. Assorted points and ink colors available.

Felt-point Pen Ink. A special permanent ink designed for use in felt-point pens; writes on most surfaces; available in several colors.

Ferrotype Plate (Chrome Tin). Flat metal sheet, usually copper, with a chrome-plated finish. Used to produce a gloss finish to photographic paper prints. Also used to produce Seal Transpara film transparencies.

Film Laminator (Cold Process). A compact cold process laminating machine for use with laminating film with a special pressure-sensitive adhesive backing. Also used for making picture transfer transparencies from pictures printed on clay-coated paper.

Film Laminator (Heat Process). An electrical machine which laminates clear or matte plastic film to paper or lightweight cardboard stock. Can also be used to produce picture transfer transparencies from pictures printed on clay-coated paper.

Filmstrip Projector. Projection device for projecting filmstrips; also used for preparing large visuals from filmstrips.

Filmstrip Tracing Visual. A series of eight filmstrips containing chalkboard illustrations which can be projected on a projection screen or any drawing surface for tracing.

Fixing. Liquid chemical removal of unexposed silver salts from developed photographic film and paper to prevent further action of light thereon.

Flatbed Printing Machine. Hand-operated ink printing machine for producing posters, signs, showcards, TV graphics, etc. Printing can be done on such surfaces as paper, cardboard, plastic, and acetate.

Flocking. Short fibers or pile or other particles are blown onto a design printed with an adhesive ink to which they adhere.

Font. An assortment of metal type (or molds) all of the same type face and point size, consisting of the complete alphabet, numerals, and punctuation marks.

Format. The distinctive and recurring treatment of a page or pages, usually of a publication, achieved through page size, stylized composition, and makeup. Also the preliminary concept of a proposed advertising piece.

Fototype Composition Paper Type (Letter). Black opaque letters printed on paper tabs for use when precision hand typesetting is required. Letters are inserted in a composing stick. Many letter styles and sizes available.

Frisket. Essentially a stencil which is cut on a photograph, acetate, or artwork to protect certain areas from airbrushing or aerosol-can spraying.

Frisket Film. A thin film with a special rubber-base adhesive on the back, ready to use when peeled off; will adhere to photographs, artwork, etc.

Frisket Film Maskoid. Liquid frisket medium for use on artwork to block out desired areas. May be applied with brush, pen, or ruling pen.

Frisket Knife. Small-bladed cutting device with a plastic or wood handle especially designed for cutting frisket film, film, color and shading sheets, composition adhesive type, and the like.

Frisket Paper. A slick-surfaced paper with a special rubber-base adhesive on the back, ready to use when peeled off. Will adhere to photographs, artwork, etc. Some frisket papers require a coating of rubber cement for use.

G

Gestefax Overhead Transparency Film. A specially surfaced transparent film for making positive-reading overhead projection transparencies with an electronic stencil cutter.

Glass Cutter. A metal tool for cutting, or inscribing designs on, glass.

Glossy. As distinct from matte. A photographic paper which when ferrotyped presents a slick, shiny surface, preferred for reproduction.

Gold Ink. Gold in ready-to-use ink solution for lettering, drawing, etc. For use in pen, brush, or airbrush.

Gold Tablet. A pure-gold tablet which is soluble in water; used for lettering, illuminating, and water-color painting.

Gold Transfer Foil. A gold transfer sheet that allows writing, lettering, and drawing in genuine 23-karat gold. The sheet is placed over the working surface, then written, lettered, or drawn on with a pencil, lettering stylus, or ball-point pen. Will transfer to paint, paper, plastic, metal, glass, leather. Available in sheets or rolls.

Grid Paper. Drawing paper with precision-printed grid lines.

Gummed-back Cloth Tape. Extra-strong gummed-backed cloth tape. For mending large maps, charts, and the like. Available in transparent, black and white, and colors.

Gummed-back Paper. High-quality paper with a gummed back. Available in assorted colors.

Gummed-back Paper Symbol. Die-cut symbol with a gummed back. Symbols include animals, flowers, birds, and so forth.

Gummed-back Products. Adhesive-backed articles—letters, cardboard, paper, etc.—which require the application of water to activate the adhesive.

H

Hangit Hanger. A metal hanging device for maps, charts, and other similar flat materials. Uses rollers to maintain a firm grip. Release is accomplished by a flick of the wrist.

Halftone. May refer either to artwork which is made up of actual graduation of tones as compared with solid black or solid colors, or it may apply to the plate used to print such artwork.

Harco Dura-Lam Laminating Film. A heat laminating film made of high-quality polyester film designed for use in heat-sealing or dry mounting presses.

Available in rolls and pouches (Lami-Pouch).

Heat Laminating Acetate (Film). A transparent acetate or mylar film for laminating with the aid of a dry mounting press or a thermocopy machine. (See Seal-Lamin Laminating Film and Thermocopy Laminating Acetate.)

Heat-resistant. Capable of remaining intact and immovable when exposed to high temperatures of thermocopy, diazo, and other reproduction processes which make use of heat or high-wattage lamps.

Hectograph (Gelatin) Carbon Paper. Color carbon-coated paper used in the hectograph and spirit duplication processes.

Hectograph (Gelatin) Compound. A special-formula gelatin compound for filling all types of tray or frame hectograph duplicators.

Hectograph (Gelatin) Duplicator. A machine used in the spirit duplication process for making copies of writing, drawing, etc., from a prepared gelatin surface to which the original image has been transferred.

Hectograph (Gelatin) Ink. Specially formulated ink for preparing hectograph masters. Inks are available in assorted colors.

Hectograph (Gelatin) Pencil. A special lead pencil for use with spirit and hectograph duplication; produces up to sixty good copies. Available in assorted colors.

Hectograph (Gelatin) Typewriter Ribbon. Purple carbon typewriter ribbon for use on spirit and hectograph masters.

High-contrast Photographic Film. An ortho-sensitive photographic film, specifically designed for line or half-tone reproduction in either the camera or contact printing frame. Rec-

ommended for making high-contrast photographic transparencies.

High-contrast Photographic Slide Film. A high-contrast photographic film recommended for the preparation of slides where the subject matter is high contrast in nature.

Hot-Press Printing Machine. Electric-heat printing machine for printing on plastic, acetate, paper, etc. A special color foil is required.

Hunt Bowl Pointed Pen (No. 512). A bowl-pointed extra-fine pen recommended for lettering or drawing on prepared and frosted acetate.

I

Illustration Board. Drawing paper mounted on cardboard backing. Generally recommended for finished artwork because it need not be mounted, does not warp when wet. Available in several weights and finishes.

India Ink (Black Drawing Ink). A black pigment of lampblack mixed with a gelatinous substance, used in drawing, lettering, etc. Recommended for the preparation of diazo and thermocopy copy materials.

Ink-bottle Holder. Rubber-base holder for standard ink bottle; prevents tipping.

Ink Compass. Drafting instrument for making circles in ink on paper, acetate, and other surfaces.

Inking Powder. A special powder for cleaning and preparing cloth, plastic, and photographic surfaces for inking.

Ink Riser Template. A spacing device for use between drawing or lettering template and drawing surface. Prevents ink from smearing on surface.

Irregular Transparent Curve. Transparent drafting device used for mak-

ing curves that cannot be made with a compass.

K

Kalvar Film. A photographic film containing certain diazonium salts which can be exposed by ultraviolet light and developed by heat.

Kinder Composition Plastic Type (Letter). Laterally reversed (mirror images) letters and numbers formed in white on $\frac{1}{16}$-inch black plastic rectangular pieces. Characters are hand-composed in a special composing stick or channel guide and then photographed on photographic film or paper.

Klamp-Boy Hanging Clamp (Hanger). A plastic hanging clamp with a pressure-sensitive back which will stick to any clean, dry surface. Will hold such things as papers, cards, maps, and charts.

Kodalith Film and Paper. Brand name for a high-contrast photographic paper and negative materials manufactured by Eastman Kodak for the graphic arts.

L

Label Maker. A compact embossing lettering machine which produces permanent raised letters and numerals on plastic or metal tape with plain or pressure-sensitive back. (See also Du-All TapePrinter.)

Label-maker Tape. Plastic or metal adhesive-backed tape for label makers. Available in assorted colors and widths.

Laminating Film (Cold Process). Acetate, vinyl, or mylar laminating film for use in a cold laminating machine. Film is coated with a special pressure-sensitive adhesive. (See also Con-Tact.)

Laminating Film (Heat Process). A transparent acetate or mylar film for laminating with the aid of a dry mounting press or thermocopy machine. (See Seal-Lamin Laminating Film and Thermocopy Laminating Acetate.)

Lamination. Combination of two or more dissimilar materials which function as one.

Lantern Slide Binder. Hand-operated device for attaching binding tape to lantern slides.

Lantern Slide Carbon Paper. Special carbon-surfaced paper for preparing typewritten lantern (3¼- by 4-inch) slides.

Lantern Slide Cellophane. Precut yellow cellophane for preparing typewritten lantern slides.

Lantern Slide Crayon. Specially prepared crayons for applying transparent color to etched glass or acetate. Available in several colors.

Lantern Slide Etched Glass. High-grade glass (3¼ by 4 inches) with an etched surface for preparing lantern slides. Etched surface will accept black and color pencils, slide crayons, and special slide inks.

Lantern Slide Ink. Special transparent color ink for use on etched lantern slide glass.

Lantern Slide Mounting Press. Hand-operated electric press for mounting lantern slides in cardboard mounts.

Lantern Slide Plain Glass. High-grade glass (3¼ by 4 inches) used mainly as cover glass for lantern slides.

Lantern Slide Stencil. For making lantern slides with typewriter, stencil, or pencil. Consists of thin, transparent film with special carbon paper folded on both sides. Enclosed in envelope with mat opening on one side.

Lantern Slide Vice. A hand-operated slide-binding device which holds binding tape in perfect alignment with cover glass while attaching tape. Also used for binding 2- by 2-inch slides.

Layout. The arrangement and form given to the various aspects of illustrative and reading material on any form of printed matter.

LeRoy Letter Size Adapter. Metal adapter for extending or condensing LeRoy lettering (height only). Adapter fits LeRoy scribers Nos. 1 or 2.

LeRoy Lettering Pen. A free-hand lettering pen with a special socket holder for mechanical scriber india-ink lettering pens.

LeRoy Lettering System. A mechanical tracing lettering system consisting of a scriber, template, and pen.

LeRoy Line-spacing Straightedge. A 15-inch Luxylite straightedge for use with any LeRoy template up to size 500. Shows where to place template to give first line of lettering, and determines spacing between lines best proportioned to height of lettering.

LeRoy Straightedge. A 15-inch plain straightedge made of Luxylite. Has a device to hold straightedge stationary without puncturing drawing surface, leaving both of the user's hands free to operate the scriber and template.

Letter Adhesive Mount. A paper tab, 1 by ⅜ inch, with pressure-sensitive adhesive on both sides for attaching paper and cardboard letters to walls, cardboard, and other surfaces.

Letterguide Lettering System. A mechanical tracing lettering system consisting of a scriber, template, and pen.

Letterpress. The process of printing directly from an inked, raised surface, metal plate, or master.

Line Drawing. Any drawing in which there are no middle tones and in which shading (texture), if any, is obtained with black-and-white lines or with screen overlays.

Line Negative. A photographic negative made from line copy (photograph, drawing, etc.).

Liquid Additive Adhesive. Liquid adhesive used as an additive to wallpaper wheat-paste flour. Recommended when increased adhesion is required in the wet mounting process.

Liquid Plastic Adhesive. A fast-setting white or transparent all-purpose adhesive that holds on wood, paper, cloth, glass, and all porous and semiporous materials.

Logo. Abbreviation for Logotype which pertains to the design or trademark of an institution, organization, firm, or product.

Lower Case. Uncapitalized type or letters.

Lucite. Thick, clear plastic that can be sawed, carved, cemented, molded, and machined.

Lucite Adhesive (Cement). Liquid plastic adhesive formulated for use on lucite.

M

Magnetic Board. A steel or magnetically treated presentation board to which objects may be attached with the use of metal, rubber, or plastic magnetics.

Magnetic Clip. A magnetic clip that can be attached to any steel. Will hold paper, cardboard, and other assorted lightweight objects.

Magnetic Cup Holder. A magnetic metal holder that can be attached to any steel surface. Designed for holding cups and many other objects.

Magnetic Letter. Precut letter for use on any surface regular magnets hold to. Some letters are made of injection-molded magnetic rubber; others are made of plastic and backed with tiny rubber, plastic, or metal magnets.

Magnetic Picture Hanger. Magnetic hangers with holding power ranging from 2½ to 10 pounds. Designed for use on steel walls.

Magnetic Tape (for Magnetic Board). A magnetic tape with a pressure-sensitive adhesive back; will hold display materials to any steel surface. Holds 2 or 3 ounces per square inch.

Mask. Generally an opaque plastic, cardboard, or acetate overlay for covering various parts of the visual or for progressive disclosure.

Masking Tape. An all-purpose crape finish tape. Adheres with just slight pressure. Water-repellent back. (See also Color Masking Tape, Photographic Masking Tape.)

Masonite Letter. Die-cut masonite manuscript letter for use on the flannel board, bulletin board, etc.

Master. Original material made for the purpose of reproducing additional copies.

Mat Board. Heavyweight cardboard with or without a pebbled surface. Used for mat cutting, mounting, and presentations.

Mat Cutter. Cutting device or knife designed mainly for mat-board cutting.

Matrix. The individual mold from which a letter is cast. Also the light metal template on which Varigraph fonts are engraved.

Matte (Frosted) Acetate. A non-inflammable cellulose acetate with a frosted (matte) surface on one side. Available in sheets, pads, and rolls. Surface permits drawing, lettering, coloring with pencil or pen.

Mechanical Scriber. A precision-engineered lettering instrument designed for use with a special-type lettering template. Scriber will accept a special india-ink pen, ball-point pens, styli, lead clutch, and cutting knives. (See also Mechanical Scriber Lettering Pen.)

Mechanical Scriber Ball-point Pen. Ball point pen-stylus with black and red reproducing ink for offset paper masters, and blue ink for layout work. Also used as a stylus for direct lettering on mimeograph stencils and spirit masters.

Mechanical Scriber Lead Clutch. Lead-holding device for the mechanical lettering scriber. Recommended for pencil lettering and preparing pencil layouts.

Mechanical Scriber Lettering Pen. India-ink lettering pen designed for use in the mechanical lettering scriber. Complete pen unit consists of a pen and cleaning pen.

Mechanical Scriber Lettering Pen Holder. Accepts standard mechanical scriber lettering pens. Ideal for freehand lettering and drawing.

Mechanical Scriber Reservoir Pen. Fountainlike ink pen designed for use in the mechanical lettering scriber. Large india-ink reservoir eliminates repeated filling of pen. Ink supply lasts for weeks. Assorted line-width pens available.

Mechanical Scriber Silk-screen Knife. A specially designed silk-screen knife for use in the mechanical lettering scriber.

Mechanical Scriber Stylus. Ball-tip stylus for use in the mechanical lettering scriber. Recommended for lettering on mimeograph stencils and spirit masters.

Mechanical Scriber Swivel Knife. A precision ball-bearing swivel silk-screen lettering knife for use in the mechanical lettering scriber.

Mechanical Scriber Symbol Template. Engraved symbol template for use with a mechanical lettering scriber. Symbols include people, machines, farm equipment, animals.

Mechanical Tracing Lettering System. Lettering system consisting of a mechanical scriber or instrument, template (template or matrix), and pen. Letters range in height from $\frac{1}{16}$ to 2 inches.

Metal-brush Lettering Pen. A flexible metal lettering and drawing pen that strokes like a brush. Available in widths, in some makes, from $\frac{1}{16}$ to 1 inch. (See also Coits.)

Metal Display Stand. Plated metal display stand for holding up paper, signs, and other objects up to $\frac{1}{8}$-inch thickness in upright position. Stand is 5 inches long.

Metal Interlocking Stencil Letter. Individual metal stencil letters and numerals that interlock to form a complete word. Can be separated and reassembled as needed. Complete word can be traced, sprayed with paint or ink, or applied with a stencil brush and ink.

Metal Letter. Cast aluminum or bronze letter for indoor or outdoor use.

Metal Magnet. Metal magnet that can be attached to letters, objects, etc. Will work on any surface regular magnets hold to. Available in a variety of shapes and sizes.

Metal Slide Mount. Metal, usually aluminum, container (mount) for permanent protection of slides against dust and damage.

Metal Triangle. Metal triangular instrument used in drafting. Recommended where drawing and cutting vertical and angle lines are required.

Metal T Square. T-shaped ruler for drawing parallel lines. Blade is made of flexible stainless steel.

Milex (Pro-Printer) Sign Maker. A sign-maker system consisting of a clear-plastic lettering guide, guide holding base, and lettering pen. Signs with letters ⅝ inch, ⅜ inch, and ¼ inch high can be produced.

Mimeograph. (See Stencil Duplicator.)

Mimeoscope. (See Viewing Light Box.)

Molded Plastic Letter. Molded plastic display letter with sanded, adhesive, plain, or pin back. Assorted colors, sizes, and styles available.

Molded Tile Letter. Molded tile display letter with sanded, adhesive, plain, or pin back. Assorted colors, sizes, and styles available.

Mongol Color Pencil. Water-soluble coloring pencil. Watercolor effect can be achieved by applying color with pencil, then brushing on clear water. Excellent color medium for matte (frosted) acetate.

Mounted Drawing Paper. Rag-content white drawing paper mounted on muslin for added strength and durability. Paper is used for all permanent maps, important documents, etc.

Mounting Board. A pressed-paper board suitable for mounting purposes. Available in several thicknesses.

Music Pen. A five-line ink ruling pen for use in drawing music lines.

N

Negative. The primary photographic record of an image, in which black and white values are reversed.

Newsprint Paper. An inexpensive wood-pulp for making quick drawings and work not demanding permanence. Available in sheets and rolls.

Nonproducing Pencil. Produces a light shade of blue which is non-reproducing in line work. This special color pencil is also used to block in and mark key lines on sketches and line mechanicals.

Nylon-point Pen (Permanent Ink). Fountain-type pen with a specially tapered point made of nylon or fiber which produces a permanent ink line; will write on most surfaces. Available in assorted ink colors.

Nylon-point Pen (Water-base Ink). Fountain-type pen with a specially tapered point made of nylon or fiber which produces a water-base ink line; will write on most surfaces. Available in assorted ink colors.

O

Offset Duplicating. A term used to denote a duplicating process in which an image is first transferred to an intermediate surface and thence to a receiving sheet.

Offset Master (Direct-image) Carbon Paper. A special carbon-surfaced paper for typing, drawing, or tracing on direct offset paper masters.

Offset Master (Direct-image) Eraser. Special erasing compound for making corrections and changes directly on direct offset masters.

Offset Master (Direct-image) Ink. Special ink for ruling, writing, drawing, or underscoring with pen or brush on direct-image offset masters. Can be used in a ruling pen for precision lines.

Offset Master (Direct-image) Non-reproducing Pencil. For drawing nonreproducing guidelines which will serve as guides in the preparation of layouts, forms, etc., on direct-image

offset masters.

Offset Master (Direct-image) Reproducing Crayon. For shading, drawing, illustrating, or making other bold impressions on direct-image offset masters.

Offset Master (Direct-image) Reproducing Pen. A reproducing ball-point pen used for handwriting, drawing, or underscoring on direct-image offset masters.

Offset Master (Direct-image) Reproducing Pencil. High-quality medium lead pencil which produces a reproducing image on direct-image offset masters. Used for handwriting, ruling, drawing, or underscoring. Printed copy has the same pencil-like appearance as the original copy.

Offset Master (Direct-image) Stamp-pad Ink. Specially formulated black stamp-pad ink for direct-image offset masters. Has reproducing properties necessary for offset reproduction. Suitable for general stamp-pad purposes.

Offset Master (Direct-image) Typewriter Ribbon. A water-resistant inked typewriter ribbon for use on direct-image offset masters and for general typing.

Oil Board. An oil-treated board for making stencil letter templates by hand or on a stencil-cutting machine.

Opaque. Materials which will not transmit light; non-transparent or nontranslucent.

Opaque Color Adhesive-backed Charting Tape. Plastic-base opaque color charting or drafting tape with a pressure-sensitive adhesive back.

Opaque Color Marking Pencil. Opaque color all-purpose marking pencil with a lead that writes in dense color on glass, plastic, acetate, cellophane, metal, photographs, and similar surfaces.

Opaque Liquid Color (Aerosol Can). Enamel fluorescent and metalic opaque color weatherproof paint in spray-can form.

Opaque Liquid Color (for Acetate). Water-soluble opaque color specifically formulated to adhere to acetate and similar surfaces without crawling.

Opaque Projector. An electrical device for the projection of opaque materials and flat objects. Can also be used to produce large illustrations (visuals) from small opaque originals.

Original. The piece of illustrative or printed matter to be reproduced or laminated.

Overexposure. Exposure to light or heat at too great an intensity or for too long a time.

Overhead Projector. An electrical device which throws a highly illuminated image on a projection surface by reflection from a mirror; it is placed in front of the viewers and may be used in a semidarkened or completely lighted room. Models available for accepting transparencies from 3¼ by 4 inches to 10 by 10 inches.

Overhead Projector Cellophane Roll. A clear cellophane roll designed for use on an overhead projector. A 100-foot roll is standard equipment for most projectors. It provides writing or drawing space equal to approximately one hundred standard transparencies.

Overhead Transparency Carbon Sheet. Special carbon sheet for typing or drawing directly on transparent acetate or plastic sheets. When projected, the type image appears black on the screen.

Overhead Transparency Cardboard Mount. Die-cut pressed cardboard "frame" for overhead projection transparencies. Most standard-size mounts will accept transparencies up to 8½ by 11 inches.

Overhead Transparency Cardboard Mount (Adhesive-backed). Sandwich-type cardboard mount with pressure-sensitive adhesive to permit mounting one or more cells inside.

Overhead Transparency Carrying Case. Combination carrying and storage case for overhead projection transparencies. Usually made of vinyl or pressboard.

Overhead Transparency Envelope. Large transparent plastic or paper envelope for protecting overhead projection transparencies when stored.

Overhead Transparency Hinge. Adhesive-backed mylar hinge designed for attaching overlays, masks, etc., to overhead projection transparencies.

Overhead Transparency Pin Registration Board. A pressed-wood or formica-covered board with registration pins for preparing art for transparencies and a registration device for finished transparencies.

Overhead Transparency Pin Registration Punch. A special punch used for preparing film, acetate, paper, etc., for perfect registration.

Overhead Transparency Plastic Mask. Heavy, white translucent plastic sheet for sliding or hinging mask on overhead projection transparencies. Used as a mask to prevent the image, or part of it, from reaching the projection screen.

Overhead Transparency Plastic Mount. White high-impact plastic overhead projection transparency mount; waterproof, nonwarping, and reusable.

Overhead Transparency Plastic

Pointer. Used in place of a finger or pencil in pointing out portions on an overhead transparency. Made of transparent plastic.

Overhead Transparency Plastic Track. Black or clear plastic tracks for overhead transparency sliding masks. Attached to transparency mount with a heavy-duty stapler.

Overhead Transparency Stapler. A special heavy-duty stapler designed for attaching hinged overlays, masks, and plastic tracks on overhead transparency mounts.

Overhead Transparency Storage File. Specifically designed steel file cabinet for overhead projection transparencies.

Overhead Transparency Tape. Masking tape for attaching film, acetate, masks to overhead transparency mounts.

Overhead Transparency Tracing Visual. Mounted transparencies, measuring 10 by 10 inches, of outline maps of all major countries of the world. Maps can be projected on a projection screen or on any drawing surface for tracing.

Overhead Transparency Typewriter Ribbon. A typing ribbon which produces opaque type directly onto clear acetate sheets. Available for most models and makes of typewriters.

Overlay. Refers mainly to one or more transparent sheets containing color, text, opaque masks, etc., attached to a base overhead projection transparency.

P

Pantograph. A precision-made drawing instrument consisting of a metal or wood frame with adjustable joints. Used to make enlargements or reductions of original art by movement of the tracing point actuating a pencil point held in contact with a drawing surface for the reproduction.

Panto-Varigraph Lettering System. A precision pantograph-type lettering instrument for reproducing, in enlarged size, an outline or solid letter up to 8 inches high from a single matrix (template). Over 100 letter styles available.

Paper Adhesive-backed Letter. Die-cut paper display letter with a pressure-sensitive adhesive back that will adhere to most clean surfaces. Assorted styles, sizes, and colors available.

Paper-base Binding Tape. (See Passe-partout Binding Tape.)

Paper Cutter. A device used to cut and trim paper to required dimensions.

Paper Gummed-back Letter. Die-cut paper letter with gummed back. Assorted styles, sizes, and colors available.

Paper Letter. Die-cut paper letter; can be attached to a surface with rubber cement, dry mounting tissue, adhesive-backed (two sides) paper tabs, etc.

Parchment Paper. Genuine parchment paper is made of sheepskin or goatskin. Other parchment papers are made of Japanese vellum or fine paper having a texture resembling parchment.

Parlab Projection Film. A thermocopy film with a variety of applications. Any thermocopy reproducible original can be copied. Halftone prints up to 85-line screen on uncoated stock can also be copied. The Parlab process can produce multicolored transparencies; diazo masters; litho negatives, positives, or overlays for commercial art.

Passe Partout. A picture mounting in which glass, picture, backing, and often a mat are bound together, as by strips of gummed paper or cloth-base tape along the edges.

Passe-partout Binding Tape. Gummed-back paper tape in assorted colors. Used for binding pictures, mats, photographs, etc.

Paste-up. Layout, copy, lettering, etc., mounted into position on mounting board or drawing paper ready for the camera.

Paste-up Layout Sheet. Paste-up layout sheet designed mainly for the preparation of artwork for electronic stencil-cutting machines. Nonreproducing grid lines printed on each sheet.

Paste-up Letters. Letters printed on paper, cardboard, or thin plastic which may be put together to form words and heading for use on a paste-up. (See also Composition Adhesive Type and Composition Paper Type.)

Pelican (Pelikan) Graphos Fountain Pen. Fountain-type drawing and lettering pen. Sixty interchangeable nibs (points) are available. Excellent pen for technical drawing, lettering, sketching, or ruling.

Pen Cleaner. A liquid cleaning solution for removing dried ink from pens and drawing instruments.

Pen Holder. Plastic, wood, or metal holder for drawing and lettering pens.

Pen Humidifier. A revolving reservoir pen storage container and humidifier. Humidified interior prevents ink in pen points from drying out.

Pencil Compass. Metal drawing device for making circles with a pencil or lead insert. Compass holds half-length pencil securely, assuring no change in arc radius.

Pentel Pen (Black). A fine-line ny-lon-point pen containing an opaque black water-base ink. Recommended for preparing thermocopy originals.

Perforating (Pounce or Tracing) Wheel. A small, metal cutting device with teeth for perforating patterns, signs, letters, etc., for transfer to a desired surface.

Perspective Grid Paper. Drawing paper with precision-printed perspective grid lines. (See also Grid Paper.)

Photodrawing. The technique of making and using photographs to convey dimension, position, identification, and spatial-relationship information in the same manner as engineering drawings.

Photograph Eradicator. Eradicator consists of two solutions, A and B, for instant and total deletion of unwanted areas or sections on photographs.

Photographic Enlarger. An optical device used for making photographic prints and transparencies which are larger than the intermediate from which they are made; can also be used to prepare large visuals from small transparent originals.

Photographic Masking Tape. A black and fully opaque tape for making masks, blocking out negatives, and for other photographic uses.

Photographic Opaque. Red, black, or gray liquid medium for retouching and opaquing photographic film. Soluble in water and can easily be washed off for corrections. Can be applied with brush, pen, or ruling pen.

Photographic Print Dryer. Photographic device used to dry photographic prints. Drum-type dryers can be used to mount dry backing cloth (Chartex) to the back of charts, maps, prints, etc.

Photographic Print Tray. Flat plastic, styron, enameled, or stainless-steel tray used for processing photographic prints and films.

Photographic Silk-screen Film. Pre-sensitized silk-screen film used in a direct photographic method to transfer fine-line lettering, visuals, halftones for silk-screen reproduction.

Photostabilization Process. A rapid photographic process which uses photo-sensitized papers and films containing part of the developing and fixing agents required for processing. A special processing machine is required. No darkroom is needed for use.

Phototype Composing Machine. Photographic machine which composes and photographs display type and lettering on photo-sensitized paper and film. Assortment of type faces and sizes available.

Picture Hanger (Gummed-back Cloth). Strong gray gummed-back cloth with metal reinforced eyelet. For hanging maps, charts, etc.

Picture Rubber Stamp. Assorted pictures on rubber stamps mounted on easy-to-hold wood blocks. Ideal for elementary school use and pictorial chart and graph making.

Picture Transfer Film. Special-surfaced film for making picture transfer transparencies from pictures printed on clay-coated paper. (See also Cold Laminating Acetate, Color Lift Film, Con-Tact, Seal Transpara-Film, and Transfer Film.)

Planotype Letter. A pliable plastic opaque or transparent letter with a pressure-sensitive backing.

Plastic-base Binding Tape. Waterproof vinyl binding tape with a pressure-sensitive back. Available in assorted colors.

Plastic Shading Plate. Textured plastic plate for adding shading, depth, tone, and texture to illustrations, letters, etc., on duplicating stencils and spirit masters. Assorted patterns available.

Pushpin. Plastic or metal head pin with a ground steel point. Plastic head pins available in assorted colors.

Plastic Slide Mount. Polyethylene or molded plastic one- or two-piece mounts for slides. Available with or without cover glass.

Plastic Spray (Aerosol Can). A transparent acrylic fixative in spray-can form that gives photos, drawings, artwork, etc., the protection of glass without its disadvantages.

Plastic Triangle. Transparent plastic triangular instrument used in drafting. Recommended for drawing vertical and angle lines.

Pliable Plastic Adhesive. A white pliable mounting adhesive that will stick to any clean, dry surface.

Pliable Plastic Letter. Die-cut letter made from a pliable plastic that sticks, on contact, to most smooth surfaces.

Polarizing (Technamation) Materials. Specialized materials for creating simulated realistic motion in overhead projection transparencies, slides, and other visual aids. Motion is achieved through the control of variably oriented polarized light.

Polarizing (Technamation) Spinner. A hand-operated or motor-driven rotating device containing a polarizing filter which is positioned in front of or below the projection lens.

Polaroid Land Camera. Photographic camera designed for use in the Polaroid Land system. Films available for producing black-and-white and color photographic prints and black-and-white line or continuous-tone transparencies.

Polaroid Land Projection Film (Photographic). Two films for producing slides with Polaroid Land cameras: type 146-L (PolaLine) specifically designed for producing $3\frac{1}{4}$- by 4-inch slides from line-copy originals; type 46-L for producing continuous-tone slides.

Positive. An image of the original copy corresponding to same in lights and shades.

Poster. Usually a large printed card, often illustrated, posted to advertise or publicize something.

Poster Board. A smooth pressed-paper board for posters, signs, and showcards. Takes pen and ink, poster colors, tempera, watercolors, airbrush, and silk-screen process. Assorted colors available.

Poster Paint. Water-base paint developed mainly for poster work. Can be used with pen, brush, and airbrush.

Pounce Paper. Granular-surfaced paper designed for pounce pattern work. Surface holds paper in place while pouncing.

Prepared (Specially Surfaced) Acetate. A crystal acetate (plastic) with a special coating on both sides that will accept poster paints, watercolors, inks, and dyes without crawling. Available in both sheets and pads.

Pressure-sensitive Adhesive. Broadly, any group of adhesives which do not have to be moistened or have heat applied for use; sticks to a clean, dry surface on contact. Wax adhesives belong to this group.

Pressure-sensitive Adhesive (Aerosol Can). Liquid adhesive in spray-can form, having characteristics similar to wax and rubber cement adhesives. For permanent and removable mounting. Will bind paper to most smooth surfaces.

Printed Paste-up Letter. (See Composition Adhesive Type and Composition Paper Type.)

Proportion. The relationship existing between the different dimensions of artwork, or the relationship existing between a dimension in enlarged or reduced size.

R

Razor Blade. Commercial single-edge razor blade with square corners suitable for most cutting jobs. Each blade protected by a heavy paper sheath.

Reducing Glass. The opposite of a magnifying glass. Used to judge how artwork and other copy will look when reduced to printing size.

Register. Exact matching in position successive overlays of color, lettering, etc.

Register Mark. Combinations of printed circles and cross lines placed on artwork, generally outside the image or copy area. When register marks exactly coincide, the multiple overlays are in perfect register.

Reprocessed X-ray Film. The least expensive of the clear acetate films. Usually has a slight bluish cast which does not alter the appearance of colored inks and adhesive sheets when applied to the surface. (See also Clear Acetate Sheet.)

Reprolith. Ansco brand of high-contrast photo-sensitive materials for photographic reproduction.

Reservoir Pen. Fountain-type pen designed for india-ink drawing, lettering, and so forth. Available in eight line widths. Keuffel & Esser and Letterguide pens can be used in mechanical lettering scribers.

Reservoir Pen Holder. Special holder for reservoir pens which permits hand use of the pen.

Reversal. Artwork or copy reversed to form white or clear on a black or opaque background.

Revolving Tray. A plastic revolving tray for holding a variety of graphic tools and materials.

Reynolds Printasign Printing Machine. A high-speed graphic typewriter printing machine for printing posters, signs, showcards, television graphics, etc. Printing can be done on virtually any flat surface that will accept ink.

Round-hole Paper Punch. Heavy-duty hand-operated round-hole paper punch. Adjustable gauge to assure uniform punching from sheet edge and permits varying distance.

Rubber Cement, Pressure-sensitive. A clear transparent cement made from pure rubber. A single coat mounts one material to another. Material coated with rubber cement may be removed and remounted without applying additional cement.

Rubber Cement, Regular. A transparent liquid adhesive made from specially treated rubber, blended to a formula best suited for joining various types of materials together.

Rubber Cement Dispenser. An airtight glass or plastic container for rubber cement. Most containers have adjustable-length sliding brush. Available in ½-pint to 1-quart sizes.

Rubber Cement Eraser. An eraser, usually made of pure crepe rubber, used to remove excess dry rubber cement from the mounting surface.

Rubber Cement Thinner (Solvent). A liquid used for thinning or reducing rubber cement. Also used as a thinner for frisket work. Can be used for cleaning metal type, rollers, stencils, and electros.

Rubber Magnet. Adhesive-backed magnetized rubber sheet or strip that can be cut with scissors. Magnets can be attached to cutout letters, cardboard, objects, etc., for use on a magnetic board or any steel surface.

Rubber Stamp Printing Set. Die-cut rubber letters, numbers, symbols, etc., mounted on easy-to-hold wood blocks. Most sets come complete with aligning guide, guide ruler, and stamp pad. Assorted styles and sizes available.

Rug Binding Tape. A rugged binding tape made of cotton drill. Applied to cloth mounting with a hand iron. Available in assorted color rolls.

Ruling Pen. A drafting instrument designed for drawing precision ink lines on opaque and transparent surfaces.

S

Scissors. A small metal cutting tool with two opposing cutting blades.

Scotch Magic Mending Tape. A translucent matte-finish acetate film tape that becomes clear upon application to a surface. Will adhere to most clean, smooth surfaces and is resistant to heat and moisture.

Scott Letter-engraving Machine. A pantograph-type engraving machine. Engraves letters on plastic laminate materials. Nameplates, desk signs, and door markers are a few of the items produced with the machine.

Scratchboard. A high-quality white-coated paper board for scratchboard work. Surface is coated with india ink and scratched off with a scratch-board tool to complete the drawing. A brilliantly contrasting black-and-white drawing results. A precoated black scratchboard is also available.

Scratchboard Tool. A special metal tool for use on scratchboard. A variety of tools is available to achieve various line effects.

Seal-Lamin Laminating Film. A mylar-base laminating film which provides permanent protection against wear and tear, stains, moisture, and many acids. Requires a dry mounting press for application. Available in regular (smooth) or matte-finish rolls.

Seal Transpara-Film. Clear mylar film, coated with a thermoplastic adhesive, used in the Seal Transpara-Film process. Color or black-and-white transparencies can be made from pictures printed on a clay-coated paper. A Seal Transpara-Film kit and dry mounting press are required.

Selfkote Thermocopy Film. A heavy-gauge clear-plastic film to which Selfkote charging fluid is applied with a special applicator. Coated film is processed as any other thermo-copy transparency film in a thermo-copy machine; the results—a direct-reading image on a clear, transparent background.

Sharpening Stone. Arkansas and India sharpening stones for knives, blades, ruling pens, drawing instruments, etc. India stones are recommended for rough sharpening and hard Arkansas stones are recommended for finishing.

Shelf Life. The period of time during which sensitized material may be kept before exposure without loss of speed, contrast, or quality.

Sign Cloth. Durable coated or treated cloth especially designed for outdoor signs, banners, charts, etc.

Silk-screen Process. A reproduction process in which heavy-bodied inks are squeezed through a stencil mounted on a fabric (formerly silk) or sometimes metal screen. Best suited for display work and short runs, the photographic stencil has made the process popular also for decals, printed circuits, etc.

Silver Ink. Silver in ready-to-use ink solution for lettering, drawing, etc. For use in pen, brush, or airbrush.

Silver Tablet. A pure silver tablet which is soluble in water; is used for lettering, illuminating, and watercolor painting.

Singletone Drawing Paper. High-quality drawing paper with one invisible shading (texture) pattern brought out with the application of a chemical developer. A variety of shading patterns is available. (See also Doubletone.)

Slide Binding Tape. Paper-, cloth-, or plastic-base tape for slide binding. Some tapes are gummed-back; others have a pressure-sensitive adhesive back. Assorted colors available.

Slide Label. (See Adhesive-backed Paper Tab.)

Slide Marker. Circular paper slide marker with gummed or pressure-sensitive adhesive back. Plain or numbered markers are available.

Slide Projector. Projection instrument designed to accept transparent slides. Slide projectors most commonly used today are 3¼- by 4-inch, 2¼- by 2¼-inch and 2- by 2-inch models.

Slide Storage File. Metal or plastic file for orderly storage and filing of slides.

Speedball Auto-Feed Lettering Pen. Fountain-type pen designed for accepting all standard Speedball lettering and drawing pens.

Speedball Lettering Pen. Metal lettering and drawing pen. Fits into a metal, plastic, or wood pen holder. Ideal for lettering, cartooning, uniform line drawing, poster making, etc. Four point styles available. Special pens available for left-handed users.

Spirit Duplicator. A manually operated or completely automatic duplicating machine which prints on paper materials from tissue to card stock. A special spirit master, prepared by hand or produced on a thermocopy machine, is required. Recognized as one of the most inexpensive reproduction methods, with paper copies costing as little as ½ cent each.

Spirit Duplicator Acetate Master. A combination transparency for overhead projection and spirit master. The plastic master can be drawn, written, and typed on. Master is then used to run off paper copies on spirit duplicator and also projected on an overhead projector.

Spirit Duplicator Color Carbon Paper. A special color-dye carbon sheet for adding color to spirit masters. Assorted colors available.

Spirit Duplicator Correction Pencil. A special pencil for correcting errors on spirit masters. A razor blade should first be used to remove as much of the carbon deposit as possible.

Spirit Duplicator Paper Master. A paper and carbon sheet unit required for spirit and hectograph duplicating.

Spirit Duplicator Pencil. Designed for use on spirit duplicator and hectograph masters.

Spirit Duplicator Prepared Master. Ready-to-use spirit duplicating masters, available in many subject areas. About one hundred sharp, clear copies can be produced from each master.

Spirit Duplicator Stylus. Small metal-pointed device for use on spirit and hectograph masters and mimeograph stencils. Styli available for ruling, shading, lettering, etc.

Spirit Duplicator Thermocopy Acetate Master-Transparency. A specially coated, transparent acetate combined with a special carbon-coated paper sheet for producing a projection transparency and also a master for reproducing paper copies on the spirit duplicator. Master must be processed with a thermocopy machine.

Spirit Duplicator Thermocopy Paper Master. A thin paper sheet, combined with a special carbon-coated paper for producing spirit duplicator masters with a thermocopy machine.

Spray Sign Kit. A complete sign-making kit which includes letters, numbers, symbols, aerosol-spray inks, and instructions for making signs, posters, etc. Letters are placed on desired surface and sprayed around thoroughly with spray inks.

Stamp Pad. Flat metal container for rubber stamp ink. Usually ink pad is constructed of felt or foam rubber. Assorted-color ink pads are available.

Stamp Pad Ink. Special inks for stamp pads. Assorted colors available.

Staple Gun. A powerful high-compression machine for driving wire staples into wood, plaster, masonite, and similar materials.

Stapler. A hand-operated machine for driving wire staples into paper, cloth, and similar materials.

Steel Ruler. Flat stainless-steel calibrated straightedge, used for drawing, cutting straight lines, measuring lengths, etc.

Steel Straightedge. Stainless-steel ruler-type device, used for cutting and ruling mats, paper, leather, glass, etc. (See also LeRoy Straightedge.)

Stencil. A sheet of material in which an image is cut by perforating or other means and through

which ink can be forced to create an image on a receiving sheet.

Stencil Art Book. Easy-to-trace stencils in book form. Books include stencils of animals, alphabet, space art, flowers, etc.

Stencil Brush. Round bristle brush for all stenciling work.

Stencil Duplicator (Mimeograph). A machine for making copies of written or typewritten matter or drawings by means of a stencil cut on a typewriter, electronic stencil cutter, or with a stylus.

Stencil Duplicator Art. Easy-to-use drawings created by professional artists. Designed primarily for preparing visuals for stencil (mimeograph) duplication. Can also be used for preparing overhead projection transparencies and slides.

Stencil Duplicator Compass Stylus. For making circles on stencils simply and quickly without damaging the stencil.

Stencil Duplicator Lettering Guide. Transparent plastic lettering stencil guide for use, with a stylus or lettering guide pen, on mimeograph stencils and spirit masters. Assorted styles and sizes available.

Stencil Duplicator Shading Wheel. Special shading tool for adding a texture pattern to drawings, letters, etc., on mimeograph stencils and spirit masters. Fine, medium, and coarse shading styli available.

Stencil Duplicator Stylus. Metal-point drawing, writing, and lettering tool for use on mimeograph stencils and spirit masters.

Stencil Duplicator Symbol Template (Guide). Transparent plastic outline symbol template for use on mimeograph stencils and spirit masters; also for general use. A stencil stylus or ball-point pen is required

for tracing symbol on stencil or master.

Stencil Ink. Opaque ink for use with metal interlocking-letter and oil-board stencils. Applied with a stencil brush, airbrush, or spray can.

Stencil Ink (Aerosol Can). Opaque ink in an aerosol spray can for use with metal interlocking-letter and oil-board stencils.

Stencil Letter-cutting Machine. A hand-operated letter-cutting machine for cutting stencil letters out of stencil oil board.

Stencil Paper. A semitransparent, oiled paper which retains sharp lines and is easy to cut. Used as a stencil on all surfaces.

Stencil-tracing Lettering System. A lettering system consisting of a transparent template (guide), guide holder (some systems), and either a pen or pencil for tracing each character. Assorted letter styles and sizes available.

Straightedge. A piece or strip of wood, metal, etc., having a perfectly straight edge used in drawing lines, testing plane surfaces, etc.

Symbol Template (Guide). Transparent plastic outline symbol template for general use, or on mimeograph stencils and spirit masters. Symbol can be traced with pen, pencil, stylus, or ball-point pen. Templates covering almost every major subject area are available. (See also Mechanical Scriber Symbol Template.)

T

Tape Compass. A beam compass designed for use with a tape pen. Produces 2- to 18-inch diameter circles with narrow-width charting tape.

Tape Cutter (for Color, Shading, and Symbol Tapes). Plastic or metal cutting tool for opaque and transparent charting tapes. Some cutters use standard single-edge razor blades.

Tape Dispenser. Metal or plastic device for holding and dispensing all types of adhesive-backed tape. Some models are designed for holding two and three rolls of tape.

Tape Edger. A manually operated device for reinforcing and protecting edges of papers, documents, overhead transparencies, maps, etc., by applying a tape edge. Edges materials up to $\frac{1}{16}$ inch thick. Uses tape up to 1 inch wide. (See also Edging Tape.)

Tape Pen (Dispenser). A precision drawing instrument for applying charting tapes to drawing surfaces. Pen can be used freehand, or with a straightedge or irregular curve.

Technical Fountain Pen (Acetate Ink). A nonclogging fountain pen which uses acetate (plastic) drawing inks. Regular india and drawing inks can also be used in the pen. Some models are available with interchangeable points or nibs.

Technical Fountain Pen (Drawing Ink). A nonclogging fountain pen which uses india or regular drawing inks. Some models are available with interchangeable points or nibs.

Template, Lettering. An opaque or transparent plastic lettering guide for use with a mechanical lettering scriber, lettering pen, or stylus.

Template (Guide) Rack. A metal rack with flexible wire separations for holding transparent curves, triangles, lettering guides, etc.

Template (Templet) Lifter. Plastic rod with beveled edge for lifting templates or pressure-sensitive materials.

Thermocopy. A generic term applied to a copying process using infrared light and the heat emitted by an infrared lamp. The original copy should be prepared in black ink or lead pencil or printed with a carbon-base ink.

Thermocopy Color Pen. Nylon- or felt-point pen that can be used for applying color to the surface of positive-reading thermocopy transparencies.

Thermocopy Duplicating Stencil. (See Thermocopy Stencil.)

Thermocopy Laminating Acetate (Film). A thin, transparent acetate sheet with a thermoplastic coating for use in a thermocopy machine. Provides a transparent protective surface for printed matter, visuals, photographs, etc.

Thermocopy Machine. A heat copying machine which exposes and develops specially coated films and papers, with a printed original, simultaneously.

Thermocopy Printed Originals. Ready-to-use art printed on white paper for making overhead projection transparencies in a thermocopy machine. Printed originals are available in more than twenty subject areas such as health, foreign languages, religion, mathematics, science, and social studies.

Thermocopy Printed Paste-up Letter. Black opaque letter printed on a white gummed-back perforated sheet, for producing overhead projection transparencies with a thermocopy machine. The 3M Company's transparency lettering kit contains more than 2,200 letters, numerals, and characters plus a supply of grid sheets to facilitate designing layouts for better visuals.

Thermocopy Reproducing Ball-point Pen. A standard ball-point pen with thermocopy reproducible ink.

Thermocopy Reproducing Nylon-point Pen. A nylon-point pen with ink that can be reproduced in a thermocopy machine.

Thermocopy Reproducing Pencil. A pencil with lead that can be reproduced in a thermocopy machine.

Thermocopy Stencil. A heat-imaging stencil for the stencil (mimeograph) duplicator. Copy to be duplicated is placed inside the stencil set and run through any thermocopy machine. The burned stencil is mounted on the stencil duplicator for duplication.

Thermocopy Transparency Film. Specially surfaced film for use in the thermocopy process. Film is not sensitive to light, but reacts to heat radiated by the image area of the original when exposed to infrared light. Exposure and developing are simultaneous in a thermocopy machine. (See also Parlab Projection Film, Selfkote Thermocopy Film, 3M Transparency Film, and Transmate Film.)

Thermoplastic Adhesive. A specially formulated adhesive that becomes activated when subjected to heat. Heat laminating films and dry backing cloth (Chartex) are treated with this type of adhesive. (See also Dry Mounting Adhesive and Dry Mounting Cement.)

3M Drymount Laminating Film. A thin, transparent film with a pressure-sensitive adhesive back for preserving and giving support to printed materials and flat specimens. A cold laminating film.

3M Transparency Film. Brand name for the 3M Company thermocopy film.

Thumbtack Lifter. A metal device for removing thumbtacks easily, quickly, and safely.

Tracing Cloth. Fine-quality cloth for tracing purposes. For use where original drawings must be made on a material that can withstand much handling and will last indefinitely. Pencil or pen can be used on the surface. Available in rolls and sheets.

Tracing Paper. Fine-quality translucent paper for all tracing purposes. Available in several weights, in rolls and sheets.

Transfer Carbon Sheet. A quality artists' transfer carbon paper that produces sharp grease-free color lines. These lines can be easily erased. Available in several colors.

Transfer Film (Picture Transfer). Clear, transparent film with a pressure-sensitive adhesive back for preparing overhead projection transparencies from pictures printed on clay-coated paper. No equipment or chemicals are required. (See also Cold Laminating Acetate.)

Transfer Tracing Paper. (See Transfer Carbon Sheet.)

Translucent Materials. Materials that are partly transparent, permitting only a portion of complete light to pass through. Frosted glass and matte acetate are examples.

Transmate Film. Coated (both sides) film for use in a thermocopy machine. Surfaces will also accept direct typing, ball-point pen and nylon-point pen inks. Film costs about one-half as much as regular thermocopy film.

Transparent. Materials which transmit light and are capable of being seen through. Clear glass and acetate are examples.

Transparent Color Marking Pencil. A pencil that has been especially created for use with overhead projection equipment. Leads are smooth and strong and appear in deep transparent color when projected. Markings can be removed with a damp cloth.

Transparent Liquid Color (Aerosol Can). Transparent color in aerosol spray cans. Color adheres to most surfaces, including glass and plastic. Dries instantly on contact.

Transparent Liquid Color (Alcohol Base). A water-resistant transparent liquid color with an alcohol base for use where permanent, durable transparent color is required.

Transparent Color Adhesive-backed Sheet. Vivid transparent color printed on the underside of a thin acetate film with a pressure-sensitive adhesive back. Used in the preparation of transparencies, color separations, posters, charts, graphs, etc. Assorted colors available.

Transparent Color Adhesive-backed Tape. Vivid transparent color printed on the underside of a thin acetate tape with a pressure-sensitive adhesive back. Used in the preparation of transparencies, color separations, posters, charts, graphs, etc. Assorted colors and tape widths available.

Transparent Plastic Letter. An opaque or transparent color reusable plastic letter made of Planoflex. Various types faces, sizes, and colors available.

Transparent Watercolor. Water-base transparent color for use where removable or water-base color is required. Can be applied with brush or airbrush.

Transparentizer. A plastic-impregnating solution which increases the translucency of matte and semi-translucent papers, films, and acetates. Some solutions are available in aerosol spray cans.

T Square. T-shaped metal, plastic, or wood ruler for drawing parallel lines; also used as a support for lettering equipment. (See also Cam-Lock T Square and Metal T Square.)

Two- by Two-inch Slide Glass. Thin, clear cover glass for preparing 2- by 2-inch slides.

Two- by Two-inch Slide Mounting Press. Hand-operated electric press for mounting 2- by 2-inch (35mm) slides in cardboard mounts.

Two- by Two-inch Slide Notcher. Hand-operated metal device for notching two- by two-inch slides for correct positioning in projector. Can also be used to notch other sizes of cardboard slide mounts.

Two- by Two-inch Slide Vise. A hand-operated slide-binding device which holds binding tape in perfect alignment with cover glass while attaching tape. Also used for binding lantern slides.

U

Unitech Lettering System. Lettering system consisting of a mechanical scriber, template, and lettering pen. Letters range in height from $\frac{1}{16}$ to 2 inches.

Upper Case. Capital letters.

V

Varigraph Lettering System. A mechanical tracing lettering system consisting of a head writer (mechanical scriber), matrix (template), and lettering pen. Hundreds of different type sizes in condensed, normal, and extended faces can be obtained from one matrix.

VariTyper Typewriter. A typing machine which is capable of using a wide variety of type faces. In addition, copy can be justified on this machine.

Velcro-backed Plastic Letter. Molded plastic letter with velcro "hook" tape attached to the back for use on velcro (Hook N' Loop) presentation boards.

Velcro Board. A unique presentation board with unbelievable holding power. Surface of board is nylon loop fabric. Flat and three-dimensional materials attached to the board must be backed with a special nylon "hook" tape.

Velour Paper. Medium-weight paper with a surface of velvetlike textile fabric. Ideal for preparing display materials and for use on the flannel board. Assorted colors available.

Viewing Light Box (Tracing Board). A translucent working surface, with incandescent bulbs or fluorescent tubes as a light source. Used in drafting, color overlay work, photographic opaquing and retouching, etc. Some units are designed especially for mimeograph stencils.

Vinyl Plastic Pressure-sensitive Letter. Die-cut vinyl plastic letter with a pressure-sensitive adhesive back that will stick to most surfaces. Assorted styles, sizes, and colors available.

W

Watercolor Brush. Small red sable or ox-hair brush used with water-base inks, paints, etc. Ideal for retouching, spotting, opaquing, and for cleaning up lettering and type to be reproduced.

Watercolor Pencil. Watercolor pigment processed and set in pencil form. May be used to simulate a painting by applying a water-saturated brush to areas where pencil has been applied. Recommended color medium for matte acetate. (See also Mongol Color Pencil.)

Watercolor Stamp Book. Water-soluble leaves (pages) of transparent colors. Color is obtained by touching a wet brush or cotton swab to a color page, or by dissolving a page in water.

Wax Adhesive. A colorless odorless, and stainless wax adhesive used for mounting three-dimensional objects (lightweight) as well as flat materials on almost any dry surface.

Wax Coating Machine. Electrical device for heating and applying adhesive wax. Wax coaters range from small hand-held spreaders to automatic paper-fed machines capable of handling large sheets.

Wheat-paste Flour. A special-formula dry flour designed for preparing the paste used for wallpaper hanging. Ideal for wet mounting.

White Correction Paper. An opaque white paper with a pressure-sensitive adhesive back. For masking out errors and making corrections on clean surfaces.

White Correction Tape. An opaque white paper tape with a pressure-sensitive adhesive back. For masking out errors and making corrections on clean surfaces.

White Ink. Dense white ink for drawing, lettering, marking, etc. Many brands are water-soluble.

White Opaque. A liquid white opaquing medium for use on most surfaces where corrections are to be made. Won't chip, crack, or peel. Can write, type, or draw over areas where liquid has been applied.

Wood Letter. Precision-made plywood or birch-wood letter for indoor or outdoor use. Assorted styles, sizes, and colors available.

Wrico Adapter Pen. Special Wrico brush pen used for obtaining different effects with the same lettering guide (Wrico Sign-Maker).

Wrico Brush Pen. Metal brush pen designed for use with Wrico Sign-Maker guides. Ideal for producing 1/16- to 1/4-inch lines which are clean-cut, full, and solid without excess ink. Recommended for use only with black india ink.

Wrico Scriber Lettering System. Lettering system consisting of a mechanical scriber, pen, lettering guide, and guide holder.

Wrico Sign-Maker Lettering System. Stencil-tracing lettering system consisting of brush pen, green transparent plastic lettering guide, and guide holder. Designed for sign and poster making.

Wricoprint Lettering System. Stencil-tracing lettering system consisting of Wrico standard lettering pen, transparent plastic lettering guide, and guide holder.

Wricoprint Pen. Special lettering pen designed for use with Wrico standard stencil lettering guides. Can be used as an india-ink pen for ruling, irregular curves, symbol templates, etc. Seven line-width points available.

X

Xerographic Transparency Film. A clear nonsensitized film for making positive-reading overhead projection transparencies with any model Xerox copier. (See also Arkwright and Zelar Transparency Film.)

Xerography. A positive-to-positive process developed by the Xerox Corporation and utilizing a light-sensitive, selenium-coated plate which carries a positive electrostatic charge. Where exposed to light, the charge is dissipated, leaving a latent image to which negatively charged black powder will adhere. The powder image can afterward be transferred and fused to other positively charged surfaces such as both unsensitized paper and metal offset plates. It is a dry process.

Xerox Machine. Copy machine used in the xerography process.

Y

Yardstick Beam Compass. Consists of two metal parts that fit standard-size yardstick. Adjusts easily and makes accurate circles up to 66 inches in diameter.

Z

Zelar Transparency Film. A clear nonsensitized film for making positive-reading overhead projection transparencies with any model Xerox copier. Available in clear, matte, and color films (see also Arkwright and Xerographic Transparency Film).

ANNOTATED BIBLIOGRAPHY

The publications annotated below and on the following pages have been included in this book to help supplement its contents. It should be pointed out that the extent to which a publication treats a technique included in the book may range from partial to extensive coverage. Chapters which each publication supplements are indicated by boldface numbers in parentheses following most entries. Publications which have no chapter reference indicated are included for their value in contributing to a better understanding of the preparation and utilization of instructional media. Following the title or author(s) of each publication is the publisher or distributor. The names and addresses of publishers and distributors can be found in the Address Directory.

Adams, Ansel E.: POLAROID LAND MANUAL, Morgan & Morgan, Inc., Hastings, N.Y., 1963.
Covers the Polaroid Land system, including everything from latest equipment, films, Polacolor, and filters to lighting, exposure, development control, copying, and slides. A complete technical data section is included in the book. **(5)**

Alexander, Mary Jean: HANDBOOK OF DECORATIVE DESIGN AND ORNAMENT, Tudor Publishing Company, New York, 1965.
Book contains over one thousand basic and representative decorative designs for study and reproduction, showing how geometric, floral, animal, and other motifs have been developed and used. Written for amateur and professional artists, art teachers, or handicrafters. **(1)**

Allcock, Hubert: HERALDIC DESIGN: ITS ORIGINS, ANCIENT FORMS AND MODERN USAGE, Tudor Publishing Company, New York, 1962.
Over five hundred illustrations trace the history and meaning of heraldic symbols and devices as they have evolved from medieval coats and shields to the trademarks in today's advertising. Includes special chapters on family coats of arms and how to design them, heraldry in advertising and trademarks today, American and world coats of arms. **(1,3)**

AMATEUR FILMSTRIP PRODUCTION,

Ohio State University Teaching Aids Laboratory, Columbus, 1958.
Pamphlet 7 dealing with a simple approach to producing instructional filmstrips with a 35mm camera. **(1, 3,5)**

ANYONE CAN CREATE A LIVELY BULLETIN BOARD, Hayes School Publishing Co., Wilkinsburg, Pa.
This book shows how to make flat or three-dimensional cutouts out of inexpensive materials, how to make pleasing arrangements, etc. Includes bulletin-board ideas for language, art, music health, physical fitness, and general nature. **(1,4)**

ART-WORK SIZE STANDARDS FOR PROJECTED VISUALS (No. S-12), Eastman Kodak Co., Rochester, N.Y., 1965.
A booklet dealing with size standards for projected visual artwork. **(1,3,5)**

Auval, Kenneth L.: SERIGRAPH: SILK SCREEN TECHNIQUES FOR THE ARTIST, Prentice-Hall, Inc., Englewood Cliffs, N.J., 1965.
A book written for the professional artist, art student, or amateur who wishes to exploit the unique characteristics of the silk-screen medium as an expressive pictorial tool. All operations of fine-art screen printing are covered. **(1,4)**

BASIC TITLING AND ANIMATION, (No. S-21), Eastman Kodak Co., Rochester, N.Y., 1962.
A pamphlet covering planning, equip-

ment, artwork preparation, titling, and techniques of animation basic to the production of an animated film. **(1,3,4)**

Bathurst, Leonard H., and Bruce Klein: A VISUAL COMMUNICATIONS SYSTEM, William C. Brown Book Co., Dubuque, Iowa, 1966.
A detailed, nontechnical, self-instructional book which describes all the procedures necessary for the production of paper and/or transparent thermocopy materials. Includes illustrations and instructions on the use and preparation of other thermocopy products such as spirit masters, laminating film, and offset plates. **(1,2,3,4,5)**

BETTER BULLETIN BOARD DISPLAYS, University of Texas at Austin, Instructional Media Center, 1961.
Arranged so that a teacher may use its pages for bulletin-board ideas, this handbook is designed specifically to acquaint the teacher with resources available for use and construction of the bulletin board. **(1, 3,4)**

BETTER MOUNTING, Seal, Inc., Derby, Conn., 1966.
A manual dealing with materials, equipment, and methods of dry mounting. Manual contains complete information on dry-mounting tissue, dry backing cloth, laminating film, and transparency-making film and materials. **(2)**

Biegeleisen, Jacob I., and M. A. Cohn: SILK-SCREEN TECHNIQUES, Dover Publications, Inc., New York, 1963.
A complete, copiously illustrated course in silk-screen techniques. Full directions for building silk-screen out of inexpensive materials; explanations of five basic methods of stencil preparation (paper, blockout, tusche, film, and photographic). (1,3,4)

Blakeslee, H. W.: ILLUSTRATORS' ELLIPSE TIPS, Michael's Artist and Engineering Supplies, North Hollywood, Calif.
Written for all users of ellipse guides. Shows correct ellipse use in isometric, dimetric, and trimetric drawings, plus basic principles and development. Includes isometric protractor and isometric gear-teeth underlays. (1)

Bogorad, A. D. (ed.): IT'S FUN TO DRAW, Tudor Publishing Company, New York.
A book with over one thousand show-how sketches and drawings to guide the beginner every step of the way from portraits to poster layouts. The Munsell color chart is also included. (1,4)

Boughner, Howard: POSTERS, Pitman Publishing Corporation, New York, 1962.
A booklet for the amateur poster maker. Covers planning, lettering, color, etc. Several pages are devoted to commercial posters. (1,3,4)

Bourges, Jean: HOW-TO GRAPHICS, Bourges Color Corp., New York, 1968.
An excellent new book on copy preparation, retouching, color separation, line and halftone reproduction. (1,4,5)

Bowman, William J.: GRAPHIC COMMUNICATION, John Wiley & Sons, Inc., New York, 1967.
A text which integrates every existing field of graphic practice under a common visual philosophy by identifying the range of ideas which can be visually presented. Offering a design methodology to translate ideas into visual statements, the author illustrates each text element with design models which can serve as a basic graphic guide for reference use in industrial or classroom situations. (1)

Bretz, Rudy: TECHNIQUES OF TELEVISION PRODUCTION, 2d ed., McGraw-Hill Book Company, New York, 1962.
A comprehensive description of the tools and techniques of television production. A reference rather than a text, presented in nontechnical, comprehensive language, as valuable to the commercial broadcaster as it is to the educational broadcaster. (1,2,3,4)

Brown, James W., Richard B. Lewis, and Fred F. Harcleroad: AUDIOVISUAL INSTRUCTION: MEDIA AND METHODS, 3d ed., McGraw-Hill Book Company, New York, 1969.
This revised and rewritten text continues to emphasize practical information about the use and preparation of instructional media to plan and carry out learning activities. It covers all types of audiovisual materials and methods, printed books, reference materials, free or inexpensive materials, with particular attention to their interrelated uses. (1,2,3,4,5)

Brown, James W., Richard B. Lewis, and Fred F. Harcleroad: AUDIO-VISUAL INSTRUCTIONAL MATERIALS MANUAL, 3d ed., McGraw-Hill Book Company, New York, 1969. A revised and rewritten manual which provides exercises (things to do) dealing with the practical problems of choosing, using, and inventing instructional materials and operating audiovisual equipment. (1,2,3,4,5)

Brunner, Felix: A HANDBOOK OF GRAPHIC REPRODUCTION PROCESSES, Hastings House Publishers, Inc., N.Y., 1964.
A book devoted to a comprehensive coverage of major graphic reproduction processes; included are gravure and lithography. Over four hundred illustrations. (1,3,4)

Burtis, Eric F., and James E. LeMay: THEY SEE WHAT YOU MEAN, G.A.F. Corp., New York, 1959.
A well-illustrated text on the preparation of overhead projection transparencies. It covers subjects ranging from masking, mounting, and preparation of originals to the use of color and presentation techniques. (1,3, 4,5)

Callahan, Genevieve, and Lou Richardson: HOME ECONOMICS SHOW-HOW AND SHOWMANSHIP: WITH ACCENT ON VISUALS, Iowa State University Press, Ames, 1966.
An idea-packed book which presents fresh, unusual, and practical ways of bringing homemaking information to life. Written especially for teachers, extension workers, and professional women who use visual aids in presenting home economics information. (1)

Cardamone, Tom: ADVERTISING AGENCY & STUDIO SKILLS, Watson-Guptill Publications, Inc., Cincinnati, Ohio, 1959.
A leading commercial artist explains the basic technical procedure of art studios and advertising art departments: paste-ups, mechanicals, printing processes and specifications, hundreds of invaluable tricks of the trade. (1,2,3,4)

Carmel, James H.: EXHIBITION TECHNIQUES: TRAVELING AND TEMPORARY, Reinhold Publishing Corporation, New York, 1962.
Covers planning and design, costs, lighting, packaging, and transportation. Includes information on exhibit construction. (1,3)

CARTOONING, Higgins Ink Co., Brooklyn, N.Y.
A fully illustrated booklet of styles used by America's top comic strip,

gag, and political cartoonists plus text on humor. (1)

Cataldo, John W.: LETTERING: A GUIDE FOR TEACHERS, Davis Publications, Inc., Worcester, Mass., 1966.
This book contains a fresh approach to the evolution of letter forms and symbols with basic strokes clearly explained and illustrated. (3)

Cavanagh, J. A.: LETTERING AND ALPHABETS, Dover Publications, Inc., New York, 1955.
This reissue of Lettering offers a full discussion, analysis, and illustration of eighty-nine basic hand lettering styles. Hundreds of technical hints on makeup, construction, artistic validity, strokes, pens, and brushes may be reproduced without permission. (3)

Cochern, George W.: LEARNING TO DRAW WITH THE MICROPOINT FLEXY, Micropoint, Inc., Sunnyvale, Calif., 1965.
An excellent booklet dealing with the use of a felt- or nylon-point pen or marker for drawing simple cartoons. Clear step-by-step sketches enable the beginner to draw simple cartoons without difficulty. (1)

Coffman, Joe W.: TECHNOLOGY OF THE DIAZOTYPE PROCESSES, Tecnifax Corp., Holyoke, Mass., 1957.
A detailed booklet dealing with the diazo process. (1,4,5)

Cohn, R., and M. Estrin: ORNAMENTAL ALPHABETS, Tudor Publishing Company, New York, 1955.
A collection of rare and unusual alphabets for every theme and purpose, from a headline to a billboard. Included are "mood" alphabets; geographic, object, people, and animal alphabets; theatrical alphabets; gay 90s alphabets; and many others. (3)

CREATIVE TEACHING, 3M Company, St. Paul, Minn., 1966.
A booklet dealing with the creation,

preparation, and utilization of 3M infrared transparency films. (1,3,4,5)

Cross, A. J. Foy, and Irene F. Cypher: AUDIO-VISUAL EDUCATION, Thomas Y. Crowell Company, New York, 1961.
Presents in outline form with illustrations a chapter on each of the audio-visual materials. Included are explanations on television, teaching machines, instructional materials centers, and the role of audiovisual techniques in international education. (1,5)

Croy, Peter: GRAPHIC DESIGN AND REPRODUCTION TECHNIQUES, Hastings House Publishers, Inc., New York, 1968.
A comprehensive text and reference source on all stages of the transformation of design to printed page, along with a range of graphic materials and mediums and nearly all the printing methods currently in use. (1,4,5)

Cutler, Merritt D.: HOW TO CUT DRAWINGS ON SCRATCHBOARD, Watson-Guptill Publications, Cincinnati, Ohio, 1960.
A thorough exploration of the scratchboard technique. An ideal guide for the professional interested in commercial possibilities and the amateur seeking an interesting and vital approach to the technique. (1)

DAILY BULLETIN BOARDS FOR ALL OCCASIONS, Hayes School Publishing Co., Inc., Wilkinsburg, Pa.
Actual miniature bulletin boards are laid out and pictures are included to guide the reader in creating fresh and distinctive bulletin boards. Shows how scraps and other readily available materials can be used. (1,3)

Dale, Edgar: AUDIO-VISUAL MATERIALS IN TEACHING, 3d ed., Holt, Rinehart and Winston, Inc., New York, 1969. Recognized as one of the leading books in the area of instructional technology. Deals with the selection,

utilization, preparation, and administration of audiovisual materials. (1, 2,5)

D'Amelio, Joseph: PERSPECTIVE DRAWING HANDBOOK, Tudor Publishing Company, New York, 1964.
A complete instruction manual and reference guide on the fundamentals of perspective for students, artists, illustrators, architects, and designers. Hundreds of clearly labelled drawings and diagrams illustrate basic concepts such as "picture plane," "vanishing line," and "cone of vision" and all basic and special techniques of determining perspective heights, widths, and depths; correcting distortions; working with shade and shadow; etc. (1)

DeKieffer, Robert, and Lew W. Cochran: MANUAL OF AUDIO-VISUAL TECHNIQUES, Prentice-Hall, Inc., Englewood Cliffs, N.J., 1958.
A revised basic text for short courses in audiovisual education. Includes information related to preparation and utilization of basic instructional materials. (1,2,5)

Denno, Raymond E.: HOW TO CREATE CLASSROOM BULLETIN BOARDS, Standard Oil Company of California, San Francisco, 1957.
A sixteen-page booklet of basic information on planning and producing bulletin boards. Shows the process involved in creating classroom bulletin boards, providing meaningful learning experiences for students. (1)

————: CREATING SOCIAL STUDIES AND SCIENCE BULLETIN BOARDS, Standard Oil Company of California, San Francisco, 1958.
This sixteen-page booklet suggests ways in which teachers and students may make effective use of classroom space. Special emphasis is given to relating petroleum to social studies and science. (1)

————: USING THE OPAQUE PROJECTOR, Squibb-Taylor, Inc., Dallas,

Texas, 1958.

A well-illustrated booklet dealing with use of the opaque projector on all educational levels; included are suggestions for using the projector in industry and the professions. Suggests use of the projector as a drawing aid. (1)

Denstman, Harold, and Morton J. Schultz: PHOTOGRAPHIC REPRODUCTION: METHODS, TECHNIQUES AND APPLICATIONS FOR ENGINEERING AND THE GRAPHIC ARTS, McGraw-Hill Book Company, New York, 1963.

This book completely covers the entire field of photographic reproduction. A complete, up-to-date, and authoritative guide, it is designed to guide the technician in the efficient performance of his task. Every reproduction task is explained in simple, step-by-step fashion and each technique is discussed in relation to other techniques. (1,3,4)

DESIGNING INSTRUCTIONAL VISUALS, University of Texas at Austin, Instructional Media Center, 1968. This handbook gives the concerned educator a better understanding of the design requirements which must be met in producing efficient instructional visuals.

DIAZOCHROME SLIDES FOR VISUAL COMMUNICATION, Tecnifax Corp., Holyoke, Mass., 1956.

A booklet published by a manufacturer of diazo materials and equipment that deals with the preparation and use of diazo slides for visual communication. (1,4,5)

Dortch, Barbara: HOLIDAY THINGS CHILDREN CAN MAKE, Maco Magazine Corp., New York, 1966.

A practical and well-illustrated booklet covering a variety of holiday display things that can easily be made by teachers or children. An excellent source of ideas for bulletin boards. (1)

DUCHART MANUAL FOR SELECTING

AND ORDERING CHARTS, Business Reports, Inc., Larchmont, N.Y., 1960. An illustrated manual on chart making. Over fifty kinds of charts are illustrated. Designed for use with Duchart system charts. (1,3,4)

Dunavan, Caryl C., and Emma Fantone: TEACHERS MAKE: SLIDES, TRANSPARENCIES, OPAQUES, TAPE RECORDINGS, Audio-Visual Office, New Jersey State Department of Education, Trenton, 1961.

A do-it-yourself booklet for classroom teachers. Deals with a number of techniques for the local preparation of audiovisual instructional materials. (1,5)

East, Marjorie, and Edgar Dale: DISPLAY FOR LEARNING: MAKING AND USING VISUAL MATERIALS, Holt, Rinehart and Winston, Inc., New York, 1952.

Aimed at showing the classroom teacher as specifically and clearly as possible how to prepare visual instructional materials and how to use them in and out of the classroom. (1,2,3,4,5)

EASY TO MAKE BULLETIN BOARDS, Hayes School Publishing Co., Inc., Wilkinsburg, Pa.

A collection of creative bulletin boards for classroom or halls. Bulletin boards for holidays, special days and occasions. All subjects including health, citizenship, science, and current events are included. (1)

Eboch, Sidney C.: OPERATING AUDIO-VISUAL EQUIPMENT, 2d ed., Chandler Publishing Co., San Francisco, Calif., 1968.

This revised manual explains and illustrates, step by step, the operation of all types of audiovisual equipment. Instructions are also included for mounting materials for opaque projection and for preparation of handmade slides and overhead projection transparencies. (1,2,4,5)

Edel, D. Henry, Jr. (ed.): INTRODUCTION TO CREATIVE DESIGN,

Prentice-Hall, Inc., Englewood Cliffs, N.J., 1967.

Develops a creative-design instinct with various mental procedures and associated application systems. Gives up-to-date technical information at key points throughout the book. Covers the entire design process in a well-organized manner with supporting information and examples in basic form. (1,3,4)

EDUCATIONAL DISPLAYS & EXHIBITS, University of Texas at Austin, Instructional Media Center, 1965. This handbook discusses purposes, advantages, and guidelines for exhibits. Provides a rich source of ideas for both display and bulletin board. Information about dioramas is also included. (1,3,4)

Erickson, Carlton W. H.: ADMINISTERING INSTRUCTIONAL MEDIA PROGRAMS, The Macmillan Company, New York, 1968.

An outstanding handbook for instructional-media program directors and a useful reference for graduate students in communication. Contains fifteen chapters dealing with acquiring, organizing, distributing, implementing, and evaluating various media. One chapter deals with the implementation of media-preparation services.

Erickson, Carlton W. H.: FUNDAMENTALS OF TEACHING WITH AUDIO-VISUAL TECHNOLOGY, The Macmillan Company, New York, 1965.

A heavily illustrated textbook dealing with the fundamentals of audiovisual technology. Chapter 6 deals with the preparation of simple instructional materials. (1,2,3,4,5)

Erickson, Jane D., and Adelaide Sproul: PRINTMAKING WITHOUT A PRESS, Reinhold Publishing Corporation, New York, 1966.

Demonstrates how to adapt printing techniques for use without a press. Over 125 illustrations. (1,3)

Estrin, Michael: 2,000 DESIGNS, FORMS AND ORNAMENTS, Tudor Publishing Company, New York, 1947.
A collection of copyright-free classic, baroque, and modern ornaments embracing the entire field of decorative design, including a huge variety of borders, crests, scrolls, monograms, and figures from all periods and countries. **(1,3)**

FELT BOARDS FOR TEACHING, University of Texas at Austin, Instructional Media Center, 1957.
This handbook contains a wealth of ideas for use of the felt board as a teaching device, explains basic materials used in construction of the felt board, and describes how it may be utilized for effective presentation. **(1)**

Finstad, Charles: VU-GRAPHICS: A MANUAL ON VU-GRAPH PROJECTION, Charles Beseler Co., East Orange, N.J., 1952.
A booklet dealing with the utilization of the overhead projector and techniques for preparing projectables. **(1,3,4,5)**

Freedman, Edward H.: HOW TO DRAW, Bantam Books, Inc., New York, 1965.
Teaches how to make fine, recognizable drawings of buildings, furniture, cars, people, animals, and countless other things as easily as one can sign his name. **(1)**

Frye, Roy A.: GRAPHIC TOOLS FOR TEACHERS, 3d ed., E & I Printing Co., Austin, Texas, 1965.
Describes a variety of techniques and methods for preparing inexpensive instructional materials. **(1,2,3, 4,5)**

Garland, Ken: GRAPHIC HANDBOOK, Reinhold Publishing Corporation, New York, 1966.
Written for today's graphic designer who is concerned with the proper use of graphic design in periodicals, packaging, production information, directional signs, promotion devices, film credits, etc. **(1,3,4)**

Garrett, Lillian: VISUAL DESIGN: A PROBLEM SOLVING APPROACH, Reinhold Publishing Corporation, New York, 1966.
Designed to unite thought processes and sensory processes to generate creative ideas in any area of the visual arts. Useful as an organized text. **(1)**

Gerstner, Karl L.: DESIGNING PROGRAMMES, rev. ed., Hastings House Publishers, Inc., New York, 1968.
Fresh and fascinating ideas for publications designers and art directors. **(1,3,4)**

Gill, Bob: ILLUSTRATION: ASPECTS AND DIRECTION, Reinhold Publishing Corporation, New York, 1964.
Shows the way that modern graphic artists solve their illustration problems. **(1)**

GRAPHIC PRESENTATION, Defense Supply Agency, Department of Defense, 1967. Order from Superintendent of Documents, U.S. Government Printing Office, Washington, D.C.
A handbook prepared basically as a guide for effective use and economic development of the visual aid as a management tool. **(1,3,4)**

Goblirsch, Margaret and Katherine M. Daly: CLASSROOM PAPER-CRAFT PROJECTS AND PATTERNS, Fearon Publishers, Inc., Palo Alto, Calif., 1962.
Easy-to-read instructions for teachers and children to make a variety of paper figures and decorations from inexpensive materials. **(1)**

Gordon, Jay E.: MOTION-PICTURE PRODUCTION FOR INDUSTRY, The Macmillan Company, New York, 1961.
A complete guide to the successful operation of a film department. One section is devoted to art and animation. **(1,3,4,5)**

GRAPHIC TIPS: ADVERTISING LAYOUT FUNDAMENTALS, nuArt Company, Chicago, Ill., 1967.
This booklet deals with the fundamentals of advertising layouts. Step-by-step illustrations included. **(1,4)**

GRAPHIC TIPS: BASIC TOOLS AND THEIR APPLICATIONS, nuArt Company, Chicago, Ill., 1962.
This booklet deals with the fundamentals of using basic drawing tools and aids such as drawing pencil, T square, ruler, protractor, compass, ellipse guide. **(1)**

Guptill, Arthur L.: PENCIL DRAWING STEP BY STEP, Reinhold Publishing Corporation, New York, 1959.
A complete study of modern pencil design methods. Includes 250 illustrations. **(1)**

Hales, John, and Roger Manvell: THE TECHNIQUE OF FILM ANIMATION, Hastings House, New York, 1966.
An authoritative book covering every stage of producing animated films for entertainment, advertising, education, and research. Includes descriptions and examples of every type of animation technique. Over 200 excellent illustrations. **(1,5)**

Hamilton, G. E.: HOW TO MAKE HANDMADE LANTERN SLIDES, Keystone View Co., Meadville, Pa. 1940.
A booklet describing how to make lantern (3¼- by 4-inch) slides in color on etched glass, typewritten slides on cellophane with carbon paper. **(1,4,5)**

HANDMADE LANTERN SLIDES, Ohio State University Teaching Aids Laboratory, Columbus.
Pamphlet No. 5 dealing with techniques and materials for preparing handmade lantern slides. **(1,4,5)**

Hartsell, Horace (ed.): INSTRUCTIONAL GRAPHICS FOR TELEVISION, Educational Media Laboratories, Austin, Texas, 1968.
A packet of materials which includes

instructor and participant manuals, overhead projectables and a sound filmstrip. Designed for use in pre-service and in-service education workshops. (1,3,4,5)

Hartsell, Horace C., and Wilfred L. Veenendaal: OVERHEAD PROJECTION, Henry Stewart, Incorporated, Buffalo, N.Y., 1960.
This booklet not only tells how the overhead projector can be used but also details specifically its application in methods of demonstration, dramatization, group discussion, illustrated lectures, etc. Includes techniques and methods for preparing projectables. (1,4,5)

Hartung, Rolf: CREATING WITH CORRUGATED PAPER, Reinhold Publishing Corporation, New York, 1966.
A book on the creative use of corrugated paper as a practical and artistic craft material. Over 150 illustrations. (1)

Hass, Kenneth B., and Harry Q. Packer: PREPARATION AND USE OF AUDIO-VISUAL AIDS, Prentice-Hall, Inc., Englewood Cliffs, N.J., 1955.
Practical information and all the know-how that is needed to prepare and use instructional materials to the greatest advantage, whether for use in the classroom, factory, or office. (1,2,3,4,5)

Hatton, Richard G.: THE HANDBOOK OF PLANT AND FLORAL ORNAMENT, Dover Publications, Inc., New York, 1960.
A collection of 1,200 line drawings of plant and floral ornaments that will reproduce excellently. Selected from woodcuts and copperplate engravings. (1)

Hawken, William R.: COPYING METHODS MANUAL, American Library Association, Chicago, Ill., 1966.
A modern, comprehensive book of copying methods dealing with the processes, methods, techniques, and types of equipment which can be used for reproducing printed sheets and documents. (1,3,4,5)

Heitner, Louis: INTRODUCTION TO OFFSET, Scholastic Products, Brooklyn, N.Y., 1964.
A book written mainly for the commercial artist beginner interested in the preparation of artwork for offset reproduction. Well written and illustrated. (1,2,3,4)

Herdeg, Walter (ed.), and John Halas: FILM AND TV GRAPHICS, Hastings House Publishers, Inc., New York, 1967.
An exciting book dealing with the field of animated films from the graphic-arts viewpoint. Contains outstanding examples of international film and television graphics from the world's major producing centers. The more than one thousand illustrations include stills, sequences, story boards, roughs, titling, and announcement slides. (1)

Horn, George F.: BULLETIN BOARDS, Reinhold Publishing Corporation, New York, 1962.
A how-to-do-it book dealing with classroom bulletin boards. Covers design, organization, layout, and effective exhibitions with bulletin boards. (1,3)

————: HOW TO PREPARE VISUAL MATERIALS FOR SCHOOL USE, Davis Publications, Inc., Worcester, Mass., 1966.
A book that can be used to create timely visual aids that add drama to presentations, capture interest, help to visualize the abstract. Text covers tips on the use of color, gives suggestions for lettering titles, and includes a list of inexpensive materials needed for the preparation of visual aids. (1,2,3,4)

————: POSTERS: DESIGNING, MAKING, REPRODUCTION, Davis Publications, Inc., Worcester, Mass., 1966.
A book that brings together in a single volume all the elements for successful poster making. Designed to help one design and execute posters that catch and hold attention. (1,3,4)

Hornung, C. P.: A HANDBOOK OF EARLY ADVERTISING ART, Dover Publications, Inc., New York, 1956.
One of the largest collections of copyright-free early advertising art ever compiled. Volume I contains some 2,000 illustrations of agricultural devices, animals, old automobiles, birds, buildings, Christmas decorations, etc. Volume II, devoted to typography, has over four thousand specimens. (1,3)

————: HANDBOOK OF DESIGNS AND DEVICES, 2d ed., Dover Publications, Inc., New York, 1946.
A collection of 1,836 basic designs and variations, carefully reproduced, which may be used without permission. Variations of circle, line, bar, triangle, square, cross, diamond, swastika, pentagon, star, scroll, etc. (1,3)

HOW TO KEEP YOUR BULLETIN BOARD ALIVE, Ohio State University Teaching Aids Laboratory, Columbus. Pamphlet No. 6 dealing with preparation of materials for the classroom bulletin board. (1)

HOW TO MAKE AND USE THE FELT BOARD, Ohio State University Teaching Aids Laboratory, Columbus.
Pamphlet No. 3 dealing with the preparation and use of the felt board in teaching. (1,2)

HOW TO MAKE A PASTE-UP LAYOUT FOR YOUR GESTEFAX, Gestetner Corp., N.Y.
A booklet of instructions for preparing artwork for an electronic stencil cutter. (1,2,5)

HOW TO MAKE TRANSPARENCIES WITH A XEROX COPIER USING ZELAR FILMS, Sepsco Films Div., Chamblee, Ga., 1968.
A small booklet containing instructions and illustrations on the use of Zelar films for making overhead

transparencies with a Xerox copier.

HOW TO USE KODAK AUTOPOSITIVE MATERIALS (No. Q-23), Eastman Kodak Co., Rochester, N.Y., 1955.
This booklet gives specific handling recommendations for the use of Kodak Autopositive film. Includes instructions for making transparent positives from photographic negatives. (5)

INSTRUCTIONAL DISPLAY BOARDS, University of Texas at Austin, Instructional Media Center, 1968.
Explains the use of felt, hook and loop, magnetic, peg, and marking boards.

Jacobson, Jurt I., and L. A. Mannheim: ENLARGING, 19th ed., Friedman, Inc., New York, 1943.
This book on enlarging emphasizes color enlarging and a wide range of applications from photography to graphic design. (5)

Jacques, Faith: DRAWING IN PEN AND INK, Golden Press, Inc., New York.
An authority on pen-and-ink techniques explains all the fundamentals of this medium, treating materials, methods, design, and other aspects. (1)

Kelley, Gaylen B., and Phillip J. Sleeman: A GUIDE TO OVERHEAD PROJECTION AND THE PRACTICAL PREPARATION OF TRANSPARENCIES, Chartpak Rotex, Leeds, Mass., 1967.
A booklet dealing with the creation, preparation, and utilization of overhead projection transparencies. The preparation section of the booklet deals mainly with the use of pressure-sensitive transparent materials. (1,3,4,5)

Kelley, Marjorie: CLASSROOM-TESTED BULLETIN BOARDS, Fearon Publishers, Inc., Palo Alto, Calif., 1961.
Booklet containing photographs of bulletin boards in classroom use, showing how many creative teachers have solved their bulletin-board problems. (1)

———— and Nicholas Roukes: MATTING AND DISPLAYING THE WORK OF CHILDREN, Fearon Publishers, Inc., Palo Alto, Calif., 1957.
Presents many practical suggestions to improve exhibits of children's artwork, written materials, science collections, and other projects, both in the classroom and at school science fairs and other displays. (1)

———— and ————: LET'S MAKE A MURAL, Fearon Publishers, Inc., Palo Alto, Calif., 1958.
A teacher's how-to-do-it booklet with examples and illustrations of mural techniques and activities for the classroom. (1)

Kemp, Jerrold E.: PLANNING AND PRODUCING AUDIOVISUAL MATERIALS, 2d ed., Chandler Publishing Co., San Francisco, Calif., 1968.
With the aid of over five hundred visuals, this revised book provides a guide to the planning and producing of audiovisual materials for classroom, self-instruction, information programs, and special training programs. Every step in each process is well explained and illustrated. (1,2, 3,4,5)

Kinder, James S.: AUDIO-VISUAL MATERIALS AND TECHNIQUES, American Book Company, New York, 1965.
A well-written basic text dealing with the selection, preparation, utilization, and administration of instructional materials. (1,2,5)

KINDERGARTEN AND PRIMARY BULLETIN BOARDS, Hayes School Publishing Co., Inc., Wilkinsburg, Pa.
Seasonal subjects for every month of the school year are included in this bulletin-board publication designed for use on the kindergarten and primary grade levels. (1)

Koskey, Thomas: BAITED BULLETIN BOARDS, Fearon Publishers, Inc., Palo Alto, Calif., 1954.
All aspects of bulletin-board planning and arrangement; recommended by art and audiovisual educators. (1)

————: CREATIVE CORRUGATED CARDBOARD, Fearon Publishers, Inc., Palo Alto, Calif., 1957.
A how-to-do-it booklet providing many examples of the uses of corrugated cardboard in making picture frames, decorative borders for displays, three-dimensional exhibits, seasonal and holiday decorations, and other classroom creations. (1)

————: BULLETIN BOARDS FOR HOLIDAYS AND SEASONS, Fearon Publishers, Inc., Palo Alto, Calif., 1958.
An "idea" booklet covering all school holidays and months of the school year. (1)

————: HOW TO MAKE AND USE FLANNEL BOARDS, Fearon Publishers, Inc., Palo Alto, Calif., 1961.
A booklet for classroom teachers showing the application of a variety of shapes, sizes, and types of flannel boards. (1)

————: BULLETIN BOARDS FOR SUBJECT AREAS, Fearon Publishers, Inc., Palo Alto, Calif., 1962.
A booklet containing ideas and sources for bulletin boards in such subject areas as English, social studies, mathematics, fine arts, business, industrial arts, science, and language. (1)

————: BULLETIN BOARD IDEA SOURCES, Fearon Publishers, Inc., Palo Alto, Calif., 1963.
Explains where to get bulletin-board ideas and how to adapt them for use in the classroom or school. (1)

Krampen, Martin (ed.): DESIGN AND PLANNING 2, Hastings House Publishers, Inc., New York.
This book explores such questions

as: How will the new computer technology affect graphic design? The designer? The total design environment? Included is a selection of challenging articles originally presented at the 1966 Design and Planning Seminar at the University of Waterloo, Ontario. (1)

Krulik, Stephen, and Irwin Kaufman: HOW TO USE THE OVERHEAD PROJECTOR IN MATHEMATICS EDUCATION, National Council of Teachers of Mathematics, Washington, D.C., 1966.
Both general and detailed suggestions for effective use at a minimum of cost. Includes directions for making and storing projectables and a listing of materials needed. (1,5)

Landon, Edward A.: PICTURE FRAMING, Tudor Publishing Company, New York, 1962.
A revised, updated edition of a comprehensive book on the techniques of picture framing. Contains nearly 300 illustrations and photos that show how easy and inexpensive it is to make picture frames and reveals a host of "professional secrets" formerly unavailable outside the trade. Includes information on tools and equipment. (2)

LANTERN SLIDES AND HOW TO MAKE THEM, Bausch & Lomb, Inc., Rochester, N.Y., 1949.
A booklet that deals with the utilization and preparation of handmade lantern slides. (1,4,5)

Laughton, Roy: T.V. GRAPHICS, Reinhold Publishing Corporation, New York, 1966.
First comprehensive survey of world television graphics. Profusely illustrated. (1)

Leach, Mortimer: LETTERING FOR ADVERTISING, Reinhold Publishing Corporation, New York, 1956.
A manual for students and professionals in the field of graphic arts, discussing the techniques of hand lettering in a variety of styles. (3)

LEGIBILITY STANDARDS FOR PROJECTED MATERIALS (No. S-4), Eastman Kodak Co., Rochester, N.Y., 1956.
A pamphlet dealing with the legibility of visuals and lettering to be projected. Includes information on direct viewing versus projection, multiple-use artwork, drafting standards, pictorial materials, and so forth. (1,3,5)

Lehner, Ernest: THE PICTURE BOOK OF SYMBOLS, Tudor Publishing Company, New York, 1956.
A reference book containing over one thousand signs, symbols, and pictographs, from prehistoric times to the atomic age. Subject categories range from arts and sciences to love and magic. (1,3)

LETTERING, Higgins Ink Co., Brooklyn, N.Y.
A booklet dealing with thirty-four distinctive type and script alphabets plus nineteen pages of manuscript engrossing—a good source book. (3)

LETTERING TECHNIQUE, University of Texas at Austin, Instructional Media Center, 1965.
A booklet covering such lettering techniques and aids as hand lettering, stencil lettering, precut letters, and mechanical lettering devices. (3)

Levitan, Eli L.: ANIMATION ART IN THE COMMERCIAL FILM, Reinhold Publishing Corporation, New York, 1960.
A course in cartoon drawing with a full description of film production. Contains over 250 line drawings. (1)

————: ANIMATION TECHNIQUES AND COMMERCIAL FILM PRODUCTION, Reinhold Publishing Corporation, New York, 1962.
Covers every phase of film animation from story board to finished film in production sequence. Contains 500 illustrations. (1,5)

Lidstone, John: DESIGN ACTIVITIES FOR THE ELEMENTARY CLASSROOM, Davis Publications, Inc., Worcester, Mass., 1966.
An elementary art teaching guide which includes twenty-two creative things to do in the classroom. Activities include mural making, classroom sculpture, potato printing, monoprinting. (1)

Liechti, Alice, and Jack Chappel: MAKING AND USING CHARTS, Fearon Publishers, Inc., Palo Alto, Calif., 1957.
A booklet with instructions for the preparation and use of classroom charts. More than sixty charts are included. Shows a variety of subjects, uses, and ideas for chart making for all grade levels. (1,3,4)

Linse, Barbara: WELL-SEASONED HOLIDAY ART, Fearon Publishers, Inc., Palo Alto, Calif., 1956.
A booklet containing more than seventy ideas and examples (illustrated) for classroom decorations and creative activities built around major school holidays. Includes basic instructions for many projects. (1)

LOCAL PRODUCTION TECHNIQUES, University of Texas at Austin, Instructional Media Center, 1967.
A useful handbook to assist classroom teachers in the designing and preparation of simple instructional materials. Topics include dry mounting, laminating, spray lettering, lettering guides, and projection for production. A suggested list of supplies and equipment required for local production is included. (1,2, 3,4,5)

Longyear, William: TYPE AND LETTERING, Watson-Guptill Publications, Cincinnati, Ohio, 1961.
A revised and expanded textbook which shows hundreds of full alphabets and one-line type specimens, many in a variety of sizes and weights. Recommended for type specifiers and designers since it covers the mechanics of typography,

printing terms and measures, proof-reading and copy-editing marks and presents examples of good type arrangement. (3)

Loomis, Andrew: CREATIVE ILLUSTRATIONS, The Viking Press, Inc., New York, 1947.
Practical art instruction for the advanced practioner who seeks commercial outlets. (1)

————: THREE-DIMENSIONAL DRAWING, The Viking Press, Inc., New York, 1958.
Art instruction with special emphasis on perspective. (1)

Lord, John, and Robert H. Harson: HANDBOOK FOR PRODUCTION OF FILMSTRIPS AND RECORDS, Dukane Corp., St. Charles, Ill., 1962.
This handbook contains the technical data necessary to produce filmstrips and sound slide films according to standards now widely accepted by the industry. (1,3,5)

Luzadder, Warren J.: BASIC GRAPHICS FOR DESIGN ANALYSIS, COMMUNICATION AND COMPUTER, 2d ed., Prentice-Hall, Inc., Englewood Cliffs, N.J., 1968.
Written for the computer age. One will find helpful information related to computer-aided design and automated drafting of engineering components and systems. An introduction to design, sketching, and creative thinking is included. Over 1,000 illustrations. (1)

Lynch, John: HOW TO MAKE COLLAGES, The Viking Press, Inc., New York, 1961.
Full instructions for creating handsome designs with scissors and paste, cloth, paper, bits of photographs, and odd materials. (1)

MacDonald, Byron J.: THE ART OF LETTERING: THE BROAD PEN, Reinhold Publishing Corporation, New York, 1966.
A how-to-do-it book which presents its subject in such a simplified way that it can be used by anyone, amateur or professional, who wants to learn the art of lettering with the broad pen. Includes numerous examples of the commercial use of the alphabets in advertisements, posters, book jackets, testimonials, and awards—all done by the author. (1,3)

Magnan, George: VISUAL ART FOR INDUSTRY, Reinhold Publishing Corporation, New York, 1961.
A guide to the techniques of and opportunities for artists in industry. Includes instructions for the preparation of technical illustrations, handbooks, manuals, charts, graphs, etc. (1,3,4)

MAKING BLACK-AND-WHITE TRANSPARENCIES FOR OVERHEAD PROJECTION (No. S-7), Eastman Kodak Co., Rochester, N.Y., 1958.
A pamphlet dealing with the preparation of overhead projection transparencies. Includes information on adding color and making additional duplicate slides. (1,4,5)

Mambert, William A.: PRESENTING TECHNICAL IDEAS: A GUIDE TO AUDIENCE COMMUNICATION, John Wiley & Sons, Inc., New York, 1967.
Deals with communication problems in business and industry. Written mainly for managers, scientists and engineers, marketing and sales personnel, teachers, writers, and anyone who wants to be a better communicator of technical information. (1)

Maurello, S. Ralph: THE COMPLETE AIRBRUSH BOOK, Tudor Publishing Company, New York, 1955.
A comprehensive manual on airbrush technique. Over four hundred illustrations, diagrams, and photographs accompany step-by-step instructions on equipment, operation of the brush, rendering, retouching, and working methods. Contains examples of outstanding work by such famous artists and illustrators as Bomar, Varga, and Teague. (1,4)

————: HOW TO DO PASTE-UPS AND MECHANICALS, Tudor Publishing Company, New York, 1960.
An instructional book on the preparation of art for reproduction. Chapters of step-by-step text and pictures cover materials and tools, cutting and trimming, paste-up procedures, cropping and scaling, use of "cold type" and photo-lettering, and the technique of color separation. Over three hundred drawings and photoillustrations are included. (1,2,3,4)

Mayer, Ralph: THE ARTIST'S HANDBOOK OF MATERIALS AND TECHNIQUES, The Viking Press, Inc., New York, 1957.
Deals with every art medium in use today. Written for the artist and art student. (1,3)

McCALL'S GOLDEN DO-IT-BOOK, Golden Press, New York, 1960.
A well-illustrated book dealing with the use of a variety of techniques for preparing drawings, display materials, letters, murals, etc. (1,3)

McGiffin, Vida B. and Orissa F. Kingsbury: CREATING THE YEARBOOK, Hastings House Publishers, Inc., New York, 1962.
Covers every aspect of creation and production of today's yearbook, with useful reference material. (1,2,3,4)

Meilach, Dona Z., and Elvie Ten Hoor: COLLAGE AND FOUND ART, Reinhold Publishing Corporation, New York, 1964.
How to create pictures with torn and cutout papers. Includes over 100 illustrations. (1)

Meyer, Franz S.: HANDBOOK OF ORNAMENTS, Dover Publications, Inc., New York, 1957.
One of the largest collections of copyright-free traditional art in print. Contains over 3,000 line cuts from Greek, Roman, medieval, Islamic, Renaissance, and other sources. (1)

Meyer, Jerome S.: THE KEY TO MECHANICAL DRAWING, Ottenheimer,

Inc., Baltimore, Md., 1964.
An introduction to mechanical drawing. Includes instructions on the correct use of instruments. Also shows how to draw simple and elementary designs, shop drawings, perspectives and isometrics, neatly and accurately, to any scale. **(1,3)**

Meyers, Hans: 150 TECHNIQUES IN ART, Reinhold Publishing Corporation, New York, 1963.
An encyclopedic manual of ideas for teachers and students. Includes seventy illustrations.

Minor, Ed: SIMPLIFIED TECHNIQUES FOR PREPARING VISUAL INSTRUCTIONAL MATERIALS, McGraw-Hill Book Company, New York, 1962.
This manual fills the need for a single publication covering all basic techniques necessary for the preparation of visual instructional materials. **(1,2,3,4,5)**

MODELS FOR TEACHING, University of Texas at Austin, Instructional Media Center, 1956.
A booklet which defines and describes various types of educational models. Offers suggestions for their selection and utilization, illustrates methods of constructing certain models, and investigates commercial sources for them.

Mooney, Bob T.: OVERHEAD PROJECTION SERIES, THE, Educational Media Laboratories, Austin, Texas, 1967.
A manual concerned with the effective utilization of the overhead projector as a versatile and flexible teaching device. Contents include sections dealing with all stages of planning and producing overhead projectuals.

Morlan, John E.: PREPARATION OF INEXPENSIVE TEACHING MATERIALS, Chandler Publishing Co., San Francisco, Calif., 1963.
This manual contains instructions for preparing a wide variety of teaching materials. Topics include mounting and preserving, lettering, bulletin-board utilization, display and study devices. **(1,2,3,4,5)**

MOUNTING TRANSPARENCIES IN GLASS (No. E-36), Eastman Kodak Co., Rochester, N.Y., 1965.
A booklet covering, in detail, the preservation of 2- by 2-inch slides with glass mounts. **(2,5)**

Muller-Brockman, Josef: THE GRAPHIC ARTIST AND HIS DESIGN PROBLEMS, Hastings House Publications, Inc., New York.
A book written mainly for designers of painted media advertisements, posters, packages, and scale tools. Also recommended for classes in advertising art. Includes over 700 illustrations. **(1,3)**

Nelms, Henning: THINKING WITH A PENCIL, Barnes & Noble, Inc., New York, 1964.
A self-instruction book dealing with fundamentals of drawing with a pencil. The book was designed for (1) those who wish to use drawing as a tool for thought and communications but lack knowledge of how to make drawings and (2) those who are accustomed to drawing but want to enlarge their graphic vocabularies and extend the range of fields in which they can apply the abilities that they already possess. **(1)**

Nelson, Leslie W.: INSTRUCTIONAL AIDS: HOW TO MAKE AND USE THEM, 3d ed., William C. Brown Company Publishers, Dubuque, Iowa, 1961.
Includes a variety of instructional materials which can be prepared and used by the classroom teacher to make his teaching easier and more effective. **(1,2,3,4,5)**

Nerdinger, Eugene: ALPHABETS FOR GRAPHIC DESIGNERS AND ARCHITECTS, Reinhold Publishing Corporation, New York, 1965.
Selects alphabets that comply with today's business-world needs and illustrates their derivation. **(1,3)**

Nesbitt, Alexander (ed.): DECORATIVE ALPHABETS AND INITIALS, Dover Publications, Inc., New York, 1959.
No payment, no permission needed to reproduce any one of 3,924 different letters, covering 1,000 years. **(3)**

OPAQUE PROJECTOR, THE, Ohio State University Teaching Aids Laboratory, Columbus.
Pamphlet No. 9 dealing with the use of the opaque projector in the classroom. **(1)**

OPAQUE PROJECTOR, THE, University of Texas at Austin, Instructional Media Center.
A booklet prepared in response to specific suggestions concerning application of the opaque projector in various areas of education. Shows how the projector can be utilized in professional and industrial training programs also. **(1)**

OVERHEAD SYSTEM: PRODUCTION, IMPLEMENTATION AND UTILIZATION, THE, University of Texas at Austin, Instructional Media Center, 1967.
A practical handbook to help school administrators, supervisors, and teachers design and prepare overhead projection transparencies. Major transparency-making techniques are included. Suggestions for the implementation of a local overhead projection program are discussed. **(1,3,4,5)**

PHOTODRAWINGS (No. P-22), Eastman Kodak Co., Rochester, N.Y., 1957.
A pamphlet dealing with the technique of photodrawing or photodrafting, as it is sometimes called. Includes information on equipment and materials, preparation of the master drawing, blueprint reproduction. **(1,5)**

PHOTOGRAPHIC PRODUCTION OF SLIDES AND FILMSTRIPS (No. S-8),

Eastman Kodak Co., Rochester, N.Y., 1960.
A data book intended to suggest means of producing slides and filmstrips by using, in most cases, readily available equipment and materials. **(1,5)**

PLANNED AND ILLUSTRATED BULLETIN BOARDS, Hayes School Publishing Co., Inc., Wilkinsburg, Pa.
A book designed to stimulate classroom participation and meet the need of individual classroom situations. Easy-to-follow directions for having an A-1 bulletin board in halls or rooms. **(1)**

PLANNING AND PRODUCING VISUAL AIDS (No. S-13), Eastman Kodak Co., Rochester, N.Y., 1960.
A pamphlet produced for the person interested in the planning and preparation of visual aids. **(1,3,4,5)**

PREPARING COPY FOR CAMERAS, Addressograph-Multigraph Corp., Cleveland, Ohio, 1961.
A booklet dealing with the preparation of art and copy for photo-offset reproduction. **(1,3,4)**

Price, Charles M.: FOOT-HIGH LETTERS: A GUIDE TO LETTERING, Dover Publications, Inc., New York, 1961.
A complete alphabet of classic Roman letters, each 1 foot high, each on a separate 16- by 22-inch plate. In addition to an accompanying description, each plate contains nine 2-inch–high forms of letters in various type faces, such as Caslon and Empire. **(3)**

Pringle, B.: CHALK ILLUSTRATION, Pergamon Press, New York.
Presents in work-study form the role of graphic illustration in teaching and gives practical information on the making of illustrations for the classroom. Topics covered, among others, are: using the blackboard; the strip diagram; shading and coloring; blackboard instrument work. **(1,4)**

PRODUCTION OF 2- BY 2-INCH SLIDES, University of Texas at Austin, Instructional Media Center, 1958.
A booklet which describes physical properties of 2- by 2-inch slides and the advantage of producing them locally; discusses production techniques of black-and-white and color slides and describes equipment needed. A list of sources is also included. **(1,5)**

PROJECTS, Higgins Ink Co., Brooklyn, N.Y.
A booklet containing instructions for ten popular projects including map and chart making, paper decorating, spatter and airbrush, textile dyeing, and bookbinding. **(1,3)**

Pula, Fred John: APPLICATION AND OPERATION OF AUDIOVISUAL EQUIPMENT IN EDUCATION, John Wiley & Sons, Inc., New York, 1968.
A how-to-do-it manual dealing with the hardware and software associated with instruction. One chapter deals with the production of audiovisual media.

Randall, Reino, and Edward C. Haines: BULLETIN BOARDS AND DISPLAY, Davis Publications, Inc., Worcester, Mass., 1961.
A book that combines basic design with imaginative use of materials that offer a fresh new source for making bulletin boards and displays that sparkle with originality. **(1)**

READING AND LIBRARY BULLETIN BOARDS, Hayes School Publishing Co., Wilkinsburg, Pa.
A book designed especially for the creation and preparation of bulletin boards for reading rooms and the library. **(1)**

Robinson, Karl D.: LINE PHOTOGRAPHY FOR THE LITHOGRAPHIC PROCESS, Morgan & Morgan, Inc., Hastings, N.Y., 1948.
A well-written graphic-arts book dealing with the principles of line photography as it applies to the lithographic process. **(1,3,5)**

Ross, George F.: SPEEDBALL ELEMENTARY ALPHABETS, Hunt Manufacturing Co., Philadelphia, Pa.
A booklet covering the making of Roman, Gothic, manuscript, and text alphabets with Speedball lettering pens. **(3)**

————: SPEEDBALL TEXTBOOK, 19th ed., Hunt Manufacturing Co., Philadelphia, Pa., 1965.
A practical manual on all lettering forms. Written mainly for use with speedball lettering pens. **(3)**

Roukes, Nicholas: CLASSROOM CRAFT MANUAL, Fearon Publishers, Inc., Palo Alto, Calif., 1960.
A booklet containing photographs and/or drawings illustrating easy step-by-step techniques for presenting craft activities in the elementary school. **(1)**

Ruby, Doris: BULLETIN BOARDS FOR THE MIDDLE GRADES, Fearon Publishers, Inc., Palo Alto, Calif., 1960.
A booklet containing over thirty bulletin boards keyed to subject areas for grades 4 through 6. Easy-to-use patterns, many of them three-dimensional. **(1)**

————: 4-D BULLETIN BOARDS THAT TEACH, Fearon Publishers, Inc., Palo Alto, Calif., 1960.
A booklet for kindergarten and primary grade teachers. Contains dual-purpose, direct, dimensional, and diversified bulletin boards for instructing children. **(1)**

Ruder, Emil: TYPOGRAPHY: A MANUAL OF DESIGN, A. I. Friedman, Inc., New York.
A fundamental treatise by a distinguished Swiss typographer and teacher. Every conceivable typographic problem in relation to texture, weight, color, legibility, pacing, and leading are explained. Over five hundred illustrations. **(3)**

Sands, Lester B.: AUDIO-VISUAL PROCEDURES IN TEACHING, The

Ronald Press Company, New York, 1956.
A textbook designed to give an understanding of the procedures appropriate to audiovisual methods at every level of education. Useful as a reference guide in evaluating and enriching the work of teachers.

Schlemmer, Richard W.: HANDBOOK OF ADVERTISING ART PRODUCTION, Prentice-Hall, Inc., Englewood Cliffs, N.J., 1966.
Provides the advertising artist with a working knowledge of the processes of printed reproduction, and of the techniques with which artwork is best prepared in order to be acceptable to these processes. **(1, 3,4)**

Schultz, Morton J.: THE TEACHER AND OVERHEAD PROJECTION, Prentice-Hall, Inc., Englewood Cliffs, N.J., 1965.
A comprehensive treatment of ideas, uses, and techniques associated with overhead projection. Although techniques mainly related to the preparation of transparencies by the thermocopy process are included, a major portion of the book deals with the use of the overhead projector in the teaching of a variety of subject-matter areas (reading, language arts, social sciences, etc.). **(1,5)**

Scuorzo, Herbert E.: PRACTICAL AUDIO-VISUAL HANDBOOK FOR TEACHERS, Parker Publishing Co., West Nyack, N.Y., 1969.
Filled with many new how-to-do-it ideas, plans, examples, and extensive audio-visual projects for classroom instruction at every grade level and for every scholastic subject. Special attention is given to slides and filmstrips, overhead projection, chalk- and display boards, flat graphics, mounting and lettering. **(1,2,4)**

Shaw, Robert: PRACTICAL LETTERING, Tudor Publishing Company, New York, 1955.
A complete self-instruction course in drawing and designing the basic letter forms, including the new script and brush styles, with scores of complete hand-lettered and type alphabets for study and reproduction. **(3)**

Shelly, Williams: PAPER SCULPTURE IN THE CLASSROOM, Fearon Publishers, Inc., Palo Alto, Calif.
A booklet providing basic information on paper-sculpture techniques, with a number of ideas for creating interesting models and displays out of paper. **(1)**

Shokler, Harry: ARTISTS' MANUAL FOR SILK SCREEN PRINT MAKING, Tudor Publishing Company, New York, 1960.
Revised edition of a book recognized to be a complete guide to the art of serigraphy and silk-screen printing. Covers building of equipment; the master sketch; analysis of color; application of tusche, crayon, and glue; mixing of paint; choice of paper; methods of printing; and more. Includes shop notes for teachers. **(1)**

Shores, Lewis: INSTRUCTIONAL MATERIALS, The Ronald Press Company, New York, 1960.
Written as an introductory textbook for prospective teachers. Contents include some instruction related to techniques for preparing instructional materials. **(1,2,3,5)**

Sides, Dorothy S.: DECORATIVE ART OF THE SOUTHWESTERN INDIANS, Dover Publications, Inc., New York, 1961.
An album of authentic designs (both pre- and post-conquest) from the pottery, textiles, and basketry of the Navaho, Hopi, Mohave, Santo Domingo, and over twenty other Southwestern groups. Designs include birds, clouds, butterflies, etc. Material can be used without permission or payment. **(1)**

SIMPLE WAYS TO MAKE TITLE SLIDES AND FILMSTRIPS (No. T-44), Eastman Kodak Co., Rochester, N.Y., 1959.
A pamphlet dealing with equipment, materials and techniques for making slides and filmstrips. **(1,3,4,5)**

Spears, James: CREATING VISUALS FOR TV: A GUIDE FOR EDUCATORS, Division of Audiovisual Instruction, NEA, Washington, D.C., 1962.
A well-illustrated booklet dealing with the preparation of visuals for educational television. Includes a variety of production techniques. **(1,3)**

Stankowski, Anton: VISUAL PRESENTATION OF INVISIBLE PROCESSES, Hastings House Publishers, Inc., New York, 1966.
How to present in a visual, easily understood form the latest developments of science and technology is the fascinating problem dealt with in this book. Among the topics discussed are: functional symbols, fields of vision, transmitting information, advertising suggestions. Examples are included. **(1)**

Stasheff, Edward, and Rudy Bretz: THE TELEVISION PROGRAM: ITS DIRECTION AND PRODUCTION, A. A. Wyn, Inc., New York, 1962.
A comprehensive treatment of the nature of the television medium with specific, simple explanations of the duties, artwork, and science which become the craft of the television producer and director. A well-written how-to book. **(1,3)**

Stone, Bernard, and Arthur Eckstein: PREPARING ART FOR PRINTING, Reinhold Publishing Corporation, New York, 1965.
A book that contains all the essential information that graphic artists and students must know to do an effective job. Based on the authors' course at New York University. Over 250 black-and-white illustrations. **(1, 2,3,4)**

Stoner, Charles: PEN TIPS ON CARTOONING, Hunt Manufacturing Co., Philadelphia, Pa., 1949.
Manual dealing with the use of

Speedball lettering pens for cartooning. Written for the amateur cartoonist. (1)

Taubes, Federic: THE QUICKEST WAY TO DRAW WELL, The Viking Press, Inc., New York, 1958.
The fundamentals of drawing, with complete instructions for using pencil, pen, brush, or crayon. (1)

————: BETTER FRAMES FOR YOUR PICTURES, The Viking Press, Inc., New York, 1968.
A complete how-to-do-it book, updated with information about new time-saving preparations. (2)

Taylor, E. A.: A MANUAL OF VISUAL PRESENTATION IN EDUCATION AND TRAINING, Pergamon Press, New York, 1966.
A comprehensive manual for the preparation and use of projected and nonprojected instructional materials. Well-written and illustrated chapters cover chalkboards and charts; magnetic materials; flannelgraph, plastigraph and cellograph; pegboard techniques; models; still projection; moving projection; overhead projection; copying and duplicating processes; and more. A detailed list of materials and equipment sources is also included. (1,2, 3,4,5)

TEACHER MAKES HIS OWN CHART, THE, Ohio State University Teaching Aids Laboratory, Columbus, 1961.
Pamphlet No. 12 dealing with the techniques and materials for preparing simple charts for classroom use. (1,3,4)

TECHNICAL ILLUSTRATION, Higgins Ink Co., Inc., Brooklyn, N.Y.
Three-dimensional, axonometric, and perspective drawing. Modern industrial illustration. Contains over one hundred illustrations. (1)

TECHNIQUES, Higgins Ink Co., Inc., Brooklyn, N.Y.
A how-to-do-it booklet in basic and advanced techniques with pen, brush, and airbrush. (1)

Thomas, R. Murray, and Sherwin G. Swartout: INTEGRATED TEACHING MATERIALS, David McKay Company, Inc., New York, 1963.
An enlarged and revised textbook dealing with the selection, utilization, preparation, and administration of instructional materials. (1,2,3,5)

Thompson, Tommy: THE BASIC BOOK OF LETTERING, The Viking Press, Inc., New York, 1968.
Contains everything the professional or student needs to know about creating original lettering styles and designing new type faces. Profusely illustrated with specimen alphabets. (3)

Trittem, Gottfried: ART TECHNIQUES FOR CHILDREN, Reinhold Publishing Corporation, New York, 1964.
A book which presents all the techniques of which a child is capable, from drawing to modeling and printing. More than forty techniques are explained. (1,3)

Turner, Ethel M.: TEACHING AIDS FOR ELEMENTARY MATHEMATICS, Holt, Rinehart and Winston, Inc., New York, 1966.
Specific instructions are given for constructing and using seventy-nine elementary mathematics teaching aids. Each aid is illustrated in full color. (1,3)

Uhl, Ronald M.: OVERHEAD PROJECTOR TRANSPARENCIES: HOW TO MAKE THEM, Visual Arts Press, Washington, D.C., 1963.
Entire manual devoted to methods, techniques, and processes for preparing overhead projection transparencies. (1,3,4)

USING TEAR SHEETS FOR TEACHING, University of Texas at Austin, Instructional Media Center, 1956.
A booklet which explores expanded uses of tear sheets through better layout and mounting techniques. The format of this handbook is such that ideas from almost every page may be used for bulletin-board layouts. (1,2)

Vangerow, Oskar: SCRAPING TECHNIQUE, Arthur Brown & Brother, New York, 1959.
A description of the technique used in scratchboard work augmented by numerous illustrations. (1)

VARIGRAPH OPERATING MANUAL, Varigraph, Inc., Madison, Wisc.
A comprehensive manual on the operation of Varigraph lettering equipment. Written in simple terms so that the beginning user can follow instructions without difficulty. Included are instructions on layout, letter spacing, retouching, etc. (3)

Verry, H. R.: DOCUMENT COPYING & REPRODUCTION PROCESSES, Morgan & Morgan, Inc., Hastings, N.Y., 1958.
Methods, equipment, practical survey. Carbon, offset, direct positive, diazo, Verifax, Thermofax, Kalfax, xerography, Electrofax, hectograph, stencil, etc. (1,5)

Vessel, Matthew F., and Herbert H. Wong: SCIENCE BULLETIN BOARDS, Fearon Publishers, Inc., Palo Alto, Calif., 1960.
An all-science bulletin-board booklet written mainly for elementary classroom teachers. Includes ideas for most of the scientific problems taught in school at the elementary level. (1)

Wainwright, Charles A.: THE TELEVISION COPYWRITER, Hastings House Publishers, Inc., New York.
Written by a veteran TV commercial maker. Deals mainly with creating successful television commercials. Takes one behind the scenes and examines the creative process in detail, from idea to finished film. Book includes contributions by more than twenty top creative people. Illustrated with storyboards. (1)

Weagley, Richard P.: TEACHING WITH THE OVERHEAD PROJECTOR, Instructo Products, Philadelphia, Pa., 1963.
A booklet that deals with the utilization of the overhead projector and

the preparation of projectables. (1, 4,5)

Weseloh, Anne: E-Z BULLETIN BOARDS, Fearon Publishers, Inc., Palo Alto, Calif., 1959.
A step-by-step booklet, photographically illustrated, on bulletin boards. Many of the photographs are in full color. Written mainly for classroom teachers. (1)

WHAT TO DO FOR BULLETIN BOARDS, Hayes School Publishing Co., Inc., Wilkinsburg, Pa.
Contains many fully illustrated, completely worked out bulletin boards covering every school holiday. Explains how to construct bulletin boards with inexpensive materials. (1)

WHAT TO DO FOR KINDERGARTEN AND PRIMARY ART, Hayes School Publishing Co., Inc., Wilkinsburg, Pa.
An activity book for primary and kindergarten teachers. It has everyday ideas with simple and easy work to develop hand control and coordination. Gift ideas with paper sculpture, crayons, clay, and paint; all to be made from easy, available, and inexpensive materials. Includes detailed instructions for teachers. (1)

WHAT TO DO IN ELEMENTARY ART, Hayes School Publishing Co., Inc., Wilkinsburg, Pa.
A book especially created to help the busy teacher. Detailed and complete with graphic instructions and simplified easy-to-follow illustrations and text. Includes decorative handcraft, complete program for all holidays, special days, and in-between days. (1)

WHY AND HOW OF MAKING A CHART PRESENTATION, THE, Oravisual Co., Inc., St. Petersburg, Fla., 1956.
A booklet dealing with the preparation and use of charts. Includes information on visuals, letterings, etc. (1,3)

Wiley, J. Barron: COMMUNICATION FOR MODERN MANAGEMENT, Business Press, Elmhurst, Ill., 1966.
Treats the entire range of industrial communication techniques. Written mainly for modern management. Included are sections dealing with the preparation of opaque and transparent visual aids. (1,2,3,4,5)

Wirth, Kurt: DRAWING: WHEN-HOW, Hastings House Publishers, Inc., New York.
Written by a noted Swiss artist—graphic designer, who states that this book challenges the doctrine that only acceptable language is documentary. For, by following this doctrine, the graphic designer deprives himself of many other possibilities which, now as ever, any lively minded designer should review when considering how to tackle a problem. In short, the graphic designer must know how to draw. (1)

Wittich, Walter A., and Charles F. Schuller: AUDIOVISUAL MATERIALS: THEIR NATURE AND USE, 4th ed., Harper & Row, Publishers, Incorporated, New York, 1967.
A complete general-reference book for the classroom teacher and professional user of instructional materials. Several chapters include information and instruction dealing with the preparation of a variety of visual instructional materials. (1,2,3,4,5)

Wolchonok, Louis: DESIGN FOR ARTISTS AND CRAFTSMEN, Dover Publications, Inc., New York, 1953.
Contains step-by-step instructions for the creation of more than 1,000 designs and shows how to create design that is fresh, well-founded, and original. Included are detailed exercises, with instruction hints, diagrams, and details. (1,3)

INDEX

The index has been designed to assist the reader in locating information, instructions, and sources related to the contents of this book with minimal effort. An honest effort has been made to include a limited number of reliable manufacturers, distributors, or organizations from which the item selected can be obtained or additional information requested. Page references in boldface refer to the Glossary, pages 255–275. Letters and numbers in parenthesis refer to coded sources in the Address Directory, pages 246–254.